DICTIONARY
OF
REAL ESTATE

DICTIONARY
OF
Real Estate

Jae K. Shim, Ph.D.
Joel G. Siegel, Ph.D., CPA
Stephen W. Hartman, Ph.D.

Business Dictionary Series

John Wiley & Sons, Inc.

New York • Chichester • Brisbane • Toronto • Singapore

Copyright © 1996 by John Wiley & Sons, Inc.

All rights reserved. Published simultaneously in Canada.

Library of Congress Cataloging-in-Publication Data:

Shim, Jae K.
    Dictionary of real estate / by Jae K. Shim, Stephen W. Hartman,
Joel G. Siegel.
        p.   cm. — (Business dictionary series)
    Includes bibliographical references.
    ISBN 0-471-01336-6 (cloth : alk. paper). — ISBN 0-471-01335-8
(paper : alk. paper)
    1. Real estate business—Dictionaries.   2. Real property—
Dictionaries.   I. Hartman, Stephen.   II. Siegel, Joel G.
III. Title.   IV. Series.
    HD1365.S48   1996
    333.33'03—dc20   95-16514

ROBERTA M. SIEGEL, *Loving Wife and Colleague*
ABRAHAM J. SIMON, *Intellectual and Great Friend*
MARC LEVINE, *Scholar and Dear Friend*
ADRIAN FITZSIMONS, *Brilliant Intellectual and Great Guy*
J.G.S.
CHUNG, CHRISTINE, *and* ALLISON SHIM, *Loving Family*
J.K.S.
ALAN GERARD *and* STEPHANIE REGINA HARTMAN, *Daddy's Special Children*
S.W.H.

PREFACE

This dictionary has the following features: over 3,000 terms that cover all areas of *real estate* including principles and practice, finance, economics, appraisal, escrow, property management, office administration, law, agency and ethics, investments, accounting, math, use of computers and software, construction, and architecture. It is packed with examples, applications, diagrams, charts, figures, and computer usage.

This book is a complete dictionary that is a must for every real estate investor, sales agent, broker, mortgage lender, escrow officer, contractor, and other related professional.

The *Dictionary of Real Estate* will be of great assistance to businesspeople and students wishing to understand the use of real estate terminology in their work or study. The dictionary provides definitions, examples, illustrations, and practical applications needed for success in planning and analyzing real estate possibilities and their implications.

In a business conference or in a college course, you are apt to hear a real estate term that you may not have heard of before or heard of but do not know its meaning and usefulness. You must know the meaning of the term and its application for your particular job or class of studies. You may be confused in reading a book on real estate or business because the terminology is strange. You may have to communicate with real estate professionals in your work. Having a copy of this reference source handy will give you explanations and demonstrations to help you handle daily encounters and solve problems.

Real estate is ever-changing and new terms emerge. You must keep up-to-date to have a competitive edge. Emerging real estate phenomena must be known for the future. All areas of real estate that a reader currently faces or may be confronted with in the future have been addressed.

The definitions are clear, comprehensive, and illustrative. Both the layman and seasoned professional can effectively utilize this Dictionary to accomplish his or her purpose.

ACKNOWLEDGMENTS

We thank Ruth Mills for her outstanding editorial assistance on this book. Her efforts are much appreciated. We thank Nancy Marcus Land for her excellent work during the production stage. Thanks also to our research assistants Catherine Carroll and Zheng Ye for their excellent work. We specially thank Marvin Milich, J.D., CPA, a renowned, leading expert in real estate, for his outstanding suggestions.

HOW TO USE
THIS DICTIONARY

The dictionary is in alphabetical order. When a term has more than one possible definition, the other definitions have also been provided. A term may be used in a different context in different real estate sectors. Readers must decide the context that the term is relevant for their specific needs since many terms may be used in different ways.

Cross-referencing of terms are in italics within the body or end of the entry.

When a term may be referred to in another manner, it is indicated by a "see also" reference.

abandonment: The voluntary giving up or surrendering of property rights without transferring the title to another party. Abandonment includes the actual act of leaving the property with the purpose of not returning. The primary determinant of the act of abandonment is the willful intention to forsake one's right to the property in question.

In abandonment, property normally reverts to one with a prior financial interest, such as a mortgagee. Abandonment does not absolve financial responsibilities associated with a piece of property.

Property abandonment usually occurs when a property owner is experiencing extreme financial stress. For example, a homeowner abandons his or her home after experiencing an extended period of unemployment, leaving the owner without the financial ability to pay the mortgage and taxes.

abate: To eliminate, nullify, or reduce. See also *abatement.*

abatement: Decrease or elimination of an existing condition.

(1) *Lease or rent abatement.* A reduction in the cost of the lease or elimination of the rent during a certain period of time. For example, in order to induce a party to rent office space, a rent abatement is implemented, providing free rent for the first three months.

(2) *Property tax abatement.* Providing a property owner a reduction or elimination of property taxes for some specific purpose. For example, certain states provide property owners a homestead exemption, reducing taxes if the homeowner claims the property as the principal residence.

ability to pay: Real estate buyer's financial ability to make interest and principal payments on a mortgage. Depends on factors such as liquidity and cash flow of the borrower. A lower credit rating will require the borrower to pay a higher interest rate on the loan.

absentee owner (landlord): Property owner or landlord who resides elsewhere.

absolute fee simple: An estate limited absolutely to the property owner and his or her heirs. There are no applicable limitations or terms to a fee simple estate. An absolute or fee simple estate provides absolute rights to the entire estate to be lawfully used and disposed of as determined by the owner with complete descendent rights.

absolute liability: Legal responsibility dictated by some jurisdictions when an individual's activities are deemed

1

incompatible with public policy, regardless of whether the action was intentional or negligent. If an individual homeowner's dog bites a delivery person, the homeowner has legal liability for any injuries.

absolute sale: Ownership of property transfers from the seller to the buyer when the contract is signed by the parties.

absorption rate: Projection of the annual sales or occupancy rate of a real estate property. For example, the estimated new houses to be sold in a particular location is 200 per year. The real estate company X anticipates having 30% of the market. The annual absorption rate would be 60 homes.

abstract: An abridged copy or summary of a document. See also *abstract of title.*

abstract of judgment: Summary of a judicial decision in a legal case.

abstract of title: Chronological summary of information from the public record concerning a parcel of real estate. Includes evidence of title, such as maps, plots, and other aids. It applies to all conveyances, including mortgages, deeds, judgments, liens, charges, estates, or other liabilities to which the land may be subject. For example, to obtain title insurance, an abstract of title would be required to guarantee the existence of a clear title.

abstraction approach: Valuation method to determine land value based on a percentage of the site value relative to the total market value of the property. Reference is made to the values of similar properties. Assume properties similar to the site in question have ratios of land value to total property value of about 40%. If the property value is appraised at $200,000, then the land value would be estimated at $80,000.

abstractor: Individual who secures information from public records to validate titles.

abusive tax shelter: Overstating expenses, such as depreciation, or other illegal write-offs by real estate owners are considered abusive tax shelters by the Internal Revenue Service. If the write-offs are disallowed, the taxpayer must pay back taxes, interest, and penalties.

abut: Boundaries of two or more contiguous properties with no intervening land. The two properties shown in the figure abut each other and the lake. See also *adjacent.*

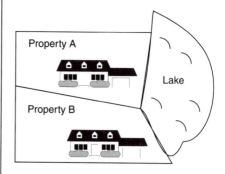

abutment: A supporting structure.

abutter's rights: A visible right associated with the property. The property should be visible at a distance by others, and the occupants should be able to see the outside street. The occupants are entitled to the rights of viewing, light, and air.

abutting: Property that is adjoining or bordering another property. An example is a driveway that is adjacent to the neighbor's property. See also *abut; abutment; abutter's rights.*

accelerated cost recovery system (ACRS): System of depreciation for tax purposes mandated by the Tax Reform Act of 1986. The type of property determines its class. Instead of providing statutory tables, prescribed methods of depreciation are assigned to each class of property. For 3-, 5-, 7-, and 10-year classes, the relevant depreciation method is the

200% declining balance method. For 15- and 20-year property, the appropriate method is the 150% declining balance method, switching to the straight-line method when it will yield a larger allowance. For residential rental property (27.5 years) and nonresidential real property (31.5 years), the straight-line method is applied. A taxpayer may make an irrevocable election to treat all property in one of the classes under the straight-line method. Property is statutorily placed in one of the classes. The purpose of ACRS is to encourage more capital investment by businesses. It permits a faster recovery of the asset's cost and thus provides larger tax benefits in the earlier years.

accelerated depreciation: Method recognizing higher amounts of depreciation in the earlier years and lower amounts in the later years of a fixed asset's life. Some equipment, for example, is more efficient early on and generates greater service potential; higher depreciation is experienced in those years. Over time, depreciation expense moves in a downward direction and maintenance costs tend to become higher; thus the accelerated depreciation results in fairly even charges to income. The greatest tax benefits from depreciation are enjoyed in the earlier years. See also *accelerated cost recovery system (ACRS); double-declining balance; sum-of-the years' digits (SYD) method.*

acceleration clause: A clause inserted in a mortgage, note, bond, deed of trust, or other credit vehicle that allows the lender to request monies due. Usually, such a clause becomes operational when there has been a default in payments of interest or principal, or both. Thereafter, the entire principal sum is "called in" and becomes due and payable. This would precipitate a foreclosure in the case of real estate, or bankruptcy action if the monies were not paid at the time

of the call. For example, Bill missed three payments on his home mortgage and did not notify the mortgagee. A clause in the mortgage states that in the event of three missed payments, the full principal of the mortgage accelerates. Bill must now pay the entire mortgage principal.

acceptance: Agreeing to an offer with the expectation of possessing it. Generally, a binding contract is effected when one party to a business arrangement accepts the offer of the other. Depending on the nature of the offer, an acceptance may be implied, partial, oral, or written.

(1) *Contracts:* Explicit acceptance or agreement to the terms and conditions of an offer.

(2) *Drawee:* Promise to pay either a time draft or sight draft. Typically, the acceptor signs his/her name after writing "accepted" on the bill along with the date. An acceptance of a bill effectively makes it a promissory note: The acceptor is the maker and the drawer is the endorser.

(3) *Deed:* The act of obtaining formal property ownership.

(4) *Insurance:* Occurs when the insurance company agrees to accept an insurance application and issue a policy.

access right: The right of a property owner to freely go to and return from an adjoining highway without interference. The figure illustrates a highway access right to Property C intersecting Property A and Property B.

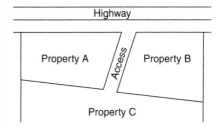

accession: The right of a property owner to have and enjoy all of the advantages of property ownership including air rights, mineral rights, riparian rights, and rights to alluvion, as well as man-made improvements. However, a possessor of the property, other than the property owner, is entitled to the increase in property value created by improvements made to the property when the value of the skill, labor, and improvements exceeds the value of the property.

accessory building: A building that is secondary to the main structure on the property. Examples include a shed, garage, gazebo, or stable.

accommodation: An act or service performed for another person as a favor, having no expectation of receiving compensation. Can be made to an accommodation party by lending one's name for the purpose of securing a note or receiving credit.

accommodation endorser, maker, or party: The endorser's, maker's, or party's credit to whom a loan is granted as an accommodation for the payee. The accommodation endorser or maker actually signs his or her name to a loan note in order to accommodate some other individual. The accommodation endorser, maker, or party receives no compensation or other consideration for extending his or her good name and credit.

accretion: A natural process of adding soil to land, usually by water action, leaving earth or sand deposits. This can take place through unusual events such as flooding or storm conditions, or cyclical events such as seasonal variations in tidal patterns. Any natural soil additions created through accretion usually belong to the property owner. See also *alluvial; alluvion.* (See top of right column.)

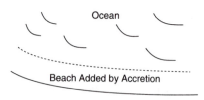

Original Beach

accrual: Recognizing revenue when earned and expenses when incurred regardless of when cash is received or paid. This differs from cash basis accounting, which records revenues and expenses only when cash is received or paid. A real estate service business may use either method.

accrual of depreciation: Depreciation that has not been recorded at the end of the accounting period. For example, if depreciation on an office building is $50,000 per year and six months has not been entered yet, the accrual is $25,000 so that depreciation will be stated correctly in the income statement.

accrual method: Accounting method in which revenue is recognized as earned and expenses are recognized as incurred regardless of when cash is received or paid. See also *accrual of depreciation.*

accrued interest: Interest that accrues and will be paid when a property is sold if the rental income does not cover the mortgage payments.

accusation: Charge of improper conduct by an individual or business. An example is a hotel owner accusing a guest of stealing hotel property.

acknowledgment: Proclamation by an authorized official verifying the individuals signing a document or deed and that they have done so freely. See also *notary public; verification.*

acoustical material: Sound-absorbing materials usually applied to walls and ceilings. Includes sound-absorbing tiles, mineral compositions, cork, wood, and special plasters made from vermiculite and other porous materials. See also *acoustical tile.*

acoustical tile: Sound-absorbing tiles designed to reduce the deflection and reverberation of sound waves. Used on walls and ceilings are made of cork, minerals, fiber, or insulated metals, depending on the type of installation.

acquisition: Function of securing ownership or controlling interest over a property or other object of interest. Occurs either through a purchase or a merger.

acquisition cost: Total price of purchasing property, including the amount of the property, cost of appraisal fees, attorney's fee, commission, credit report, hazard insurance, document preparation fee, loan application fee, mortgage insurance application fee, mortgage insurance premium, mortgage taxes, pest inspection, property survey, tax stamps, and title insurance. For example, John purchased a home for $150,000 plus $6,000 in costs, including appraisal fees, attorney's fee, mortgage broker commission, property survey, tax stamps, and title insurance. John's total acquisition cost was $156,000. See also *closing cost.*

acquisition loan: Money borrowed for the express purpose of acquiring property through a purchase transaction. For example, a building contractor obtains an acquisition loan from a bank to purchase a particular piece of property, and then obtains a construction loan to build homes for resale purposes.

acre: Two-dimensional land measure equivalent to:

4.046856E+07 square centimeters,
4046.856 square meters,
4.046856E-03 square kilometers,
627,2640 square inches,
43,560 square feet,
4,840 square yards,
.0015625 square miles, or
10 square chains.

For example, a survey of Smith's property shows that it is 5.2018 acres of land.

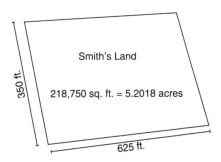

acre-foot (foot-acre): Measure of volume equal to 43,560 cubic feet or 325,850 gallons. An acre-foot equals a one-acre area one-foot deep. Primarily used in measuring the volume of coal and water.

act of god: Unpreventable action occurring without the intervention of man, normally associated with violent natural occurrences such as droughts, earthquakes, floods, hurricanes, lightning, monsoons, pestilence, tornadoes, and wind storms. A physical occurrence, usually accidental in nature and an outcome of the natural universe having no relationship to the actions of man. For example, an individual files an insurance claim to indemnify the damages caused to his roof by the effects of a hurricane.

action:
(1) In the legal sense, a suit brought before a court of law in the form of a complaint, demanding a legal right from another party. It has all the procedures accompanying any judicial action, including a court adjudication and its enforcement or denial.
(2) In real estate, a procedure brought before the court to repossess or regain specific properties or hereditaments. Those based on the right of property are termed droitural and those based

on the right of possession are termed possessory.

action in personam: Judicial proceeding against the person rather than against the person's property. Seeks to have the individual perform the terms of a contract, provide a service, or repair a loss. In common law, it seeks the payment for a debt or damages incurred. For example, John sues to enforce a contract whereby Bill agreed to paint the outside of his house for an agreed-upon consideration.

action in rem: Judicial proceeding against property, or more literally, "against the thing." While in legal theory an action in rem occurs only against property, in actuality it consists of a legal action between parties for the purpose of attaching or disposing of property owned by them. Examples include dividing or selling all or a portion of real estate, foreclosing a mortgage, or implementing a property lien.

active participation: Involvement in real estate ownership and management on a continuing basis as contrasted to passive participation. The tax laws provide greater tax benefits when the owner actively participates in real estate property and rentals.

actual age: Chronological (real) age of property. For example, a house that was constructed 20 years ago has an actual age of 20 years. See also *effective age.*

actual notice: Actual and direct knowledge by a potential property purchaser of the terms of a property transaction. Such knowledge would include all details in the public record relating to the title and title search, land surveys, liens, or other financial interests in the property, as well as access, air, mineral, or water rights.

There are two categories of actual notice: express and implied. In express no-tice, it has been clearly established that the purchaser was personally shown all relevant details of a transaction, whereas in implied notice, it is assumed that an individual's knowledge was sufficient to cause an interest in further investigation and inquiry. For example, in an express actual notice, an individual is shown a property survey detailing the extent and physical traits of the property. In an implied actual notice, an individual is informed that a piece of property is being auctioned because of unsatisfied property liens, but the details of the liens are not given. His knowledge of their existence should prompt him to research the size and nature of the liens.

addendum (addenda): An attachment, clause, or section added to an agreement or contract specifying additional terms or requirements. For example, an addendum to a contract for a sale agreement would/that state a previous lien must be satisfied prior to the issuance of a new mortgage to purchase the property. Addenda commonly added to real estate contracts relate to financing and property survey requirements.

add-on-interest: Interest that is figured into the total cost of a loan over its entire life. The interest is added to the principal and divided by the number of monthly payments to determine the amount of the monthly payment. For example, if Bill borrows $1,500 at an add-on interest rate of 9% for 5 years, then the total cost of the loan would be $1,500 $\times$ 9% $\times$ 5 years = $675.

Using the add-on interest method to determine Bill's monthly payment, $675 would be added to $1500, dividing the sum by the number of monthly payments to be made. This results in a monthly payment of $36.25, calculated as follows:

5 years × 12 months = 60 monthly payments

$$\frac{\$1500 + \$675}{60} = \frac{\$2175}{60} = \$36.25$$

This would be much higher than a monthly simple interest payment of $27.25.

additional first-year depreciation (tax): Property value of up to $10,000 that of a taxpayer may elect to treat as an expense rather than as an asset. It applies only to personal property, not real property.

adhesion contract: Legally enforceable, standardized contract offered by a business for a product or service on a "take it or leave it" basis. Under its terms, the consumer has no opportunity to negotiate the terms or conditions of the agreement and can only be satisfied by accepting it. An adhesion contract puts the consumer at a serious disadvantage. An example would be a real estate lease agreement where the terms are non-negotiable.

adjacent property: Property that is close to, although not actually touching, another piece of property. See also *adjoining property.*

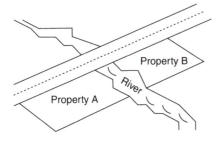

adjoining owners: Property owners whose property touches a common property. Adjoining owners have a legal right to be notified when a zoning variance or change in licensing in the common property is being formally considered. (See top of right column.)

Adjoining Owner A | Common Property | Adjoining Owner B

adjoining property: Property that shares a common border, is contiguous, and touching. See also *adjacent property.*

adjournment of closing: Act of postponing a closing for another day or place. Adjournments of closing can occur for a variety of reasons including the lack of an appropriate closing statement, one or more parties being unable to be present, or an irregularity in the title report or credit check. If both parties agree to the adjournment, the closing may be rescheduled. In the event of a cancellation, the purchase contract may be jeopardized, dependent in part on the cancellation clause.

adjudication: Formal decision by a court of law in an action brought before it. The court reaches a final determination for all parties in the case before it. For example, Smith sues Jones in small claims court for three months' rent owed on an apartment. The court declares that Jones owes Smith the three months' rent and issues an adjudication order for a salary garnishment to recover the rent.

adjudication order: See *decree; judgment.*

adjustable rate mortgage (ARM): Also called variable or flexible rate mortgage. A mortgage where the interest rate is not constant, but changes over time. ARMs often have attractive beginning interest rates, called teaser rates, and monthly payments. However, there is the risk that payments will increase. Benefits of ARMs include:

(1) Lower starting interest rate (usually about 2 percentage points less than a fixed rate) and lower beginning payments, resulting in dollar savings.

(2) Lower cap rates—the maximum interest rate a borrower might pay for a loan.

(3) Lower payments if interest rates drop.

(4) Greater availability and less processing time for loans compared to fixed-rate mortgages.

(5) Usually assumable by a borrower, which is helpful when selling.

(6) The possibility of prepaying the loan without penalty.

Drawbacks of ARMs include:

(1) Higher monthly payments if interest rates increase.

(2) Negative amortization. When monthly payments do not cover all of the interest cost, the uncovered interest cost is added to the unpaid principal balance. This means that after making many payments, the borrower could owe more than he or she did at the time the loan was initially taken out.

(3) The initial interest rates last only until the first adjustment, usually six months. Further, the promotional, or tease rate is usually not distinguished from the true contract rate. The latter is based on the index tied to the loan.

A borrower should prefer a fixed rate loan rather than an ARM if he or she:

- Plans to be in the same home for an extended time period. However, an ARM is preferred if he or she is buying a starter home or anticipates moving or being transferred in a couple of years.
- Does not anticipate income increasing.

- Has other significant debts, such as auto loans.
- Wants the predictability of fixed payments.

When seeking an ARM, the following checklist of questions may be asked of lenders:

- What is the initial loan rate, the annual percentage rate (APR) and the points? What other costs besides interest are involved?
- What is the monthly payment?
- What index is the loan tied to? How has the index changed in the past? Does the rate always move with the index?
- What is the lender's margin above the index? The margin never changes during the loan period. The ARM interest rate equals the index rate plus the margin.

EXAMPLE: Bob is comparing ARMs of different lenders. Both ARMs are for 30 years and amount to $65,000. Both lenders use the one-year Treasury index, which is 10%. However, Lender X uses a 2% margin, and Lender Y uses a 3% margin. The difference in margin impacts the initial monthly payment:

Lender X
ARM interest rate   12% (10% + 2%)
Monthly payment $668.60 at 12%

Lender Y
ARM interest rate   13% (10% + 3%)
Monthly payment $719.03 at 13%

- How long will the initial rate be in effect? Will there be an automatic increase at the first adjustment period, even if the index has not changed? What impact will this have on monthly payments?
- How many times can the rate change?

- Is there a "cap" (ceiling) on each rate change and how will the limit affect monthly payments?
- Is private mortgage insurance (PMI) required, and if so, what is the monthly cost?
- Is there negative amortization?
- Is the mortgage assumable?
- Is a prepayment penalty involved?

See also *creative financing; renegotiated rate mortgage (RRM); variable rate mortgage (VRM).*

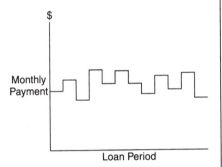

adjusted basis: Cost measuring method for tax purposes where the cost is reduced because of depreciation and increased because of the cost of capital improvements. For example, the adjusted basis of measuring the cost of a home would be increased by the cost of a permanent improvement, such as the installation of central air conditioning.

adjusted gross income (AGI): Federal tax term applicable to the difference between the taxpayer's gross income and adjustments to income. Adjustments to income include deductions for individual retirement accounts (IRAs) and Keogh pension plans. Pension funds may be invested in real estate. AGI is the basis for determining the eligibility and limitations of other components in calculating the taxpayer's tax, such as for miscellaneous expenses (2% of AGI).

adjusted price: Price of a bond or note plus accrued interest.

adjusted sales price:
(1) The net sales price of a piece of property where the commissions and other closing costs are subtracted from the actual sales price.
(2) In appraisal, the price of a comparable piece of property after differences between it and the property in question are accounted for.
(3) In income taxation, the selling price of a home is reduced by the cost of improvements. For example, the comparable property is the same as the property in question except the comparable property has a one car garage and the subject property does not. Therefore, the selling price of $125,000 for the comparable property is reduced by $5,000. The adjusted sales price is $120,000.

adjusted tax basis: Original cost of property plus additional capital expenditures made to it less the accumulated depreciation. The realized gain or loss for tax purposes is the difference between the selling price and adjusted basis. Assume an office building was bought for $500,000 and $200,000 of capital improvements were made to it (e.g., roof, paneling, burner). If the accumulated depreciation was $100,000, the adjusted cost basis of the property for tax purposes is $600,000. If the property is then sold for $620,000, the taxable gain is $20,000.

adjuster: Insurance company employee who settles the damage to insured property. The insured is contacted, the property is assessed, a valuation is made, and a recommended amount of reimbursement is made by the insurance company.

adjustments in appraisal: Changes in the value of a subject property based on the value of a comparable property. The differences can be expressed in percentages or dollars that collectively provide an indication of the value of the subject property. Adjustments in appraisal of a comparable property affect the overall value of the subject property. For example, an appraisal is made of a four bedroom home with a comparable home having only three bedrooms which sold for $125,000. The additional bedroom in the subject home is appraised at $15,000, giving the subject home an adjusted sales price of $140,000.

ad litem: Literally translated, "for the suit." In practice, one where a guardian has been appointed to protect the interests of the suit on behalf of an individual who is either an infant or legally incapacitated.

administrative discretion: Authority of an individual appointed to a governmental position to use their judgment and discretion in interpreting the intent of the law when making a decision or implementing a policy. For example, a building inspector is required to render a judgment as to whether a non-branded form of insulation material, falling within a certain range of insulation values, conforms with the building code.

administrator: Court appointed male who manages an intestate's property including all assets and liabilities. A male estate manager designated by a will is an executor. See also *intestate*.

administrator cum testamento annexo (C.T.A.): A will where the decedent's nomination of an executor/executrix is flawed, requiring an administrator to be appointed by the court and annexed to the will. The executors either were never named, incompetent, or declined to carry out the requisite functions. For example, a decedent named a brother to be the executor of his will, but the brother moved abroad and is unable to function as the executor. At a court hearing, an attorney is appointed administrator C.T.A. to manage the estate for the heirs.

administrator's deed: Deed used to convey an intestate's real property through a court appointed administrator. The administrator is legally empowered to convey the property deed to the heirs. See also *intestate*.

administratrix: Court-appointed female administrator of an intestate's property. A female estate manager designated by a will is termed an executrix. See also *intestate*.

adobe construction: Method of construction using sunbaked blocks made of soil mixed with straw. In the United States, this style of construction is chiefly used in the Southwest. It is also used in Latin America as well as other arid parts of the world.

adult community: Housing projects specifically designed to meet the community needs of the increasing number of individuals who are largely retired, having no small children. Adult communities are found in group projects including condominiums, cooperatives, townhouses, apartment complexes, and planned communities. Normally, adult communities are characterized by low maintenance, high security, and lifestyle recreational programs.

ad valorem: Literally translated, "according to value." See also *ad valorem tax*.

ad valorem tax: Tax levied in proportion to the value of property. The most common is that levied by localities on real property; however, it can also be levied on personal property, such as an automobile. For example, if a home is assessed at $150,000 and the ad valorem tax rate is 1.5%, then the tax would be $150,000 × 1.5% = $2,250.

advance:
(1) An increase in the price or market value of real estate.
(2) Money given to an employee of a real estate business before it is earned or incurred, such as an advance against salary or a cash advance for travel expenses.
(3) Prepayment received for work, goods, services or contracts to be performed later. Some contracts stipulate an advance before completion (e.g., construction project).
(4) Money from a lender to a borrower in advance of a loan.

adverse: See *adverse land use.*

adverse environmental effects: Negative impact on living or working conditions associated with property or land developer actions.

adverse land use: Open occupation of real property contrary to the interests of the property owner; implies the lack of recognition of the property owner.

adverse possession: Acquisition of land through prolonged and unauthorized occupation under an evident claim or right, in denial or opposition to the title of another claimant. Adverse possession is a statute of limitations that prevents a legal owner from claiming title to the land when the owner has done nothing to evict an adverse occupant during the statutory period. The courts demand proof before they permit adverse possession. For example, the claimant must show proof that he or she has maintained actual, visible, continuous, exclusive, hostile, and notorious possession and must be publicly claiming ownership to the property.

advocacy role: Position taken by a real estate consultant representing the best interests of the client.

aerial photos: Photographs of land areas taken by cameras mounted in aircraft or satellites. Aerial photos are extremely useful in interpretation of the Earth's surface features, both natural and manmade. Archaeologists, civil engineers, foresters, geologists, geographers, hydrologists, soil scientists, and those studying urban growth make extensive use of aerial photographs. Aerial photographs are also made of land or a group of homes for a prospective buyer's use.

While aerial photography can assist in developing maps, they differ from maps in one important way. A map has a uniform or controlled scale. The aerial photograph, on the other hand, does not have a constant or uniformly changing scale. When a vertical photograph is taken of a nonhorizontal surface, distances that are of equal length on the ground will appear unequal on film because of topographic irregularities.

Aerial photographs have two primary uses: mapmaking and interpretation. Numerous instruments are used in making maps from aerial photographs. One of the functions of many of these instruments is to remove distortion resulting from axial tilt.

Perhaps the most important characteristic of aerial photographs is that they can be viewed stereoscopically, or in three dimensions. This is true whether they are black-and-white, color, infrared, or any other special type. Stereoscopic effect enables photo interpreters to extract many kinds of useful information from aerial photographs. Using aerial photographs, the geologist can identify rock types, determine geologic structure, and obtain information that will assist in the search for petroleum and mineral deposits.

aesthetic value: Value added to property because of its intrinsic artistic, beautiful, and favored location. For example, a parcel of property located high on a bluff overlooking a beautiful lake is worth significantly more than surrounding properties that are not located on the bluff.

affidavit: Written statement or declaration, made under oath before a licensed individual, such as a notary public. In an affidavit of title, the seller (the affiant) identifies himself or herself and his or her marital status, certifying that since the examination of title on the contract date, there have been no judgments, divorces, bankruptcies, unrecorded deeds, unpaid repairs, or defects in title known to him or her and that he or she is in possession of the property.

affirm: To confirm, ratify, verify, and accept a transaction that can be canceled.

affirmation: Serious confirmation and verification that a written contract or affidavit is true, bonafiable, and valid. For example, a buyer is about to sign a contract to purchase a piece of property from a broker representing the seller who issues an affirmation that the contract represents the true terms of the property.

affirmative action: Federal and state programs prohibiting any form of preferential treatment or discrimination based on age, national origin, race, religion, sex, or other personal characteristics, using deception and quotas, to prevent equal access to employment and other societal opportunities, such as voting and housing. Beginning with several federal civil rights acts, most particularly the Civil Rights Act of 1964, and subsequent state legislation, affirmative action programs encourage equal opportunities and open access for all. Real estate brokers and agents are prohibited from steering clients toward one type of neighborhood rather than another based on ethnicity or race. For example, an agent hindering a minority family from buying a home in a particular neighborhood by steering them to another would be violating the law.

afforestation: Creating a forest cover on a land area not previously forested. Not only increases the aesthetic value of the land, but helps to prevent erosion thereby improving the environment.

a-frame: Outside shape of a structure that has the shape of an inverted V or an A, hence, the name.

after-acquired title: Doctrine by which the title of real property previously unsuccessfully transferred because of the lack of possession by grantor automatically passes to the previous grantee upon acquisition. This is based on the acquisition of title by estoppel. For example, an individual sells real property to a buyer but makes a faulty delivery of the title since the property is in probate from an inheritance . The property is subsequently coveyed to the buyer under the after-acquired title doctrine when the seller successfully acquires the property after completion of the probate process.

after-completion costs: Expenditures incurred subsequent to the building of a structure. An example would be the cost of wallpaper after a house was built to specification.

after-tax cash flow: Cash flow from income-producing property, reduced by income taxes related to the property's income. A tax loss providing a tax savings from the shelter of income earned outside the property is added to the cash flow earned by the property. Assume a property generates $5,000 per year of cash flow, and in the first year of ownership, depreciation and interest deductions result in a tax loss of $6,000. Assuming a tax rate of 40%, the loss saves $2,400 ($6,000 × 40%) of taxes. The after-tax cash flow is

$7,400 ($5,000 + $2,400). See also *before-tax cash flow; cash flow*.

after-tax equity yield: Net return rate earned on an equity investment in real estate after deducting any interest costs and taxes. Assume a purchase of real estate for $500,000 cash and the balance of $300,000 on mortgage. The property generates annual cash flow of $70,000 after interest and before taxes. If taxes are $20,000, the after-tax cash flow is $50,000. After one year, the property is sold for $900,000 net of tax. The gain on sale is therefore $100,000 ($900,000 − $800,000). The total return is $150,000 on an $800,000 investment providing a yield rate of 18.8%.

after-tax rate of return: Rate of return after income taxes that a real estate investor can keep out of current income (such as rental income or interest income) and capital gains or losses on the property.

age-life depreciation: Depreciation method based on the anticipated useful life of the property, allowing for normal wear and tear.

agency:
(1) Relationship between two people or entities in which one is a principal and the other is an agent representing the principal in activities with other parties. This relationship stems from a contract wherein the agent is retained by the principal to handle transactions with a third party. This arrangement may exist with real estate.
(2) A governmental unit, such as a department, committee, or council.
(3) Buying or selling property for a client.

agenda: List of items to be accomplished or considered in a preplanned meeting. For example, the closing for Abel's property included an agenda of documents to be signed and transactions to occur.

agent: Individual having the authority to act on the behalf of another and represent his or her business interests. A real estate agent is associated with a real estate broker for the purpose of renting or selling real property to the public. For example, an individual gives a listing to a real estate agent for the purpose of selling his or her home.

agreement of sale: Contractual agreement between a seller and a buyer for a future sale; statement of accord setting forth terms and conditions obligating the seller to sell and the buyer to buy a piece of property. Normally, requires an earnest money deposit equalling 10% of the total price of the property, states a description of the property, and has a time limitation to complete the sale.

For example, Joyce's broker prepared an agreement of sale to sell a home to Paul. Both principals signed it. The agreement provides that the price of $300,000 is to be paid at closing, contingent on Paul's ability to obtain a $75,000 mortgage at an 8% interest rate. See also *offer and acceptance; contract of sale*.

agricultural property: Property zoned and used for farming including the raising of crops and livestock. The designation of property as agricultural causes it to have a much lower property tax rate than other property classifications.

agricultural use value: Value of agricultural land as determined by its ability to produce crops and livestock. Several factors determine agricultural use value. An important consideration is the amount of arable land on the property, that is, property which is not disrupted by rock outcroppings, untillable terrain, or trees and other overgrowth. A second factor is the proximity to an adequate water supply. While plant nutrients can be added with fertilizer, water cannot be replaced. Agricultural properties located in extremely arid regions will have less ability to produce crops and support livestock, reducing the use value. A third factor is the climatic location of agricultural land. Properties located in northern climates have shorter growing seasons than those located in more temperate areas. Climate also determines the types of crops that can be raised, while temperature extremes negatively affect agricultural use value.

air rights: Rights to the use of open air space over property, including commercial aircraft flight paths, the erection of signs, buildings, railroad rights of way, and the rights to preserve an open view by preventing the building of obstructions. Condominium owners retain the air space within their individual units. Air rights can be sold fee simple or leased. For example, Mr. Smith leased the air rights to the roof of his building bordering an interstate highway to a company for the construction of an advertising billboard.

aka: Also known as. In a contract or other document, an individual may be referred to as AKA. For example, a married woman may customarily use her maiden name interchangeably. Therefore, a contract stipulates her maiden name as AKA.

alcaide: Governor of a fortress, custodian, jailer, or warden.

alcove: Normally small recess in a room extending to the floor. Originally an alcove was vaulted or separated from the rest of the room by an arch.

alias: Syn. for AKA. Another name by which a person is known. Alias is a generic term describing a name that could be fictitious or a nickname. For example, John Smith's alias is Long John Silver.

alien: Foreign-born individual not qualifying as a citizen of the country in which he or she resides. The extent of an alien's legal rights depend on the legal system of the country in which he or she resides. Aliens in the United States have the full legal protection and rights guaranteed by the Constitution.

alienation: Voluntary and purposeful conveyance of property from one person to another through the transfer of title and possession. Alienation of property includes all voluntary methods of transferring property. For example, at the closing the alienation occurs with the signing of the deed by the seller.

alienation clause: Stipulation in a contractual agreement either allowing or forbidding the right to transfer property from one person to another. For example, a comprehensive insurance policy has an alienation clause voiding the policy in the event the property owner transfers ownership of the property to another individual.

allegation: Accusation, charge, claim, inculpation, or statement of a party to an action against a respondent. An allegation establishes the circumstances to be proved in a formal action before the court. An example would be a landlord accusing a tenant of damaging the apartment or office.

alley: A narrow passageway between buildings providing secondary rear access. Frequently an alley occurs within a relatively well-developed complex of buildings. An alley not only provides access for pedestrians, but also can provide access for emergency and service vehicles.

alley influence: Impact resulting from a real or side alley on the worth of an abutting property. This may be particularly important to a business property.

all-inclusive trust deed (AITD): See *wrap-around mortgage (trust deed)*.

allocation method: Approach used to allocate the price paid for two or more properties based on their fair market values. Assume land and building are bought for $900,000. The appraised values of the land and building are

$400,000 and $800,000, respectively. The allocated cost to the land and building are $300,000 and $600,000, respectively, determined as follows:

	Appraised Value	Allocated Cost
Land	$ 400,000	$300,000
Building	800,000	600,000
Total	$1,200,000	$900,000

allotment:
(1) Allocation of real estate made on some equitable basis to prospective buyers.
(2) Part of an appropriation that may be encumbered or expended during a budget allotment period, which is usually a period of time less than one fiscal year. Bimonthly and quarterly allotment periods are most common.

allowance for vacancy and income loss: Provision made in evaluating and valuing rental or income-producing property for the income lost from unoccupied premises. An example would be an owner of an office building that estimates its occupancy rate and makes a loss provision for vacant offices.

alluvial: Soil, sand, and gravel deposited on land, usually a shoreline, as the result of flooding or tidal action. The property owner normally acquires property rights to the alluvial accretion or deposit.

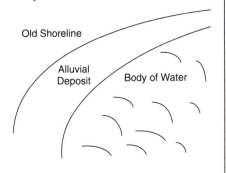

alluvion (alluvium): See *alluvial.*

alta title policy: See *American Land Title Association (ALTA).*

alternative mortgage instrument (AMI): Type of mortgage which is not based on a constant interest rate.

ambulatory: Covered passage or sheltered area within the walls of a building, or between the columns and walls of a circular building. Provides a sheltered walking area within a building's confines.

amenities: Those features associated with the location and design primarily of residential property, structures, and appurtenances that enhance overall living quality. The term is more associated with aesthetic value rather than pure monetary considerations although amenities can enhance overall property value. For example, the amenities of a home might include a beautiful ocean view, well designed and maintained gardens, and a well shaded patio. See also *amenity value.*

amenity value: Value added to property from its associated amenities. For example, the proximity to a water view and well-developed landscaping added $50,000 to the value of the home.

American Institute of Architects (AIA): Founded in 1857 and located in Washington, DC, with over 54,000 members, throughout the United States, the AIA has 301 local groups in all 50 states. A professional society of architects promoting excellence in architectural design, professionalism, and continued training. It sponsors educational programs with schools of architecture, graduate schools, elementary, and secondary schools. The AIA maintains a 30,000 volume library including print collections, archives, drawings, and rare books. It also sponsors annual honor awards recognizing outstanding design achievements nationwide. It publishes the monthly *American Institute of Architects-Memo.*

American Institute of Real Estate Appraisers (AIREA): Merged with Appraisal Institute (AI) in 1991.

American Land Development Association: Trade group of predominately land developers. The organization can be reached at 1200 L Street, N.W., Washington, DC 20005; (202) 371-6700.

American Land Title Association (ALTA): Organization founded in 1906 and located in Washington, DC, ALTA has over 2,400 members in 40 states. It fosters uniformity and quality in title abstract and insurance policies. It publishes the monthly *Capital Comment,* the bimonthly *Title News,* and the annual *Directory of Members.* See also *title company.*

American Planning Association (APA): Founded in 1978 and located in Washington, DC, the APA has 26,000 members with 45 regional groups throughout the United States. The APA encourages the best techniques and decisions for the planned development of communities and regions. It provides extensive professional services including publications for professionals and laypeople and its Planning Advisory Service furnishes extensive information and research, including an inquiry-answering service. Also provides specific research reports on planning, zoning, and environmental regulations. It maintains a sizable professional library containing books, pamphlets, comprehensive plans, zoning ordinances, and environmental reports. The APA also works in conjunction with local, national and international governments and organizations. Biennially it publishes the *AICP Roster,* the *Jobmart,* and the *Journal of the American Planning Association.*

American Real Estate Society (ARES): Founded in 1985 and located at Cleveland State University in the College of Business, Cleveland, OH, ARES has 950 members, consisting primarily of college professors interested in real estate finance, investment, development, valuation, marketing, and related activities. ARES members actively conduct research and exchange real estate market, finance, and development-related information and investment concepts. It participates in professional real estate education through the ARES case studies series which is available to the industry. The society grants annual awards for the best professional real estate related research papers. It publishes an occasional newsletter, a membership directory, and the *Journal of Real Estate,* as well as other publications.

American Real Estate and Urban Economics Association (AREUA): Founded in 1965 and located in Bloomington, IN, AREUA has 15,500 members consisting of educators, behavioral scientists, state and local school system research directors, research specialists, and graduate students. It publishes a journal and a semiannual newsletter.

American Society of Appraisers (ASA): Founded in 1952 and located in Washington, DC, ASA has 6,000 members. The society is primarily concerned with the advancement of the appraisal profession including its teaching, certifying, and testing. In addition, ASA actively seeks to establish the ability of its professional members to act as professional experts and witnesses as well as establish recognition of the profession in property value economics by educational and governmental institutions. The society awards the professional designation of ASA to senior members having at least five years' valuation experience after successfully passing written and oral examinations. It also awards the designation of FASA to Fellows chosen from the senior members by the ASA board of governors for outstanding services to the profession.

American Society of Real Estate Counselors (ASREC): Founded in 1953 and located in Chicago, IL, ASREC has 850 members. A society of real estate professionals providing a counseling service on real estate purchase and investment decisions through a negotiated fee rather than charging a commission. Members have the CRE (Counselor of Real Estate) title. The society maintains a speaker's bureau and conducts educational campaigns. It publishes a directory and the semiannual *Real Estate Issues.*

amortization: Gradual reduction of a loan amount over time, such as paying off the principal on a mortgage. See also *amortized loan; amortization schedule; depreciation.*

amortization schedule: Schedule showing the breakdown of each loan payment that consists partly of interest and partly of principal. The interest component of the payment is largest in the first period (because the principal balance is the highest) and subsequently declines, whereas the principal portion is smallest in the first period (because of the high interest) and increases thereafter as, shown in the following example.

EXAMPLE: Assume that a business borrows $2,000 to be repaid in three equal installments at the end of each of the next 3 years. The bank charges 12% interest. The amount of each payment is calculated as follows:

Table 4 (see Appendix) factor at 12% for 3 years = 2.402. The amount of each payment equals:

$$\frac{\$2,000}{2.402} = \$832.64$$

The following amortization schedule can be set up:

Year	Payment	Interest	Repayment of Principal	Remaining Balance
0				$2,000.00
1	$832.64	$240.00[a]	$592.64[b]	$1.407.36
2	$832.64	$168.88	$663.76	$ 743.60
3	$832.64	$ 89.23	$743.41[c]	

[a] Interest is computed by multiplying the loan balance at the beginning of the year by the interest rate. Therefore, interest in year 1 is $2,000 (0.12) = $240; in year 2 interest is $1,407.36(0.12) = $168.88; and in year 3 interest is $743.60(0.12) = $89.23. All figures are rounded.
[b] The reduction in principal equals the payment less the interest portion ($832.64 − $240.00 = $592.64)
[c] Not exact because of accumulated rounding errors.

A monthly amortization schedule (monthly repayment program) based on a 9%, 6-year $1,000 amortized loan is:

Year	Principal	Interest
1	$132.92	$90.00
2	144.88	78.04
3	157.92	65.00
4	172.14	50.78
5	187.63	35.29
6	204.51	18.41

A graph of monthly mortgage payments is:

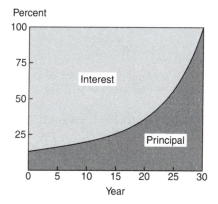

amortized loan: Loan paid off in periodic equal installments which includes varying portions of principal and interest during its term. Examples include mortgage loans and most commercial loans. The periodic payment may be computed by dividing the principal loan amount by a Present Value of an Annuity of $1 factor (see Table 4, Appendix). See also *amortization schedule; rule of 78.*

EXAMPLE: Paula has a 40-month loan of $5,000 for her new roof at a 12% annual interest rate. She wants to find out the monthly loan payment.

Note that i = 12%/12 months = 1% and the Table 4 factor at 1% for 40 months = 32.8347

Therefore,

$$\frac{\$5,000}{32.835} = \$152.28$$

Another approach to compute the monthly payment is to use Table 5 in the Appendix. It gives the monthly payment needed to pay off a $1,000 installment loan for a given annual interest rate and term.

EXAMPLE: Bill takes out a $15,000, 12%, 48-month home improvement loan. He wants to know the monthly installment payment. Using Table 5, he follows these three steps:

Step 1: Divide the loan amount by $1,000:

$15,000/$1,000 = 15

Step 2: Find the payment factor from Table 5 for the interest rate and loan maturity:
The Table 5 payment factor for 12% and 48 months is $26.34

Step 3: Multiply the factor obtained in Step 2 by the amount from Step 1:

$26.34 × 15 = $395.10

His monthly installment loan payment is $395.10.

amortized mortgage: Mortgage where the interest and principal have been fully paid by the mortgagee. For example, the total amortization of a $60,000 mortgage over 30 years at 10% interest would include total interest payments of $129,555.46 plus the original principal of $60,000 for a total payment of $189,555.46.

anchor tenant: Major tenant, such as a nationally known department store, in a shopping center who determines the success or failure of the center's ability to attract shoppers and helps the secondary tenants succeed. Often, the anchor tenant will be granted favorable lease terms in order to attract and keep them in the shopping center. See *Triple A Tenant.*

ancillary: Secondary or subsidiary building or structure in a structural complex. For example, the security checkpoint is an ancillary building at the condominium complex entrance.

ancillary administrator: Out-of-state or out of jurisdiction administrator appointed to probate a decedent's property when there is no executor or executrix. The ancillary administrator performs all necessary estate responsibilities to close the estate.

annexation:

(1) *Municipality:* Legal process by which a municipality expands its territory to include part of an adjacent unincorporated area. The law of annexation is defined by state law, and annexation normally requires a ratification vote by both the incorporated municipality and the area to be annexed.

(2) *Fixtures:* Act of permanently attaching a fixture to a building, making it a part of the structure. Such fixtures are attached by concrete, nails, or screws and are considered a permanent part of the structure itself. For example, the electrical fuse box and interior wiring are annexed to the building and cannot be removed at the time of sale.

annual cap: Amount the interest rate of a variable rate mortgage can be raised or lowered in any consecutive 12-month period. For example, a 9% variable rate mortgage has a $2\frac{1}{2}$% annual cap. Thus, in a 1-year period, the interest rate could either be raised to $11\frac{1}{2}$% or decreased to $6\frac{1}{2}$%.

annual debt service: Required total annual interest and principal loan payments. For example, the monthly payments on a 30-year, $94,999.75 mortgage are $869.00, and the first year's total interest payment is $9,952.52 and the total principal payment is $475.48 for a total annual debt service of $10,428.

annual mortgage constant: See *mortgage constant.*

annual percentage rate (APR): True measure of the effective cost of credit for real estate purchases. It is the rate a borrower actually pays (including interest, points, and loan origination fees) expressed as a percentage rate per year. The lender must, according to the Truth in Lending Act (Consumer Credit Protection Act), disclose to a borrower the effective annual percentage rate (APR) and the total finance charge. The borrower can then compare the costs of the alternative loans. Banks often quote their interest rates in terms of dollars of interest per hundred dollars. Other lenders quote in terms of dollars per payment. This may confuse borrowers. APR eliminates this confusion. The calculation of the effective APR for different types of loans is presented below.

Single-Payment Loans. The single-payment loan is fully paid on a specified date. Two methods to compute APR on single-payment loans are the simple interest method and the discount method.

(1) Simple Interest Method. Interest is computed only on the amount borrowed (proceeds). The formula is

$$\text{Interest} = p \times r \times t$$

$$= \text{Principal} \times \text{Rate} \times \text{Time}$$

$$\text{APR} = \frac{\text{Average annual finance charge}}{\text{Amount borrowed or proceeds}}$$

EXAMPLE 1: Carol took out a single-payment loan of $1,000 for two years at a simple interest rate of 15%. The interest charge is $300 ($1,000 $\times$ 15% $\times$ 2 years). The APR is

$$\text{APR} = 15\% \ (\$150/\$1,000)$$

With the simple interest method, the stated simple interest rate and the APR are always identical for single-payment loans.

(2) Discount Method. Interest is computed and then deducted from the amount of the loan. The difference is the actual amount the borrower receives. In effect, the borrower prepays the finance charges.

EXAMPLE 2: Using the information from Example 1, the actual amount received is $700 ($1,000 − $300), not $1,000 to be paid back. The APR then is

$$\text{APR} = 21.43\% \ (\$150/\$700).$$

21.43% is the rate the lender must quote on the loan, not 15%.

The discount method always gives a higher APR than the simple interest method for single-payment loans at the same interest rates.

Installment Loans. Most consumer loans use the add-on method. There are several methods for calculating the APR on add-on loans. They are: (a) the actuarial method, (b) the constant ratio method, (c) the direct ratio method, and (d) the N-ratio method.

(a) The actuarial method is the most reliable in computing the APR and the one lenders most use. The interest is computed on unpaid balances of principal at a fixed rate, with each payment applied first to interest and the balance to principal. Because this approach involves complicated formulas, annuity tables available from the Federal Reserve and member banks or computer programs are typically used.

(b) The constant ratio method estimates the APR on an installment loan by the use of a simple formula. However, it overstates the rate significantly. The higher the quoted rate, the greater the inaccuracy. The constant ratio formula is

$$APR = \frac{2MC}{P(N + 1)}$$

where M = number of payment periods in one year, N = number of scheduled payments, C = finance charges in dollars (dollar cost of credit), and P = original proceeds.

(c) The direct ratio method has a more complex formula but is still easier than the actuarial method. It slightly understates the APR relative to the actuarial method. The direct ratio formula is

$$APR = \frac{6MC}{3P(N + 1) + C(N + 1)}$$

(d) The N-ratio method provides a more accurate estimation of the APR than either the constant ratio or the direct ratio method for most loans. The results of the N-ratio method may be either slightly more or less than the true rate, depending on the maturity of the loan and the stated rate. The N-ratio formula is

$$APR = \frac{M(95N + 9)C}{12N(N + 1)(4P + C)}$$

EXAMPLE 3: Assume Carol borrows $1,000 to be repaid in 12 equal monthly installments of $93.00 each for a finance charge of $116.00. The APR under each of the four methods is

computed as follows (Assume an annuity table or computer program gives an APR of 20.76%):

Actuarial Method

The APR under this approach is 20.76%, obtained from an annuity table or computer software.

Constant Ratio Method

$$APR = \frac{2MC}{P(N + 1)}$$

$$= \frac{2 \times 12 \times 116}{1000(12 + 1)}$$

$$= \frac{2784}{13000} = 21.42\%$$

Direct Ratio Method

$$APR = \frac{6MC}{3P(N + 1) + C(N + 1)}$$

$$= \frac{6 \times 12 \times 116}{3 \times 1000(12 + 1) + 116(12 + 1)}$$

$$= \frac{8352}{40508} = 20.62\%$$

N-Ratio Method

$$APR = \frac{M(95N + 9)C}{12N(N + 1)(4P + C)}$$

$$= \frac{12 \times (95 \times 12 + 9) \times 116}{12 \times 12 \times 13 \times [4(1000) + 116]}$$

$$= \frac{1599408}{7705152} = 20.76\%$$

These approximation formulas should not be used if variation exits in the amounts of payments or time periods between payments such as when one payment is unusually high.

Some financial institutions charge fees for a credit evaluation, a loan application, or for life insurance. The lender adds these fees to the finance charge as a component of the APR calculations.

EXAMPLE 4: Bank A will give a 7% business loan if Carol puts 25% down. Hence, if she takes out a $4,000 loan she will finance $3,000 over a three-year period with carrying charges amounting to $630 (7% × $3,000 × 3 years). She will make equal monthly payments of $100.83 for 36 months.

Bank B will give $3,500 on the same loan. Carol must pay $90 per month for 48 months. Which is the best loan for her? (Use the constant-ratio formula).

The APR computations (using the constant-ratio formula) follow:

Bank A:

$$APR = \frac{2 \times 12 \times 630}{3000(36 + 1)}$$

$$= \frac{15120}{111000} = 13.62\%$$

Bank B:

$$APR = \frac{2 \times 12 \times 820}{3500(48 + 1)}$$

$$= \frac{19680}{171500} = 11.48\%$$

For Bank B the total cost is $4,320 ($90 × 48). The total credit cost is $820 ($4,320 − $3,500).

Based on the APR, Carol should select Bank B. See also *effective annual yield; effective interest rate.*

annual percentage yield (APY): See *effective interest rate.*

annuity: Equal periodic payments or receipts. Examples of an annuity are annual rental receipts from a real estate investment and cash dividends from a real estate firm's preferred stock. There are two types of an annuity. They are: (1) an ordinary annuity, where payments or receipts occur at the end of the period; and (2) an annuity due, where payments or receipts are made at the beginning of the period.

annuity in advance: See *annuity due.*

annuity in arrears: See *ordinary annuity.*

annuity due: An annuity where the payments are made at the beginning of each month, quarter, or year depending on the period specified in the terms of the contract.

annuity factor: Factor used to determine the equal periodic payment (e.g., yearly, monthly) associated with a real estate transaction. Used to obtain the equal monthly lease payment, based on the lessor's desired rate of return, and the regular monthly mortgage payment. An annuity factor is used for both a present value of annuity or future value of annuity problem. The equal payment may be at the end of the period (ordinary annuity) or at the beginning of the period (annuity due). The annuity factor is computed and then it is looked up in the appropriate present value or future value of annuity table to arrive at the solution to a problem.

EXAMPLE: A 10-year lease agreement is signed for property worth $100,000 today. The lessor's desired rate of return is 10%. The equal year-end lease payment is computed below:

Present value of ordinary annuity

$$\text{Present value of property} \quad \frac{\$100,000}{6.1446} = \$16,274$$

Annuity factor for n = 10, i = 10%

annul: To abolish, cancel, do away with, eliminate, invalidate, or make null and void. For example, to annul a contract is to render it useless, as if it had never occurred.

ante: Prefix meaning coming before or in front of something else. For example, an antechamber, anteroom, or anteportico.

antenuptial agreement: Agreement negotiated between two individuals about to enter into matrimony; deals with issues of the distribution of property and support should the marital union dissolve or either spouse die. Such agreements are normally developed when there is a substantial amount of property involved.

anti: Prefix meaning:
(1) opposed or against something, as in antitrust or antisemitism.
(2) opposite, as in anticyclical or anticlimax.
(3) imputing strife, as in anti-king or antimanifesto.
(4) neutralizing or restorative, as in anticorrosive or anti-friction.

anticipated holding period: Time period for which one expects to keep property such as a real estate investment. For example, a real estate investment trust (REIT) often specifies in its prospectus how many years it expects to hold on to the property before sale.

anticipation: Expecting or looking forward to something happening. An example is expecting a fall in real estate prices so that a new home may be bought in the near future.

anticipatory breach: Terminating a contract prior to the time when actual performance is to occur. An example is when one party to a real estate contract announces he will not honor its terms even though he signed it. If the breach is through conduct instead of declaration, it is referred to as voluntary disablement.

anti-deficiency legislation: Statutory authority to meet a budgetary shortfall through increasing revenue by enacting a temporary surcharge or permanent tax increase. Budgetary deficiencies occur either because of unanticipated expenditures or decreases in actual as compared to projected revenue collections.

antitrust laws: Government laws designed to improve market efficiency, encourage competition, and curtail unfair trade practices by reducing barriers to entry, breaking up monopolies, and preventing conspiracies to restrict production or raise prices in the real estate industry.

There are three major antitrust laws: the Sherman Antitrust Act of 1890, the Clayton Antitrust Act of 1914, and the Federal Trade Commission Act of 1914.

apartment: Unit of one or more rooms usually connected to a multifamily complex of similar units; however, it can also be the only unit constructed within a single family home. Normally, the purpose of an apartment is to serve as rental housing or to house other related individuals, such as a mother-in-law. An apartment is never owned by the occupant and is managed by a property owner or manager. See also *duplex; multifamily housing; resident manager.*

apartment (building): Dwelling unit within a multifamily structure, usually used as rental housing. An apartment building is a structure with individual apartment units and a common entrance and hallway. Garden apartments, however, have individual entrances. Apartments vary in size from small, one-room units to large, multi-bedroom units. Apartment buildings may be as small as a one-story duplex to a high-rise building with hundreds of units, including retail and office space. See also *multifamily housing.*

apartment house: Multi-family housing complex of rental apartments managed by either the property owner or a resident manager. As of 1990, there were 32,923,000 rental units in the United States. However, 64.2 % of all housing units were owner occupied.

appearance: Extremely important consideration for real estate valuation. When trying to sell real estate, prospective buyers are very aware of appearance in that it gives an indication as to how well the property has been maintained and cared for. Secondly, appearance simply makes a property more attractive and pleasing to the eye allowing the seller to ask and get a higher selling price.

appellant: Party who petitions a lower court decision to the next higher court or moves a dispute from one jurisdiction to a higher level. For example, Jane Doe sought to overturn a lower court decision finding her guilty of a felony by appealing to the state's court of appeals.

apportionment:
(1) A division or assignment based on a plan or proportion. An example is prorating certain property expenses, such as insurance and taxes, between buyer and seller.
(2) Segregating property into individual parcels by tenants is common.

apportionment of basis: Allocating the price paid to purchase two or more properties based on their appraised values. Assume $950,000 is paid to buy land and a building having appraised values of $600,000 and $400,000, respectively. The apportioned cost basis is:

	Appraised Value	Apportioned Cost Basis
Land	$ 600,000	$570,000
Building	400,000	380,000
Total	$1,000,000	$950,000

apportionment clause: Contractual provision requiring apportionment.

appraisal: Valuation assessment of real property by an expert third party for the following purposes:
(a) developing a realistic market price.
(b) setting a market value at the time of death when probating an estate.
(c) dividing the value of real estate between the property and structural improvements.
(d) establishing insurable value.
See also *appraiser.*

appraisal approach: Three basic methods for setting values on property: (1) The cost approach estimates the replacement value of real property. (2) The comparable sales approach compares properties with other similar properties, thereby estimating the market value. (3) The income approach compares the net income a property will return to an investor. See also *appraisal report; comparable sales; cost approach; income approach; market comparison approach.*

appraisal of damage: Also called assessment of loss or loss appraisal. Analysis of property loss. Usually done by a professional appraiser, often with the insurance industry, and in connection with an insurance claim. Appraisers take into account the quality and quantity of the property and its age, value, and degree of damage. See also *assessed valuation; assessment.*

appraisal date: Date of the valuation of property, usually contained in a report. This is significant since property values change over time.

appraisal fee: Fee charged by a professional appraiser for an appraisal and appraisal report.

appraisal institute: Members are professional valuers and appraisers of real estate. Located at 225 North Michigan Avenue, Chicago, Illinois 60611, (800) 732-7732.

appraisal methods: Techniques used in valuing property. Includes comparable sales, cost approach, income approach, and market comparison approach.

appraisal process: Written report or affidavit by an appraiser that includes the date and purpose of the appraisal, a description of the property and all structures, street address, zoning, assessed valuation and taxes, highest and best use of the property, an appraisal method discussion, a history of the property and the area, the appraiser's licenses and qualifications, assumptions and limitations, and final value estimate of the property.

appraisal by summation: See *cost approach.*

appraiser: Individual having the necessary certification, education, and experience to professionally evaluate real estate market value. May act as an expert witness before a court of law regarding the process of evaluating property as well as giving testimony concerning real estate market value.

appreciation: Increase in the value of real estate. For example, property increased in fair market value from $500,000 to $600,000, resulting in an appreciation of $100,000. See also *capital gains or losses; return; yield.*

appreciation equity: Equity interest of an owner in the increase in value of the property over time. For example, if an investor owns 30% of a commercial property that has increased in value by $100,000 since it was purchased, the investor has experienced a $30,000 increase in his equity interest.

approximate compound yield: Measure of the annualized compound growth of a real estate investment.

appurtenance: Item that is part of something else that goes with the property. Examples are gardens and barns. The deed covers the real property and all that is attached to it.

appurtenant structures: Structure not directly belonging to a property but considered a part of it through the use of an easement of common consent. An adjunct to a main property that enhances the utility and enjoyment of the property. For example, access to a bathhouse on a shared beach. See also *appurtenance; right of access; right of way.*

a priori:

(1) Impact of a cause (reason) on something. For example, the failure to maintain a building in proper working order may cause breakdowns (e.g., oil burner, water leaks from roof).

(2) Theoretical base rather than actual experience. For example, in theory, when interest rates decrease, house prices should increase because of lower mortgage rates. However, the interest rate decline had no actual significant effect on the prices of homes.

arable: Land that is suitable for tilling and growing of crops. For example, a great majority of the land in the midwestern region of the United States is arable and cultivable.

arbitrage: Profiting from price differences when the same asset is traded in different markets. For example, simultaneously buying one contract of silver in the Chicago market and selling one contract of silver in the New York market, locking in a profit since at that moment the price on the two markets is different, provided the selling price is higher than the buying price. It is also the process of selling overvalued and buying undervalued real estate so as to bring about an equilibrium where all real estate are properly valued.

arbitrageur: One who engages in arbitrage.

arbitration: Process where a grievance or contract dispute is referred to an impartial arbitrator or a panel of arbitrators for the purpose of arriving at a mutually acceptable solution, avoiding the necessity of a judicial settlement. The arbitrator(s) hears the evidence and arrives at a decision. It is faster and less expensive than having a court action.

arcade: Arches, either roofed or open, mounted on a series of pillars to form a passageway or walkway. May or may not be attached to a building. Often used as a decorative and functional entranceway to a building. (See top of page 25.)

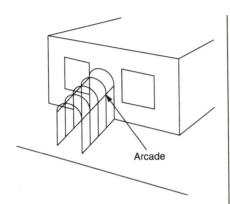

Arcade

arch: Structure designed to span an open space between two supporting members. Designed to bear weight and add support to a structure. Often used as a support structure in a bridge.

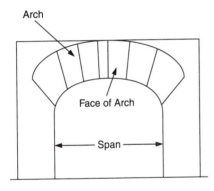

Arch

Face of Arch

Span

architect: An individual, educated, trained, and licensed in the principles of designing structures, and rendering drawings, specifications, bidding requirements. Sometimes also does overall management of the building project.

architect's punch list: List of architectural design items needing to be corrected and resolved prior to finalizing a building design.

area: Two-dimensional, circumscribed space having measurable dimensions. For example, a building lot is 70 ft. wide

and 100 ft. long, therefore, the total area of the building area is 7,000 sq. ft (70 x 100). Buildings and property are described in terms of total area.

arm's-length transaction: Transaction between unrelated entities or individuals acting in their own interest. An example is a real estate transaction carried out where the buyer and seller are not in communication with each other, and both parties are acting in their best financial interests. It is presumed that the prices used are the appraised values of the property being exchanged.

arrears:

(1) Payments made at the end of a time period.

(2) Late or overdue payment. Payments which are in default. An example is unpaid rent on an apartment.

arroyo: Dry ravine formed by water runoff. Found in arid areas, and not suitable building areas since they may flood whenever a significant rainfall occurs.

artesian well: Drilled well where water rises through the opening because of naturally occurring water pressure. Normally a pipe is inserted into the outlet to direct and control the water flow.

asbestos: Fibrous, fire-proofing material that was used in buildings and homes for insulation. It has been shown to be a possible health hazard and is a potential liability for purchasers. For example, the City of New York paid millions of dollars to remove it from school buildings.

as is:

(1) Term for secondhand or damaged items sold without a seller's warranty. The purchaser accepts delivery of goods in the condition found on inspection before acquisition, regardless of defects or damage. The buyer must inspect the items carefully, since the responsibility

of determining their condition falls on him or her.

(2) Not warranting the condition of real estate.

ask price: Listed and initial price for a piece of real estate. Normally considered to be a negotiable starting point in the eventual sale of the property. See also *bargain; listing; negotiable.*

asked price: Also called offering price, ask price, or asking price.

(1) The price at which real estate is offered for sale. Typically, it is the lowest price at which one can buy the property.

(2) For real estate mutual funds, the current net asset value per share plus sales charges.

assemblage: Process of combining two or more parcels of real estate into one.

assessed value: Amount set for real estate or other property by a government as a basis for levying taxes. For example, a local tax assessor may value property at $50,000. If by statute, properties in this jurisdiction are assessed at 70% of market value, the individual's assessed valuation then is $35,000 and property taxes will be based on this assessed value.

assessment:

(1) *Valuation.* Evaluation of property by a taxing authority for the purpose of levying a property tax. For example, the municipality gave an assessment of $150,000 for a home located in the suburb.

(2) *Taxation.* Actual amount of property tax levied on real property and due to the taxing authority. For example, the annual property tax assessment was $4,500 on a residential home.

(3) *Proportionate charge.* Payment share for a common charge apportioned to several property owners in a property association. For example, each unit was

assessed $500 to repair the condominium's pool.

(4) Special tax levied by government for repair or improvement, such as for sidewalks, sewage systems, and landscaping.

(5) Amount paid as compensation for damages made on the individual who wins a legal action in a real estate dispute.

assessment cycle: Period of time between valuations of property for tax purposes in a given locality.

assessment district: Any geographic taxing division where the legally chosen representatives are charged with the responsibility of assessing taxable property and collecting tax revenue.

assessment ratio: Relationship between a real estate's assessed valuation and its market value. The assumption is it is a current market value ratio. This requires continuous updating that rarely occurs. For example, if a home's assessed valuation is $50,000 and its market value is $250,000, then the assessment ratio = 50,000/250,000 or 20%. Dividing the assessed valuation by the assessment ratio produces the market value.

assessment record card: Physical record card where the date of the last assessment valuation and its results, as well as a property description are kept. More sophisticated assessment records are kept on computerized data bases.

assessment roll: Public record in an assessment district listing the assessed valuation of all its assessed property. The total assessed valuation is used by the taxing jurisdiction to determine the millage rate required to raise needed revenues.

assessor: Governmental representative charged with the responsibility of officially evaluating real property for ad valorem taxation purposes.

asset: Economic resource that is anticipated to provide benefits to a business. May be tangible or intangible and is expressed in money or is convertible into money. Examples of tangible assets are land, buildings, and automobiles. Examples of intangible assets are goodwill, trademarks, trade names, and copyrights.

asset depreciation range (ADR): Range of depreciable lives allowed by the Internal Revenue Service (IRS) for a particular asset. It is used to determine class lives for property, plant, and equipment.

assign: To transfer to another's rights under a contract.

assignee: Individual or business to which all rights (usually intangible) to property have been transferred. For example, in payment of a debt Jones transfers all rights to the lease on a piece of rental property to Smith.

assignment: Total transfer of one's rights under a real estate contract to another.

assignment of mortgage: Transfer of an assumable mortgage from the old owner to the new owner. An example is transferring a low interest mortgage to the buyer of a home.

assignment of policy: Right of a party, the assignor, to allocate the benefits of certain insurance policies to a third party, the assignee. Insurance on real estate may assign the policy to protect the property for those having an insurable interest. Thus, the assignee would have a risk involved, as in the case of a bank financing the property. Normally, the assignment is done through an endorsement whereby the insurance benefit rights are transferred. However, property and casualty policies usually are nonassignable except when the insurance company has given its permission. If property and casualty insurance policies are assignable, the beneficiaries are legitimate assignees. See also *assignment.*

assignment of proceeds: Agreement to transfer funds to a third party. For example, an agreement may stipulate that an insurance company will pay someone other than the insured for a reimbursable loss caused by damage to real property.

assignor: Individual or business transferring a right or benefit to another person or business. An example is the transfer of a lease agreement to real property.

assumable mortgage: Mortgage agreement permitting the loan liability to be transferred to a purchaser of the property with no change in its terms. However, if the mortgage has a due-on-sale clause, then it is not assumable.

assume: To undertake or take on a responsibility or duty. See also *assumable mortgage.*

assumption: Obligation taken on by a person who did not obtain it originally, but agrees to honor the terms of the existing obligation as a condition for the transaction. By assuming the loan rather than taking subject to the loan, the buyer becomes personally liable on the debt. See also *assumption of mortgage; deed of trust.*

assumption agreement: See *assumption of mortgage; deed of trust.*

assumption clause: Provision in a mortgage permitting the owner of property to transfer the mortgage to a buyer.

assumption fee: Charge assessed a mortgagor by the mortgagee when assuming a pre-existing mortgage. The assumption fee is often included in the closing costs when purchasing property.

assumption of mortgage (deed of trust): Buyer agrees to accept the responsibility for the existing mortgage. The seller is not relieved of the obligation unless the lender agrees to release it. Many lenders charge points and increase the interest rate when a mortgage is assumed.

assurance: Giving of a promise or guarantee to the receiver to instill confidence. An example is a contractor's guaranteeing the homeowner of the quality of the electrical work. See also *insurance*.

at-risk rules: Taxpayer can deduct losses only to the degree of risk. Amounts are restricted to the cash investment and the debt from which the taxpayer is personally liable. Assume the taxpayer incurs losses from real estate activities of $50,000. If the cash investment and personal debt incurred were $45,000, the most that could be deducted as losses is $45,000. There is an expansion of the at-risk amounts to real estate only to include certain nonrecourse loans from qualified lenders.

atrium: Originally a rectangular room with roof open to the sky and acting as the central, most important room in Roman architectural home design. By the third century B.C. the atrium house had become overwhelmingly popular in Italy. Its use gradually declined under the Roman Empire, when it was replaced by garden houses.

   The modern atrium is a large area forming a courtyard within a building, often enclosed by glass and open to sunlight. An atrium may be several stories high providing environmental functionality and appeal.

attachment: Legal term of the writ authorizing the taking of property or rights because of legal action. Its purpose is to protect the property to satisfy a judgment in favor of the plaintiff.

attachment date: Day the attachment of property under a judicial order becomes effective.

attest: Formal statement by an auditor, after thorough examination and con-

sideration, as to whether a real estate company's financial statements fairly present financial position and operating results. With an attest, the public accountant provides an objective evaluation to aid financial statement users.

attestation clause: Provision at the end of a document, such as a will, wherein the witnesses sign that the instrument has been executed before them. This may be useful involving transfers of real estate.

attic: Accessible room or space between the roof rafters and ceiling joists of a structure. May be unfinished or completely finished.

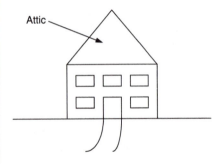

attic fan: Used to cool the attic by removing hot air.

attorney-at-law: An individual who has been admitted to practice law in his or her state. He or she is approved to represent clients, and can conduct the usual activities, such as drafting legal documents, providing legal advice, and representing clients in courts, regulatory agencies, and other entities.

attorney in fact: Power of attorney giving permission for a lawyer to represent a client.

attorney of record: Attorney whose name officially appears in permanent records of a case or an appeal thereto, or on the appearance docket. It gives public notice of the attorney who is handling the case.

attornment: Tenant agrees to a replacement landlord. Assume Landlord A became bankrupt and was replaced by Landlord B. Landlord B was recognized by the tenants to be the new owner.

attractive nuisance: Hazard or condition located on a premises that may attract and be dangerous to children. A property owner having an attractive nuisance must take prudent care to prevent children from having access and being exposed to the danger. For example, a homeowner installs an inground swimming pool on his property and constructs a fence to avoid an attractive nuisance.

attribution: Also called constructive ownership. Situation where the tax law assigns to one taxpayer the ownership interest of another taxpayer. For example, under the law, a father is considered to constructively own the real property actually owned by his son.

auction market: Where property is sold to the highest bidder. The last (highest) bid price is accepted when the auctioneer announces "sold."

audit: Examination of the financial records of a business to uncover errors and other irregularities. Involves looking at source documents to determine the legitimacy of transactions. An evaluation of internal control is also made. A unit of the business, such as a division or department, may also be investigated to determine if there is adherence to the company's procedures and operations and to corporate policy. A compliance audit determines whether the company is complying with specified rules and regulations.

automatic renewal clause: Provision in an agreement in which its renewal is a matter of course at the end of its initial term. An example is a lease contract which gives the lessee the right to renew it.

auxiliary lane: Supplementary narrow pathway, such as to a building.

average office occupancy: Average number of business days an office space is being used.

average tax rate: See *effective tax rate.*

avigation: Aerial navigation that may interfere with a property owner, such as creating undue noise. The value of land near an airport may decline in value for this reason. Further, airport congestion may have a negative impact.

avigation easement: Right of a property owner located adjacent to an airfield to use the air space above a certain distance to fly an airplane. However, the owner may not be allowed to put structures, signs, or trees on the property that may place aircraft in danger, such as near the runway.

avulsion: Removal of land by the action of water. See also *erosion.*

awning: Rooflike cover that extends over any place to provide shelter from the sun, rain, or wind.

awning window: Covering on the top exterior of a window.

axial growth: Land expansion resembling a "star." The star's center is the city, and major thoroughfares going away from the city are depicted.

azimuth: Angle from north or south of a property. When a real estate appraiser does surveying, it is looked at clockwise from north. It may assist in determining the form or boundaries of land.

baby boom generation: Americans born between the end of World War II and the 1960s when the veterans of World War II were in the family formation stage of their lives. A tremendous surge or "boom" in the birthrate occurred. This generation was responsible for significant consumer demand in the economy, starting with housing.

back-end fees: Commissions received by a syndicator when real property is sold. The fees typically occur after the investors receive their initial investment plus the specified return.

backfill: Dirt around a building's foundation for support. Holes are filled in.

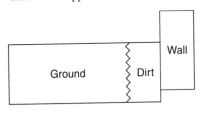

back taxes: Taxes owed due to nonpayment, underreporting, or omission (unknowingly or intentionally) from a prior year. The taxing authority will demand the back taxes, including possible fines, penalties, and interest.

backup contract: Secondary written agreement to purchase real property in the event the initial contract is not signed. For example, Joe sells his home to Fred contingent on Fred obtaining a mortgage. In the event this does not materialize, Joe has a backup agreement to sell this property to Bob.

bad faith: Intent to deceive or never to carry out the provisions of an agreement. An example is being dishonest in a real estate contract.

balance sheet: Statement of financial condition for a real estate business at the end of a reporting period listing all of its assets, liabilities, and stockholders' equity. Assets are what the company owns while liabilities are what is owed. Assets less liabilities equals net worth. The accounting equation for a company is: Assets = Liabilities + Stockholders' Equity. The balance sheet is categorized into major groupings of assets, liabilities, and stockholders' equity. For example, asset groupings include current assets, fixed assets, intangible assets, investments, and deferred charges. The balance sheet is static and historical in nature. See also *financial statements.*

balancing the books:
(1) Reconciling the records to show agreement. An example is a bank reconciliation in which the balance per

books (depositor's records) equals the balance per bank (bank's records).
(2) Agreement of the records to physical amounts. An example is comparing the value of rental property to its actual existence.

balcony:
(1) Platform extending beyond (external to) the regular apartment or premises and enclosed by a railing. It is a desirable feature to most tenants.
(2) Highest floor in a theater. It is more difficult to see the show, but the tickets are cheaper.

balloon:
(1) Type of loan where the final payment is substantially greater than the previous payments; also termed partially amortized loan. A debt agreement might stipulate a balloon payment when future refinancing is expected.
(2) Last lease payment for a leased asset. It includes the residual value of the asset, which is often greater than previous rental payments made during the lease period.

balloon clause: Provision in a mortgage that requires the final payment to be substantially more than all other payments.

balloon loan: Loan having the last payment either (1) more than twice the amount of any other payment, or (2) a payment arising from the lender's "call" provision. The term loan (or straight loan) is a form of balloon loan. See also *balloon.*

balloon payment: Last installment payment, substantially greater than the previous installment payments. The unpaid balance of a long-term loan is paid off in a lump sum at the end of the loan term. See also *balloon; balloon loan.*

balloon-note mortgage: Partially amortized and requiring a lump sum (balloon) payment at maturity.

band of investment: Way to determine the capitalization rate of income property for valuation purposes by weighting the rate of interest and source of financing in percentage terms.
EXAMPLE:

Financing source	$\times$	Interest rate	$=$	Weighted average
Debt 80%	$\times$	10 %		= 8.0%
Equity 20%	$\times$	6%		= 1.2%
Band interest rate				= 9.2%

bank: Financial institution that services savings and checking accounts, provides loans, and deals with negotiable instruments. Stringent federal and local regulations exist over banking activities. The three major types of banks are commercial, savings, and savings and loan associations. Various kinds of real estate loans are available from banks at attractive interest rates. However, the borrower should "shop around" since rates vary among banks.

bank letter:
(1) Provided by a commercial or savings bank to the real estate company itself or to another party for documentation purposes. Such a letter may be needed by a prospective condominium owner to document his bank balance for a condominium board deciding whether to accept him; also a prospective tenant in a forthcoming shopping mall may request the real estate developer to provide such a letter to confirm his assertions of financial stability to complete the mall.
(2) Letter of credit promising the future availability of financing under a line of credit.

bankruptcy (business): Situation in which a business' debts exceed the fair market value of its assets. A judicial order discharges the debtor partially or fully for unpaid obligations, and the creditors receive distributions of assets from the debtor's property under supervision of the court. Chapter 11 of the Bankruptcy Law provides for reorganization in which the debtor keeps possession and control of the business, while the debtor and creditors work together to resolve the financial issues.

bankruptcy (personal): Legal mechanism available for a person who is "over his head" financially and is unable to meet his financial obligations. The individual can file for bankruptcy to eliminate some or all of his debts. Under Chapter 7 of the Bankruptcy Law, often referred to as straight bankruptcy, the intent is to liquidate assets to pay the debts. However, the bankrupt individual can claim specified property as "exempt" and retain them as basic needs of life, e.g., house, auto, and clothing. Once declared bankrupt, the individual cannot be discharged from debts again for six years. Under Chapter 13, often referred to as a wage-earner plan, the assets are not liquidated. Rather, interest and late charges are eliminated and arrangements are made to retire some or all of the debts over several years. However, bankruptcy will not discharge all the debts. Debts that cannot be eliminated include taxes, child support, alimony, student loans, and debts incurred through fraud. An attorney can advise on bankruptcy issues and help obtain the greatest benefit from the second chance.

bargain: Something that is of good value for the money and an attractive deal. An example is buying a house inexpensively because the homeowner is anxious to sell (e.g., job relocation or illness).

bargain and sales deed: Involves the transfer of property from one individual to another for a consideration in the form of sale. It is the most widely used type of real estate deed with a period of bargaining followed by a sale. May be with or without covenant. The bargain and sale deed without covenant allows the grantor to make no warranty as to title to the property.

barn: Enclosed building that stores agricultural products (e.g., hay, livestock, or farm equipment).

barter: Exchange of products or property between individuals in which no cash is paid. Each party must recognize income based on the fair market value of the product or property received. An example is when a plumber performs services to a homeowner in exchange for part of the homeowner's property.

base:
(1) Bottom of something used as support.
(2) Most essential element.
(3) Type of interest rate used when computing compound interest equal to: $(1 + i)$.
(4) Justification of an argument or position.
(5) Typical amount or measure for comparison.

baseboard: Wooden piece placed at the spot where the floor intersects the wall. An example is a protecting or finishing molding.

base and meridian: Surveyor's use of hypothetical lines to portray a property's position. North to South is the meridian line while East to West is the base line.

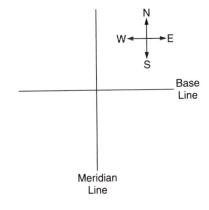

base line: Latitude line selected as a reference in the rectangular survey system.

base molding: Wood strip on the top of a baseboard.

base rent: Monthly fixed rental payment. An additional amount above the minimum rent may be charged, such as that based on a percentage of sales or profits. Further, additional rent may be assessed to cover operating costs, such as maintenance and sanitation. For example, if the constant rent is $1,600 and an additional 2% is added based on sales of $100,000, the total rent would be $3,600 ($1,600 + $2,000).

base shoe: Wood strip (molding) at the bottom of a baseboard.

basic industry multiplier: Percentage of a geographic location's population to the number of persons employable by a basic industry in that area. A basic industry is one that draws income from outside the locality for its product or service. The industry not only generates jobs directly but also indirectly creates jobs for related services (e.g., store clerks, auto repair mechanics, waiters). The industry not only attracts workers from outside the area but also their families. Assume the town of Greenvale has a multiplier of 5. This means that for one new job created in the basic industry the population of that town is increased by 5.

basis: Figure or value which is the starting point in computing gain or loss, depreciation, depletion, and amortization. For example, in an asset sale, "gain" is proceeds minus basis, where "basis" is the amount on which depreciation is calculated.

basis point: Unit of measure for the change in interest rates for loans. One basis point equates to 1 percent of 1 percent, that is, 0.01 percent. Therefore, one hundred basis points = 1 percent.

bathroom: Room with a bathtub, shower, toilet, and sink. Most houses have more than one bathroom, increasing their value.

batten: Board used when connected as a floor. It may also be used as a strip in a wall or door.

bauhaus style: Style of architecture originating at the German Bauhaus, or architectural institute, in the 1920s associated with the International School of Architecture. The Bauhaus style emphasized functional and simple building design. The houses had no decoration and were smooth white blocks constructed of steel, reinforced concrete, and integral walls of glass. See also *international architecture.*

bay window: Window designed in an alcove extending outside the structure. A bay window makes a home look more attractive and adds light, as well as providing a better view.

beam: Primary horizontal support for a structure such as a house. It may be a large piece of wood, stone, iron, or other material that lies across the walls, and serves as support of the principle rafters.

beamed ceiling: Horizontal supports for the ceiling of a structure.

beam right agreement: Arrangement between neighbors permitting one of them to put a beam for support on another neighbor's wall.

bearer instrument: Unregistered stock or bond that pays the holder dividends (if stock) or interest (if bonds) as well as the selling price when sold (if stock) or principal (if bonds are held to maturity). Bearer means the security does not list the owner's name, but rather payment is made to whoever presents the coupon. An endorsement of the instrument is not required for transfer.

bearer stock: Has not been registered on the company's books. It belongs to the person holding it. See also *bearer bond; bearer instrument.*

bearing value: Nature and ability of soil and other materials to withstand weight of a structure (e.g., foundation of a house).

bearing wall: Aids in supporting a building.

bedrock: Solid rock that lies underneath soil providing a foundation on which to construct a building.

before-and-after method: Way to determine how much to pay an owner whose property is taken by the government under emminent domain.

before-tax cash flow: Cash flow before subtracting income taxes. For example, after deducting debt service of $30,000 from a net operating income of $40,000, Paul has a before-tax cash flow of $10,000. See also *after-tax cash flow; cash flow.*

belt highway: Principal highway designed to divert traffic around a major urban area in order to limit congestion and expedite traffic flow. A belt highway is connected to the urban area by main highways and streets. For example, the Capital Beltway, routes I95 and I495, surrounds Washington, DC and diverts traffic around the city although major access arteries intersect it.

benchmark: Standard unit of comparison. The comparison has to be of similar items. The item is expressed as being below, above, or the same as the universal unit. For example, the median selling price of a home in a state may serve as a benchmark for the selling prices of homes.

beneficial interest: Unit of ownership in a real estate investment trust.

beneficial use: Right to peaceful enjoyment of property while the legal title is held by one person and the property is used by another. For example, for two months Smith rents a beach house to Jones. During the rental period, Jones has the right to beneficial use of the beach house and property, including beach and boating access.

beneficiary: Individual who will receive an inheritance upon the death of another. The proceeds of an insurance policy may be in the form of a lump-sum annuity. Real estate also passes to the beneficiary.

beneficiary statement: Lienholder's statement as to the unpaid balance on a trust deed note.

benevolent association: Nonprofit charitable entity, such as one providing housing for the homeless.

bequeath: To pass property by will to an heir. Strictly speaking, real estate cannot be bequeathed to an heir, it must be devised. However, if it becomes clear the purpose of the testator was to devise real estate, it can be ruled that the intent was to devise. For example, Mary bequeathed her wedding gown, automobile, and diamond ring to her daughter.

bequest: Transfer of personal property via a will as a gift to the recipient.

berm:

(1) That portion of exposed beach formed by waves depositing sand as they dissipate on the beach. The size of the berm commonly varies with the season. In the summer, the waves move sand onshore and the berm increases; however, in the winter waves erode the berm and move the sand offshore.

(2) Bank of earth, sometimes paved, which is used to deflect surface runoff, indicate property limits, or change terrain.

(3) Highway shoulder.

betterment: Replacement of a major component of property by another component that will result in better performance capability. Increases overall efficiency of the property. An example is an improved home heating system.

beveled siding: See *clapboard.*

B horizon: Subsoil that is beneath the A horizon and above the C horizon of the earth.

biannual: Occurring two times per year; also called semiannual. On the other hand, biennial means occurring each two years.

bid: Offering price. For example, Smith places his home for sale at the ask price of $199,900. Jones makes a bid of $189,000 for the home. Typically, the final price is a compromise of the two prices.

bid and asked: Term used in the real estate industry describing the price requested by a property owner vs. the price a buyer is willing to pay. Bid is the highest price a purchaser is willing to pay while asked is the lowest price a seller is willing to accept. Together, the two prices constitute a quotation in a real estate listing. See also *spread.*

bid price:

(1) Price a buyer is willing to pay, or bid, for a certain piece of property. It is the highest price offered to buy the property.

(2) Price per share that shareholders receive when they redeem their shares in a real estate corporation.

biennial: Occurring every 2 years. For example, a variable rate mortgage has a provision to adjust the interest rates biennially. See also *biannual.*

bilateral contract: Legal agreement between individuals (or entities) who both agree to do or not to do some act.

bilateral listing:

(1) Agreement where the broker and the seller agree to mutual performance. The broker agrees to advertise the property at the agreed sale terms with the intention of putting together buyer and seller, while the seller agrees to sell and deliver the listed property.

(2) Simultaneous listing with two separate realtors.

bi-level: Two-story house where the front door is located above the first floor but below the second floor. An example is a split-level or high ranch house.

bill of sale: Formal document for the transfer of title to personal property and chattels. It states that the property has been paid for and that no outstanding liens exist on it. This is the buyer's receipt that gives him or her the right to sell the property at a later date. There may be a need to register the bill of sale at a county office.

binder:

(1) Temporary and symbolic payment showing good faith and obligating two or more individuals until a final transaction takes place. The binder is typically returned if the final agreement is not consummated.

(2) Deposit paid to secure the right to buy a house based on the agreed terms. It is a temporary deposit until there is a contract.

(3) Written memorandum of the contract terms of insurance that provides temporary protection to the insured pending final approval by the insurance company.

binding arbitration: Term used in a real estate dispute in which an independent third party listens to the arguments of two parties and issues a judgment with which both parties must comply. May be voluntary or compulsory. It is voluntary if the parties have agreed to it but is compulsory if a government authority requires it. A person may engage in a real estate contract and agree that any dispute be arbitrated.

bi-weekly (mortgage) loan: Fixed interest rate loan in which the payments are made every two weeks, but the payment is one-half the amount of a regular monthly fixed-rate mortgage with the same amortization schedule. It is a bi-weekly accelerated mortgage reduction payment plan which enables a borrower to payoff his or her current 30-year mortgage in approximately 20 years. These payment plans provide a sizable build-up of equity, saving the borrower a significant amount of interest. These plans do not change existing mortgages. The borrower is not reapplying or refinancing anything, so there are no points, no need for costly appraisals, and no credit restrictions. Rather than making one monthly payment, he or she makes a half payment each 14 days. This results in 26 half payments yearly, or an extra monthly payment each year, accomplishing:

• The reduction he or she will achieve on the loan more than doubles, even in the short term. For example, on an 11%, 30-year, $125,000 loan, after three years in the bi-weekly program he or she would have $6,099 in equity available, as opposed to $1,891 if he or she had stayed on the regular monthly plan.
• The loan is shortened if the owner keeps his or her property for the full term of the loan. A typical 30-year loan is completely paid off in a little more than 20 years, with a savings of more than $142,000 in interest per every $125,000 borrowed.

Biweekly payment plans are offered by several firms that are retained to serve as money managers to aid the owner. Once in the program, everything is automatic. Each 14 days an electronic wire transfer of half his or her monthly payment is sent from his or her local bank. After the second monthly half-payment, the funds are combined and the entire payment is transferred to the lender.

When seeking a biweekly loan, consider the following:

• A reasonable, one-time start-up fee.
• Reasonable wire transfer fees.
• The program holds the borrower's funds in a major bank.
• Interest is paid on all funds held.
• The borrower has the ability to go off, and back on, the program or transfer at no additional fee.

blanket mortgage: Single mortgage or other encumbrance that covers more than one piece of real estate. For example, a developer buys a large tract of land and plans to subdivide the land into 100 lots and then build homes on the lots. Rather than going to the expense and time of obtaining 100 separate mortgages, one blanket mortgage covering all the lots is obtained. Since the developer will probably be developing a few lots at a time, the mortgage will include a partial release clause which means that as the debt is paid, individual lots will be released from the mortgage. Thus, the developer can pay off part of the mortgage, have a certain number of lots released, build on the lots and then sell them free and clear from the lien that still exists on the unreleased lots.

blanket rate: Uniform charge for transportation and delivery of household items to a homeowner within a particular locality.

blended loan: Refinancing by a borrower (e.g., mortgage) in which the new interest rate takes into account the interest rate on the prior loan and the prevailing current interest rate in the market. An example of such a loan is a wraparound mortgage.

blended rate: Interest rate that exceeds the rate on the old loan but is less than the rate on new loans. It is usually offered by the lender to encourage home buyers to refinance existing, low-interest rate loans as an alternative to assuming the existing loan. For example, Roberta wishes to sell a home to Susan. Susan can assume the existing loan of $80,000 at an interest rate of 5%. Susan could get a new loan at a rate of 10%. Roberta's lender offers the option of refinancing the loan for $100,000 at a blended rate of 8%.

blind pool: Limited partnership in which limited partners rely on the general partner to choose specific properties after the funds are available. For example, each of 1,000 investors contributes $25,000 into a limited partnership. The general partner has not yet selected the property to be bought, so the investment money is considered a blind pool.

blind pool syndicate: Money raised by a syndicate promoter and placed into a fund prior to selecting the specific property in which funds will be invested.

blind trust: Giving one's approval to another, e.g., a fiduciary, to manage his or her finances. This arrangement may exist when there is a possible conflict of interest. A blind trust would be suitable for a legislator involved with an industry in which he or she has a real estate interest.

block:
(1) Rectangular area bounded on all sides by consecutive streets. It is part of a platted area.
(2) Substantial amount of real estate properties to be sold together.
(3) Group of houses, apartments, or businesses in one area, such as on Foster Avenue between Charles Street and Blake Street.

(4) Substantial amount of stock of a real estate company, such as 50,000 shares or any quantity worth more than $500,000. Due to the effect of such a large number of shares on the market during any one trade, special handling is typically needed, by which buyers or sellers are prearranged. Block trading is often undertaken by institutional investors. A block sale applies only to previously issued stock.

blockbusting: Illegal practice of inducing panic selling in a neighborhood for financial gain. Such selling may arise because of the threatened move to the area of a particular racial or ethnic group.

blueprint:
(1) Architectural plan of a structure in the form of a picture in white on a blue background. Contains lines and solid shapes and aids in the planning, outlining, and construction of a building.
(2) Guide to follow in performing some act.

blue sky laws: Refers to state statutes protecting the public against securities frauds of real estate companies. Include regulations over the licensing of brokers, new securities, registrations, and formal approvals by applicable government agencies. The term initially arose when a judge ruled that a certain stock had about the same worth as a patch of blue sky.

board of appeals: See *Board of Equalization.*

board and batten: Kind of siding for wood frame houses where the joints in the usually vertical siding are covered by narrow strips of wood called battens. The battens are nailed over the joints.

board of directors: Group of individuals elected by a real estate company's stockholders to run the firm in accord with the corporate charter. The Board is appointed by senior management and usually is comprised of top management executives (inside directors) and external representatives (outside directors). The Board has substantial influence over the policies of the company's business.

board of equalization: Governmental body that reviews property tax assessment procedures.

board foot: Cubic unit of measure for a board one-foot long, one-foot wide and one inch thick, or 144 cubic inches. These measurements are not actual, since they are stated prior to finishing and planing the wood.

board measure (B.M.):
(1) Method of measurement lumber using the board foot cubic measure. The board measure is used to estimate quantities and prices of lumber materials.
(2) Method of estimating lumber potential from trees.

board of realtors: Local group of real estate brokers who are members of the State and National Board of Realtors. Meets regularly with their membership and helps determine licensing requirements as well as managing the multiple listing service of their service area. They may also provide additional services to their members.

board of trustees: Organizational governing group. Either an appointed or elected body overseeing the management of an organization and rendering advice on current issues. Members are legally responsible for their decisions. For example, the Seaview Condominium Association has an elected Board of Trustees responsible for overseeing the professional management of the condominium, and making major financial decisions regarding member assessments for maintenance and repairs, as well as determining member rules.

boilerplate: Standard language in real estate contracts and prospectuses—usually in small print.

bona fide: A Latin term meaning "in good faith," without deceit such as with the sale of a real estate property.

bona fide purchaser: Buyer who is acting in good faith, is not aware of any outstanding claims or rights of others to the property, and has given valuable consideration as part of the business transaction.

bond beam: Continuous beam on top of supporting walls, usually constructed of concrete and often having steel rods for additional strength placed within it. Supplies lateral support as well as distributing concentrated vertical loads along the wall. See also *tie beam.*

bond net lease: Lease where, in addition to the rent, the lessee pays the taxes, insurance, and maintenance. As a guarantee for the lessor, the lessee posts a bond payment equivalent to one year's tax, insurance, and maintenance payment.

bond for title (deed): Mutually binding property sales contract where the title remains with the seller until the purchase price is paid by the buyer. It is a contract to convey title in the future upon satisfaction of contract terms.

bone structure: Skeleton (bones) of a building.

book:
(1) When used as a noun (usually plural), refers to journals or ledgers.
(2) When used as a verb, refers to the recording of an entry.
See also *book value; plat book.*

book cost: Expenditures incurred to initially purchase property, including incidental costs necessary to put the property into existing use and location. This cost is then depreciated over the asset's life (except for land, which is not depreciated).

book value: Net worth of property as shown on the balance sheet. It equals gross cost less accumulated depreciation. Because book value is based on historical cost it differs from market value. For example, if $3,000,000 was paid for an office building which is now 25% depreciated, its book value is $2,250,000 ($3,000,000 − $750,000).

boom:
(1) Sudden and dramatic increase in activity or prices. An example is the sharp increase in home prices because of new recreational facilities in the area.
(2) Rapid economic prosperity.

boot: Tax term referring to cash or property of a type not included in the definition of a nontaxable exchange. The receipt of boot results in an otherwise tax-free transfer becoming taxable to the extent of the smaller of the boot's fair market value or the realized gain on the transfer.

boring test: Examination of the load-bearing capabilities of terrain by taking bore samples of the subterranean strata.

borrower risk: Liability a borrower assumes. These include:
(1) Due to unforeseen circumstances, the borrower may lose the financial ability to repay the principal and interest of a loan placing the collaterized property at risk of foreclosure. For example, due to a company downsizing, the borrower loses his job and no longer has the financial ability to maintain mortgage payments on his home.
(2) In the case of an adjustable rate mortgage, rising interest charges may make the payments unaffordable, placing the mortgaged property at risk of foreclosure.
(3) In the event of a depreciating asset, the loan value may exceed the value of the collaterized asset. For example, an individual assumes a $200,000, 30-year mortgage on a home having an initial appraised value of $250,000; however, because of a falling real estate market, the appraised value of the home falls to $150,000. The homeowner becomes "locked-in" to the mortgage. Even if the home were sold at the $150,000 market value, the homeowner still has a $50,000 liability from the $200,000 mortgage.
(4) In the event of the death of the borrower, payments on a loan will become a liability of the heirs.

botel: Guest accommodations offered by some marinas to mariners. These services are similar to those offered to motorists by motels.

bottomland:
(1) Land adjacent to a lake, river, or stream that can also be part of a flood area.
(2) Land at the bottom of a valley or glen. Normally, this land is very fertile as the top soil from the land at the higher elevations has flowed down to the bottomland over time.

boulevard: Main street having a divider either in the center or between the curb and sidewalk with trees, grass, or other shrubbery.

bowstring truss: Beam, girder, or truss with the top portion being in the shape of a bow and the bottom portion being straight across and connecting both ends of the top portion.

box construction: Method of construction where vertical siding is attached to a horizontal framing structure. Often found in the design of agricultural buildings.

bracing: Structures added to framing to increase overall strength and stability. Various types of bracing include cables, rods, struts, ties, shores, additional framing, etc. Bracing can be used singly or in combination.

bracket: Any structure projecting from a wall or other vertical element for the purpose of providing support for a weight or other object. For example, a bookcase is constructed consisting of several lateral boards mounted on supporting wall brackets.

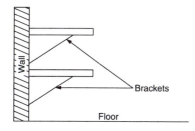

branch office: Office created by an organization in another location for the purpose of providing localized services. Is an integral part of the main organization, but may not have all of the resources or, in some cases, the authority of the main organization. For example, a major real estate brokerage establishes a branch office in another city employing several real estate sales personnel. While it has full communication, including the sharing of multiple listing services, with the main brokerage office, it cannot independently approve listing agreements or make advertising commitments.

breach: Violating a law, commitment, duty, or obligation through commission or omission. The responsibilities of an agreement or guarantee are not met.

breach of contract: Failure, without sufficient reason, for one or both parties to perform the terms of a real estate contract. Breach requires unequivocal, decisive, and absolute refusal to carry out the agreement. When a breach takes place, the damaged party may recover the resulting losses. It is also possible to sue for performance if recovery is inadequate.

break-even:

(1) Occupancy rate at which rental income of a property pays for operating expenses and debt service, leaving no residual cash flow.

(2) The level of sales of a real estate business where total revenue equals total costs. There is no profit or loss.

breather roof: Roof constructed on a storage tank designed to expand and contract directly with the level of stored materials (usually liquid). Its design prevents the loss through vaporization of the stored materials, as well as the escape and intermingling of gaseous vapors with the outside air.

breezeway: Covered walkway, open to the outside, connecting two parts of a building or two buildings. A breezeway protects pedestrians from the elements but provides open access to the outside.

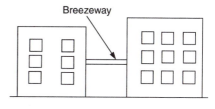

brick cavity wall: Brick wall where a space or cavity is left between the inner and outer walls and is usually filled with insulation.

brick masonry: Method of constructing a brick, block, or stone wall using mortar in various overlapping patterns. The brick pattern is extremely important in terms of adding strength and stability to the wall. The two types of brick used are those used to tie a wall together longitudinally, termed stretchers, and those used to tie it together transversely, termed headers. There are twelve brickwork bonding patterns having individual structural and decorative attributes. The American bond method is shown below:

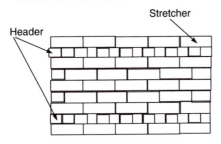

brick veneer: Nonload bearing layer of brick covering a wall for decorative purposes only. The wall is usually constructed with wood framing or masonry block.

bridge loan:
(1) Also called swing loan. Short-term loan that is made in anticipation of permanent longer term loans. The interest rate on such a loan is usually higher than on longer term loans. An example is a temporary loan made to allow for a closing on the purchase of property before permanent mortgage financing.
(2) A business loan in which cash is received for a specific transaction, and repayment will be from cash flows from an identifiable source. The purpose of the loan and the source of repayment are related; hence the reference bridge loan. An example is an advertising agency contracting to produce a TV commercial for the XYZ Real Estate Corporation. The total contract price is $500,000, but the agency wants about $200,000 in financing to produce the commercial. The loan is a bridge loan because it supports a particular event and the source of repayment is identifiable (completing the commercial). Another example of a

bridge loan is property financing in which the loan is to be paid from the sale of the real estate.

bridging:
(1) Supporting the joists of a floor with small pieces of wood.
(2) Providing temporary financing, such as a short-term loan, to a real estate developer before long-term financing can be obtained.

broker (real estate): Person licensed by a state to perform real estate activities listed for compensation on behalf of both buyers and sellers. For example, a broker may be hired by a prospective buyer or tenant looking for suitable property.

brokerage:
(1) Licensed broker employed to represent and match buyers and sellers. Usually employs several real estate agents in an office.
(2) Commission or fee charged to sell real estate or perform related real estate services. For example, the brokerage fee on a $200,000 real estate sale at 6 ½% was $13,000 ($200,000 × 6.5%).

brokerage administration: Administering and directing the activities of a real estate brokerage firm to assure they are in compliance with regulations and policies.

broker's agreement: Contract to act on the behalf of a principal in selling real estate. The principal agrees to pay a commission to the broker when a buyer is produced who is ready, willing, and able to meet the agreed upon terms of the sale. See also *listing agreement.*

brooder house: Heated structure needed to raise fowl.

brownstone: Houses attached by either side of the same wall. Typically has a stoop to the first floor of a 5- or 6-story brick structure with a flat roof. These townhouses were built in the nineteenth century. (See top of page 43.)

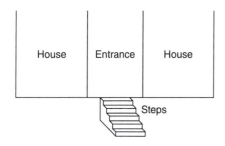

btu: British thermal unit—a unit of energy associated with the creation of heat. Prior to 1929, it was defined as the amount of heat required to raise the temperature of 1 pound of water 1 degree Fahrenheit (from 59.5° F to 60.5° F). In 1929, it was redefined as being equivalent to 251.996 calories, 778.26 ft-lb, or in electrical units, approximately one-third watt-hours. In the United States, the BTU is a standard measure of the heat-producing capabilities of various heating appliances, furnaces, and fuels.

bucket shop: Derogative term describing a high-pressure telemarketing office where sales personnel often use extremely exaggerated claims as well as intense sales practices to convince targeted clients to make real estate purchases.

budgeting:
(1) Estimating all income and expenses for an accounting period.
(2) Financial forecasting, planning, and controlling. It involves using a budget to set and accomplish short-term objectives ensuring that actual goals are consistent with budgeted goals.

budget mortgage: Involves monthly payments for property taxes and insurance, besides principal and interest. The tax and insurance payments are put into an impound account (also called an escrow or a reserve account). For a residential mortgage this means one-twelfth of the property taxes and property insurance each month. For the borrower, the advantage is the spreading out of these annual expenses into 12 equal payments. For the lender, who normally places these funds into an impound or reserve account, the advantage is the assurance that these expenses will be paid when due. For example, Kim borrows $100,000 on a 20-year budget mortgage at 10% interest. Her monthly mortgage payment is $1,260, which includes $965 principal and interest, $250 taxes, and $45 insurance.

buffer zone: Strip of land that separates one land use from another. An example of buffer zones could be a park area. Alternatively a buffer zone could be an apartment building intermingled in a single-family residence area.

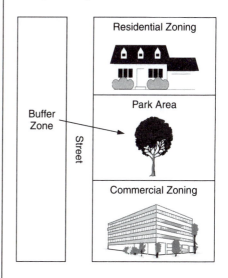

builder breakdown method: See *quantity survey method.*

builder warranty: Limited-time warranty against defects, offered by builders to new home purchasers. Normally effective for a relatively short period of time, such as one or two years.

building capitalization rate: Rate of return of capital invested in building improvements. Is segregated from land investments and provides a method of separating property income streams between improvement and land investments. Normally the yield is stated as an annual rate of profit per dollar of investment.

Three factors are necessary in order to correctly compute the building capitalization rate:

(1) The amount of the investment.
(2) The size and duration of the income stream.
(3) The eventual resale proceeds.

The building capitalization rate may be expressed as $R = I / V$ where $V =$ the capital value, $I =$ the annual net income, and $R =$ the capitalization rate necessary to attract investors. For example, if $100,000 was invested in a building and it resulted in $10,000 income over 10 years, then the formula would be $R = \$10,000 / \$100,000$ or $R = .10$ or a 10% return.

building code: Municipal or state ordinance enforceable under the police powers of the state and locality controlling alterations, construction methods and materials, size and setback requirements, use, and occupancy of all structures. Building codes have specific regulations covering all aspects of construction including electrical, foundation, heating and air conditioning, insulation, plumbing, and roofing systems. Building codes are designed to maximize the health, welfare, and ambiance of the residents. For example, a builder wishes to construct a new home development, but each home must have no less than 1,500 sq. ft. of living space and be located on at least $\frac{1}{3}$ of an acre.

building construction: Methods and materials used in designing and fabricating a building.

building density: Concentration of buildings in a given geographic area. Higher building density patterns have several affects. Without careful planning, high density can be associated with crowding, crime, environmental stress, and traffic congestion. Issues such as air rights and access rights assume great importance. Balancing property uses between commercial, industrial, and residential become prime considerations in property zoning. Property in high building density areas has greater value than in low density areas because of the balance between supply and demand.

building energy performance standard (BEPS): Criterion used to measure the annual utilization of energy by a building.

building life: Estimated life of a building. Under the 1992 federal tax law, the IRS' General Depreciation System (GDS), using accelerated depreciation for property placed into service after 1986, allows a depreciation period of 31.5 years for nonresidential real property and 27.5 years for residential rental property. Farm buildings are given a life of 20 years.

The IRS' Alternative Depreciation System (ADS), using straight-line depreciation, allows 40 years for nonresidential real and residential rental property and 25 years for farm buildings.

For a business, there is a difference between the total life of a building and its useful life. The total building life is greater than the useful life.

building line: Line established by a building or zoning code beyond which a building structure may not extend. Certain exceptions to the building line for sidewalks, steps, and uncovered entrance ramps may exist. For example, a building code specifies a building line where no structure may be built within 30 feet of a street curb. See also *building setback.*

building loan agreement: Agreement where a lender gives money to a builder at various stages of construction. For example, after the foundation and rough plumbing are constructed, the lender will give ⅛th of the total loan to the builder. See also *construction loan.*

building and loan associations: See *savings and loan association.*

building owners and managers association international (BOMA): Founded in 1908 and located in Washington, DC, BOMA has 7,500 members and 10 regional groups and 6 state groups. It consists of managers, owners, investors, and developers of commercial office buildings. The basic purpose of the organization is to advance the office building industry, sponsor conferences and deliberations, provide education, distribute information, and establish standards. Its educational unit offers certification courses to be a Real Property Administrator (RPA), Facilities Maintenance Administrator (FMA), and Systems Maintenance Administrator (SMA). BOMA has a library, operates a placement service, does research, and offers programs.

building paper: See *building permit.*

building permit: Approval given by a local municipality to construct a particular structure at a specific location. The permit may contain certain provisions that require builder compliance.

building residual technique: Appraisal method for determining a building's value under the following criteria:

(1) The land value can be easily determined from comparable sales or other methods.

(2) The building on the land is not the highest and best use.

(3) The building is aged and/or seriously deteriorated.

As a building ages and deteriorates, it becomes increasingly difficult to estimate its economic value. The building residual technique estimates a building's value on the basis of the residual building income after adjusting for land value.

For example, a 40-year old apartment building produces a net income of $20,000 annually after taxes. Using the comparable sales method, the land value is estimated to be $80,000. A building capitalization rate is estimated at 9% and the building is calculated to have a future economic life of 20 years. Using a straight-line method of capitalization, it is possible to estimate the total value of the building and land:

Estimated land value =	$80,000
Total net annual income =	$20,000
Land capitalization at	
$80,000 × 9% =	$ 7,200

Net income residual to building $12,800
Building rate:

(a) 9% interest on investment
(b) 5% recapture rate (100%/20 year life)
    14%

Building value $12,800/.14 = $91,428.57

Total value of property:	
Estimated land value	$ 80,000.00
Calculated building value	91,428.57
Total	$171,428.57

building setback: Municipal ordinance stating the distance from a curb or property line where the building of a structure is prohibited. Also states the distances from a boundary line where construction is permitted. Building setbacks are intended to provide access space and/or preserve environmental character.

built-ins:

(1) Subunit integral to a larger unit. Are usually associated with furniture, for example, the wall with a built-in bookcase.

(2) Permanent fixture or appliance which is not intended to be portable and cannot easily be removed. A home has an installed wall oven and it is considered to be a built-in appliance.

built-up method: Approach to determining a capitalization rate for use in valuing property so as to arrive at a suitable purchase price. To the risk-free interest rate is added a risk premium to cover the greater risk. If the risk-free rate is 6% and a risk premium of 3% is necessary to compensate for the property's poor liquidity, the built-up total capitalization rate would be 9%.

bulkhead:

(1) Retaining wall constructed along water with solid earth behind it. It extends the effective shoreline and protects the land from tidal action.

(2) That portion of a wall located beneath a storefront window.

bulk sales law: Statute designed to protect lenders if a seller secretly sells substantially all of the business property. The objective of the law is to safeguard against defrauding creditors.

bullet loan: Intermediate debt (5 to 10 years) without periodic payments but the entire amount (balloon payment) is due at the maturity date. If full payment is not made, the lender may foreclose on the property. Stiff prepayment penalties typically exist.

bumper strips: Timber wood situated on the exteriors of a loading deck to safeguard it from damage resulting when trucks unload and load.

bundle of rights theory: Those legal rights that are a part of the ownership of property. These rights include the rights to occupy and use, peaceful enjoyment, bequeath, construct a structure, lease, sell, mine, and improve.

bungalow: Small one-story frame house or cottage. It usually has a front porch that can be open or enclosed. (See top of right column.)

burn-off: Reducing the prepaid items on a debt agreement.

business cycle: Regular pattern of expansion (recovery) and contraction (recession) in total economic activity surrounding a growth trend, including the impact of economic variables such as employment and inflation. At the peak of the cycle, economic activity is high compared to trend, but at the trough (valley) of the cycle, the low point in economic activity is reached. The business cycle influences corporate earnings, cash flow, and expansion. See also *depression; recession.*

business day: Standard days when an organization is open and conducts business. Business days exclude weekends and holidays. For example, when a contract states an action must occur within a stated number of business days, only those days during the week, from Monday to Friday and excluding recognized holidays, can be counted.

business opportunity: Favorable occurrence providing a good chance for success, usually in financial terms. An example is buying real estate property that is expected to sharply increase in value because it was bought at a low price and because economic conditions are expected to significantly improve.

butterfly roof: Inverted gable roof design where the two sides slope upward from the center to the eaves with a valley in the middle. The roof resembles the wings of a butterfly, hence, the name. See also *double pitch*.

buy-back:

(1) Agreement to sell real estate with a pre-arranged reverse but at an established price. This may not be legal in some instances, and any resulting losses may not be tax deductible.

(2) Arrangement to rescind specified policy limitations on the insured if further coverage is bought from the insurer.

buy-back agreement: See *buy-back*.

buy down: Cash payment to a lender so as to lower the interest rate on a loan a borrower must incur. The lower rate may apply for all or a part of the loan term. For example, a builder has a tract of homes for sale. To accomplish a sale of the house, the builder arranged for a buy down loan with a lender to pay discount points so that the lender can offer a loan at a lower interest to the buyer. This can apply for the life of the loan at the cost of about 8 discount points for each point of interest rate reduction, or it can apply for a shorter period, such as the first three years of the loan.

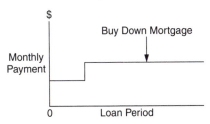

buyer's broker: Broker employed by and therefore loyal to the buyer.

buyers' market: Market situation in the housing industry in which a buyer has strong position. There may be few buyers and many sellers. Thus, a buyer can negotiate better prices and terms (e.g., quality assurance and closing dates).

buyer's policy: Insurance or maintenance policy taken out by a buyer of real or personal property. Examples are a policy offered by a contractor to repair a structure for problems over the next five years and a termite policy.

buying power:

(1) Financial ability and soundness of a business or individual to afford the purchase of property.

(2) Worth of the dollar in real terms considering inflation. For example, in inflationary times $1 buys less today than it did one year ago.

buying power index (BPI): Average of income, retail revenue, and population of a locality as a percentage of the entire United States. It reflects the economic status of a particular region.

buy-out estimate: Estimated price at which a partner in a partnership can buy out another partner. There are several methods for developing a buy-out estimate including market comparisons, appraisals, or multi-year projections of market appreciation.

buy-sell agreement: Partnership agreement where the parties consent to purchase the interest of those leaving the partnership while those leaving similarly consent to sell their interests to the other partners. This is an important agreement for a partnership in the event of the death or disability of one or more partners or the occurrence of some other specified event.

bylaws: Regulatory rules that have to be followed by the organization in conducting its activities. For example, the bylaws established by a real estate company may stipulate self-imposed requirements between the company and its stockholders on how the company should perform its duties. Bylaws may also be established among owners of property (condominiums and cooperatives) or tenants (apartment renters) in conducting activities of concern to them.

cabinet work:
(1) Craft of one who fabricates fine cabinets, furniture, or woodwork.
(2) General term describing interior wood finish work performed by cabinetmakers instead of carpenters.
(3) Built-in cabinets, cupboards, counters, shelves, etc.

cadastral map: Map within a governmental jurisdiction showing the boundary lines and ownership of all real property. A cadastral program produces the cadastral map.

cadastral program: Performance of a complete inventory of real property within a jurisdiction. A cadastral program is usually completed by the property assessor and results in the production of a cadastral map.

caisson foundation: Constructed in place by filling holes drilled through to bearing strata with concrete.

california bungalow: Small, early twentieth century, one-story house or cottage.

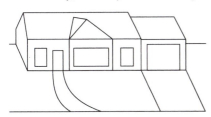

california ranch: Long, one-story house with the roof sloping toward the ground, often having skylights and contemporary windows.

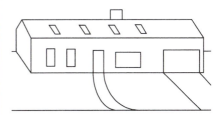

camber:
(1) Mildly convex arch built into a load bearing beam, girder, or truss to counteract any load bearing stress placed on it.
(2) Slight slope designed into a structure such as a driveway or roadway for runoff.

cancel: Null or void something; revoke or destroy; rescind or set aside; abandon; abolish; repeal; surrender; waive; terminate. In real estate, to void a buy or sell order, price, or quantity. The cancellation may be associated with new instructions.

cancelable agreement: Contractual clause allowing one or both parties to terminate the agreement if a specified occurrence takes place. This is a cancellation clause, which allows the agreement to become null and void, thereby allowing the parties to end their duties. The cancellation stipulation protects the interests of each participant if one is damaged.

cancellation:
(1) Voiding an order to buy or sell real estate.
(2) Prematurely terminating an insurance policy.
(3) Voiding a negotiable instrument by nullifying or paying it.

cancellation clause: Contractual provision describing the terms under which coverage may be terminated. An insured or insurer may cancel a policy (such as a property and casualty insurance policy) before its expiration date. Generally, a written notice of cancellation must be sent. The insurance company then refunds a part of the premium as stipulated in the insurance contract.

cantilever:
(1) Bracket used to support an extended eave or cornice on the outside of a house.
(2) Truss or beam projecting beyond its base and supported by its strength and rigidity, for example, a balcony.

cantilever beam: Beam that is supported only at one end.

cantilever construction: Method of construction where part of the structure is supported by a cantilever beam or truss.

capacity:
(1) In real estate, the amount of development dollars an area can profitably support.
(2) Ability of a service business (e.g., real estate brokerage) to render services based on human and physical resources and constraints.
(3) Manufacturing capability of a production business such as a manufacturer of wood.
(4) Amount of traffic a highway design can support.
(5) Structural load carrying capability.

capacity of parties: Legal competence of parties to be held responsible for the terms of a contract or to be brought into the courts. Those who are under the legal age, are mentally incompetent, or under the influence of a substance do not have legal capacity.

cape cod colonial house: Early American style 1½ story house with a steep gable roof covered with shingles. The bedrooms are on the first floor, but the attic is often finished and made into additional bedrooms. Typically, the cape cod colonial has a front doorway in the center with windows on both sides. With variations, this style house has been extremely popular throughout America.

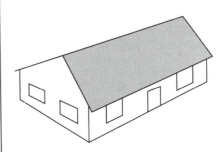

capital appreciation: Increase in the value of property. The appreciation may arise from many possible reasons, such as inflation, construction of higher priced homes in the neighborhood, tax incentives, and lower interest rates on mortgages.

capital assets:
(1) Any asset purchased for use in production over long periods of time rather than for resale. It includes land, buildings, plant, and timber reserves.
(2) In taxation, property held by a taxpayer, except cash, inventoriable assets, merchandise held for sale, receivables, and certain intangibles.
(3) Fixed assets usually consisting of tangible assets, such as plant and equip-

ment, and intangible assets, such as a patent.

capital expenditure: Outlay for a new fixed asset or an outlay that becomes part of the cost of an existing fixed asset. Examples are the costs for a new roof, aluminum siding, and central air conditioning that become part of the cost of the house. Capital expenditures increase the value of the property. The cost of the fixed asset can then be depreciated.

capital gains distribution: Income for investors arising from net long-term profits of a real estate mutual fund realized when the portfolio is sold at a gain. Profits from sales of real estate securities are passed on by fund managers to shareholders at least annually.

capital gains or losses: Any gain or loss from selling of capital assets. The gain or loss is the difference between the net selling price and cost basis. The two types of capital gains or losses for tax purposes are long term (to be held more than one year) and short term (to be held one year or less). Capital gains are net after all costs have been deducted. Capital gains and losses are reported on Schedule D of IRS Form 1040. They include sales of real estate.

capital improvements: Costs incurred in connection with real property that increase its cost basis or worth, such as a new roof, an additional room, or paneling a room.

capitalization:
(1) Multiplying the average gross or net operating income of rental property by an appropriate factor to determine the value of the property. The capitalization rate depends on factors such as neighborhood, stability of rental payments, risk, quality of tenants, historical occupancy rate, etc. For example, if rental property generates gross income per year of $500,000 and a suitable multiplier is 5 times,

the property would be valued at $2,500,000.
(2) To take advantage of something such as capitalizing on a buying opportunity of a house.
(3) Charging expenditures made to an asset such as charging the cost of a house with a new roof.
(4) Recording leased property as an asset. See also *capital lease.*

capitalization rate: Also called cap rate or income yield. A useful way to compute the rate of return on a real estate investment. It equals the net operating income (NOI) for the first year divided by the total investment. That interest rate that, when applied to the earnings of an investment, determines its market value. The lower the cap rate, the higher the risk to the investor and the higher the asking price. Whether property is overpriced depends on the rate for similar property in the market. There are two drawbacks to this approach: (1) it is based on only the first year's NOI, and (2) it ignores the appreciation in property value.

EXAMPLE: Assume that net operating income = $20,000 and acquisition price = $250,000. Then, the cap rate is 8.0%. If the market rate is 12%, the fair market value of similar property is $20,000/12% = $166,667. The property appears overpriced. See also *income approach.*

capitalize: Recording an expenditure having a benefit of more than one year to the cost of the property. For example, the cost of a new roof, kitchen, or basement increases the cost basis of the house. Upon sale, the gain or loss for tax purposes is the difference between the selling price and adjusted cost basis. If the home is used for business, depreciation on the capital improvements may be deductible for tax purposes.

capital lease: Rental in which the lessee obtains major property rights. Although not legally a purchase of property, theoretical substance governs over legal form and requires that the leased property be recorded as an asset on the lessee's books. The asset equals present value of the minimum lease payments (excluding executory costs which are reimbursements to cover the lessor's costs such as insurance, maintenance, and taxes) and the present value of the bargain purchase option. A capital lease exists if any one of the following four criteria is met: (1) the lease transfers ownership of the property to the lessee at the end of the lease term; (2) there is a bargain purchase option; (3) the lease term is 75% or more of the life of the property; and (4) the present value of minimum lease payments equals or exceeds 90% of the fair market value of the property.

capital markets: Markets for long-term bonds and equity securities of real estate companies. For example, many large companies are listed on the New York Stock Exchange (NYSE). Smaller companies are listed on the American Stock Exchange (AMEX) and the regional stock exchanges. Further, securities are traded through brokers and dealers on the over-the-counter market.

capital recapture:
(1) Return of the principal invested in real estate. It excludes income earned.
(2) Collection of a previously written-off bad debt.

capital recovery: How much of an investment made in real estate has been recovered expressed in dollars or in percentage terms. For example, if $100,000 has been invested in a property for which $60,000 has been received by the owner, 60% of that investment has been recovered.

capital turnover: Number of times a given amount of capital assets turn over to generate sales over a given period of time.

cap rates (CAPS): Maximum interest rates a borrower might pay for an adjustable rate mortgage. It controls the amount of change in the rate when it adjusts. The first number is the maximum increase allowed for one period of adjustment; the second is the total increase allowed over the life of the loan. A value of zero shown for the first number means that the loan permits negative amortization. A payment cap limits how much the payment due on the loan can increase or decrease.

capricious value: Arbitrary value assigned to real property without any scientific or technical reason. It is a personal decision based on a hunch. An example is a potential seller of a home significantly overstating the value of it relative to its real market value because of emotional attachment.

caption: Heading of a document, such as a real estate report.

capture rate: Proportionate share of an item to total items in the population. An example is a real estate firm that is selling 60% of the total new homes in a community.

carpet strip: Small piece of carpet often placed under a door or at an entrance to a doorway.

carrying charge: Cash outlays required to maintain an investment position. For example, raw land which produces no income involves carrying costs for taxes and debt service costs if financing is used. Carrying costs incidental to home ownership include property taxes and insurance.

carryover basis: Basis for the valuation of property acquired from a decedent for tax purposes. The unified transfer tax in 1976 provides for the valuation of property to be the adjusted basis immediately preceding death. This adjusted basis is then further adjusted with respect to such aspects of a transfer as appreciated property, election of fair market value for personal items, and exceptions for small estates.

case: Legal action between a plaintiff and defendant. An example is a lawsuit brought before the court for damaging rental property.

case law: See *common law*.

casement window: Window normally mounted on hinges in a window casing. It swings outward to open.

cash basis: Method of accounting in which expenses are recorded when cash is paid and revenue is recorded when cash is received. The cash basis can be used for a service business. It can only be used for a company that has inventory if there is a risky customer and uncertain collection period. See also *accrual method*.

cash equity: Amount invested in property in cash.

cash equivalency:
(1) Revising the selling price of real property to reflect what it would be worth if typical financing was available.
(2) How much real property would be sold for if all cash was involved. For example, a seller wants $300,000 for his property from a buyer who agrees to pay him $50,000 in cash and $250,000 in monthly payment notes over 10 years. If the buyer were willing to pay all cash, the seller would not have to worry about possible default of the debt, and would therefore be willing to accept $275,000.

cash flow:
(1) Cash revenue from product sales or services rendered less cash expenses. It is different from accrual earnings.
(2) The money available after deducting operating expenses and mortgage payments from rental revenue. For example, Bill buys an office building

generating the following operating revenues for the first year:

Gross rental income	$100,000
Less: Vacancy loss	15,000
Effective gross income	85,000
Less: Operating expenses	30,000
Net operating income (NOI)	55,000
Less: Debt service	40,000
Cash flow before taxes	$ 15,000

cash flow before taxes: See *before-tax cash flow; cash flow*.

cash rent: Rentals received in cash rather than on credit.

cash throw-off: Difference between cash revenue less cash expenses before taxes associated with rental property or a real estate investment.

cash value: Expected market value of property if sold today.

casing:
(1) The exposed trim and molding surrounding a door or window.
(2) Woodwork which encases a pipe or structural member.
(3) Method of creating a form for the pouring of concrete, for example, for forming a tie beam.

casualty loss: Loss arising from the partial or complete destruction of property resulting from circumstances of a sudden, unanticipated or unusual nature. Examples of circumstances are storms, floods, and fires to real property. These circumstances must be identifiable as the proximate cause of such a loss for classificatory purposes. Individuals may deduct a casualty loss as an itemized deduction to the extent of any amount not compensated for insurance or otherwise if: (1) the loss is incurred in a trade or business; (2) the loss is incurred in a transaction entered into for profit; and (3) the loss is caused by fire, storm, shipwreck, or other casualty or by theft. In a business, casualty losses are typically shown as an extraordinary item net of tax in the income statement. For example, if the casualty loss is $10,000 and the company is in the 35% tax bracket, the after-tax loss presented in the income statement is $6,500.

cause of action: Legal claim with enough basis in fact to have a lawsuit. An example is when one party refuses to honor contractual commitments. This occurrence (cause) provides that fact necessary to sue in a right of action.

causeway:
(1) Paved roadway constructed above lowlands such as a swamp.
(2) Roadway in ancient Egypt connecting the valley temple with a pyramid.

caveat actor: If action is undertaken in conformity with contractual provisions, legal responsibilities arise. The concept is that the person taking action must "beware."

caveat emptor: Latin term meaning "let the buyer beware." The buyer purchases at his or her risk, in the absence of fraud. This does not obligate the seller to volunteer information. However, legal statutes mandate full disclosure by the seller of known defects or problems in the property.

caveat subscriptor (venditor): Reference to let the vendor beware. Without specific exemptions, the vendor is obligated for action by the buyer for any explicit or implied modifications in the contract or warranty.

caveat vendor: "Let the seller beware" that he may be held legally accountable for deficiencies in the property sold. For example, a seller fails to disclose to the buyer structural damages in the property. The seller is responsible for any repair costs necessary to fix the property and/or damages caused by the defective property.

cavity wall: Hollow masonry wall consisting of an inner and outer wall with dead air space between them. The air space provides increased thermal insulation. Cavity walls are not used in northern climates since water entering the cavity will freeze.

cease and desist order: Judicial order prohibiting a person or business from doing something. This dictate may be issued by the court when unlawful conduct or activity is occurring. An example is when a homeowner's actions against another is improper, such as the playing of loud music all night or throwing garbage on the other homeowner's lawn.

cease and desist petition: Statement filed by a homeowner showing a premises' address and notifying a state's Secretary of State that such premises are not for sale and the homeowner does not wish to be solicited by real estate brokers. This puts real estate brokers on notice that such premises has no implied invitation to be solicited.

ceiling joist: A joist to which a ceiling is attached. A ceiling joist usually consists of several small 2″ x 4″ boards nailed or mortised to the sides or bottom of overhead joists to which the ceiling is attached.

ceiling loan: Maximum loan that can be borrowed by a potential debtor. A ceiling loan represents the topmost credit that can be extended. For example, newlyweds Judy and John Smith were advised by the bank that based on their income and credit history, the ceiling loan they could borrow would be $40,000 for home improvements.

ceiling rate: Also called price control or rent control. A controlled or administered price that is set for property by a federal or local agency typically in extraordinary circumstances. For example, the Office of Price Administration during World War II placed maximum prices on items, which were rationed because of excess demand.

cement block: See *concrete block.*

central business district: Primary business district of a city or urbanized area having the area's major governmental offices, professional, and retail businesses represented.

central city: Major city in a metropolitan area. For example, New York City is the central city in the New York Metropolitan Area.

certificate: Written document by an official granting agency and signed by an empowered official certifying that some specific act including the fulfillment of certain requirements has occurred on a given date. Examples include a certificate of insurance or a certificate of occupancy.

certificate of beneficial interest: Document stating one has an ownership interest but not direct control in an asset, estate, or business. While one shares in the benefits of ownership including profits, the direct control is left to others. In a business, a certificate of beneficial interest entitles one to a share in the profits of the business, but direct control is provided by management.

certificate of eligibility: Certificate issued by the government showing evidence that the veteran is qualified and the amount of guarantee available to obtain a VA loan. It is one of the documents necessary to obtain a VA-guaranteed loan for the purchase of real estate. See also *certificate of reasonable value (CRV).*

certificate of insurance: Document describing the benefits and provisions for people or businesses covered by group insurance.

certificate of no defense: See *estoppel.*

certificate of occupancy (CO): Certificate usually granted by a jurisdiction's building department certifying a specified premise has satisfactorily complied with all zoning and building ordinances. This certification is a prerequisite for occupancy for its designated use and often the transfer of title at a sale.

certificate of reasonable value (CRV): Certificate showing the appraised value of the property and maximum VA guaranteed loan a veteran under GI guaranteed mortgage loan may obtain from a private lender. See also *certificate of eligibility.*

certificate of sale: Certificate issued to the buyer at a judicial sale, such as an execution sale. After the time for redemption has expired, the holder of the certificate is entitled to a deed.

certificate of title: An attorney's opinion of the status of a title, which is attached to the abstract of title.

certification:

(1) Written statement by a responsible individual or entity of the correctness and reliability of something. For example, a corporate officer certifies that certain conditions have been met.

(2) Written permission to do something, such as receiving a real estate franchise.

(3) Issuance of an unqualified audit opinion on a real estate company's financial statements by a Certified Public Accountant (CPA).

Certified Assessment Evaluator (CAE): Credential awarded by the International Association of Assessing Officers to appraisers of real property working for a government body.

certified commercial investment member: Name given by the Realtors National Marketing Institute which is affiliated with the National Association of Realtors.

certified historic structure: See *historic structure.*

Certified Property and Casualty Underwriter (CPCU): A knowledgeable person authorized to aid in the underwriting of property and casualty insurance.

Certified Property Manager (CPM): Professional certification granted by the Institute of Real Estate Management, an affiliate of the National Association of Realtors.

Certified Residential Broker (CRB): Certification granted by the Realtors National Marketing Institute, which is affiliated with the National Association of Realtors.

Certified Residential Specialist (CRS): Certification granted by the Realtors National Marketing Institute upon successful completion of an education program and the required residential sales experience. Candidates must already have achieved the Graduate of the Real Estate Institute designation.

certiorari: Writ issued by a superior court to a lower court requiring the latter to produce a record of the proceedings of a particular case. The purpose of a writ of certiorari is to review the proceedings of the lower court actions to determine if there is a legal basis for an appeal hearing at the higher court.

cession deed: Deed used to transfer property rights to a governmental authority. For example, a developer transfers property ownership rights of a dedicated sump to the local municipal government.

cesspool: Underground pit or tank used to store sewage.

cestui que trust: Trust beneficiary or an individual who is legally entitled to the property and financial benefits of a trust whose title is in another name. For example, the minor children Alan and Stephanie are the cestui que trust which is in the name of the trustee John Smith until they reach the age of majority whereupon the legal title of the trust reverts to Stephanie, the eldest, with the property of the entire trust being divided equally between the two

children when Alan, the youngest, also reaches the age of majority.

chain of title: Linkage of property ownership that connects the present owner to the original source of title.

change: Concept used in valuing real property that conditions may be altered requiring a revised estimate of market value. These conditions include a shift in the demand/supply relationship, deterioration of property, and capital improvements.

change order: Revised specifications requiring a modification in work. An example is when a customer changes his mind about how the basement should look and communicates to the contractor the change in plans.

change in principle: When a real estate company switches from one accounting method to another. Examples are changing the depreciation method on property (e.g., straight line to double declining balance), and switching from the percentage of completion construction method to the completed contract method. A change in principle is reported in the current year's income statement in an account called the "cumulative effect of a change in principle" (net of tax). Disclosure should be made of the nature and justification for the change.

chapter 7: Also called straight bankruptcy. A provision of the 1978 Bankruptcy Reform Act providing for a person's property to be divided among creditors to satisfy his/her unpaid debts. Any debtor subject to Chapter 7 is also subject to Chapter 11. See also *bankruptcy (personal).*

chapter 11: Used primarily by real estate corporations as a means of restructuring and reorganizing existing debts. Creditors must vote on a debt-paying plan and a judge must give approval. It provides protection for individual debtors with debts too large for a Chapter 13 filing. See also *wage earner plan (chapter 13)*.

chapter 13: A judicially approved plan in which a person's obligations are paid over three years. It is an arrangement for the repayment of debts which permits a credit user in severe financial straits to pay off credit obligations without declaring bankruptcy. See also *bankruptcy (personal); wage-earner plan.*

character: Credit standard judging the borrower's historical record of paying loans, among other considerations of the credit worthiness of the borrower. See also *five cs of credit.*

character of a city: Charm, ambiance and allure of a city that becomes its overall unique appeal. For example, San Francisco's character includes its large artistic community and cable cars.

chattel: Any property, tangible or otherwise, except real estate. Examples are furniture and automobiles.

chattel mortgage: Pledge of personal property, e.g., furniture, as collateral for a note. If the debt is not paid, the holder of the mortgage will receive the mortgaged property. See also *mortgage.*

chattel real: Interests and property directly connected with real property. This would include property leases, fixtures, and access rights.

chimney back: Rear lining of chimney. An acceptable chimney back lining can be achieved by plastering the interior surfaces of the chimney. A better alternative, however, is a manufactured lining of extruded fireclay. Prefabricated fireplaces often use multiwalled metal chimneys. In these chimneys, cool air from the room is introduced in the space between the flue walls at the bottom of the chimney and serves to insulate the outer shell by absorbing heat from the inner wall and discharging into the outside air above the roofline or into the room below the ceiling. Local building codes specify accept-

able minimum construction requirements for masonry chimneys as well as prefabricated fireplaces.

choose in possession: Property held by an individual, such as furniture.

chose in action: Claim or debt that may be recovered by instituting a lawsuit.

cinder block: Lightweight masonry block using cinders with a high metallic content as the major component. Cinder blocks are widely used in interior partitions.

circa: Approximate date. For example, the historic house in the middle of town was built circa 1800.

circlehead window: Half oval window. It is usually small and placed over a doorway serving a decorative purpose. In some cases, the window may be mounted with a hinge at either end to a permit opening for ventilation.

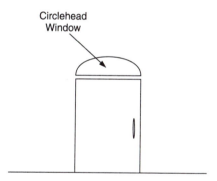

Circlehead Window

circuit breaker: Device that cuts off an electric circuit when that current becomes too strong.

cistern: Barrel, reservoir, or tank for storing rain runoff.

city plan: Large scale map of an urban area detailing land use. City plans are essential for projecting the growth, development, and redevelopment of the urban area. The major objective of a city plan is to have compatible uses, using the zoning law, as well as to preserve important environmental, topographical, and historical features of an area.

civil action: Legal proceeding to exercise a right in a disagreement between private individuals or businesses. One party seeks a remedy against the other. It does not involve a criminal situation. An example is the landlord suing the tenant for nonpayment of rent.

civil court: State court where civil disagreements are decided by the judge or jury. A written record is kept of the deliberations. In some states, civil and criminal courts are combined.

civil law: Law involving noncriminal issues such as breach of contract, libel, slander, and accidents. For example, the landlord may sue the tenant for nonpayment of rent and/or eviction.

civil rights laws: Civil rights acts passed by the U.S. Congress include those of 1866, 1870, 1871, 1875, 1964, and 1968. The first two acts gave blacks the rights to be treated as citizens in legal actions, particularly to sue and be sued and to own property. The cornerstone of the modern civil rights movement is the Civil Rights Act of 1964. This act prohibited discrimination in employment and established the Equal Employment Opportunity Commission. This major piece of legislation also banned discrimination in public accommodations connected with interstate commerce, including restaurants, hotels, and theaters. The Civil Rights Act of 1968 extended these guarantees to housing and real estate.

class action: Lawsuit brought by one or more persons of a large group for the benefit of all members of that group. For example, an investor may sue a real estate company for losses because of fraudulent financial statements.

classified property tax: Property tax that varies in rate depending on the zoning classification (use) of the property.

cleaning deposit: Nonrefundable fee to pay for the painting and cleaning of an apartment or office unit after a tenant vacates the premises.

clear title: Marketable title that is free of encumbrances and disputed interests. Clear title is essential in order to convey a general warranty deed in a transaction.

clerestory window: Window(s) situated on top of a structure to furnish air and light for the inside.

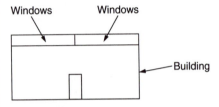

client: Individual or entity who pays for the professional services of another person or business. An example of a client relationship is that between a real estate broker and seller of a home for which a real estate commission will be earned.

closed-end lease: Involves monthly payments over a given time period. There is no charge when the lease expires. At the expiration date, the lessor sells the leased property for a gain or loss.

closed-end mortgage: Mortgage in which the collateralized property cannot be used as security for another loan. See also *open-end mortgage.*

closed mortgage: See *closed-end mortgage.*

closing: Legal process of transferring a piece of real estate to a buyer. Typically it occurs in the office of the lender, attorney, or an escrow company.

closing costs: Fees and expenses incurred by a home buyer in negotiating and financing the acquisition of a home and paid at the closing. Closing costs include the loan, loan origination fees, points, title search and insurance, appraisal charges, and other miscellaneous costs such as mortgage taxes and credit reports.

closing escrow: All of the conditions of the purchase and sale agreement have been fulfilled. The escrow agent prepares a written summary of the funds received in escrow, and the moneys paid out. The agent records the new deed with the County Recorder, and delivers a new deed to the buyer. Any remaining funds from the purchase price are then remitted to the seller. When the escrow has been accounted for, title is given to the buyer.

closing statement: Detailed financial accounting of all the credits and debits for the buyer and seller upon consummation of a real estate sale.

cloud on title: Also called a title defect. Any claim, lien, or encumbrance which, if valid, may impair the owner's title to the property. This cloud does not hinder transfer of ownership on the property, but may reduce its market value. See also *quitclaim deed*.

cluster housing: Planned subdivision where detached housing is located in close proximity to each other. Additionally, the subdivision shares common open space including parking and recreation areas.

co-brokerage: Two or more authorized brokers who agree to cooperate together representing a principal for the completion of a real property sale. For example, broker A has a listing on a parcel of property adjacent to another parcel for which broker B has a listing. Both parcels are owned by the same principal. A buyer wishes to get more favorable terms and offers to buy both parcels as a package. The principal owner of the two parcels agrees to allow broker A and B to cooperate together to realize the sale. Broker A and

B similarly agree to cooperate together and jointly reduce their commissions to consummate the sale.

code: An organized set of rules and regulations on a particular subject. Often codes are an accumulation of laws in a particular area of interest. For example, a zoning code or a building code.

code of ethics: An organized group of ethical behavior guidelines governing the day-to-day activities of a profession or organization. For example, the National Association of Real Estate Brokers (NAREB) has an extremely strict code of ethics to which all members subscribe.

codicil: A written supplement or amendment to an existing will such as one affecting the transfer of real estate upon death.

cognovit clause: Provision in a loan agreement where a debtor authorizes a judgment against him in the event of a default. These agreements are widely restricted, but when they are lawful, the creditor is empowered to appear in court and enter judgment against the debtor.

coinsurance: Arrangement the insured and insurer share on a proportional basis the payment for a loss. For example, in property insurance, it is a clause requiring policyholders to buy insurance in an amount equal to a certain percentage of the value of the improvements to their real property.

coinsurance clause: Provision in an insurance policy that "caps" the insurer's liability by stipulating that the owner of the property that has experienced damage (e.g., fire or water damage) must have another policy that covers usually at least 80% of the cash value of the property at the time of damage, in order to collect the full amount insured. This serves as an inducement for an individual to carry full coverage.

cold canvass: Sales approach where the salesperson approaches individuals or telephones them with no previous contact seeking a sale of some product or service. The cold canvass often produces the desired results, but it requires great persistence and mettle. For example, salesman A in the sample real estate brokerage office called every telephone number in a targeted area seeking real estate listings.

collapsible corporation: A company that is terminated within 3 years. According to the tax law, a gain arising from the sale or liquidation of such a business is considered ordinary income to the individual taxpayer on Form 1040.

collar beam: A horizontal beam connecting together two rafters supporting the roof. The collar beam is located at a point substantially higher than the wall plate connecting the rafters. The high position of the collar beam provides more head room than a conventional truss where the horizontal connecting beam is at the level of the wall plate.

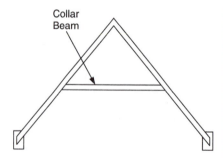

Collar Beam

collateral: Property that must be pledged for a loan. If the borrower defaults, the lender can typically seize the security such as a house.

Collateralized Mortgage Obligation (CMO): Mortgage-backed, pass-through securities that segregates mortgage pools into short-, medium-, and long-term. CMOs arose because GNMA or FHLMC mortgage-backed securities have uncertain time periods because of the possibility of prepayment of the principal balance on the mortgages. By separating mortgage pools into different time periods, investors now can buy shares in short-term (such as 5-year) or long-term (such as 20-year) pools. See also *mortgage-backed securities*.

collateral loan: Loan secured by the pledge of specific collateral. For example, Adams obtained a $10,000 loan from a bank using a $15,000 savings account as collateral.

collateral security: Property pledged to obtain a loan or credit. For example, giving as security one's home to receive a mortgage. Another example is placing stock in a real estate company as collateral to receive financing.

collusion: Secret understanding between two or more individuals to perpetrate a fraud or undertake other illegal actions. For example, a real estate salesperson and manager selling fictitious real estate property or investment trusts.

colonial architecture: Traditional style borrowed from the British Georgian architecture in the American colonial period. Colonial architecture usually has two stories emphasizing window detail and shutters.

colonnade: Grouping of several columns arranged in intervals supporting an architectural overhang, usually a roof.

color of title: Some plausible, but not completely clear-cut indication of ownership rights. It supplements a claim to title to property, but does not actually establish it.

comaker/cosigner: See *accommodation endorser, maker, or party.*

combed plywood: Plywood whose surface is given parallel scratches or grooves in the manufacturing process. It provides increased bond to adhesives, mortar, plaster, or stucco as well as giving a grain impression for painting.

combination windows: Window having both screens and storm windows that can be easily interchanged according to seasonal needs.

commercial acre: An acre of property zoned for business income-producing purposes. For example, a shopping center is located on 13 commercial acres.

commercial banks: The largest financial intermediaries directly involved in the financing of real estate. Commercial banks act as lenders for a multitude of loans. While they occasionally provide financing for permanent residential purchases, commercial banks' primary real estate activity involves short-term loans, particularly construction loans (typically six months to three years) and to a lesser extent home-improvement loans. Most large commercial banks have a real estate loan department; their involvement in real estate is through this department. Some of the largest commercial banks are also directly involved in real estate financing through their trust departments, mortgage banking operations, and real estate investment trusts (REITs). All commercial banks are either federally (nationally) chartered or state chartered. National banks are chartered and supervised by the U.S. Comptroller of the Currency. The word "national" appears in their title, and they are members of the Federal Reserve System (FRS). However, only one-third of all commercial banks are members of the FRS, even though the member banks control the majority of total bank assets. Nationally chartered banks are also required to maintain membership in the Federal Deposit Insurance Corporation (FDIC). Federally chartered banks can make real estate residential loans up to 90% of the appraised value with a maturity of not more than 30 years. However, any government insured or guaranteed loans are exempt from these limitations. State chartered banks are regulated by various agencies in their particular state, and membership in both the FDIC and the FRS is optional. Banks not members of the FDIC are normally required to maintain membership in a state insurance corporation.

commercial broker: Real estate broker specializing in the listing and selling of commercial property. This property can include apartments, businesses, hotels, industrial, retail, or wholesale uses. For example, a commercial broker assembles 15 commercial acres for a client who wants to construct a hotel.

commercial listing: List of business property.

commercial property: Business property, such as an office building, retail stores, medical center, or hotel, that operates with a profit. A risk/return relationship exists in commercial property. The return is comprised of the net rental income and capital appreciation in price. See also *residential property*.

commercial real estate: Real property usable in a trade or business. Examples are the property on which a retail store, office building, or hotel are located.

commingling of funds: A fiduciary intermingling a client's funds or one who is entrusted with funds and groups them with those of his own. This practice is considered a breach of a fiduciary relationship and a form of fraud. An example is an attorney who commingles a client's down payment on a piece of property with his own account.

commission: Charge paid to a person for services performed, usually based on a percentage of the amount received from the transaction (typically the total sales price). However, a commission may be based on other factors such as profitability. A commission is different from salary, which is a constant amount paid to an employee on a recurring basis. An example is the real estate commission earned by the real estate broker on the sale of a home paid to him by the seller. Assume a house is sold for $200,000 and the real estate commission is 6%. The commission equals $12,000. The salesperson would earn $\frac{1}{2}$ of this, or $6,000.

commissioner: An administrator appointed by the government or the courts to administer the laws relating to a government agency or court. A commissioner is a part of a government or court commission.

commission split: The method for splitting a commission between a registered real estate sales person and the sponsoring real estate broker, and between the listing broker and the selling broker, or any person regularly engaged in the real estate business in any other state. For example, at a 6% commission rate, the commission for selling a

$150,000 home is $9,000. The listing and selling broker each agree to a 50% split of the total commission. This commission, $4,500, may then be split 60% for the sponsoring broker and 40% for the real estate salesperson. Thus, the broker obtains $2,700 and the salesperson obtains $4,500–$2,700 or $1,800.

commitment:
(1) An agreement to buy real estate at a specified price and conditions. The failure to honor the commitment may result in damages.
(2) Bank commitment to lend money in connection with the purchase of real estate.

commitment fee: Charge by the lender to keep credit available to the potential borrower. Once the loan is made, interest is charged on the amount borrowed. Real estate businesses often need money available for land development and building construction. Typically, the bank will charge a commitment fee on those funds.

committee deed: A deed in which two or more people in an indenture agreement have reciprocity and obligations toward each other.

common area: Space that is available to all tenants or owners (e.g., condominiums), such as a courtyard, main entrance, elevator, and pool.

common area charges: Fees that all tenants or owners must pay for the cost of maintaining common areas. An example is the charges assessed retail stores for upkeeping the mall in a shopping center. Another example is the amount paid by owners of cooperatives or condominiums for the costs to maintain the development (e.g., landscaping).

common elements: Those parts of a condominium that are owned by all the unit owners.

common law: System of jurisprudence that is based on court decisions instead of statutes passed by a legislative body.

It is based on the principles decided by the courts. For example, in litigation over real estate matters, a review of previous court findings should be made to support the litigant's position.

community association: Generic name given for any association of property owners sharing an interest in commonly owned property. Community associations may be developed in condominium, cooperative, or housing subdivision developments. Their members have a common interest in managing common interests including maintenance and improvements.

Community Association Institute (CAI): Organization dedicated to creating and furnishing the most timely and effective advice and direction for the professional management and financing of facilities and services for condominiums, townhouse projects, open space, and other planned communities. Located in Alexandria, VA, and founded in 1973, the CAI has 13,000 members with 7 regional groups, 45 state groups, and 51 local groups. The organization conducts workshops and training seminars, sponsors competitions, and grants the National Community Association of the Year and Research Awards.

The CAI publishes the bimonthly association and industry newsletter, *CAI News,* and a bimonthly journal, *Common Ground,* which highlights the community association industry. It also publishes the monthly newsletter, *Association Law Reporter,* which covers court cases, community association legal trends, and current legislation.

community property: Property owned and held jointly and equally shared by each spouse. It is purchased during their marriage, regardless of the wage-earning situation of either spouse. A spouse may not make a gift of or dispose of community property without valuable consideration and written consent of the other spouse. Also, "necessaries" (furniture, furnishings, or fittings of the home) may not be disposed of without written consent of the other spouse. On a co-owner's death, one half belongs to the survivor as separate property. One half goes by will to the descendent devises or by succession to the survivor. Property owned before marriage, and property acquired after marriage by gift, inheritance, or by purchase with separate funds can be exempted from the couple's community property. Such property is called separate property and can be conveyed or mortgaged without the signature of the owner's spouse.

EXAMPLE: Harry and Sue are married. Before marriage, Sue inherited $100,000 worth of real estate from her uncle and kept it under her name. Under the community property laws, $100,000 is entirely her separate property.

community property laws: Statutes stipulating that the property of deceased individuals is distributed in a way that assumes that property during marriage is jointly owned and equally shared by the spouses irrespective of how much each paid. Sixteen western states have the community property doctrine. See also *community property.*

community reinvestment act: An Act, passed by Congress in order to prevent the practice of redlining and disinvestment in central city areas. Redlining is a practice whereby lenders refuse to make loans in certain geographic areas of a city. It is as if someone had taken a red pencil and drawn a line around the boundary of a neighborhood and said that no loans would be made in that neighborhood. Disinvestment is withdrawing funds and support of a particular neighborhood such as a riot-torn area.

co-mortgagor: Two or more parties signing a mortgage and sharing a joint financial obligation for the mortgage terms. Under these circumstances, co-mortgagors often have a joint property interest and consent to share a portion of the mortgage payments. For example, Smith and Robbins jointly apply and receive a mortgage to buy a home they choose to share together. Upon receipt of the mortgage and purchase of the home, they become co-mortgagors.

compaction: Method of eliminating the spaces between the solid fragments in fresh cement or mortar during the mixing process. This is done by a combination of constantly mixing, turning, centrifuging, or vibrating the mixture. The end result is to give a smoother consistent mixture which is stronger and more easily troweled.

comparables: Properties similar to the subject property that are used to estimate the value of the subject property.

comparable sales: Market analysis method where sales of similar properties in proximity neighborhoods are compared. The comparable sales methodology is extremely useful if the properties being compared are very similar and the sales are recent. It is widely used by real estate brokers to give approximate market valuations to buyers and sellers of real estate. Other factors enter into comparable sales including condition, location and property amenities. See also *comparables; market analysis; market approach.*

compensation: Money and nonmonetary consideration given to employees for work performed. The reward will typically be increased the better the job is done. Salary and fringe benefits are a major cost of a business so the amount paid must be within the financial abilities of the entity. Compensation depends on union contract and must not violate any laws (e.g., amount paid is below the minimum wage). For example, a manager of real estate properties is compensated for his work.

competent: An individual legally fit and able to undertake an activity or function. An example is a real estate broker or agent who is qualified to perform his job because he possesses the prerequisite knowledge, education, and experience. A person must be legally competent to sign a contract. A contract with a minor or severely mentally ill person may be deemed unenforceable.

competent parties: Persons considered legally capable of entering into a binding contract.

completion bond: Bond given by a building contractor to a public authority and guaranteed by a third party, usually a bonding company, that a contracted construction project will be completed within the contract period. Building contractors must be qualified in terms of meeting specific experience and achievement qualifications. Should the building contractor default, the bonding company guarantees to compensate for financial damages.

component: Part of something such as the units making up a heating or air conditioning system in a building.

component building: Structure of prefabricated units.

component depreciation: An accounting methodology for separately depreciating individual parts or elements of a building or improvement qualifying as business use or a depreciable asset under the IRS tax code. Examples might include sidewalks, roads, drainage facilities, sewers, wharves and docks, fences, landscaping shrubbery, central office telephone switching equipment, telephones, teletypewriters, computers, electrical, plumbing, heating, air conditioning and permanently secured appliances. In component depreciation, each component has its own class life and recovery period. For example, a telephone has a class life of 10 years and a recovery period of 7 years under the general depreciation system (GDS).

compounding: Paying interest on interest. The process adds earned interest to the principal so that interest is figured on a progressively larger amount.

compound interest: An interest rate that is applicable when interest in subsequent periods is earned not only on the original principal but also on the accumulated interest of prior periods. For example, assume that the initial principal is $1,000 and the annual interest rate is 10%. At the end of first year, the amount is the principal and interest, which is $1,000 + .1($1,000) = $1,000 + $100=$1,100. At the end of second year, the amount is accumulated $1,100 + .1($1,100) = $1,100 + $110 = $1,210. See also *future value; simple interest.*

compound sum: Total amount due at maturity consisting of both principal and compound interest.

con:

(1) Slang meaning a confidence scheme as in con man or con game.

(2) Prefix meaning with or together.

concentric zone theory: Land development planning model theorizing that an urban area grows in rings expanding out from the central business district. The second ring is a shifting area having manufacturing and warehousing activity, including some less prominent commercial activity. The third ring has low social economic status housing while the fourth ring has middle income housing. A fifth ring has new high social economic status housing.

concession:

(1) Right to engage in and earn from a particular activity in return for services or for a particular use.

(2) Reduced price used as an incentive.

(3) Permission or right, granted by a governmental body, to use property for a particular type of business in a specific area or place, such as a retail store or restaurant on a highway.

(4) Compensation for the underwriter's work in a new security issue of a real estate company.

conclusive presumption: Incontrovertible reality forcing a judge in a trial to find evidence to the contrary unsupportable. For example, a conclusive presumption is that water is wet and any evidence to the contrary cannot be sustained.

concrete: Substance developed from a binding cement medium with stone particles compacted together. After concrete hardens, its characteristics are very similar to stone. Concrete is an essential element in any building foundation and basement.

concrete block: Hollow building block whose dimensions are 8″ x 8″ x 16″. Concrete blocks are widely used in the construction of foundations and outer walls. They provide strength and durability.

concurrent ownership: Ownership in property by two or more persons at the same time.

condemnation: Legal action under eminent domain where the government takes ownership of privately held real estate for public use (e.g., schools, parks, or public housing) irrespective of the owner's wishes. The property owner is compensated for the appraised value of the property.

condemnation value: See *just compensation.*

conditional commitment: Agreement by a lender to loan money to suitable borrowers within a given time period but without identifying those borrowers. An example is a bank commitment given to a real estate developer to grant mortgages to financially sound borrowers.

conditional conveyance: Situation in which pledged property is held by a person or entity until the loan is paid. An example is the condition that the borrower make payments on the due date. If there is a default, the lender retains the property.

conditional endorsement: The endorser stipulates something such as that the transferee cannot use the funds for six months.

conditional fee: An estate constrained from some heirs and dedicated to others on the basis of a certain condition. For example, a testator stipulates only male heirs will be entitled to the contents of the estate. If there are only female heirs, the condition is that when one has a male child the estate passes to that heir.

conditional offer: Offer to buy real estate provided certain conditions are met. For example, an individual makes an offer to buy a house on the condition a permit is acquired allowing the rental of a guest apartment.

conditional sale contract: Real estate sales contract where possession and use is provided to the buyer, but the deed is kept by the seller until certain conditions are met. Typically, the buyer agrees to make payments until the full purchase price is met whereupon the title is placed in the buyer's name. See also *contract for deed; installment land sales contract; land contract.*

condition precedent: Condition that must be fulfilled or requires certain action before the estate granted can take effect. For example, many real estate sale contracts require payments to be made at the time specified before the purchaser may request for transfer of title.

conditions:
(1) Qualifications applying to an estate occurring when the estate is defeated or enlarged.
(2) Restrictions in a deed.
See also *condition precedent; condition subsequent.*

condition subsequent: Condition that depends on the failure or nonperformance of which an estate already granted may be overthrown. Upon the breach of the condition, the grantor has the power to terminate the estate. An example is a condition in the deed forbidding the grantee from using the premises as a liquor store.

condo conversion: Conversion of a rental apartment house to individual condominium ownership of a portion of the building. Often, the tenant is given an opportunity to "buy into" the condo conversion at a favorable price prior to it being offered on the open market. If the tenant refuses to "buy into" the condo conversion after a certain period, he or she must vacate the premises.

condominium: Ownership of a divided interest, i.e., a home ownership arrangement in which the owner has title to a housing unit within a structure, and a proportionate interest in the common grounds.

condominium owners association: Association of the owners of all condominium units in a building that is concerned with managing day-to-day matters in the building complex, including the surrounding property. These issues include maintenance and repairs as well as developing and enforcing condominium bylaws.

conduit:
(1) Distribution channel through which originating mortgage lenders distribute mortgages to the Secondary Mortgage Market. Those purchasing mortgages distributed through the conduit re-sell them using the private market system. They are often converted into standardized mortgage investments as mortgage-backed investment securities. The mortgages are serviced either by the originating lender or by a service agency.
(2) In construction, an enclosed channel or pipe used to carry electrical wiring, water, or other fluids.

(3) A long restricted passageway between two walls.

confession of judgment: Provision in a credit contract specifying that if the lender sues the borrower for late payments, the borrower accepts guilt in advance, irrespective of the reason for nonpayment.

confirmation of sale: Confirmation of a court ordered sale through the approval of the terms, price, and conditions. The court appoints a representative, either an administrator or executor in the event of an estate sale, a conservator or guardian in the case of an incapacitated individual, or commissioner in a foreclosure, to complete the sale.

confiscation:

(1) Government seizes private property, but does not provide fair and reasonable compensation for it. An example is when land is taken to build a highway with adequate compensation.

(2) Property is seized and the owner's rights abolished because of a legal violation. An example is when a home is used for an illegal activity, such as drug dealing or prostitution.

conforming loans: Loans that adhere to national guidelines by Fannie Mae, who buy the loans on the secondary market. Fannie Mae purchases mortgages to a certain dollar limit. Conforming loans typically come with a lower interest rate than larger mortgage, or jumbo loans, which are purchased on the secondary mortgage market by another federally-chartered company, the Federal Home Loan Mortgage Corporation (Freddie Mac).

conformity principle: A generally accepted appraisal principle stating properties having similar architectural, socioeconomic occupancy, and usage characteristics maximize respective market values. In contrast, nonconforming uses will reduce market respective to property valuations. For example, a middle class housing development having similar architectural and socioeconomic characteristics normally will have higher respective property valuations than a comparable neighborhood having nonconforming commercial or industrial properties.

consent: Approving or permitting an action to occur. An example is a landlord agreeing to let the tenant subrent it.

consequential damage: Unanticipated damages incurred as the result of the subsequential effects of a party's breach of responsibility or contract. Consequential damages often result in financial compensation. For example, a poorly conceived road widening project results in flooding of adjoining properties. A subsequent court action awards the property owners consequential damages.

conservator: An individual appointed by a court to manage the affairs and property of a legally incompetent party. The conservator has full decision-making authority over the affairs of the property in accordance with court-established guidelines.

conservatorship: Act of being a conservator.

consideration:

(1) Anything of value given to induce a person or entity into entering a contract. It may be money, personal services, or the trading of property. A valid contract requires adequate consideration.

(2) The amount actually received from the sale of securities of a real estate company after deducting all the expenses including taxes on the sale and commission to the broker from the gross receipts.

consolidation loan: Loan that combines smaller loans into one larger loan and typically arises from refinancing debt. It typically results in a lower overall interest rate, longer payment schedule, and lower dollar amount for each payment. Further, it is more convenient and easier when there is one loan rather than many loans.

constant payment loan: Loan mandating equal periodic payments to pay off the loan subsequent to the last payment.

construction costs: Expenditures incurred building a structure, including material and labor. Examples include bricks, walls, lighting fixtures, and beams. There are also indirect expenditures such as for permits and insurance.

construction cycle: Time period that a round (set) of regular recurring construction takes place. There may be boom and bust times in construction activity.

construction loan rate:
(1) The interest rate charged on a construction loan.
(2) The rate at which construction loan progress payments are made. See also *bridge loan; bullet mortgage; development loan.*

construction loans: Also called interim financing. A mortgage that provides the funds necessary for the building or construction of a real estate project. The project can be a residential subdivision, a shopping center, an industrial park, or any other type of property requiring financing during the time required to complete construction. Normally, the full amount to be loaned is committed by the lender, but the actual disbursement is dependent upon the progress of the construction. Funds are sometimes distributed to the borrower in a series of draws, depending upon the work required by the lender. Another method used is for the developer to submit all bills to the lender, who in turn pays the bills. In either case, interest is paid on what has been distributed and not on the total amount to be borrowed.

constructive: Meaning or definition given to an act, fact, or thing through legal or juridical interpretation. For example,

the constructive interpretation of a contested will arbitrates the distribution of the estate's contents to the heirs.

constructive annexation: The consolidation of items that have been considered a part of property but are not actually annexed, secured, or joined to it. For example, a past pattern of use over an extended period of time establishes an access right to a highway through an adjoining property. A judicial ruling subsequently establishes a constructive annexation of the access right through the adjoining property.

constructive eviction: Tenant breaks the lease because the landlord does not keep the premises habitable.

constructive market value: Estimated market price property could bring using currently accepted appraisal methods. This might not be the same as the market price at any one given time when the seller is compelled to sell under auction circumstances, but rather the highest price a willing buyer would pay in an open and fair market. See also *comparable sales; comparables; market analysis; market approach.*

constructive notice: Notice given by public record and by visible possession, coupled with the legal presumption that all persons are thereby notified.

constructive receipt: Tax concept whereby income not actually received is considered to be constructively received by a taxpayer and thus must be reported. An example is a bond interest coupon. The interest is taxable in the year the coupon matures, even though the holder delays cashing it until a later year.

constructive trust: Judicial order creating a trust for property wrongfully or illegally assumed or taken. The trust compels the person improperly assuming the title to the property to transfer it to another having a legally sustainable claim.

consumer goods: Any commercially fabricated and widely available product designed for household and personal use. Consumer goods are available in an open market place and are competitively priced.

Consumer Price Index (CPI): An average of the prices of goods and services commonly bought by families in urban areas. This indexes the most well-known inflation gauge and is often referred to as the cost-of-living index, which labor contracts, rents, and social security are tied to. The CPI measures the cost of buying a fixed bundle of goods (some 400 consumer goods and services), representative of the purchase of the typical working class, urban family. The index excluding volatile energy and food costs is often called core rate of inflation. The base year for the CPI index was 1982-84 at which time it was assigned 100. The CPI is important to landlords because it helps keep the base monthly rent in pace with inflation. The monthly rent will increase in a percentage equal to the increase of the CPI figure. The CPI figures are published around the 18th of each month by the Bureau of Labor Statistics of the U.S. Department of Labor. See also *GDP deflator; price indices; producer price index (PPI).*

contemporary: Innovative architectural designs for either single or multi level homes and other buildings incorporating innovative features, such as passive solar heating. Contemporary building plans are often developed using computer-aided design allowing great individualized creativity.

contents replacement cost protection: Optional feature included in some homeowner's insurance policies that pays the replacement cost of any personal property.

contiguous: Properties which abut and actually touch and share a common border. Properties B and C are contiguous. Property A is adjacent to properties B and C, but it is not contiguous.

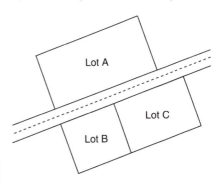

contingency: Possibility or chance that an event may occur. An action is dependent on something else happening. An example is a prospective home buyer planning to buy a home if he gets a new promotion or job.

contingency clause: Provision in a written agreement that depends on the occurrence of something else. An example is a clause in the contract stating that the purchase of a home is contingent upon getting a mortgage from the bank.

contingency fund: Money set aside for a possible loss, such as from a fire.

contingency planning: Considering future occurrences that may possibly arise. An example is having a plan in place in the event a major real estate contract is not renewed.

contingent: Something that is dependent on something else. For example, a binder put on a house by a prospective buyer is upon the approval of a parent.

contingent beneficiary: Person who will become the beneficiary if the original beneficiary dies before the insured. It is the policyholder's second election as beneficiary, dependent on the status of the primary beneficiary.

contingent commission: Fee paid only if other criteria are met. An example is a commission to be paid to a real estate broker by the owner of a house when it is sold or a commission to be paid by a landlord if a tenant is found.

contingent interest: Interest is due on a loan only if a particular circumstance occurs. An example is when interest will be charged on an obligation only when the periodic payment is past due. In this case, the interest is charged based on the number of days past due.

contingent rentals: Lease payments based on factors other than the passage of time. An example is a store in a mall paying a monthly rental based on a flat fee plus an extra amount based on sales or profitability. Disclosure should be made of the contingent rental payment and terms prior to entering into an agreement.

contingent sale: Sale that is finalized only in the case of a particular occurrence or eventuality. An example is a sale of a home contingent on the buyer obtaining a mortgage.

contingent vesting: Right to property depends on some occurrence. An example is the real estate company giving pension rights to real estate agents after they have worked five years for the firm.

continuation statement: Document submitted to a governmental agency to extend the time period for a previously approved document.

continuing commitment: Recurring obligation or assurance given. An example is when a homebuilder makes a written agreement to repair any structural damages that may occur with the house. Such commitment is automatically renewed on a yearly basis.

contour: A line on a map or drawing showing equal ground elevation points. See also *contour map.*

contour map: A map that shows land elevations. (See top of right column.)

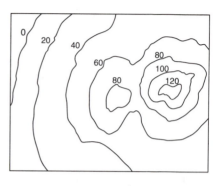

contract: Agreement between two or more individuals (or entities) whereby each party agrees to do or not to do some act. The parties have reciprocal obligations of performance or actions.

contract for deed: Method of selling and financing property whereby the buyer obtains possession, but the seller retains the title.

contract for exchange of real property: Trading of two or more properties containing separate descriptions and separate financial statements.

contract for novation: In law, substituting a suitable person or entity for an original party to a contract. It terminates the old contract and begins a new one. The new contract has the same provisions, but with a different person or entity. An example is a father's agreement to assume the mortgage of a daughter with the bank's approval.

contract price (tax): Selling price of a property less assumed mortgages by the buyer. For tax purposes, the computation of the contract price is critical. For example, Smith sells a property for $150,000 to Jones who assumes a first mortgage of $80,000. He receives $30,000 in cash and completes the financing by giving a second mortgage of $40,000. The contract price of the property is $150,000 less the first mortgage of $80,000 or $70,000 ($150,000 − $80,000) = $70,000. See also *installment sale.*

contract rate: Stated rate of interest on the face amount of a loan or installment note.

contract rent: Amount of rent specified in the lease contract.

contract of sale: Written agreement between a seller and a buyer in which the latter agrees to buy real estate property upon mutually suitable terms.

conventional loan: Mortgage loan not insured or guaranteed by a governmental agency such as the Federal Home Administration or the Veterans Administration. Such a loan is repayable in fixed monthly payments with a fixed rate and term (usually not exceeding 30 years), secured by real property.

conventional mortgage: Mortgage requiring a substantial down payment. It is usually only available to those having good credit, and has fixed monthly payments for the life of the loan. It usually has a 30-year period of fixed interest rates discharged on an amortized basis with equal monthly payments. The term "conventional" refers to a mortgage that is not FHA-insured or VA-guaranteed. Since there is no third person or entity to insure or guarantee the mortgage, the lender assumes full risk of default by the borrower. A lender's decision to make a conventional mortgage is usually dependent upon: (1) the value of the property being used to secure the debt and (2) the credit and income position of the borrower. As more and more conventional mortgages have been made, the loan-to-value ratio (relationship between amount borrowed and the appraised value of the property) has continued to increase, even though most lenders still limit the amount they will lend to no more than 80% of value unless private mortgage insurance is carried. This down payment requirement is higher than with either FHA or VA loans. As the market price

of residential real estate has continued to increase, a larger cash down payment has been required of the borrower, and thus many people have been eliminated from financing with a conventional mortgage. With both insured and guaranteed mortgages, people have been able to purchase real estate with a smaller cash down payment.

contractor:

(1) Individual or business that is engaged to do some sort of construction work for another for a fee. There are basically three types of contracting: A general contractor enters into a direct contractual agreement with the property owner for the entire construction activity. A subcontractor is employed by the general contractor to do part of the work. An independent contractor is directly engaged by the property owner to do a portion of the construction activity; a specific item. The independent contractor controls how the work is performed. An example of a contractor is one who is hired to do home improvements by the homeowner.

(2) Individual involved in a contract.

contract specifications: Details of a contract of sale including a financial statement, legal description, type of deed, place, date and time of closing of title.

contractual ability: Capability of a party to enter into a contract such as having the financial and physical resources as well as mental competency to meet contractual commitments.

contractual savings: Transaction savings realized by setting a fixed and certain price. For example, a mortgage commitment contract specifies an interest rate cap that cannot be exceeded before the loan closing.

contribution: Appraisal concept stating the value a particular improvement contributes to the overall value of a property irrespective of its actual cost. For example, remodeling a kitchen makes a $7,500 contribution to the value of a home even though it costs $4,000.

control variable: Environmental element that remains unchanged and strongly influences real estate valuations despite the cost of improvements. For example, Jones purchased a home for $150,000 and subsequently spent $50,000 on added improvements. However, the market price of the home only increased to $165,000 since the control variable was the average neighborhood price of $155,000.

conversion: Transfer of personal property or real estate of a certain type to property of a different type.

conversion proceeds: Amount received when property is changed from one use to another (e.g., apartment house to a condominium). For example, the owner of the property receives money from tenants who now want to buy their apartments. A change in ownership may also be forced such as when foreclosure occurs and the property is sold.

convertibility: Agreement to exchange real estate upon specific terms.

convey: To sell property from one to the other and transfer all title and interest. Property is conveyed by bill of sale, contract, deed or other instrument. For example, Jones conveyed the property to Smith by contract of sale and deed.

conveyance: Transfer of the title of land, real estate, or personal property from one person or entity to another. This transfer is typically made via a mortgage, trust deed, sales contract, or similar instrument.

cook the books: Falsify financial records and statements to misrepresent the financial position and operating results of the business.

co-op:

(1) Housing arrangement in which the tenants are shareholders in a company that owns and maintains the structure.

(2) Agreement between two real estate brokers in which the commissions will be shared, usually equally.

cooperating broker: Broker who, acting as an agent of the listing broker, procures a buyer.

cooperative: Also called co-ops. A corporation that owns housing units and whose tenants purchase shares in the corporation equivalent to the value of their housing unit.

cooperative apartment: Apartment building in which each resident owns a percentage share of the corporation that owns the building.

cooperative housing: An apartment ownership method in an apartment complex with stock in a corporation. Each owner has a lease on an apartment, but does not have outright ownership as in a condominium. Since there is no individual apartment ownership, cooperative shareholders cannot obtain individual mortgage financing and must pay a share of the overall mortgage and tax payments with all the other cooperative owners. Individual cooperative shareholders are at risk since they are responsible should one or more shareholders default.

corner:

(1) In land surveying, the point at which two properties intersect constituting a boundary line between the properties. A corner can be determined by either a survey or general agreement between neighbors. A surveying monument indicates the boundaries at the corner.

(2) Property bounded by two intersecting roads. See also *corner influence; corner lot.*

(3) Point at which two walls join each other at an angle.

corner influence: Additional value of property bounded on two sides by intersecting roadways. Generally speaking, corner influence adds value to property when compared to abutting inside lots. This is particularly true with commercial property. However, this is not universally true, and there are several appraisal methods of determining actual corner influence of a property.

The chief advantage of a commercial corner lot is that it has twice the street frontage an inside lot has. Corner influence steadily declines in importance as the property classifications change in the following order: retail commercial, financial, office, hotel, apartment, ordinary retail, wholesale, residential, and undeveloped or rural areas. However, for residential purposes, increased street frontage may be a disadvantage when considering the increased traffic hazard and associated environmental and noise pollution.

Corner influence includes several advantages particularly for commercial purposes:

(1) Zoning and building codes normally allow greater building area.

(2) There is greater exposure and access to automobile and pedestrian traffic.

(3) There is increased light and air.

(4) The increased exposure provides greater effectiveness for window and sign advertising.

(5) There is greater ease of access and egress.

Variations in the value of corner sites depend to a great degree on the significance of the importance of these variables. Generally, corner influence is greatest in high valuation retail sites.

A number of formulas are used in developing corner values; however, there is wide disagreement over the value of the formulas and appraisers generally acknowledge that other factors are still critical. Corner influence steadily falls in importance as the property classifications decline in the following order: financial, office, hotel, apartment,

ordinary retail, wholesale, residential, and undeveloped or rural areas. These factors include market conditions, age and condition of improvements on a corner property, and zoning restrictions. See Corner Influence Table in the Appendix.

corner lot: Land parcel bounded by two intersecting roadways. See also *corner; corner influence.*

cornice:

(1) Molded projection attached to and crowning the uppermost portion of an outside wall. The functional purpose of the cornice is to meet the roof and throw off rain water.

(2) Any wood or plaster molding on an inside wall just below the ceiling. It is ornamental in purpose giving the wall a finished appearance.

(3) Molding forming the top part of a door or window.

corporation: Business organized as a distinct legal entity with ownership evidenced by shares of stock. To form a corporation, "articles of incorporation" must be filed with the state. When approved, the state issues to the real estate company a "certificate of incorporation." The two documents in combination are referred to as the "corporate charter." Each founding stockholder receives a certain number of shares of stock. A stockholder may sell his or her shares to others. A corporation is a legal entity separate from its owners. Advantages of the corporate form are unlimited life, limited liability of owners, ease of transferring stock, ability to obtain significant funds through public issuance of securities, and professional management. There are various forms that a corporation can take depending on ownership.

corporation sole: Corporation having only one person. A corporation sole is primarily used for the purposes of a nonprofit ecclesiastic church related organization. In a church, the corporation sole is headed by a priest, minister or bishop who holds title to all church-related property. The corporation sole allows the title to pass to the successors in office rather than to the heirs of the priest, minister, or bishop.

corporeal right: Right to substantive real or personal property having tangible body and form. For example, a corporeal right to a house, property, furniture, or fixtures.

corpus: The actual, physical and tangible fact in a given situation; a substantive body of positive evidence.

correction deed: Issued to correct errors in another deed such as spelling errors in a name or an improper legal description. For example, a correction deed was issued to the property owner Smith to amend an inaccurate property description. See also *deed of confirmation.*

correlation: Degree of relationship between variables or factors affecting the real estate market and activities within that market. Correlation analysis looks at cause/effect relationships such as the impact of economic conditions on housing starts or building construction. Correlation examines how the value of one variable changes (e.g., real estate values) when the value of another variable changes (e.g., interest rates, money supply). A prediction can be made based on the relationship. A degree of correlation is measured mathematically by the coefficient of determination (r-squared). The correlation between variables may range between +1 to −1. Perfect positive correlation (variables move in the same direction) is +1. Perfect negative correlation (variables move in the opposite directions) is −1. No correlation between variables is indicated by 0.

corridor:
(1) Long interior passageway providing access to rooms.
(2) Passageway providing public access from a building interior to an exit.

corrugated siding: Siding made out of aluminum, plastic derivatives, or cement asbestos having ridges and valleys which is attached to the sides of buildings.

cosign: To sign a note on behalf of another individual and, therefore, to guarantee payment. The cosigner is responsible for the loan if the borrower defaults. Such an agreement may occur in connection to the purchase of real property.

cost:
(1) The sacrifice, measured by the price paid, to acquire real estate.
(2) An asset. The term cost is often used when referring to the valuation of acquired property. When it is used in this sense, a cost is an asset.
(3) Concepts of cost and expense are often used interchangeably. When the benefits of the acquisition of a building expires, the cost becomes an expense called depreciation.

cost approach: Notion that a buyer should not pay more for a property than it would cost to buy at current prices for land, labor, and appraisals. The following shows a calculation to derive an appraised value under this method:

Estimated land value without vacancy	$ 50,000
Estimated Construction Cost of a Similar Structure	160,000
Less: Estimated Depreciation	(10,000)
Estimated Value of Building	150,000
Appraised Property Value	$200,000

cost approach to value: Valuing real property based on the expected cost to buy property of identical value. The replacement cost to build a structure should be based on current prices. The appraisal should consider any deterioration (depreciation) to the property in question.

cost estimating: Projecting what the total cost would be to construct a structure. Costs include material, labor, and lawyers' fees.

cost of capital: Rate of return that is necessary to maintain market value of a real estate project. The cost of capital is used for project evaluation purposes. Under the net present value method, the cost of capital is used as the discount rate to calculate the present value of future cash inflows derived from the real estate project. Under the internal rate of return method, it is used to make an accept-or-reject decision by comparing the cost of capital with the internal rate of return on a given project. A project is accepted when the internal rate exceeds the cost of capital. See also *hurdle rate; cutoff rate; minimum required rate of return.*

cost of development: Expenditures incurred to develop real estate. An example is the cost to build a shopping center.

cost of funds index: Average of what savings institutions in the 11th district of the Federal Home Loan Bank System (California, Arizona, and Nevada) are paying in interest to depositors and other sources of borrowed money. The index was developed in 1981 to provide a benchmark for adjustable rate mortgages. Currently, about 10 percent of the nation's mortgages are tied to the index. When the index rises, so do interest rates on millions of home mortgages.

cost of home ownership: Expenditures paid by the owner of a house to keep and maintain it including real estate taxes, interest on a mortgage, repairs and maintenance, and capital additions (e.g., new roof, new basement).

cost of living: Cost to buy goods and services encompassed in an accepted standard level of consumption.

cost of occupancy: Expenditure paid to occupy property over a specified time period.

cost-plus contract: Agreement in which the contract price to build something is equal to the total costs incurred plus a predetermined profit. The profit may be based on a percentage of cost (e.g., 20% of cost) or a flat profit figure (e.g., $50,000). This type of contract is not good for the buyer because the contractor may intentionally overstate the construction costs to obtain a higher profit figure when profit is determined based on a percentage of total costs. If the construction costs are $100,000 and the percentage of profit is 25%, the total contract price will be $125,000.

cotenancy: When two or more individuals simultaneously have rights in a property unit (e.g., apartment). The individuals sharing the property have legal privileges and responsibilities to each other. Before a cotenant is accepted, careful consideration should be given because problems may arise.

counseling: Process of conferring and consulting with clients concerning real estate investments and developmental projects. See also *American Society of Real Estate Counselors (ASREC).*

Counselor of Real Estate (CRE): Designation given to members of the American Society of Real Estate Counselors (ASREC). A prerequisite for membership is professional experience and ethical conduct.

counterclaim: Counter action by a defendant against a plaintiff. It is an independent action and not just a denial of the plaintiff's action.

counterflashing: Substance or material used at the top of a chimney at the roof to inhibit the development of moisture and to protect the metal.

counteroffer: Initial offer to buy or sell answered with a revised offer. For example, a buyer offers $500,000 for a home put on the market. The owner rejects the offer but submits a counteroffer for $525,000. Offers and counteroffers are not limited to price, but comprise such matters as financing arrangements and apportionment of closing costs.

cove:

(1) Concave or cratered corner molding. A hollow cornice.

(2) Small navigable body of water having limited water access and egress. Coves are often secluded and act as a boating anchorage.

covenant:

(1) Agreeing to perform or not to perform some act. An example is a tenant agreeing not to sublease the apartment.

(2) Entering into a contractual commitment such as signing a three year lease.

(3) Stipulating something such as a tenant agreeing not to have a dog in the apartment.

(4) Implied or express commitment in connection with a contract or deed. An example is a restriction placed on the borrower in a loan agreement by the bank to protect its interest. Another example is requiring a real estate developer to maintain a minimum working capital and carry a minimum amount of insurance.

covenant not to compete: Legal agreement not to perform an activity similar to that performed by another individual or business. This contractual provision may be necessary to keep trade secrets, prevent taking away existing clients using the current business's methods, or otherwise seriously impair the activities of the existing business. These covenants may arise when a real estate broker sells his business, a partner leaves a real estate firm, and when an employee is hired. For example, a real estate broker who signs a covenant not to compete may prohibit him from opening up a real estate brokerage firm within 50 miles for a two-year period. This restriction is particularly important when the employee is highly qualified and will likely develop a strong customer following. However, if the restriction is very excessive, it may be legally unenforceable.

covenants running with the land: Written agreement, guarantee, pledge, or promise annexed to the land between two or more parties to do or not do something and is transferred to successive title holders. For example, in exchange for donating a parcel of land to the community, Jones adds a covenant running with the land that the property would forever be used only for educational purposes.

crawl hole (space):

(1) Any interior passage of limited height sufficiently large to allow the entrance of individuals for the purpose of gaining access to electrical, heating, plumbing, or other building subsystems.

(2) Unfinished access space below the first floor having less height than a full story. An individual must crawl through the crawl hole to gain access.

creative financing: Any financing agreement excluding a conventional mortgage from a third-person or entity lending institution. This type of financing is more prevalent when the price of real estate is too high for many buyers. See also *seller financing; balloon payment loans; wraparound mortgages; assumption of mortgage; sale-leasebacks; land contracts; alternative mortgage instruments; adjustable rate mortgage (ARM); shared equity mortgage (SEM).*

credit:

(1) A purchase of real property made on account.

(2) Loan extended to business or individuals to buy real estate.

(3) Form of trust established between a lender and a borrower.

(4) In taxation, a dollar-for-dollar reduction in taxes. An example of a tax credit is the housing rehabilitation credit.

credit application: Form used to record information about a credit applicant's ability to meet his obligations in connection with a real estate purchase.

credit history: History of an individual's credit financial transactions including a detailed payment analysis. The credit history is critical for performing a credit analysis to develop a credit rating. A credit history record of prompt and timely payments is important for a strong credit rating. A credit history is kept by major credit rating organizations and is accessible for a fee by commercial organizations as well as by individuals under terms of the Consumer Credit Protection Act. Banks and other major lenders give an individual's credit history serious consideration before extending credit or granting loans.

credit limit: Maximum credit a prospective buyer may be given. An example is the maximum mortgage a prospective home buyer may receive from the bank.

credit rating: Rating used by lenders and creditors to determine if a credit applicant should be granted credit. It depends on many factors such the applicants' job history, earnings, net worth, etc. Some companies keep credit records of people and entities. Examples of credit rating agencies are TRW (for individuals) and Dun and Bradstreet (for businesses).

credit scoring: Objective method of appraising an applicant's credit standing by assigning values to factors such as annual income, liabilities, job status, and credit history.

creditworthiness: Financial standing of a debtor as a basis to pay obligations.

creeping inflation: Gradual and steady increase in the general price level which is bearable in the near term but may result in significant long-term price increases. See also *galloping inflation.*

crossover:
(1) Plumbing connection between two water pipes in the same system.
(2) Pipe fitting shaped like the letter U permitting an intersecting pipe to be directed around another pipe.
(3) Passageway in an auditorium paralleling and between the seats allowing passage from one aisle to another.

cross tie: Supporting beam or connecting member between two walls. A cross tie gives support for wall structures.

cubic foot factor method: Along with the square foot factor method, this is the most widely used method for estimating comparable building costs. The cubic foot factor method requires the computation of the cubic contents of a building by multiplying the building area from the outside of the exterior walls times the height of the building. The average building cost for a comparable group of buildings is then divided by the cubic contents of the building to arrive at the average building cost per cubic foot.

The cubic foot factor method is used by appraisers to estimate the reproduction costs of a building. For example, if the average cubic foot cost of a certain building type is $20, and the total cubic contents of the building are 5000 cubic feet, then the estimated reproduction cost of the building is $20 × 5000 = $100,000.

cul-de-sac: Street having access only at one end and terminating with a circular turnaround area. The circular area permits automobiles to exit the street without having to use a home's driveway to turn around.

curable depreciation: Correcting depreciation by making improvements at less cost than the value added. For example, the management of an aging strip shopping center makes a decision to refurbish the windows and walkway at a cost of $2,000 per unit. Management estimates this will provide a rent increase of $100 per unit. The current neighborhood gross rent multiplier is 120. Therefore, the value added by the improvements is 120 × 100 = $12,000 per unit. This is curable depreciation since the $12,000 unit value added more than compensates for the $2,000 unit cost of the improvements.

curable penalty: Penalty charged in order to cure a previous wrong.

curb: Raised concrete border constructed along a street or a sidewalk. A curb prevents vehicles from going on the adjacent property and sidewalks as well as directing runoff into storm drains.

curb line: Property boundary demarcated by the curb.

current value: Present worth of the property which is different than the price paid for it or its book value (cost less accumulated depreciation). The current value may be determined through appraisal.

current yield: Measurement of investment return that relates current income to the investment cost.

EXAMPLE: Norman Henteleff bought a parking lot for $150,000, which generates annual revenue of $90,000. Annual expenses including property taxes, insurance, and operating expenses totals $60,000. Annual income before taxes then is $30,000. The current yield is 20%: $30,000/$150,000 = 20%

See also *return; yield; yield to maturity (YTM)*.

curtail schedule: Lessening of work assignments such as when a real estate management firm reduces the number of buildings assigned to each manager. By reducing someone's schedule, he will probably do a better job since there are less units to service.

curtesy: Husband's common law rights to the property his deceased wife owned either during the marriage or at the time of her death. The husband has life estate rights in the deceased wife's property. State laws differ on curtesy rights, and many states have eliminated them entirely. For example, as a result of John's curtesy right, he has a life estate with his late wife's home, but at the time of his death the home devolves to the children from her first marriage.

customer (custom) builder: Builder who builds homes or other buildings to the specification of his customer. Normally the homes and other structures are presold; however, the customer builder may also build a few on speculation or "spec houses." The customer builder builds only a few homes at a time, whereas the developer uses mass production in producing many homes at once.

customer's extras: Features a home buyer orders from a custom builder or developer when purchasing a home. For example, a customer may order a two-car garage when buying a home requiring an additional charge.

D

damage deposit: Prepayment to cover any physical damage other than normal deterioration caused by the tenant.

DBA (Doing Business As): Certification by a state that a principal is doing business under an assumed name. The certificate also states the address where the business is being conducted. The primary purposes of the DBA certificate are:
(1) Registration of a business and its assumed name giving the principal's name and address.
(2) Protect the business name from being used by others.
(3) Provide a public source of redress.

dead end street: Street terminating at one end with only one outlet. A dead end street is not a through street. See also *cul de sac.*

dead storage: Storage of inactive items, including automobiles, for a certain period. Normally, a storage facility, charging a fee, provides dead storage of items. To prevent deterioration, dead storage often is in a controlled atmosphere facility.

debenture: Unsecured long-term debt. There is no collateral or lien on the property. A debenture can only be issued by a financially sound borrower with an excellent credit rating because no security is given. There are two types of debentures: senior and junior (subordinated to the senior issue).

debt:
(1) Money or services owed by one party to another party. The debtor may have to pledge an asset for a loan, such as a mortgage on his or her house. Principal and interest payments are required. Debt may either be current or noncurrent. See also *amortized loan; loan; mortgage loan; straight loan; term loan.*
(2) Entry on the left side of an account.

debt financing: Raising money by mortgages and borrowing the money directly from financial institutions. The presence of debt financing provides financial leverage, which tends to magnify the effects of increased operating profits on the individual's and corporation's returns. Interest is tax deductible. Further, leverage is desirable as long as the borrowed funds produce a return in excess of their cost. However, too much debt can result in higher levels of financial risk in meeting the principal and satisfying interest payments. Excessive debt will make it more difficult to raise funds and will increase further borrowing costs.

debt-to-income ratio: Ratio of monthly debt payments to monthly gross income. Lenders use a housing debt-to-income (DTI) ratio (house payment divided by monthly income) and a total DTI ratio (total debt payment including the house payment divided by monthly income) to determine whether a borrower's income qualifies a buyer for a mortgage.

debt limit: Maximum amount of debt an individual or business can borrow in order to buy real estate.

debtor: Individual who has a legal obligation to pay money to another.

debt service: The interest and principal paid on a loan. Debt service is normally paid biweekly, monthly, quarterly, or annually depending on the terms of the loan. For example, the table gives the first twelve $869 monthly payments on a 30-year $95,000 loan at 10.5% interest. Note that the initial interest payments are substantially higher than the principal payments, but begin declining as the principal payments steadily increase. See also *amortization.*

decedent: One who has died with a valid will in effect.

decent: When an owner of real estate dies intestate, having no enforceable will, the property descends, by operation of law, to the owner's inheritors.

deciduous: Relating to trees or shrubs normally found in temperate climates. Deciduous trees shed their leaves in the fall. Deciduous woods such as pine, oak, maple, redwood, and spruce are widely used for making furniture. Pine is a very commonly used deciduous building material.

deck:
(1) Flooring in a structure.
(2) Open structure with flooring erected outside a main building. A deck can have different levels with direct access to the main structure. It is usually constructed of wood having a creative design. In a home, a deck is often used for entertainment purposes and is recreational in nature. In a commercial building a deck is designed to be attractive and add to the ambiance. For example, a

Debt Service

Amount of Loan:	$95,000.00	Term of Loan:	30 Years
Monthly Payments:	$869.00	Yearly Interest:	10.500%
Total Interest Paid:	$217,844.50	Total Payout:	$312,844.50

Payment	Amount	Interest	Principal	Interest to Date	Remaining Balance
1	869.00	831.25	37.75	831.25	94,962.25
2	869.00	830.92	38.08	1,662.17	94,924.17
3	869.00	830.59	38.41	2,492.76	94,885.76
4	869.00	830.25	38.75	3,323.01	94,847.01
5	869.00	829.91	39.09	4,152.92	94,807.92
6	869.00	829.57	39.43	4,982.49	94,768.49
7	869.00	829.22	39.78	5,811.71	94,728.71
8	869.00	828.88	40.12	6,640.59	94,688.59
9	869.00	828.53	40.47	7,469.12	94,648.12
10	869.00	828.17	40.83	8,297.29	94,607.29
11	869.00	827.81	41.19	9,125.10	94,566.10
12	869.00	827.45	41.55	9,952.55	94,524.55

restaurant may have a deck where the clientele is served in suitable weather.

(3) Roof structural surface where a roof covering system is applied. See also *deck roof.*

decking:

(1) Wide boards, generally two inches thick, attached to flooring or roofing joists acting as the floor or roof of a structure.

(2) Light gauged ribbed metal sheets used for supporting a roof or floor.

deck roof: An open surface constructed on top of a flat roof. Normally, a railing is constructed on the sides of a deck roof. See also *deck.*

declaration: Legal record used to create a condominium. It encompasses the description of the property, common elements, ownership units, and acceptable uses of the residence.

declaration of homestead: Statement filed with a governmental authority declaring property a homestead for the purposes of securing a homestead exemption. The declaration of homestead has no effect on the property title and is not a conveyance. For example, Bill Jones makes a declaration of homestead to the municipality for his home in order to qualify for a homestead exemption of a 25% property tax deduction.

declaration of trust: Written acknowledgment by an individual holding title to property that it is being held in trust for another. For example, a trustee signs a declaration of trust that the property title is being held in trust for a minor child.

declaratory judgment: A binding judicial determination of the rights and standing of litigants. A declaratory judgment does not result in any relief for the action brought before the court. It merely determines whether there is a justiciable action between the litigants. A subsequent judicial action between the parties determines any relief on the declared justiciable action. For example, a landlord seeks a declaratory judgment against a tenant for behavior causing several complaints by tenants in an effort to determine grounds for eviction. In the declaratory judgment, the court rules the landlord has grounds for eviction under the terms of the rental lease agreement. The landlord subsequently sues the tenant for eviction in a separate court action.

declining market: Market condition in which sellers exceed buyers, thereby causing prices to fall. In real estate, declining markets may result from unfavorable business conditions and high interest rates.

decree: Decision rendered by a court of law. An example is requiring a tenant to pay the landlord for a breach of the rental agreement.

decrement: The act or process of decreasing in size. The total amount of decrease. For example, as the result of a storm there was a 50-foot decrement in the size of the beach.

dedication: Property given and accepted as a grant to the public. For example, a real estate developer may purchase land to build an office complex, but dedicates part of the land to the community as a park for public relations. In so doing, the real estate developer has given up its ownership to that portion of the land.

deed: A written, legally enforceable document used to transfer title to real estate. See also *quit claim deed; warranty deed.*

deed of confirmation: Used to rectify errors made in a previous deed. Such errors can include incorrect spelling of a name, inaccurate property description, or an improper execution. It is often referred to as a correction deed. For example, a deed of confirmation is issued to correct a previous bargain and sale deed which incorrectly spelled the owner's name, Adam, as Adaim.

deed covenant: Any of a number of types of covenants agreeing to do or not to do something that is attached to the title and is passed from one owner to the next. For example, a deed covenant may prohibit a type of architecture or building material in order to preserve the character of a particular community. See also *covenant running with the land.*

deed description: Property description contained in a title deed. A deed description is intended to inform a reasonable person where property is located. It can be described by metes and bounds, by reference to a lot on a filed map by monuments, or by a government survey. A street address may be used, but it is not the best method. The deed description should also include any street rights, or rights of neighbor's property. See also *legal description.*

deed in lieu of foreclosure: Legal document that conveys real estate to the lender after the borrower defaults on his or her mortgage payments. The borrower should demand cancellation of the unpaid balance and a confirmation letter from the lender. The lender is relieved of the inconvenience of foreclosure proceedings actions. It is a voluntary act by both borrower and lender.

deed of release: Upon satisfaction of a mortgage or other debt payments, the deed releases property, or a portion of it, from the incumbrance. Often it is used in circumstances where a deed of trust is held by a trustee until a debt payment, usually in the form of a mortgage, is made.

deed restrictions: Written statement in a deed limiting the number, type, size, and use of property. An example would be a deed restriction stating the described property can only be used for

educational purposes. It is illegal for deed restrictions to be imposed against individuals because of color, creed, nationality, race, or sex. See also *deed covenants.*

deed of trust: Also called trust deed. A document that conveys title to a neutral third party (trustee) during the period in which the mortgage loan is outstanding as collateral for a debt.

deed recording fee: The fee charged by a governmental jurisdiction to enter in the public record the deed and other documents affecting the title to property at the time of a transaction. For example, Smith buys a home from Abel. At the closing, Smith pays a $67 deed recording fee and a $65 recording fee for the mortgage.

de facto: Latin for in deed, in fact, in reality, actually. An act or fact that occurs as a matter of practice and reality as distinguished from de jure, meaning a lawfully and rightfully occurring act. A de facto action or occurrence is accepted as a matter of fact, but is illegal or illegitimate. For example, a homeowner has been notoriously using the premise as a de facto two family house, although the single family residence zoning makes this an illegal practice.

de facto contract: Contract that intends to convey property from one individual to another, but is defective in one respect. For example, a de facto property contract intends to convey the property to another owner, but there never was any consideration.

default: Failure of a debtor to pay principal and/or interest at the due date. If a default occurs, the creditor may make a claim against the debtor's property in order to recover the amount owed.

default charge: Penalty charged if an amount owed on the purchase of real estate is not paid on time. For example, if a monthly payment of $1,500 is not paid before the tenth of the month, a default charge of $25 may be assessed so that the late payment will total $1,525.

default judgment:

(1) Judgment against a defendant who does not respond to the plaintiff's lawsuit or fails to appear in court at the hearing or trial date. An example is a contractor who sues a homeowner for not paying for services rendered, and the homeowner fails to respond to the action. The judge may issue a default judgment for the fee.

(2) Judgment issued by the court against the defendant without the person responding in his own defense.

defeasance clause: Provision guaranteeing the return of title to a mortgagor upon satisfaction of a mortgage's conditions and terms. Causes the discharge of a mortgagee's estate interest in a property.

defeasible: Clause in a contract, title, or mortgage that is subject to being annulled, repealed, or revoked upon the satisfaction of a claim or completion of a future event. For example, a defeasance clause annuls all of a mortgagee's estate interest in a property upon the satisfaction of all terms and conditions of a mortgage.

defeasible title: Title that can be made null and void or defeated upon the satisfaction of a claim or the completion of some future contingency.

defective title: Flaw in an otherwise proper title. A title obtained through error or fraud without proper signature or consideration or other improper action. A defective title is null and void having no effect on the original title. For example, Smith bought a piece of property and obtained a bargain and sale deed, but it did not have a proper signature from a previous owner's wife, and it was therefore deemed to be a defective title.

defendant:

(1) *Civil:* Individual against whom a court action is brought by a Plaintiff for restitution of property or satisfaction of a complaint. An example is a tenant who is being sued for nonpayment of rent by the landlord.

(2) *Criminal:* Individual accused of a crime such as a real estate developer accused of fraud.

deferred interest mortgages: Financing technique aimed at those people who only plan to live in a house for a short time. Under this mortgage, a lower interest rate and, thus, a lower monthly mortgage payment is charged. Upon the selling of the house, the lender receives the deferred interest plus a fee for postponing the interest that would normally have been paid each month.

deferred maintenance: Factor in real estate appraisal. A type of physical depreciation owing to lack of normal upkeep, such as broken glass and doors and discolored paint that negatively impacts the value of property.

deferred payments: Money payments to be delayed for a future date or extended over a period of time.

deficiency: Additional tax liability that the IRS deems to be owed by a taxpayer. A taxpayer can argue the correctness of a deficiency with the IRS. There can be an appeal to the Tax Court without paying the tax.

deficiency judgment: Judicial finding that the debtor owes an amount exceeding the value of the collateral put up for the defaulted loan.

deflation: General decrease in prices. It is the opposite of inflation and different from disinflation, which is a decrease in the rate of price increases. Deflation results from a reduction in the money supply.

delinquency: Being behind in a payment on a tax or debt (e.g., mortgage) when due (on the due date of payment or before the grace period).

delivery: Transfer of property from a seller to a buyer.

delivery basis: Method of revenue recognition based on delivery instead of sale.

demand loan: Also called demand note. A loan with no established maturity period, callable on demand by the lender for repayment. The interest on this type of loan is calculated on a daily basis and billed at fixed intervals.

demise:

(1) Transfer of an estate by bequest, or contract for a stated time period or life.

(2) Making of a charter or lease for a specified time period.

demised premises: Leased or rented property. For example, a rented apartment in an apartment building is considered to be a demised premise.

demising clause: Provision in a lease whereby the landlord (lessor) leases and the tenant (lessee) takes the property.

demographics: Evaluation of housing requirements based on family size, ages, occupations, marital status, and other population characteristics.

demolition: The total destruction, razing, tearing down, breaking into pieces or pulverizing of a structure on a building site. Demolition usually occurs when clearing a building site either as preparation for building a new structure or eliminating a hazard.

demolition insurance: An insurance policy indemnifying a property owner up to the limits of the policy against fire or other hazard requiring the total destruction and removal of the structure.

demurrer: Defendant's legal objection to the prima facie sufficiency of a judicial pleading. It is a motion to dismiss an action on the ground there is no apparent equity violation, the court has no jurisdiction to rule, or that the pleading is insufficient to be considered by the court. For example, while a defendant admits to constructing a fence having an architectural design to which the complainant objects, the fence is legally erected within the property and zoning laws of the jurisdiction. Considering these factors, the defendant issues a demurrer stating there is not sufficient cause to have the matter considered before the court.

density: Distribution of population over a given area of land. For example, the population density per square mile for the United States is 69 inhabitants.

density zoning: Placing limitations on property development by controlling the number of structures in a given area in order to control population density. For example, a density zoning regulation of a community requires that a home cannot be built on fewer than two acres.

depletion: Physical exhaustion of a natural resource (e.g., oil, coal). It is a tax deductible expense.

deponent: One who acts as a witness and gives written testimony under oath.

deposit: Also called earnest money. Money deposited with an individual for security for the performance of some contract. This is intended to show his/her willingness to follow through with the purchase agreement. Deposit or earnest money can be forfeited if the depositor defaults on the terms of the contract. For example, if the property is not bought, the buyer typically loses the money put up unless there is some escape clause, such as the deposit being subject to the approval of a relative.

deposition: Discovery of information before trial in which a stenographer records the statements made by a witness under oath. The statements are made to answer questions posed by the attorneys to both parties. The witness may either be a party to the action, or an independent person (e.g., expert witness).

deposit receipt: Written acknowledgment that money has been paid by someone as a deposit into an account or for the purchase of property or services. Examples are a receipt given by the bank for a deposit made to a savings or checking account, a receipt given to a buyer of real estate who has made a down payment, and a receipt given to a homeowner by a contractor for an advance payment for future services to be rendered.

depreciable life: Economic or physical life of a fixed asset. The property is depreciated over the period benefitted.

depreciable real estate (tax): Under current tax law, real estate is depreciated under either the straight-line method or modified accelerated cost recovery system (MACRS) method. See also *MACRS*.

depreciated cost (taxation): New cost less accumulated depreciation to date.

depreciation:
(1) Decrease in the value of property because of use, obsolescence, deterioration, wear and tear, or the passing of time.
(2) Spreading out of the original cost over the estimated life of the fixed assets such as plant and equipment. Depreciation reduces taxable income. Among the most commonly used depreciation methods are the straight-line depreciation and accelerated depreciation, such as the sum-of-the-years'-digits and double-declining balance methods.
(3) Decline in economic potential of limited life assets originating from wear and tear, natural deterioration through interaction of the elements, and technical obsolescence. To some extent, maintenance (lubrication, adjustments,

parts replacement, and cleaning) may partially arrest or offset wear and deterioration.

depreciation (tax): Allocation of the cost of fixed assets, such as plant and building, over the life of the asset. Depreciation is due to physical use and/or obsolescence. Depreciation reduces taxable income, but does not reduce cash. The two depreciation methods allowable on the tax return are straight-line and modified accelerated cost recovery system (MACRS). Under the straight-line method, depreciation is the same amount each year. Under MACRS, each item of property is assigned to a property class. The property class establishes the depreciation time period. For example, residential rental property is depreciated over 27.5 years while nonresidential real property is depreciated over 31.5 years.

depreciation basis: Amount subject to depreciation which equals the initial cost less the estimated salvage value.

depreciation recapture: Part of a capital gain (the amount of a gain on depreciable assets) constituting tax benefits previously taken and taxed as ordinary income.

depressed market: Market condition in which the prices of real property are declining because of a lack of demand normally associated with a general economic slowdown.

depth tables: Table demonstrating the relationship between the depth of a building lot from the street frontage and its market value. Street frontage is the greatest asset of a land parcel. The property value decreases as the distance from the street increases. Many different tables have been developed to measure the relationship between property depth and property value as a percentage of the front foot value of a standard lot. Examples of depth table rules include the 4-3-2-1 Rule, Davies Rule, Hoffman Rule, Hoffman-Neil Rule, Jerrett Rule, Newark Rule, Milwaukee Rule, Cleveland Rule, and Somers Rule. Depth tables have the most applicability in high class retail areas with the least importance in industrial or urban areas.

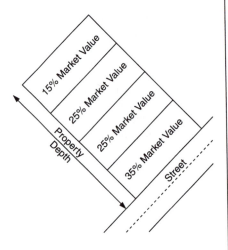

deraign: To acquit, exonerate, absolve, or discredit allegations. For example, the jury deraigned the accused of all fraud charges and returned a verdict of innocent.

dereliction:
(1) Intentional property abandonment or desertion with no hope of returning or recovery.
(2) Recovering land from the water as the sea withdraws below the usual water line. This is the opposite of alluvial.

derivative title: Transfer of title based on a preceding title transfer or conveyance. A derivative conveyance increases, ratifies, moderates, renews or transfers the stake created by the original conveyance. For example, an income property owner creates a derivative conveyance whereby all the lease income is assigned to his son.

derived demand: Secondary demand created from a primary agent or facility. For example, a large office complex creates a derived demand for a retail stationery outlet where tenants can purchase office supplies and newspapers.

description: Formal or legal description of property and its dimensions included in deeds, leases, listing agreements, rental agreements, and sales contracts. For example, a property deed gives a property description which includes the lot and block as well as the subdivisions.

descriptive memorandum: Method of describing a real estate property offering by a developer in lieu of a prospectus.

design: Architectural plan which may include blue prints of a property project. Designs must meet technological and zoning requirements.

desist and refrain order: Court or government regulatory order to stop doing something, such as not showing minorities certain neighborhoods.

detached housing: Free-standing residential housing constructed on its own building lot. Detached housing is the typical type of housing found in suburban developments.

deterioration: Value of property is reduced from usage over time. The problem is worsened when repairs and maintenance have not been made. An example is an apartment building that has been run down and vandalized.

developer: Individual who creates property improvements by making homes, shopping centers, and other commercial buildings for a profit on an area of land. The developer organizes and plans the development and supervises its construction as well as managing all the business elements of the project. For example, Smith purchases 40 acres of commercial property at a cost of $15,000 per acre. He then constructs a shopping center consisting of 30 store fronts with one main anchor tenant. He subsequently leases the stores to tenants and manages the property.

developer's equity: Financial interest a developer has in a development. The interest may be a direct investment or a percentage interest in the overall profit. For example, a developer contractually agrees to build a development with a guaranteed developer's equity of 15% of the project's net annual profit for a period of 15 years.

developer's profit: The sum of money a developer earns in a development project after all costs have been paid. This is the offset to the investment risk, as well as time and labor the developer has invested in the development's outcome.

development: Process of developing an area by planning and building homes, shopping centers, schools or churches. The development process includes the construction of streets, sewers, utilities, parks, and other resources. For example, Jones, a developer, buys a large building parcel and obtains a development loan for the purpose of building an entire community including installing streets, utilities, and parks as well as constructing 75 homes. He begins selling the homes as the project progresses to raise additional capital to pay for the development loan and finish the project.

development cost: All the costs involved in constructing a development project including the cost of acquiring a parcel of land, paying for contractors' labor, materials as well as taxes and development loan interest costs.

development loan: Loan used by a developer for the purposes of paying development costs. A development loan is paid by unit sale proceeds. See also *construction loan.*

development, neighborhood, stage: Point at which a housing development becomes a neighborhood. After an initial housing development is sold and the new owners become established, the neighborhood stage begins. The construction of a housing development assures similar age and architectural design structures. In an economic sense, a neighborhood is distinguished by similar property values typifying a normal housing development. Neighborhoods usually have place names often identified with the original subdivision and have boundaries associated with streets.

devise: Gift of real property as stipulated in a will.

devisee: One who receives real property under a will.

devisor: A testator/testatrix who donates real property.

dictum:
(1) Judge's remark in a court ruling not in and of itself embodying the law. A dictum merely illustrates or amplifies the ruling.
(2) Arbitrator's ruling. For example, in a rent dispute between a landlord and a tenant, an arbitrator's dictum reduced the renter's payment by $35.

dimensional shingles: Shingles that are manufactured in uniform, rather than varied, sizes.

dimension lumber: Standard precut lumber sizes for lumber industry needs. The typical sizes are 2 to 5 inches thick by 5 to 12 inches wide.

direct capitalization: A capitalization method which divides a property's first year net operating income by an estimated general capitalization rate to develop a total property estimate. For example, an income property produces a first year net operating income (NOI) of $30,000, and the market indicates a general capitalization rate of 10% for comparable properties. The direct capitalization estimate of the value of the total property would be ($30,000/.10) or $300,000.

direct costs:
(1) Costs in erecting a new building involved with either site preparation or building construction, including fixtures, in contrast to indirect costs which include building permits, land survey, and overhead costs such as insurance and payroll taxes.
(2) Costs that can be directly identified with the costing object such as a piece of property and department. Examples are direct payroll and advertising outlays made directly to a particular property.

directional growth: The direction in which a community is growing. Directional growth is measured over time, and its path strongly influences current and future market values of those properties clearly in its path.

direction of least resistance: Tendency to go to the party or situation of the lowest level of opposition. For example, if a real estate development is having financial difficulties, the contractor or bank least likely to complain should be asked first to extend the payment due date.

direct reduction mortgage (DRM): A fully amortized mortgage necessitating periodic payments of both interest and principal. In the early years of the loan, the share of principal is smaller and the interest larger, a condition that gradually reverses as the end of the period approaches. The periodic payment may also consist of taxes and insurance.

direct sales comparison approach to value: Appraisal approach where property values are estimated by comparing current comparable sales. For example, a home owner wishes to sell his home, and wants to know its market value. The real

estate agent uses the direct sales comparison approach to value and shows the homeowner that current neighborhood comparable sales indicate the market value of the home is $175,000. See also *market approach.*

direct steam system: Heating system dependent upon radiators in each room of the structure. The steam goes from the boiler through pipes to the radiators. A two-pipe system should be employed for larger structures.

discharge: Removing a debt by making full payment. A mortgage discharge is a document formally specifying that a mortgage debt has been paid. It is typically recorded in a local property deeds office.

discharge of bankruptcy: Court order whereby the bankrupt debtor is forgiven of his or her debts. Even though the debtor is no longer obligated for discharged debts, the bankruptcy remains in his credit report for 10 years.

discharge of lien: An order withdrawing a property lien after a claim is paid by other means.

disclaimer:
(1) Giving up an ownership claim to property.
(2) Renunciation of a claim to real property. For example, land becomes dilapidated and the absentee owner disclaims any ownership to it.

disclosed principal: In a principal-agent transaction or contract where a third party knows the name of the principal the agent represents. This is a typical setting in real estate situations. In this arrangement, the agent is not legally bound under the written or oral agreement.

disclosure: See *full disclosure.*

disclosure statement: A written statement of a borrower's rights under the Truth-in-Lending Law or a statement of all financing charges, which must be disclosed by a lender. See also *full disclosure; regulation z.*

discount:

(1) The difference between future (or face) value and present value of a payment.

(2) A reduction in the amount due for early payment.

(3) Discount loan.

(4) Taking into account all available good or bad news about a real estate property in evaluating its current price. It is called discounting the news.

discounted cash flow: A method to estimate the value of a real estate investment, which emphasizes after-tax cash flows and the return on the invested dollars discounted over time to reflect a discounted yield. The value of the real estate investment is the present worth of the future after-tax cash flows from the investment, discounted at the investor's desired rate of return.

EXAMPLE: Carol wants a rate of return of 10% on property offered for sale at $150,000. She anticipates that rents can be increased each year for five years. He/she expects that after all expenses she would have an after-tax cash flow of $6,000, $6,200, $6,400, $6,600, and $6,800 for each year. It is expected that this property can sell for $180,000 at the end of the fifth year. Carol would be willing to pay how much for this property?

We can set up the present value table as follows:

Using this technique the investor would be willing to pay $135,892 for this property. See also *discounted cash flow (DCF) techniques.*

discounted cash flow (DCF) techniques:

(1) Methods that involve discounting the future cash flows generated by an income property. These techniques are used primarily for valuation.

(2) Methods of selecting and ranking investment proposals such as the net present value (NPV) and internal rate of return (IRR) methods where time value of money is taken into account.

discount loan: A loan in which the entire charge is subtracted up front from the face value of a loan. The proceeds received is the face value of the loan less this deduction, which increases the effective interest rate. Assume Bill borrows $50,000 from the bank at a 12% interest on a discount basis. The effective interest rate is:

$$\frac{\$6,000}{(\$50,000 - \$6,000)} = \frac{\$6,000}{\$44,000} = 13.6\%$$

See also *annual percentage rate.*

discount points: An additional fee imposed by lenders on home mortgages payable in cash at the time of the closing. For example, if 3 points are charged on a $200,000 mortgage, the charge would be $6,000 ($200,000 × 3%). In selecting a mortgage, interest rates and points (if any) should be taken into account.

Years	Present Value After-Tax Cash Flow		Total of $1 at 10%	Present Value
1	$ 6,000		.909	$ 5,454
2	6,200		.826	5,121
3	6,400		.751	4,806
4	6,600		.683	4,508
5	6,800		.621	4,223
Sell property		$180,000	.621	$111,780
Present value of property				$135,892

discount rate:
(1) The interest rate used to convert future receipts or payments in connection with real estate property to their present value. The cost of capital (cut-off, hurdle, or minimum required rate) is used as the discount rate under the net present value (NPV) method.
(2) Also called the rediscount rate. The interest rate charged by the Federal Reserve Bank to its member banks for loans. A change in the discount rate will have a significant impact on the real estate market. For example, a change in rates on mortgages will soon follow.
See also *capitalization rate.*

discrimination: Unequal treatment and denial of opportunity to individuals based on race, color, creed, nationality, age, or sex. The Civil Rights Acts passed by the U.S. Congress included those of 1866, 1870, 1871, 1875, 1964, and 1968. The first two acts gave blacks the rights to be treated as citizens in legal actions, particularly to sue and be sued and to own property. The Civil Rights Act of 1964 prohibited discrimination in employment and established the Equal Employment Opportunity Commission. This landmark legislation also banned discrimination in public accommodations connected with interstate commerce, including restaurants, hotels, and theaters. The Federal Fair Housing Act of 1968, included as Title VII of the Civil Rights Act of 1968, prohibited discrimination in the sale or rental of residential housing. For example, a real estate agent may not engage in the practice of steering an individual into certain neighborhoods based on racial discrimination.
Housing equality for racial minorities has not been achieved. Housing abandonment continues in sections of many central cities, while the return of high-income households to other central city neighborhoods has displaced lower-income residents. See also *affirmative action; civil rights laws.*

discriminatory inducement: Real estate property incentive offered for reasons other than individual merit. A discriminatory inducement is an effort to get an individual to buy or sell, rent, or lease real estate through the unfair use of bias. For example, a property manager offers an individual a significantly lower rental rate in an apartment because of racial preference.

disinflation: A lessening in the inflation rate. This may occur during a recession when insufficient demand prevents sellers from passing on higher prices to prospective buyers of houses. See also *deflation.*

disintegration:
(1) The transformation of a racially integrated neighborhood housing pattern into segregated housing.
(2) Deterioration, destruction, or decay.

dispersing force: Those factors causing the movement of people, industry, and business from the central city to the outside central city areas, suburbs, and/or small cities. Elements of the dispersing force are need for increased space, high rentals, commutation times, crime, pollution, and the need for natural ambiance.

disposable income: Personal income minus personal income tax payments and other government deductions. It is the personal income available for people to spend or save; also called take-home pay. It may be a critical factor to consider by prospective home buyers.

dispossess proceedings: Legal action by an owner of property to oust or exclude an individual or business from using the property. An example is a landlord that seeks a court order to eject a tenant for the nonpayment of rent. The landlord wants to regain possession of the property.

distraint: Landlord's act of seizing a tenant's property to satisfy defaulted rent payments. To distrain a tenant's property the landlord must give proper legal notice and is often accompanied by changing the locks. The landlord may place a lien on the tenant's property. Distraint is limited by local law.

distressed property:

(1) Foreclosed real estate or subject property in a bankrupt estate.

(2) Income property which is making an inadequate return and has a negative capitalization rate.

distributee: An heir to an individual who died intestate and is entitled, under the distribution statute, to a portion of its proceeds. After all claims against the estate are satisfied, the distributee will receive his or her share of the estate.

distribution approach: The apportioning, disbursing, dividing, offering, or parceling out of property among individuals.

(1) *Probate:* Court order to divide up and distribute the contents of an estate after the satisfaction of all claims against it. The estate is divided between all distributees.

(2) *Securities Offering:* A public securities offering by an issuer or underwriter.

(3) *Statutes of Distribution:* State laws controlling the distribution of individuals' intestate estates to all distributees.

distribution title: Probate court approved title issued to the distributee of an individual's intestate estate.

divestiture:

(1) Surrendering voluntarily or involuntarily ownership of property or an interest therein. Examples are the loss of property from fire, the sale of the property, or government seizing of property for nonpayment of taxes.

(2) Court order to give up possession or the right to property such as in the case of an antitrust action to eliminate a monopolistic advantage of a real estate company in a particular area.

division fence: Fence constructed at a property line or other division point separating a subdivision or a homesite. It marks the point of separation between two separate properties.

doc: Abbreviation for the word document.

dock: Structure built into the water from the land providing a facility for boats to tie up. A dock will often provide utility access.

doctrine: Legal rule, principle, or tenet.

document: Any recorded materials including letters, photographs, inscriptions, text, reproducible computer file, official or legal forms. A document is any tangible information including letters, contracts, photographs, electronic or paper files, x-rays, receipts, or other material evidence.

documentary evidence: Any written evidence or tangible material which can be reproduced as written material which is coherent and related to the subject at hand. This includes documents, contracts, inscriptions and written instruments of all types and related evidence including electronic and paper files, photographs or other admissible non oral evidence. For example, as documentary evidence of the commission owed to a real estate broker, a signed listing agreement was entered into evidence.

document stamp: Tax imposed by some state and local governments to record into the public record property deeds and mortgages. For example, at the time of the closing of the sale of a house, the buyer had to pay $350 for a state document stamp to record the mortgage.

dollar and percentage adjustments: Modification in the amount of money involved for some justifiable reason.

An example is when a contractor agrees to take a lower rate because the homeowner is not pleased with the quality of the work performed. Another example is when the seller of a house downwardly adjusts the selling price because the buyer notices on the closing date that water is leaking from the ceiling that will require the replacement of the roof.

dome: A convex vaulted curvature often spherical in shape usually built atop of a building. Domes can be constructed of any material including masonry, wood, glass or steel. They can be decorative or functional in nature.

Dome

domicile:
(1) A person's permanent and legal place of residence. While an individual may have one or more residences, it is only possible to have one permanent address.
(2) The state where one has a permanent legal address. The individual is therefore subject to paying California taxes and votes using the California residence. For example, Smith's domicile is in California.

domiciliary administrator: Being an administrator in the state where an individual was domiciled at the time of death. The domiciliary administrator is considered the primary and principal estate administrator.

dominant tenement: Property having an easement right through another adjoining property. The property through which the easement passes is considered to have the servient tenement.

Roadway	Servient Tenement	Dominant Tenement
	Parcel A	Parcel B
	Easement	

donee: One to whom a gift or bequest is made. For example, as the donee, the library received a large cash contribution it used for making a new wing on the building.

donor: One who donates or gives a gift or bequest. For example, Smith made a cash bequest in his will to his long time friend and companion, John, who was the donee.

dormer: Vertical window built through a sloping roof having its own gable and forming its own roof line.

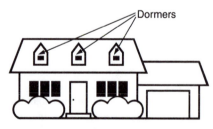
Dormers

double declining balance depreciation method: Accelerated method in which a fixed percentage factor of two times the straight-line rate is multiplied each year by the declining balance of the fixed asset's book value. For example, if property has a 20-year life, the straight-line rate is 5% (1/20). Therefore, the double declining rate is 10%.

To compute the annual depreciation expense, the asset's book value at the beginning of the period is multiplied by the double declining rate. Although salvage value is not included in the initial calculation for depreciation, a fixed asset cannot be depreciated in the last year below its salvage value.

EXAMPLE: A building costs $500,000 and has an estimated life of 10 years. The estimated salvage value is $50,000. The depreciation on the building for the first three years follows:

Year	Computation	Depreciation	Book Value
0		$500,000	
1	20%* × $500,000	$100,000	400,000
2	20% × 400,000	80,000	320,000
3	20% × 320,000	64,000	256,000

*|1/10| = 10%, 10% × 2 = 20%.

double-digit inflation: Annual rate of inflation of 10% or higher.

double floor: A floor where the binding joists support the common joists above and the ceiling below.

double framing: A construction method of using twice the number of framing members to provide additional structural strength.

double hung window: A sash window having two vertically moving sashes respectively offset by sash weights. Each sash closes a different part of the window.

double pitch: Roof design having two different pitches. See also *gambrel roof.*

doubling up: Having two families live in a residence designed for only one family. This violates single-family residence zoning.

dower: The legal right of a widow to a portion of her deceased husband's real property.

down payment: Partial payment needed of the purchase price when a house is purchased. The down payment represents an element of the total cost. See also *earnest money.*

downspout: Rainwater pipe attached to a roof gutter channeling the run off down and away from the building.

downzoning: Rezoning of land from a higher density use to a lower density use.

dragnet clause: Mortgage clause causing the mortgagor to pledge additional properties, mortgaged or not, as collateral to the present mortgage. Failure to pay any of the other mortgages causes a foreclosure on the dragnetted property even if its payments are current.

drainage easement: The right to drain water through another's property through a ditch, pipe, or trench. See also *drainage right of way.*

drainage right of way: A land owner may not divert or redirect a natural occurring waterway from his or her property causing damages to another property. Waterway is normally construed to mean streams and rivers having well-defined channels and borders.

draw:

(1) To periodically withdraw money during construction stages as defined in a construction loan. For example, after the building contractor completed the first stage of construction including construction of the foundation and installation of the rough plumbing, he was able to withdraw a 15% payment from the construction loan.

(2) To write out a check or money payment or draft.

(3) To compose and write a document such as a contract, deed, petition, or will.

(4) To constitute a jury to hear a court action through a name selection process. For example, in order to hear the fraud case brought before the court, the

attorney for the prosecution and defense drew a jury from 40 people who were subpoenaed to appear before the court to be considered as jurors.

driving time radius: Time it takes to drive to an outlying area from a major urban area. The driving time radius can radically affect real estate values in outlying areas of major metropolitan regions. Unless there is a unique attraction, the greater the driving time radius, the less value outlying property will have in relation to urban property values.

droitural action: One based on the whole body of the law. A lawful right is being exercised.

dry mortgage: Creates a lien against the mortgagor's property, but does not permit a lien against his or her personal assets. See also *nonrecourse.*

drywall: Any walls constructed without using concrete or mortar. Drywall materials include sheetrock, gypsum, plywood, styrofoam, and pressed fiber. See also *drywall construction.*

drywall construction: The construction of stone or block walls without using concrete or mortar. Drywall construction is a traditional building technique used for stone field wall construction. Newer building blocks have been designed using precise fitting joints eliminating the need for concrete and mortar. See also *drywall.*

dual contract: Illegal practice of having two contracts for the same transaction. One contract may be used as a subterfuge to achieve the second contract. For example, an unethical real estate broker suggests developing two sales contracts for a parcel of property. For the purpose of getting a higher bank appraisal, the second contract has a considerably higher price than the first real sales contract. This is a form of fraud.

dual divided agency: Representation of two or more parties in a transaction by the same real estate agent.

dual listing: Listing where a real estate broker represents both the buyer and seller creating two principals. A real estate broker has a fiduciary relationship to represent a principal's interests exclusively. A dual listing occurring without the knowledge of both parties causes the real estate broker to violate the principal's fiduciary relationship, and therefore is illegal. However, if both the buyer and the seller are aware of and agree to the dual listing, then it is not illegal.

duct:

(1) Pipe or conduit for electrical wiring.

(2) Enclosed conduit made of metal or other appropriate materials for transferring low pressure hot or cold air throughout a structure.

due-on-sale clause: Provision allowing the lender to require full payment of the mortgage when the initial buyer resells the property or effectively prevents a new buyer from assuming the loan.

dummy: Individual acting in the place of someone else in order to conceal their identity. In a real estate transaction, a dummy buys a parcel of real estate in his or her name and then re-sells the property to a third party in order to prevent undue publicity or the loss of leverage when negotiating the original selling price. This is also called acting as a strawman or one standing in for another.

duplex:

(1) Structure have two dwelling units under the same roof.

(2) Two-story apartment unit.

durable power of attorney: Legal instrument permitting one to grant others general or specific powers for administering their finances.

duress: Act of forcing an individual or business to do something against their will. It is a legitimate defense in court to reverse the effect of the compelled act. An example is threatening the life of a family member so that a person signs a contract to buy expensive vacant land.

Dutch colonial: Early American architectural housing style stressing a gambrel roof and overhanging eaves.

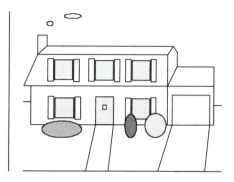

early Georgian: Home prominent in Williamsburg and typical of those in Georgia in the 1700s. The homes usually were 2 to 3 stories, in rectangular form, with double hung windows, two high chimneys, and simple exterior.

earnest money: A deposit in advance of the down payment on a real estate purchase as an indication of good faith. See also *escrow.*

earthquake insurance: Comprehensive insurance policy rider or available as a separate policy indemnifying property against damages caused by an earthquake or volcanic eruption. Damage claims can be filed for each earthquake and related shocks occurring more than 72 hours after the initial shock. Earthquake insurance does not cover losses from fires, floods, explosions, or tidal waves.

easement: Legal right or privilege, such as that arising from a contract, to use land owned by another person or business for a specific purpose. The use should be reasonable for the circumstances.

easement appurtenant: Burdens one parcel of land (the servient estate) for the benefit of another parcel (the dominant estate).

easement in gross: Not attached to any parcel of land but merely a personal right to use the land of another.

easement by necessity: Created by law usually for the right to travel to a landlocked parcel of land.

easement by prescription: Acquired by adverse land use for a statutory period of time.

eastlake house: Nineteenth-century style home architecture featuring three dimensional ornamentation, made by hand using a chisel and gouge.

easy credit: Situation in which very few prospective buyers of real estate are rejected by lenders. This may be due to ample money supply, lower interest rates, and/or relaxed credit standards. See also *easy money; tight credit.*

easy money: Increase in the amount of money available for businesses and people to buy real estate because of lower interest rates. Easy money stimulates spending on investment such as houses. See also *easy credit; tight money.*

eaves: That part of a roof which projects beyond the sides of the building. The eaves keep rain overflow off the sides of a building structure and seal the roof rafters. (See figure at top of page 98.)

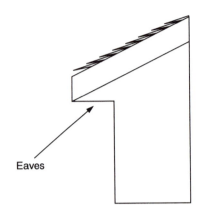

Eaves

economic base analysis: Appraisal method that examines current and future economic conditions in a particular location to help in deriving property values.

economic capacity of land: Ability of the size of the land to accommodate the desired economic purpose. An example is having enough space to build a supermarket to meet the needs of the community.

economic force: Power or strength of economic factors and variables influencing the real estate market. For example, real estate values may decline in times of recession because people cannot afford to buy homes. In economically depressed neighborhoods, property values decline.

economic indicators: Measures looking at the past, current, and future direction of the economy. They may have an impact on the real estate market. Each month government bodies, including the Federal Reserve System, and several economic institutions publish economic indicators. These consist of the following general categories:

(1) Measures of general economic performance, including gross domestic product (GDP), personal income, capital expenditures, corporate earnings, and inventories.

(2) Price indices measure the inflation rate. The Consumer Price Index (CPI),

a well-known inflation measure, is used as the cost-of-living index, which is related to employment contracts and social security. The Producer Price Index (PPI) monitors raw materials and semi-finished goods and measures prices at the early stage of the distribution cycle. It reflects changes in the general price level, or the CPI, before they actually occur. The GDP Implicit Deflator is another index of inflation that is used to isolate price changes in GNP calculations from real changes in economic activity.

(3) Measures labor market conditions and signals conditions in employment such as the unemployment rate, average workweek in manufacturing, applications for initial jobless claims, and hourly salary rates.

(4) Money and credit market indicators include the money supply, consumer credit, the Dow Jones Industrial Average (DJIA), and the Treasury bill rate.

(5) Index of leading indicators consists of 11 data series comprising the money supply, business formation, stock prices, vendor performance, average work week, new orders, contracts, building permits, inventory change, layoff rate, and change in prices. Business activities are examined as an indication of a change in the economy.

(6) Measures for major product markets that apply to segments of the economy such as housing, retail sales, steel, and automobile. Examples include housing starts, construction permits, auto sales, and retail sales.

Economic indicators show a home buyer or a real estate investor something about national and local economic conditions. Industry trends are also revealed. See also *index of leading economic indicators; lagging indicators.*

economic life: Expected period that property will provide benefits. It is typically less than the physical life of the property because the property continues to have physical life regardless of inefficiency and obsolescence. Depreciation is usually based on the economic life.

economic obsolescence: Loss of property value due to external forces or events.

economic rent: The amount of rent a property could command in the open market. See also *market rent.*

economic value: Worth of property based on the relevant economic factors (e.g., state of the economy, unemployment rate).

economies of scale: Situation in which the average cost of construction declines as building size and volume is expanded. Some of the reasons are: (1) increased specialization and division of labor, (2) better use and specialization of labor, and (3) use of more efficient or high-tech building equipment.

effective age: How old an item is, such as a home, based on its condition. This differs from chronological age which is the age of the item from its acquisition date. The effective age will be older if the home has not been properly maintained. For example, an office building might be 10 years old, buy effectively it is 15 years old because upkeep and repairs have not been made.

effective annual yield: See *effective interest rate.*

effective interest rate:
(1) Real rate of interest on a loan. It is the coupon rate divided by the net proceeds of the loan. Assume Sharon took out a $1,000,000, one year, 10% discounted loan to buy real estate. The effective interest rate equals:

$$\frac{\$100,000}{(\$1,000,000 - \$100,000)} = \frac{\$100,000}{\$900,000}$$

$$= 11\%$$

In this discount loan, the proceeds received is only $900,000, which effectively increases the cost of the loan.

(2) The effective annual yield, also called the annual percentage yield (APY). Different kinds of investments have different compounding periods. For example, some banks pay interest quarterly. If an investor wants to compare investments with different compounding periods, she must place them on a common basis. It is used for this purpose and is computed as follows:

$$APR = (1 + r/m)^m - 1.0$$

where r = the coupon stated rate and m = the number of compounding periods per year. Assume that a bank offers 6% interest, compounded quarterly, then the APR is:

$$APR = (1 + .06/4)^4 - 1.0$$

$$= (1.015)^4 - 1.0$$

$$= 1.0614 - 1.0$$

$$= .0614$$

$$= 6.14\%$$

This means that one bank giving 6% with quarterly compounding, while another bank offering 6.14% with annual compounding, would both be paying the same effective interest rate.

effective rate of return: See *effective interest rate.*

effective tax rate: Equals the tax divided by taxable income. For example, if the tax is $30,000 on taxable income of $120,000, the effective tax rate of the business is 25% ($30,000/$120,000).

egress: Passageway exiting from property. An egress may lead to a roadway or some other form of exit.

ejectment: Steps taken to remove someone from the real property who does not have a contractual basis to be there.

An example is the landlord removing homeless people who have moved into a vacant building. Another example is the landlord seeking to remove a holdover tenant beyond the lease term.

eleemosynary: Charitable gesture, such as when real estate is donated to a charity. The fair market value of the donated property may be tax deductible as a charitable contribution.

elevation: How tall a structure is from some point (e.g., ground level).

elevation map: Representation on a flat surface of any region that depicts the elevation of that region.

11TH District Index: A cost of funds index that most adjustable rate mortgages (ARMs) written in California in recent years are tied to. Computed by the Federal Home Loan Bank of San Francisco, it reflects the cost of deposits at savings and loans in California, Arizona, and Nevada.

Elizabethan style: English architecture. Generally has two levels with the second level typically overlaying the first story. It usually has half timber stucco walls. The roof is high and the chimney is sculptured.

Ellwood, L. W.: Name of an appraiser of real estate who initiated the Ellwood method based on a multiplier of mortgage-equity to determine the value of income-producing property.

emblements: Annual crops raised by a land tenant. The tenant has the right to the emblements, or crops, even after the lease has expired. For example, a tenant's lease expires the first week of August, but the crops do not mature until the third week of August. The tenant has the right to harvest the emblements he or she has cultivated.

eminent domain: Governmental right to take private property for public use as long as fair compensation is paid to the owner. Land for schools, parks, roads, public parking, highways, and other social and public purposes is obtained in this manner. A condemnation proceeding is required when the government exercises this right.

employing broker: Licensed real estate broker who employs a licensed real estate salesperson for the purpose of selling or renting real estate. The employing broker must pay commissions to the real estate salesperson for successful real estate transactions.

empty nesters: Describes a husband and wife or widow(er) whose children have been raised and moved out of the home. This creates a situation where the home becomes too large for their needs and creates a burden. Under these circumstances, the empty nesters often choose to sell the home and move into a condominium, cooperative, or apartment.

encroachment:
(1) Infringement on the property or rights of another individual or business.
(2) Structure or part thereof, such as a building, that obstructs or overlaps another property.

encumber: To create an encumbrance.

encumbrance:
(1) Debt secured by a lien on property.
(2) Commitments related to unfilled contracts for real estate. The purpose of encumbrances are to prevent further expenditure of funds considering the commitments already made.

end loan: See *permanent mortgage*.

endorsement:
(1) A signature on a draft or check by a payee prior to the transfer to a third party. A payee provides such an endorsement when transferring this draft to the payee's bank. Checks can be endorsed in three different ways. In a blank endorsement, once this instrument is signed, it becomes negotiable and can be used by anyone. A restrictive endorsement limits the use of the check to a single purpose. "For deposit only" is written on a check

when it is deposited by mail. If the check is lost in the mail and subsequently found, it cannot be cashed. A special endorsement is used when the check is used to pay someone else. All that is required is to indicate the payee and sign. (2) A statement attached to an insurance policy (such as property and casualty insurance) changing the terms of the policy.

endowment: Funds or property bestowed upon a person or an institution. The income is used to serve a specific purpose for which the endowment was intended. An example is an endowment fund set up to provide supplemental income to a distinguished researcher at the university.

energy tax credit: Tax credit aimed at encouraging the conservation of natural resources, as well as the development of alternative resources.

enforceable: An agreement, debt, judgment, or law which can be operationalized, put into effect, fulfilled, completed, executed, or performed. For example, a financial agreement has an enforceable clause permitting a lien to be placed on a subject property in the event of default.

English half-timber architecture: Originally describing buildings of the 16th and 17th century built in England with strong timber foundations, supports, knees, and studs. The walls were filled with plaster or brick. In American architecture, the English half-timber architecture has been combined with the English Tudor design using a wood beam over stucco exterior design.

English Tudor: A house having brick or stucco siding mixed with some wood. The house usually is two or more stories.

entity:
(1) Separate economic unit subject to financial measurement for accounting purposes. Examples are a real estate corporation, real estate partnership, and trust.
(2) Individual, partnership, corporation, and so on permitted by law to own property and engage in business. Affiliated legal real estate entities may exist such as those consolidated for financial reporting. Here, two or more companies operate under common control.

entrepreneur: Individual who has the initiative to start an enterprise with its associated responsibilities, obligations, and risks. The entrepreneur usually hires people to work for him. An example is a real estate brokerage or property management firm.

environmental impact statement: Report that contains information regarding the effect of a proposed project on the environment.

Environmental Protection Agency (EPA): Independent agency, established in 1970, in the executive branch of the U.S. government "to permit coordinated and effective government action on behalf of the environment." The EPA consolidates in a single body the administration of all federal environmental legislation, ranging from the Refuse Control Act of 1899 to the most recent statutes concerning environmental pollution including the Clean Air Act of 1963, the Water Quality Act of 1965, and the Solid Waste Disposal Act of 1965. The agency supervises environmental quality and seeks to control the pollution caused by solid wastes, pesticides, toxic substances, noise, and radiation. It has established special programs in air and water pollution, hazardous wastes, and toxic chemicals, and sponsors research in the technologies of pollution control. Ten regional offices facilitate coordination of pollution control efforts with state and local governments.

environmental regulations and controls: Federal, state, and local pollution control laws, codes, and regulations. Federal regulations include the Refuse Control Act of 1899, the Clean Air Act of 1963, the Water Quality Act of 1965, and the Solid Waste Disposal Act of 1965 as well as the Super Fund Act of 1980 that reserves funds for cleaning up toxic waste sites. See also *Environmental Protection Agency (EPA).*

Equal Credit Opportunity Act (ECOA): U.S. law making it illegal to discriminate when giving credit based on factors such as race, color, religion, marital status, national origin, and age. A lender must respond to credit applications within 30 days. If the application is denied, reasons must be given. The Federal Trade Commission enforces the provisions of the act. Exceptions to the protection of the law are individuals who do not have contractual capacity (minors) and individuals who are noncitizens and whose status might affect a creditor's rights and remedies in the case of a default. The purpose of this law and Regulation B, which was issued by the Board of Governors of the Federal Reserve System, was to assure that lenders would not treat one group of applicants more favorably than other groups except for reasonable and justifiable business reasons. Strict rules have been established to require fair dealing in all aspects of a credit transaction including that dealing with the purchase of real estate.

equitable conversion: Legal doctrine applied in some states when death prevents the seller of property, who has signed a real estate sale agreement, from completing the sale. Under these circumstances, equitable conversion mandates the contract is still binding on both the buyer, having signed the sale agreement, as well as the seller's representative. Despite the fact the title has not been conveyed, equitable conversion vests property rights with the buyer. See also *equitable title.*

equitable lien:
(1) Written contract or court judgment placing a lien on a parcel of property as collateral for a loan. An equitable lien may be applied as a matter of fairness and equity.
(2) Right of a property owner to have his or her property used in satisfying a loan.

equitable owner: The person identified to receive the benefit of property held in trust.

equitable title: The right to demand that title be conveyed upon payment of the purchase price.

equity buildup: The increase in a person's equity in real estate due to the reduction in the mortgage loan balance and price appreciation.

equity cushion: Ownership interest in property that is above the minimum needed to meet uncertainties or a downward trend in real estate market.

equity kicker: Privilege of a real estate investor or lender to participate in the profitability generated from property. This is in addition to any principal, interest, or dividends.

equity lending: Bank financing to a homeowner based on his dollar equity in the home. For example, if a house is appraised at $300,000 but the owner owes $100,000, his equity is $200,000. If the bank lends him 75% of the appraised value as a safety measure, the amount of the loan will be $150,000. The interest rate typically fluctuates such as being based on the change in the prime interest rate. Interest expense is tax deductible to the homeowner.

equity mortgage: Financing of a home based on how much equity the homeowner has in it. For example, a homeowner receives a loan of 85% of the property's appraised value less any outstanding obligations on the property. The interest rate is typically a variable one.

equity participation: Lender has an equity interest in the property that is the subject of the loan. This is in addition to principal and interest payments on the mortgage. The lender shares in the increase in market price of the property as well as any net income generated (e.g., rental revenue less rental expenses).

equity in property: Amount by which the appraised value of property exceeds the debt balance. If property has a fair market value of $300,000 while the mortgage balance is $120,000, the owner's equity in the property is $180,000.

equity purchaser: An individual or business that buys someone else's equity in property but may not assume any responsibility for a loan balance.

equity rate of return: Return before taxes on the capital invested in real estate property.

equity of redemption: Borrower's right to redeem his property by immediately paying off the loan balance and any related costs (e.g., interest, penalty fees). An example is a homeowner who makes full payment on his mortgage to prevent an imminent foreclosure.

equity reit: Type of real estate investment trust (REIT) whose investment money is used for the purchase of a portfolio of specific properties to be managed in order to generate investment return through current income and capital gain.

equity sharing: Arrangement whereby a party providing financing gets a portion of the ownership.

equity-to-value ratio: Percent of the purchase price of property to its total appraised value. If a property is appraised at $500,000 and the price paid is $400,000, the ratio is 80%.

equity trusts: See *equity REIT.*

equity yield: Internal rate of return (IRR) ignoring taxes associated with the capital invested in property. It shows the impact of leverage on the owner's return rate. Internal rate of return considers the amount and timing of the annual cash flow from the property and the expected selling price.

erosion:
(1) Gradual decline in the value of real estate because of poor market and economic conditions.
(2) Gradual deterioration of land due to nature such as because of floods, storms, and hurricanes.

escalation clause:
(1) Provision in a rental agreement or other contract that stipulates for an increase in lease payments or in a contract price if a specified uncontrollable event occurs. Examples are escalation clauses due to higher property taxes, interest rates, fuel prices, or inflation (as measured by the consumer price index).
(2) Provision in a loan agreement or mortgage in which the entire debt becomes immediately due upon the occurrence of an item such as missing three consecutive monthly payments or when the current ratio falls below 1.0.

escape clause: Contractual provision allowing an individual or business to renege on a commitment in certain cases without being penalized. An example is a clause in a contract to buy a home contingent on obtaining a mortgage at no more than an 8% interest rate. If such mortgage is unattainable, the prospective buyer is relieved of his obligation.

escheat: The right of local government to take property when no persons are legally entitled to inherit or make claim to a deceased's property.

escrow: Arrangement in which a buyer gives a deed and/or money to an independent third party (an escrow agent) to retain until specified conditions have been met. Once met, the escrow agent releases the holdings to the seller. The escrow benefits both parties. The escrow time period is negotiated between the buyer and seller of the property. For example, a buyer of a home may demand that the seller put money into an escrow account for unanticipated repairs when the buyer moves.

escrow account: Also called reserve account or impound account. An account into which payment is made for particular expenses to assure that money will be available. An example is an account used in which the lender deposits the borrower's monthly tax and insurance payments. Another example is a special account the homeowner's attorney establishes for advance funds he receives in connection with the sale of the property. A final example is an account the seller of a home deposits funds into to pay for any unexpected repairs in the first month the buyer of the home moves in.

escrow agent: The individual responsible for an escrow account. She is the agent of both parties until the conditions of the escrow are satisfied. Once the terms have been complied with, the escrow account is closed.

escrow fees: Amount earned by the escrow agent for accumulation and monitoring the data from the various sources and for distributing same to the parties.

escrow instructions: Written proposals and acceptances applicable to the aspects of the transaction. The escrow agent must strictly follow the purchase and sale agreement.

escrow statement: Declaration by an escrow agent (independent third party) that instruments or property are being held by him in accordance with the agreement to the parties in a real estate deal. For example, a property deed and money may be held in escrow for safekeeping until some condition has been satisfied.

estate: The real and personal assets of a person at the date of death. The distribution of the assets to the heirs depends on the provision of the will. If no will exists, the distribution is based on a court order for liquidation. Court-monitored probate achieves the following purposes: determines ownership of property; establishes who is to receive the benefits; assures the correct transfer of property and the payment of debts and taxes. The executor of a will is the person chosen by the decedent during his or her lifetime to satisfy the terms of the will. Some duties of the executor are to manage property, collect estate assets, pay creditors, and distribute the remaining property. The costs of settling a decedent's estate reduce the principal. The costs to operate, maintain, and manage income-producing property are immediately expensed in the income statement.

estate on condition: A land property estate contingent upon the occurrence or lack of occurrence of a particular event whereupon it can be created, augmented, or dismantled. For example, a testator states in a will that upon his or her death certain specified parcels of land will be passed to the eldest son if he has a male child through marriage.

estate of inheritance: An estate which descends to heirs in perpetuum. In an estate of inheritance, the current tenant not only has the right to enjoy the property for life, buy his or her tenancy rights pass to succeeding generations without limit.

estate for life: Having an interest in property for the duration of one's life after which the title reverts to another party. For example, former President Eisenhower gave his Gettysburg farm to the federal government provided that his widow, Mamie Eisenhower, would have use of the estate for life. See also *life estate.*

estate in reversion: See *reversion.*

estate in severalty: Owned by one individual or sole ownership. See also *tenancy in severalty.*

estate at sufferance: The continued and illegal occupancy of property after a legal period of occupancy has expired. In an estate at sufferance the tenant occupies the property at the sufferance of the property owner, and can be ejected at the latter's whim.

estate tax: Tax paid to the federal government or state upon the death of the taxpayer based on his or her net worth. The tax is paid by the estate, not the heirs. A $600,000 exclusion exists on the property transferred. There is no tax for property transferred between spouses. See also *inheritance tax.*

estate at will: A leasehold estate that can be terminated by the lessor or lessee at any time.

estate for years: Any lease with a specific starting time and a specific ending time.

estimate:

(1) To approximate the worth or valuation of property.

(2) To give an appraisal value estimate of property. Property value appraisals are never exact, and are at best approximations of actual market values.

estoppel: Barring an act. It may occur when an individual has improperly acted resulting in an unfair advantage over another party. For example, Mr. Abel has lied to Mr. Blake about the provisions of a real estate contract. Mr. Blake signs that contract relying on the untruths that will result in detrimental effects to Mr. Blake. However, as it turns out, Mr. Abel is harmed more by the contract (e.g., the price of real estate goes against him suddenly). Mr. Abel attempts to refute the contract but will be prevented (estopped) from doing so because he initiated the offer.

estoppel certificate: Mortgagor's signed statement that the stated remaining balance of a mortgage is correct and it is a property lien. This prevents a mortgagor from later stating the facts were misrepresented, and the mortgage therefore is invalid. See also *certificate of no defense; reduction certificate; waiver of lien.*

estoppel by deed: Restraining a person or business from denying an appropriate conveyance of property evidenced by a deed he has given. For example, Mr. Cook legitimately conveys property, but later changes his mind. He will be prevented from such action.

estover: Right of a tenant to make use of a property's wood or food producing capacity to provide for his or her own necessities. For example, a tenant takes sufficient firewood to provide adequate heat in the apartment he has rented.

et al.: Abbreviation for the Latin term et alii meaning "and others." For example, a title deed that is in several people's names is referred to as William Jones et al.

et con: Legal abbreviation meaning with husband.

ethics: The integrity, morals, and principles guiding an individual's or profession's actions. For example, a licensed real estate broker/salesman maintains a fiduciary relationship with a principal (seller or buyer). In this relationship the broker/salesman acts on the behalf of the principal transacting business and handling money for a real estate contract. Maintaining the highest level of ethics in these transactions is absolutely essential for the benefit of the public and profession.

et ux: Legal abbreviation meaning "and wife." For example, a title deed in the name of John Smith and his wife is referred to as John Smith et ux.

eviction: Legal action of a landlord to remove a tenant. The tenant may have violated the lease agreement such as for the tenant's failure to pay the rent.

eviction, actual: The act of removing or dispossessing or expulsion of an individual from a premises by force or law.

eviction, constructive: The altering of a rented or leased premises by a landlord rendering it unsuitable for habitation in order to effectuate the tenant's vacating. Constructive eviction occurs when the tenant vacates the premises because of the landlord's changes made in the premises. For example, the landlord shuts off the heat and water to an apartment causing the tenant to leave.

eviction, partial: Removal of a tenant from a portion of a rented or leased premise. For example, a partial eviction occurs when a tenant forces the expulsion of a tenant from the bottom floor of a two-floor premise.

evidence of title: Document, such as a deed, which demonstrates property ownership.

ex post facto: Act occurring after the fact. For example, a property deed was issued after the property closing occurred.

exception:
(1) A right or portion of property reserved to the grantor in a conveyance by deed.
(2) Waiver of a requirement in a lease agreement such as the landlord allowing an old tenant to have a cat or dog .

excess condemnation: Taking more property in a condemnation proceeding than is required. For example, in the need to build a new high school, the school district condemned an entire farm parcel although only two thirds was actually needed.

excess depreciation: Costs taken over and above what one is entitled to. This can occur either by claiming depreciation costs exceeding actual depreciable value or by depreciating items that cannot be depreciated. Items that cannot be

depreciated include land, since it never wears out, inventory, containers, costs to demolish a building, a life interest or an interest for a term of years in a property, or income interest in a trust. For example, Smith pays $150,000 for a home on a parcel of land used for the purposes of producing rental income. Smith claims a total depreciable basis of $140,000 for the property. The Internal Revenue Service overrules the depreciable basis claiming it is excess depreciation since the land parcel is worth at least $60,000 leaving $90,000 ($150,000 − $60,000) as the allowable depreciable basis for the property.

excess income (rent): Rental income received from property that exceeds the costs of owning and maintaining the property.

exchange:
(1) See also *tax-deferred exchange.*
(2) A reciprocal transfer of property from one entity to another.
(3) A market for securities of real estate companies, such as the New York Stock Exchange (NYSE).

exclusionary zoning: Property zoning having the net effect, intended or not, of excluding the poor and minority groups from living in a particular area. Building lot size is the most frequently used exclusionary zoning method. Large property size requirements increase the cost of housing, and can serve to discriminate against those who cannot afford to live there. For example, a two-acre building lot size requirement can substantially increase the cost of housing.

exclusive right to sell: A contract with a real estate agent that pays a commission to the agent even if the property is sold to a buyer found by the owner. See also *exclusive listing; open listing.*

exculpatory clause: Contractual clause freeing a party from personal liability. For example, an exculpatory clause in a mortgage agreement provides a mortgagor the ability to surrender a mortgaged property in the event of a default without risking personal liability.

execute: To fulfill, complete, implement, perform, or carry out the terms of an agreement including completing a signature on a contract and delivering a document to the intended party. For example, at the property closing the purchaser executed the mortgage agreement and property deed including placing a signature in the required area.

executed contract: A real estate contract whose terms have been completely satisfied.

execution:
(1) Conducting a transaction such as the purchase or sale of real estate.
(2) To sign and deliver an instrument, such as a deed.

executor (male) /executrix (female): Person chosen by a testator/testatrix to handle and conduct the terms of a will to an estate. Duties include collecting and selling of properties and paying debts of the estate.

executor's deed: Conveyed by an executor. If the testator to a will does not expressly give the executor authority to convey the property, the probate court must authorize it.

executory: Unfulfilled action where something remains to be done in order to complete it. See also *executory contract.*

executory contract: Agreement in which some terms are yet to be carried out. The contract is still not fully completed. An example is when a party to a construction contract needs to do considerably more work on the building. When the work is completed, the contract will have been executed.

executory cost: Cost excluded from the minimum lease payments to be made by the lessee in a capital lease. The lessee reimburses the lessor for the lessor's expense payments. Examples are maintenance, insurance, and taxes.

exempt property: Real estate not subject to property tax such as that owned by nonprofit entities including charitable, governmental, and religious institutions.

exhaust fan: Fan with an opening to the outside air that lets stale or hot air exit the structure; usually used in a kitchen when cooking or in a bathroom that does not have a window. It is used for ventilation purposes.

expansible house: House designed to be easily expandable. For example, it may have a full basement that could easily be transformed into a finished basement or it may have an expansion attic or an unfinished second floor that could easily be expanded into two or more bedrooms.

expansion joint: Space constructed between elements of a structure permitting lateral movement due to expansion occurring from temperature increases. For example, expansion joints are constructed at spaced intervals on a bridge surface permitting expansion of the road bed during temperature increases preventing it from buckling.

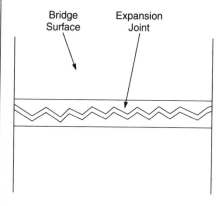

Bridge Surface   Expansion Joint

exposure: Person or business susceptible to loss on an investment, such as a high-risk speculation. See also *at risk.*

express contract: Agreement in which the promises of the parties are revealed in words, either orally or in writing.

extended coverage: Protection over and above that of an insurance policy or warranty.

extension: Giving additional time to conduct some act. An example is a financial institution giving a borrower an additional ten days to pay a mortgage payment. Another example is a landlord granting a tenant an additional week to make the rental payment.

extension agreement: Written agreement between two or more parties to extend the terms of a document. For example, a mortgage extension agreement would extend the amortization schedule between a mortgagor and mortgagee.

extensive margin: The broad use of credit to purchase a security. For example, under current (1994) rules of the New York Stock Exchange (NYSE), an investor must have at least 50% of the cost of a security in cash. An investor using extensive margin would be using the maximum credit available to purchase securities increasing the risk should the market value of the purchased securities decline and trigger a broker's call for additional cash to mark the margin to the market value.

exterior finish: The external covering finish of a structure which protects it from the elements. Exterior finish materials, including shingles, siding, and paints, are designed to resist severe weathering effects as well as providing decoration.

exterior wall: Outside wall of a structure that is exposed to the weather. The exterior wall is normally insulated to protect the interior of the structure. An exterior wall can also be a load bearing wall.

facade: External front wall to a structure.

face brick: Often termed facing brick, it is an exterior decorative brick surface. The brick is not rendered, painted, or plastered and is made of various brick materials, including clay, to give a desired effect.

face wall:
(1) A retaining wall.
(2) A structure's front wall.

facsimile:
(1) Reproduction or exact copy.
(2) In architecture, a reproduction of a building style.
(3) In telecommunications, the electronic transfer of an exact image of a document or photograph, a fax.

Fair Credit Reporting Act (FCRA): Statute regulating the use of credit information. Allows consumers such as prospective homeowners access to their credit files. It forces credit bureaus to maintain only correct information about borrowers. It requires a lender to explain how loan interest is computed. This act, which became effective April 1971, attempts to regulate the action of credit bureaus that give out erroneous information regarding consumers. First, banks and credit companies must make a consumer's credit file available to the person in question. Further, the consumer upon examining the file, has the right to correct any error that may appear in the credit reports. Second, if a creditor denies a loan to an applicant, the applicant must be given the name and address of the credit bureau that supplied the credit information to the creditor. Upon request, the credit bureau must supply the consumer with the pertinent information contained in the applicant's credit file. Finally, the act limits the access of the consumer's credit records to people who evaluate an applicant for insurance, credit, or employment; those who secure the consumer's permission; or those who secure court permission.

fair market rent: The rent a property commands in a free and open market setting.

fair market value: The amount that could be received on the sale of real estate when there exists a willing buyer and a willing seller.

falling out of escrow: One of the parties is unable to satisfy the conditions of the purchase and sale contract. For example, if the buyer cannot obtain a loan by the time escrow was to close, the contract is null and void.

false advertising: Deceptive or misleading advertising. For example, a rental advertisement claims the rental price of an apartment includes air conditioning even though the air conditioning unit has never been installed.

false personation: A criminal act of falsely representing another individual to gain profit or gain an advantage. For example, an individual who rents an apartment presenting a cash deposit to an individual giving the false personation they are the landlord authorized to make the rental agreement. In reality, the prospective renter was defrauded.

family room: Room in a home where the occupants spend their leisure time. The room often has certain amenities such as a television and/or an entertainment center.

Fannie Mae: See *Federal National Mortgage Association (FANNIE MAE).*

Farmers Home Administration (FmHA): Federal agency providing home financing to qualified people in low-income, rural areas. Currently, FmHA administers two loan programs for rural housing: (1) a direct loan program and (2) a guaranteed loan program. Properties securing such loans may not be located in urban areas and, like Federal Housing Administration (FHA) and Veterans Administration (VA), FmHA requires that the property meet certain minimum requirements. Although there is no statutory loan limit for such loans, the property must appraise for the contract sales price. Information on both loan programs is available from any office of the Farmers Home Administration.

feasibility study: Evaluation of a contemplated project or course of action, according to pre-established criteria (such as net present value, internal rate return, and payback) to determine if the proposal meets the requirements of the property owner. An analysis is also made of alternative means of accomplishing the task. An example is the feasibility of the design of a proposed shopping center. See also *capital budgeting.*

federal: Term describing any activity, regulation, agency, branch, or department of the United States government.

federal agency securities: Debt instruments of U.S. agencies such as the Federal Home Loan Bank, the Federal National Mortgage Association, the Federal Farm Credit Bureau, and Tennessee Valley Authority. Although these issues are not direct obligations of the U.S. Treasury, they still have a high credit rating.

Federal Fair Housing Law: Originally passed as Title VIII of the Civil Rights Act of 1968, it prohibits discrimination in the sale or rental of residential dwelling units or vacant land on the basis of color, national origin, race, religion, or sex. The law also prohibited the denial of participation of an individual in any multiple-listing service (MLS), real estate brokers' organization or other service, organization, or facility relating the business of selling or renting dwellings on the basis of race, color, religion, sex, or national origin. The act also prohibited a bank or other lending institution from discriminating against a person seeking a loan or other financial assistance to construct, purchase or improve a home. This includes the practice of restricting or refusing to grant mortgages and/or insurance in a defined geographic area. The handicapped, "familial" status, or those with children under eighteen, are also protected from housing discrimination under the Federal Fair Housing Law.

Judicial interpretations of the act have also included the following housing discrimination actions: refusal to show a home, preferential advertising, blockbusting, and steering.

Federal Home Loan Bank Board (FHLBB): Federal agency that monitors the federal savings and loan associations and federally insured state-charted

S&Ls. It acts as a central bank. In addition, it operates the Federal Savings and Loan Insurance Corporation (FSLIC).

Federal Home Loan Bank System: Twelve regional Federal Home Loan Banks directed since 1932 by the Federal Home Loan Bank Board (FHLBB). The FHLBB was dismantled by the extensive savings-and-loan bailout and reorganization legislation of 1989, when its regulatory functions went to the new Office of Thrift Supervision under the Treasury.

Federal Home Loan Mortgage Corporation (FHLMC): Known as Freddie Mac, the FHLMC is a stockholder-owned corporation, chartered by Congress in 1970, to provide ongoing assistance to the secondary market for residential mortgages by increasing liquidity of mortgage investments and improving the distribution of investment capital available for residential mortgage financing.

Freddie Mac purchases investment-quality mortgages from lenders and packages them as securities which are re-sold to investors such as insurance companies and pension funds. These securities are guaranteed by Freddie Mac. Freddie Mac has been instrumental in reducing mortgage financing costs thereby lowering housing costs as well as increasing the supply of residential mortgages. Since its inception in 1970, Freddie Mac has helped one in six homebuyers obtain mortgage financing.

Freddie Mac has an 18-member board of directors. Thirteen board members are elected, and five are appointed by the President of the United States.

Federal Housing Administration (FHA): Federal agency within the Department of Housing and Urban Development that provides financing to home buyers, particularly those with little cash or with a need to lower monthly payments. It insures mortgage loans that satisfy its requirements.

Federal Housing Administration Insured Mortgages: Mortgages insured by the Federal Housing Administration (FHA) designed to help to stimulate the depressed economy. In order to provide the means by which new homes could be purchased, FHA established an insurance program to safeguard the lender against the risk of nonpayment by people purchasing these homes. Under an FHA-insured mortgage, both the property and the borrower must meet certain minimum standards. The borrower is charged an insurance fee of one-half percent on the unpaid balance and can, under certain conditions, receive up to 97% financing on the appraised value of the property. If a purchaser using FHA financing is paying more than the appraised value, the difference between the appraised value and the sales price must come from the purchaser's assets. Borrowers are not permitted to obtain second mortgages to use as down payments. Also, FHA sets limits as to the maximum loan origination fee charged by the lender. The subject property must be appraised prior to the loan being made; this fee is normally absorbed by the mortgagor. FHA insures these loans for up to 30 years. Thus, the low closing costs, the relatively low down payment, and the long amortization period permitted under FHA have all aided in providing residential financing for millions of people who otherwise would not have been able to purchase a home. On a conventional mortgage, the interest rate is determined by the lender rather than by the Secretary of Housing and Urban Development. This rate is periodically raised or lowered to reflect changes in the cost of money, although historically, interest rates on FHA mortgages have been slightly below conventional mortgage interest rates. In addition, borrowers financing with FHA coverage may be charged discount points since points can be paid by either the buyer or the seller. In recent years, FHA has expanded its operation; currently, the agency administers a number of programs dealing with housing. The basic home mortgage program is normally referred to as 203(b), and the program which provides insured mortgages for low or moderate income families is referred to as 221 (d)(2).

Federal National Mortgage Association (FNMA): Also known as Fannie Mae; established by Congress in 1938 to acquire government-insured mortgages through the Federal Housing Administration (FHA). Fannie Mae became a mortgage power after World War II when it was authorized to purchase Veteran Administration (VA) loans. In 1968, it was partitioned into two entities: Fannie Mae, a private corporation serving low- and middle-income families; and Ginne Mae, part of the Department of Housing and Urban Development. Shareholder-owned Fannie Mae—the stock is traded on the New York Stock Exchange—now claims to have underwritten one in every seven mortgages in the United States. It buys single- and multifamily mortgages from a network of more than 3,000 mortgage lenders nationwide. Such purchases are financed by selling debt and mortgage-backed securities to private investors.

The mortgage purchase procedure used by FNMA is conducted through an auction process referred to as the Free Market System Auction. Periodically, the association accepts bids from approved lenders as to the amount, price and terms of existing mortgages that these lenders wish to sell Fannie Mae. Upon deciding how much money it will spend during a given time period, FNMA notifies the successful bidders (determined by those mortgages offered for sale that will generate the highest yield to FNMA), and these bidders have a certain time period in which they can choose to deliver the mortgages. Once the mortgage has been delivered to Fannie Mae, the originator of the mortgage continues to service the loan (collect monthly payments, escrow property taxes, etc.) and for this service the originator receives a servicing fee. By selling to Fannie Mae, a lender is allowed to rollover its money. That is, by selling $1 million worth of mortgages to FNMA, a savings and loan association now has $1 million that can be used to originate new mortgages. Thus, funds are provided that would not have been available had Fannie Mae not purchased the mortgages.

Federal Savings and Loan Association: Charter issued by the Office of Thrift Supervision, under the U.S. Department of Treasury, to an institution to act as a savings and loan association. A federally chartered savings and loan association, in contrast to one with a state charter, may have the ability to branch across state lines as well as make certain investments a state chartered thrift institution cannot.

federal tax lien: Placed by the federal government on an individual's real property for federal estate tax or income tax law violations. In the case of a federal estate tax lien, upon the owner's death, the estate is liable for the tax lien. In the even of a failure to pay federal income taxes, the government may seek a tax warrant causing a federal tax lien to be placed against the taxpayer's property.

fee ownership: Largest form of ownership giving the owner complete control including the development of an inheritable estate. It is also known as a fee estate. See also *fee simple.*

fees: Charges billed for services rendered. They may be on a flat basis or on an hourly rate. For example, a real estate broker may charge a flat fee of $1,000 to find an apartment for a prospective tenant. Another example is a broker charging a seller of a house a 6% fee based on the selling price.

fee simple: The largest, most complete bundle of rights one can hold in property. It expressly establishes the title to real property in the owner, without limitation. The owner may dispose of the property by sale or trade.

fee simple absolute: An estate limited absolutely to an owner and his or her heirs in perpetuity and without limitation, entitling the owner to all of the property involved as well as having unlimited ability to divide it among his heirs.

fee simple conditional: A fee estate conditioned by the provisions of the grantor or the grantor's heirs that some action occur in order to complete its conveyance. Should the condition not occur, the estate is defeated and it returns to the original grantor. For example, a grantor of a fee simple conditional estate will transfer the estate to his son provided that he completes his college education.

fee simple defeasible: The granting of a fee ownership estate that can be defeated and returned to the grantor should a certain event occur. For example, a grantor will transfer an estate to his daughter provided that she does not marry a certain named individual.

fee simple determinable: A fee estate limited by the happening of a certain event.

fence: Connected group of wires, woods, or other material surrounding real property to either protect it or act as a barrier against others. A fence often increases the value of the property.

FHA Mortgage Insurance: Mortgages insured by the Federal Housing Administration. It provides insurance to approved lenders to assure a steady source of mortgage money on FHA-approved homes at reasonable rates. The purpose is to make mortgages more attractive for lenders.

fidelity bond: Insurance coverage against specified losses that arise from the dishonest acts or defalcations of employees. This bond may be applied to persons or positions. An example is a fidelity bond taken out on a doorman or security guard.

fiduciary: Individual or institution responsible for holding or administering property owned by another. Examples of a fiduciary are executor, trustee, and executor. A fiduciary is legally responsible to act properly.

15-year mortgage: Mortgage loan where for a slight increase in the monthly payment, the loan can be paid off in only 15 years. The overall savings in interest paid to the lender over the life of the 15-year mortgage can be quite substantial, yet the monthly payment is not significantly higher.

EXAMPLE: Consider a $100,000 30-year fixed rate mortgage at 13%. The monthly payment for principal and interest is $1,106.20. Assume that one has decided to refinance his home with a fixed-rate loan at 10%. Two options are available: 30-year loan at 10% vs. 15-year loan at the same rate. The table on page 114 compares the monthly payments and total interest over the life of the two loans. In either case, the monthly payment is less than the 13% mortgage. Between 30-year and 15-year, however, the monthly payment increases about 22.45% while the savings in total interest payments over the life would be almost 57%. From this example, note that $122,495 in total interest payments can be saved by election of a 15-year loan without increasing the monthly burden and the buyer will be a 100% equity

Comparison of 30-Year vs. 15-Year Fixed Rate *Mortgage*

	30-Year	15-Year	Decrease (Percent)	Increase (Percent)
Principal	$100,000	$100,000	—	
Rate	10%	10%	—	
Monthly payment	$877.57	$1074.61	197.04	22.45%
Total interest	$215,925	$93,430	(122,495)	(56.73%)

holder in a home within 15 years instead of 30 years. See also *refinance*.

filtering down: Situation where a neighborhood is gradually occupied by progressively lower income people.

final decree: A judgment of a court issued as a final order after hearing all the evidence and material directly related to some matter before its consideration. A final decree considers all the rights to the parties on the subject matter, and finally concludes its consideration of the matter. See also *interlocutory decree*.

final value estimate: Final property appraisal estimate arrived at by applying appropriate appraisal methods.

finance charge: Fee for the cost of a loan including interest and points. Points (1 point = 1% of the total loan) are advance charges for a mortgage, whereas interest is charged over the life of the mortgage. Interest and points add to the total cost of the loan. The Truth-in-Lending Act requires any costs to be disclosed to the prospective homebuyer before final acceptance. See also *Consumer Credit Protection Act; Regulation Z.*

financial calculators: Portable electronic calculator having numerous built-in financial functions including cash flow analysis and margin calculators, mortgage amortization, present and future value, yield to maturity, and numerous other business statistics and financial ratios.

financial institutions and markets: Institutions (e.g., banks) acting as intermediaries between suppliers and users of money. They are wholesalers and retailers of funds. The financial markets are where those wanting funds are matched with those having surplus funds.

The financial markets consist of money markets and capital markets. Money markets (credit markets) are the markets for short-term (less than 1 year) debt securities such as federal agency securities, bankers' acceptances, and negotiable certificates of deposit issued by public and private institutions. Money market securities are very liquid and have a low default risk. Capital markets are the markets in which long-term securities issued by the government and business are traded. Unlike the money market, both debt-instruments (bonds) and equities (common and preferred stocks) are traded. Compared to money market securities, those of the capital market have greater default and market risks, but return a higher yield to compensate for the greater risk. The New York Stock Exchange and American Stock Exchange are examples of capital markets. These exchanges are organized markets. Further securities are traded through brokers and dealers on the over-the-counter (or unlisted) market. There are other markets such as the mortgage market which handling various real estate mortgages. A primary market refers to the market for new issues, while a secondary market deals with previously issued securities being exchanged. The New York Stock Exchange is an example of a secondary market.

financial intermediaries: See *financial institutions.*

financial leverage: Also called trading on equity. A portion of a real estate company's assets financed with debt instead of equity. It involves interest and principal obligations. Financial leverage is beneficial to real estate investors as long as the borrowed funds generate a return above the cost of borrowing. However, the increased risk can offset the general cost of capital. Financial leverage is measured by the debt-to-equity ratio. See also *leverage; trading on equity.*

financial management rate of return (FMRR): An adjustment to the internal rate of return (IRR) computation so as to improve this measure. The FMRR computation uses a risk-free after-tax rate and a customary rate for money reinvestment.

financial markets: See *financial institutions and markets.*

financial statement: Report containing financial information about a business or individual. The required financial statements for a real estate company are balance sheet, income statement, and statement of cash flows. Other supplementary reports may be presented to provide additional information about financial statues such as segmental data. An individual may prepare a financial statement, such as to obtain a real estate loan from the bank. A personal financial statement includes a balance sheet and perhaps a statement of changes in net worth.

financing fee: See *finance charge.*

financing statement: See *financial statement.*

finder's fee: Amount paid to a person or business for bringing the parties together in a business arrangement. The finder may also act in a consulting capacity. The fee may be a flat amount or rate, a percentage of the sale, or percentage of profit. For example, finder's fees are paid in matching a seller and buyer of real estate.

finish floor: Second layer of flooring material placed over the rough flooring or flooring planks in a structure. The finish floor is a polished floor often made of oak or other hardwood materials.

finish hardware: See *hardware.*

finish out allowance: Provision in a commercial lease providing a financial allowance for a tenant to finish the interior of a building according to individual requirements. For example, a retailer leases a new retail store location at a cost of $20 per square foot. Since the building has never been used before, the interior is still unfinished having only cement block exterior walls and no interior walls or finished ceiling. The lessor provides a $10 square foot finish allowance for the lessee to complete the interior of the building.

fire doors and walls: Fire resistant materials to construct a structure's doors and walls. For example, doors are made out of steel and have no windows. The walls are made out of fire-resistive materials designed to withstand high temperatures for a sustained time period.

fire insurance–standard fire policy: Also known as the 165-line policy because of the standard form used. To complete the policy additional forms and endorsements must be added to cover direct and indirect risks associated with the specific covered risk. The Standard Fire Policy is found in Section I where the property coverage of most policies are listed, including homeowner's and special multi-peril. There are four sections comprised of: (1) Declarations (a description of property and its location) covered amount, and name of insured; (2) Insuring agreements (premium amount, insured's duties and claim information; (3) Insurance conditions (circumstances suspending or restricting coverage, hazard conditions); and (4) Exclusions (hazards not covered such as war-related events).

fireproof: Materials that are inherently noncombustible. Fireproof materials are widely used in constructing exterior surfaces and include brick, aluminum siding, cement, and asbestos shingles.

fire-resistive: Materials designed to withstand exposure to fire for a defined period of time while retaining its structural characteristics. Fire resistive materials are used in interior finishes, such as wood paneling, wallboard, acoustical tile, furniture, and carpeting fabrics.

fire stop: A horizontal block built between the wall studs within covered walls to prevent fire from spreading vertically.

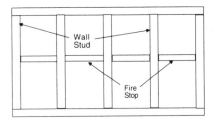

Wall Stud

Fire Stop

first lien: First right of a party, usually a creditor, to hold, keep possession of, or control the property of another to pay a debt, duty, or obligation. An example is a first mortgage that comes before other mortgages (e.g., second mortgage) over the collateralized value of property if default occurs. For example, if a home worth $300,000 is subject to a first and second mortgage of $350,000 and $200,000, respectively, the first mortgagee will receive the entire $300,000 collateralized value.

first mortgage: Initial or senior mortgage on property. It comes before all subsequent mortgages, and the mortgagee has precedence in payment if default occurs.

first refusal: See *right of first refusal*.

first user: Initial user of real estate property, such as the first tenant in a newly constructed apartment building or office building.

fiscal year: A 12-month period used by a real estate company or partnership to account for and report business operations. Typically, the fiscal year ends December 31. However, many real estate businesses use the natural business year, referring to a year ending at the annual low point in business activity or at the end of the season. For example, a business selling real estate may have its year-end on February 28 when business is slowest because of bad weather.

five C's of credit: Considerations used by lenders in appraising a prospective homebuyer's credit application. They are: (1) Character (willingness to pay), (2) Capacity (cash flow), (3) Capital (wealth), (4) Collateral (security), and (5) Conditions (economic status).

Character is an individual's honesty and capability to pay obligations. The borrower's credit history indicates how reliable the borrower is in meeting obligations. Capacity refers to the person's earning power and cash position. Capital refers to a borrower's net assets (net worth). Collateral refers to pledge property that can be sold by the lender if a loan is defaulted upon. Conditions are the economic status and a borrower's susceptibility to negative economic conditions. If money is in ample supply and interest rates are low, it is easier to obtain credit. On the other hand, when credit is tight, applicants would be more readily rejected. Once the five C's are evaluated, a borrower is assigned a credit rating classification, which will affect the default risk premium for the borrower. The more risk associated with a borrower, the higher the interest rate.

fixed price contract: Predetermined price for a contract that will be the same irrespective of the actual costs incurred to complete it. This contract is advantageous to the buyer because he knows beforehand what the price will be. It is risky to the contractor because if he significantly underestimated the actual costs when setting the price, losses may arise. On the other hand, if actual costs are much less than the estimated costs used as a basis to set the price, greater profits will arise. Therefore, careful consideration must be given to costs before contractual prices are established.

fixed-rate mortgage: A mortgage loan that is at a set specified interest rate for the lifetime or maturity of the mortgage. Unless interest rates exceed "comfortable" levels (typically about 10 percent), buyers are likely to choose this type of mortgage. According to the Federal National Mortgage Association (Fannie Mae), first time buyers often choose fixed-rate mortgages because they want the security of stable and affordable payments. Some may choose fixed-rate mortgages because they want low monthly payments throughout the loan term. For instance, because homes in some areas may appreciate more slowly than those in other areas, some people prefer to make low monthly payments so that they can put the money they save into other investments that bring greater returns. Also, buyers can reap the greatest cumulative tax deductions available over the loan term. Generally, lenders require 20% down payments on conventional fixed-rate mortgages, but with Federal Housing Administration (FHA) insurance, only 5% is required. Currently, however, FHA insurance is available only on loans less than $101,250. Also, private mortgage insurance (PMI) can help buyers purchase a home with only a 10% down payment. As the name implies, buyers purchase PMI through private companies, but lenders typically

acquire the insurance for the buyers. First-year premiums are usually between .35% and 1.65% of the total loan amount, and depending on policy requirements, buyers must pay the premiums either in advance or monthly. A twist on the 30-year fixed-rate mortgage is the shorter term fixed-rate mortgage, with either a 10- or 15-year loan term. These shorter terms require larger monthly payments than a 30-year term, but the benefits that often attract buyers include the lower interest rates, faster equity buildup, and a substantial interest savings over 30-year mortgages.

fixing-up expenditures: Payments made to enhance the appearance and condition of real estate property. In so doing, the market value of the property should increase. Examples of renovation costs are siding, painting the interior, repairing electrical problems, and putting in a new burner.

fixture: A fixed asset whose utility is derived from its physical attachment to a property and which usually cannot be removed without causing loss of value or damage. An example is a lighting fixture. A fixture, under the terms of a lease or other agreement, can be detached.

flagstone: Flat irregularly shaped stones, ranging from 1 to 4 inches thick, used for terrace or lawn walkways.

flashing: Sheet metal, often made of aluminum, used to cover a structure's open masonry or wood joints. The purpose of flashing is to prevent the penetration of water as well as to provide a drainage passageway between joints. The most common use of flashing is to cover the joint between a roof and wall.

flat: A building having one household on the first floor and a second household on the second floor.

flat fee broker: Registered real estate broker who charges a flat fee, rather than a commission, for real estate purchase and sale transactions regardless of the property's sale price. For example, Pleasant Town Realtors, a flat fee broker, charges a $3,500 flat fee for the selling of a home regardless of its selling price. No fee is charged if the property is not sold.

flat lease: Lease agreement having level payments during the contractual period. It does not have an escalation clause to allow for increased costs due to increases in inflation, taxes, or other related costs. For a landlord, the flat lease is not suitable for an extended period of time since it does not provide for increases in payments.

flat roof: Roof having less than a 10 degree slant.

flaw: Deficiency or defect existing in the way a home has been constructed. For example, the plumbing system may be inadequate. A flaw may be corrected by the builder or supplier, a refund in price given for the imperfection, or the item returned.

Flexible Loan Insurance Program (FLIP): A graduated payment mortgage (GMP) developed to overcome the negative amortization aspects of the GMP. The key to the FLIP mortgage is the use of the buyer's down payment. Instead of being used as a down payment, the cash is deposited in a pledged, interest-bearing savings account where it serves as both a cash collateral for the lender and as a source of supplemental payments for the borrower during the first few years of the loan. During the early years of the mortgage, each month the lender withdraws predetermined amounts from the savings account and adds them to the borrower's reduced payment to make a full normal mortgage payment. The supplemental payment decreases each month and vanishes at the end of a predetermined period (usually five years). By using this type of program, a borrower is likely to qualify for a larger loan than with a conventional fully-amortized mortgage.

flexible payment mortgage: Loan that allows the borrower to pay only the interest for the first few years of the loan.

flexible rate mortgage (FRM): Mortgage that has an interest rate that changes based on some event. For example, the interest rate may vary depending on changes in the prime rate or inflation rate.

float:
(1) Amount of funds represented by checks that have been issued but not yet collected.
(2) Time between the deposit of checks in a bank and payment. Due to the time difference, some real estate firms are able to "play the float," that is, to write checks against money not presently in the firm's bank account.
(3) To issue new securities, usually through an underwriter.

floating floor: Floor designed to provide sound insulation qualities. A floating floor is separated from the building's structure by the use of special resilient materials, often fabricated from fiberglass, or flexible mounting devices, including springs. Floating floor construction is used when there is a need to separate the rest of the building from noise, vibration, or a combination of these elements often produced by machinery.

floating interest rate: Interest rate on a loan that varies periodically based on some related measure. An example is a mortgage in which the interest rate is adjusted monthly depending on the prime interest rate or the Treasury bill rate. If interest rates are currently high and a prospective buyer of a home believes future interest rates will be decreasing, he should contract for a variable rate mortgage (VRM).

flood insurance: Insurance indemnifying property from flood losses and mud slides for property qualified under the National Flood Insurance Act of 1968.

flood plain: Contiguous shore area bordering a river that is subject to periodic water level increases. In the flood stage, the flood plain can be under water.

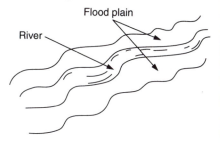

floor area ratio (FAR): The ratio between a structure's total floor area and the total land area of the land upon which it is constructed. The floor area ratio must conform with the building code's floor area specifications. The FAR is calculated by dividing the total building floor area by the total building lot square area:

$$\text{Floor Area Ratio} = \frac{\text{Building Floor Area}}{\text{Building Lot Area}}$$

For example, a building code may specify a 2.5:1 FAR indicating that a building may have 2.5 sq. ft. of floor area on every 1 sq. ft. of land area. In this case, a building occupying ½ of the building lot could have 5 stories (2.5 × ½) or a building occupying ¼ of the building lot could have 10 stories (2.5 × ¼).

floor joists: Beams providing structural floor support. Flooring is directly attached to the floor joists. See also *joist.*

floor loan: A minimum amount a lender is willing to provide on a commercial loan for a building designed to be tenant occupied. A floor loan is progressively funded as the building moves from the initial construction stage of occupancy. At its inception, a floor loan may fund up to 75% of the principal amount of the total loan and then provide additional portions of the principal as the building is constructed. For example, a corporation obtains a $2 million loan to build an office building. The lending institution provides a 75% floor on the loan, or $1.5 million for the initial building construction. After the building is 70% occupied, the lending institution will provide an additional $250,000 and when the building reaches 90% occupancy it provides the remaining $250,000.

floor plan: The arrangement of the walls and rooms in a structure. A two-dimensional horizontal scale drawing of the arrangements, size, and orientation of doors, rooms, walls, and windows of a single floor of a building structure.

flue pipe: Airtight conduit constructed within a chimney using fireproof materials to carry away combustion gases and smoke occurring in a furnace or fire box.

FNMA: See *Federal National Mortgage Association (Fannie Mae).*

forced hot air: A heating system consisting of a heating unit forcing hot air through an interconnected network of air ducts with outlets throughout the structure. Three advantages of a forced hot air system are:

(1) Rapid elevation of room temperature from forcing hot air through the outlets.

(2) The system can easily be converted into a central air conditioning system using the same ducts.

(3) A humidifier unit can easily be attached to the duct work to maintain a comfortable level of humidity throughout the building.

forced sale: Sale of property where the seller is unable to allow current market prices and conditions determine the actual selling price. In a forced sale, the property owner is selling under duress complying with court judgment specifying a specific sale date and other judicially determined sale conditions. A foreclosure sale is an example of a forced sale. Other examples occur as the result of a court decree ordering property to be sold within a specified period of time to satisfy a mortgage, judgment or tax lien.

force majeure: An unpreventable, overwhelming, and irresistible force. It is common to place a force majeure clause in a construction contract to indemnify a construction deadline in the event an act of God should occur which prevents a timely completion of the contract. For example, a contractor place a force majeure clause in a contract for the construction of a building which is to be completed within nine months. Due to an unexpectedly cold winter, the project had to be delayed three months. The inclement cold weather operationalized the force majeure clause and indemnified the contractor's failure to complete the project on schedule.

foreclosure: A legal means whereby the owner of property loses his legal rights and interests therein. It arises from a default on the part of the mortgagor in paying a mortgage lien or taxes against the property. In a foreclosure, the creditor takes over the property through a judicial order and the property is sold at auction. The proceeds received are used to pay the mortgagee any remaining balance and back taxes. The remainder is distributed to the original owner of the property.

foreclosure sale: A legal procedure to sell a mortgaged property to the highest bidder in order to satisfy a mortgage claim from a mortgagee against the value of the property. A foreclosure sale can occur from a judicial sale where a court orders the sale after hearing a foreclosure petition filed against a mortgagor by a mortgagee. A foreclosure by power of sale contained in a mortgage allows a mortgagee to have a foreclosure sale, after providing proper legal notice to a defaulting mortgagor, without the need for judicial recourse.

forfeiture: Loss of property from nonfulfillment of some duty or condition. In some cases, forfeiture is required by a court order, whereas in other cases the nonfulfillment of a contractual debt is enough to result in a forfeiture. For example, the loss of a lease can result from the failure to pay rent on time. See also *default; foreclosure.*

forgery: Act of fabricating or producing something falsely. An example is signing someone else's name on a check and cashing it.

formica: Trade name by the American Cyanamid Corporation for a plastic laminate surfacing material widely used on furniture, cabinets, counter tops and wall coverings. Formica is hard, durable, and resistant to heat, water, alcohol, chemicals, and stains.

for rent by owner (FRBO): Owner of property attempts to find a tenant himself without using a real estate broker. The owner also manages the property without the need for property management. The advantages are lower costs and the owner can select what he considers to be the best tenant.

for sale by owner (FSBO): Owner of property tries to sell it by himself and not through a real estate broker. The owner may advertise the property in the newspaper and have a "for sale" sign outside his house. The advantages to the owner are avoiding the brokerage commission and greater flexibility.

foundation: That portion of a structure providing the primary ground support. Foundations have a foundation wall forming a permanent below grade retaining wall. All modern foundations rely on concrete reinforced cement blocks or masonry as the primary construction materials.

foyer: An entrance hallway from the outside of a building. Foyers are intended as a gathering place for people either before exiting or upon entrance. For example, most movie theaters have large entrance foyers where people often stand in line before being admitted to the viewing of a movie.

franchise: Privilege granted by a franchiser to a franchisee permitting the latter to operate using the franchiser's name. The franchisee must pay a franchise fee for such right. In addition, the franchisee is typically required to use the franchiser's products. The franchisee usually receives other benefits from the franchiser such as advertising. Many real estate brokerages are franchisees.

fraud:

(1) Deliberate action by an individual or entity to cheat another causing damage. There is typically a misrepresentation to deceive, or purposeful withholding of material data needed for a proper decision. An example of fraud is when a property manager falsifies records in order to steal money.

(2) Falsification of a tax return by an individual. Examples of tax fraud are intentionally not reporting taxable income or overstating expenses. Tax fraud is a criminal act.

Freddie Mac: A real estate industry nickname for the Federal Home Loan Mortgage Corporation (FHLMC).

free and clear title: Property title having no encumbrances. In the usual sense this means a title not having a mortgage. However, other encumbrances could include judgments or additional financial liens.

freehold: Unlimited interest in property. A freehold estate may be a fee simple or life estate. Freehold estates include freehold in deed, a fee simple estate; freehold in law, an inheritable estate; and determinable freeholds, a life estate.

French Provincial: Style of home emphasizing symmetry and balance. Usually $1\frac{1}{2}$ to $2\frac{1}{2}$ stories having a steep hip roof with curved upper windows interrupting the cornice.

frontage: Linear measurement of property abutting a road or water body acting as a boundary marker. See also *frontage road.*

frontage road: Road or highway acting as a frontage boundary.

front-end money: Amount of money that must be charged or invested in the initial stage of a business transaction to demonstrate good faith as well as to help offset some expenses. For example, the customary 10% deposit on the initiation of an agreement of sale is a form of front-end money required to initiate the contract.

front foot: A property measurement of the front footage of a parcel of property adjoining the street. In urban areas, the front foot measurement is an extremely important indicator of property value and property is often evaluated on the basis of cost per front foot. Normally, the front foot measurement is the first measure shown in a property description. For example, if a parcel of property is 150 ft. x 300 ft., the former is the front foot measurement.

front money: The amount of money a developer must directly invest in order to obtain a development loan. It pays for the initial development cost including costs for items such as architectural plans, surveys, permits, legal fees, and engineering studies. Normally obtained from investors, it is sometimes termed seed money. For example, a developer raised $100,000 front money to pay for the initial development costs of a $2,500,000 project in order to obtain a $2,400,000 development loan.

frost line: The maximum depth to which the ground normally becomes frozen in a given geographic area. The depth of the frost line is an important consideration when placing or installing pipes or any other structure that can be damaged or affected by freezing conditions.

FSBO: Abbreviation meaning For Sale by Owner. This is the term used when a property owner wishes to sell property without having a listing agreement with a real estate broker.

full covenant and warranty deed: Widely used type of property deed containing five warranties:
(1) Covenant of seisin. This is an assurance the purchaser has possession of the estate in quantity and quality as was purported.
(2) Covenant of quiet enjoyment. An assurance against hostile claims to the property title.
(3) No liens and encumbrances.
(4) Covenant of further assurance. An assurance by the property seller to the purchaser that all necessary actions to perfect a title will be undertaken, should any claims arise against the title.
(5) Warranty of title.

full disclosure:
(1) Requirement to present all significant information related to a certain matter.
(2) Requirement for a real estate broker to provide all known information about the condition of the subject property.
(3) Requirement for a lender to disclose to borrowers the effective cost and terms of loans.
See also *Regulation Z; Truth-in-Lending Act.*

full warranty: Type of warranty that entitles a homeowner to full remedies for defective work done by a contractor (e.g., electrical work).

fully amortized mortgage: Mortgage that has been paid in full. The principal balance is zero.

fully indexed rate: Interest rate on an adjustable rate mortgage based on the total of the current value of an index and margin applicable to the mortgage. The rate is the basis for the computation of monthly loan payments. Assume a mortgage is indexed to the consumer price index, and it has a value of 5%. The margin on the loan is 1.5%. Therefore, the fully indexed rate will be 6.5% which is the basis for the initial year's interest rate. The interest rate will change each year depending on the change in the related index.

functional deficiency: Negative characteristics about real property which do not meet the needs of the usual occupant. Examples are inadequate lighting in the rooms and a one-car garage when a two-car garage is required.

functional depreciation: A reduction in structural value from all reasons except physical failure. For example, a commercial building having an outdated elevator or electrical wiring system is experiencing functional depreciation.

functional modern or contemporary house: Home designs developed after World War II incorporating modern technology, materials, and architecture including energy conservation methods to achieve a highly functional structure.

functional obsolescence: Also called functional depreciation. Loss of value that results from improvements that are inadequate, outdated, overly adequate, or improperly designed for today's needs. May be curable or incurable.

functional utility: A property's usefulness to the owner or lessee. For example, room size may be sufficient to a professional who wants to use his house also as an office.

fungible: Goods that are freely substitutable. It is goods of a given class or type, any unit of which is as acceptable as another, and capable of satisfying an obligation expressed in terms of the class. For example, bushels of rice are fungibles, while parcels of real estate are not.

furring: See *furring strip.*

furring strip: Insulating material attached to crevices around doors and windows to prevent air from either entering or escaping from a structure. Tacked, stapled, or glued onto the surfaces of the doors or windows, the strip is made from either artificial or animal fibers.

future advance clause: Clause in an open-ended mortgage permitting the mortgagor to borrow additional sums of money in the future pledging the same real property collateral. A construction loan has a future advance clause providing additional loan guarantees as the building project progresses.

future interest: An interest in property with the right of possession being postponed into the future until a certain even occurs. There are several possibilities where a future interest in property could occur. One possibility is a present life estate which will pass to another individual having a future interest as a fee simple estate. Other opportunities for a future interest occur with a reversion and/or a remainder.

gable: A triangular shaped end of a building where a double sloped roof meets at the top of the triangle. A gable begins at the eaves of a roof and terminates at the roof ridge. See also *gable roof.*

gable roof: A roof forming a triangle from the eaves to the ridge of the roof. See also *gable*

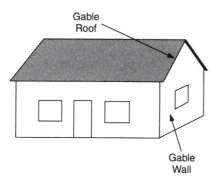

Gable Roof

Gable Wall

gain: Excess of money or fair value of property received on sale or exchange over the carrying value of the property. An example is the sale of a building when the cash received exceeds its book value. Gains also occur when the cash payment to eliminate a mortgage is less than the carrying value. An example is paying off a mortgage before its due date because it is financially advantageous to do so. See also *loss.*

galloping inflation: Also called hyperinflation. Very high rate of inflation rate.

gambrel roof: Roof having two slopes or pitches on each side. The lower slope is greater than the upper slope.

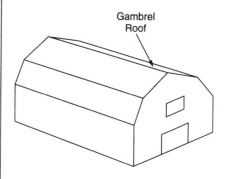

Gambrel Roof

gap loan: Temporary financing meeting a developer's financial difference between a construction loan and a permanent mortgage. For example, a developer is approved for a $1.5 million permanent mortgage once the development achieves 80% occupancy, but only has a $1 million construction loan to complete the project. In order to cover the difference between the construction loan and the permanent mortgage, the developer arranges a

$500,000 gap loan until the mortgage occupancy requirements are met.

garden apartments: An apartment complex providing tenants access to a lawn area.

garnishment: Legal proceeding whereby a person's property is attached and used to pay an obligation. The employer may withhold part of the employee's salary to the court until the debt has been paid.

GDP: See *gross domestic product.*

general contractor: Contractor who signs a contract with a property owner or developer and assumes comprehensive responsibility for completing a construction project. A general contractor will hire and pay subcontractors to complete the components of a construction project and supervise all details of the project.

general lien: A lien against all of the property of a debtor. A general lien may be obtained either through a judgment lien, where the court issues a judgment, a lien by creditors on an estate, or through federal and state tax liens. See also *specific lien.*

general partner:
(1) Managing partner of a limited partnership who is in charge of its operations. A general partner has unlimited liability. See also *limited partner.*
(2) Member of a partnership who is jointly and severally liable for all partnership debts.

gentrification: The rehabilitation and redevelopment of low-income housing into higher income housing resulting in the displacement of the low-income residents. Gentrification primarily occurs in neighborhoods close to larger urban centers because of their proximity to the central business district and urban services.

Georgian architecture: English-style architecture named after King George I–III and extremely popular in Great Britain and North America during the 18th century. A Georgian house has two to three stories and is rectangular with classic lines and ornamentation. See also *Georgian colonial architecture.*

Georgian colonial architecture: Early American architecture modeled after the English Georgian architecture, having two or three stories with a rectangular design and ample ornamentation often including a widow's walk.

gift deed: Deed that states "love and affection" as the consideration for the gifted real estate.

gift tax: Tax assessed on the transfer of property made without adequate legal consideration. This tax is imposed on the donor of a gift. The tax is based on the appraised value of the property at the time of transfer. Under the law, each parent may give each recipient $10,000 a year ($20,000 for parents electing gift-splitting) without gift tax consequences. Also, gifts of property between spouses are untaxed.

G. I. guaranteed mortgages: See *Veterans Administration Mortgage.*

GI loan: See *Veteran's Administration Mortgage.*

Ginnie Maes: Debt securities sponsored by the Government National Mortgage Association (GNMA). The objective of the GNMA is to fund high-risk mortgages for high-risk borrowers, typically in areas approved for government construction projects that have no other funding sources. The government body also offers guarantees mortgages issued by others, such as commercial banks, mortgage banks, and insurers. Ginnie Maes are backed by the United States and thus have a high credit standing. See also *Government National Mortgage Association (GNMA)*.

girder: Main structural support beam. A girder is made of steel, reinforced concrete, or timber. It is designed to support loads at different points along its length.

good faith (goodwill): In conducting a real estate transaction, each party is presumed honest and fair with no deceit. The intentions are honorable and realistic. If deception occurs without prior knowledge, the transaction, carried out in good faith, remains valid. For example, if a property deed is transferred in a good faith sale, and it later becomes obvious that a prior owner had not properly executed the certificate, the sale remains intact. However, bad faith is when an individual knowingly commits fraud or deception rendering the transaction null and void.

good repair clause: A clause that may be inserted into a purchase agreement or a lease indicating that subject property must be properly maintained in order to validate the contract. The effect of a good repair clause is to create liability for the seller or the lessee in the event subject property is found to be in need of repairs.

goodwill: Value of a company's or person's name and reputation. As a result, the business will have a competitive edge, and generate better-than-typical future earnings.

Government National Mortgage Association (GNMA): Nicknamed Ginnie Mae; established in 1968 through amendment to the National Housing Act. GNMA is a wholly owned government corporation administered by the Department of Housing and Urban Development. It does not buy mortgages; it issues pass-through securities in which interest and principal received on a pool of federally insured mortgage loans is paid to the investor. GNMA guarantees the timely payment of principal and interest on the mortgages. Because many mortgages are prepaid before maturity, investors in GNMA pools often obtain their principal investment before the maturity date. Ginnie Mae is a safe investment. See also *Ginnie Maes; mortgage-backed securities*.

government rectangular survey: Way in which the U.S. government uses to subdivide public land. Land is designated as either a base line (East-West) or principal meridian line (North-South). It is a rectangular approach to surveying the land breaking the district down to quadrangles of 24 miles. Ranges exist every 6 miles East and West of each meridian. This system is used in slightly more than 50% of the states, predominately in the West.

grace period:
(1) Period allowed after date due for payment of rent, mortgages, etc.
(2) The 30-day period subsequent to the due date permitted on insurance policies, which retains coverage even though the premium has not yet been paid.

grade:
(1) The ground elevation at a building site. The portion of a building structure which is over the grade, is termed above grade. The foundation or any subterranean portions of a building is termed below grade.
(2) Method of classifying building materials. Grades of lumber are particularly

important when choosing an appropriate building material.

(3) The rate of rise or fall of a roadway. The grade of a highway is normally expressed as feet per 100 ft. or as meters per kilometer. Ascending grades are expressed in positive numbers while descending grades are expressed in negative numbers. See also *gradient*.

graded lease: See *graduated lease*.

graded tax: Increasing tax rates with increasing levels of taxable income.

gradient: The slope of a surface inclination normally expressed as a percentage. The gradient is determined by dividing the surface change by the length of the surface:

$$\text{Gradient} = \frac{\text{Surface elevation change}}{\text{Length of the surface}}$$

For example, if the change in elevation of a surface if 40 ft. over a distance of 200 ft., then the gradient is 0.2 or 20% (40/200).

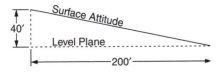

graduated lease: A rental stipulating a varying rental rate. Rental rates are determined tied to periodic appraisals or an inflation index. The provision is more common in long-term leases. For example, a 10-year graduated lease may have annual rent increases of 5%.

graduated payment mortgage (GPM): A special kind of fixed rate mortgage (conventional mortgage) in which the monthly payments are less in the beginning years and more in the later years. After five years it usually levels off for the remainder of the loan payment.

Under the level annuity, fully-amortized mortgage, each month's payment is the same. The obvious advantage is that when securing a mortgage the borrower is assured of a level or constant mortgage payment. However, for some purchasers the required monthly payment is so high that a lender will not make the loan simply because the borrower's income is insufficient. With a GPM, monthly mortgage payments start at an amount less than would be required under a level annuity payment and increase periodically over the life of the mortgage. Therefore, the borrower can finance a larger purchase than if the monthly payment were level throughout the life of the mortgage. FHA has a number of GPM programs currently available.

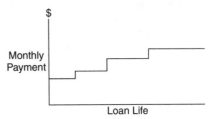

Graduate, Realtors Institute (GRI): A designation awarded to Realtors who complete a prescribed course of real estate study.

grandfather clause: Provision contained in a new policy that exempts from the rule an individual or business engaged in the real estate activity coming under regulation.

grant: To transfer a property title by deed or other instrument to another party. For example, in a closing a property deed is granted to the purchaser of the property.

grant deed: Form of deed used in the transfer of real property. It is somewhat narrower than a warranty deed in terms of covenants and warranties.

grantee: The person named in a deed who acquires ownership.

grantor: The person giving property or establishing a trust.

gravel: Loose combination of small rocks and pebbles used for a gutter, driveway, landscaping, or roadbed.

grazing rights: The right to allow livestock to graze on a certain range or grazing lands. Grazing rights can be obtained through a lease or by contractual agreement stipulating the period of time and the number of livestock that will be permitted to graze on subject properties.

green lumber: Lumber that has not had adequate time to dry and be seasoned. Green lumber may actually appear green, and can later warp as well as being more difficult to work with including cutting and nailing.

grid:

(1) Series of intersecting bars, wires, or supports as in a grating or supports in a dropped ceiling.

(2) Series of intersecting lines dividing a map or chart into equal sections.

gross area: The total floor area of a structure, in square feet, measured from the outside walls not adjusting for the actual interior useable area. Useable area is the difference between the gross area of a structure and the space consumed by internal structures, such as staircases, heating and cooling equipment, structural supports, and other erections consuming space within a building.

Gross Domestic Product (GDP): Measure of the value of all goods and services produced by the economy within its boundaries and is the nation's broadest gauge of economic health. GDP is normally stated in annual terms, though data are compiled and released quarterly. The government gives a preliminary figure every quarter and revises it twice. GDP is often a measure of the state of the economy. For example, many economists speak of recession when there has been a decline in GDP for two consecutive quarters. The GDP in real terms and percentage change from the same quarter a year earlier is a useful economic indicator. An expected growth rate of 5% in real terms would be a healthy sign of the economy. Unfortunately, there is no way of measuring whether we are in a recession or prosperity currently, based on the GDP measure. Only after the quarter is over can it be determined if there was growth or decline. In addition, an increasing number of analysts say the GDP criteria for a recession are no longer valid. Experts look upon other measures such as housing and construction activity, unemployment rate, industrial production, durable orders, corporate profits, and retail sales to look for a sign of recession.

gross income multiplier: Method to compute the price of an income-producing property by dividing the asking price (or market value) of the property by the current gross rental income. For example, if the current gross rental income = $30,000 and the asking price is $300,000, then the gross income multiplier is 10.

A property in a comparable neighborhood may be valued at "12 times annual gross." Therefore, if its annual gross rental income amounts to $30,000, the value would be taken as $360,000.

This method should be used carefully because different properties have different operating costs which must be considered in computing the value of a property. See also *gross rent multiplier.*

gross leasable area (GLA): Building's total floor area, in square feet, designed for tenant leasing. The GLA in normally calculated from the outside walls to any existing room partitions.

gross lease: A rental in which the lessor pays all operating costs such as taxes, utilities, insurance, and maintenance. It is usually a short-term lease and a common arrangement. Typically there is no provision for rent increases because of its near term nature. An example is a landlord of an office building paying all the insurance, maintenance, taxes, and utilities out of the tenant's gross rent receipts.

gross rent multiplier (GRM): The percentage of the selling price of property to its gross rental income. It is used to value an income-producing property. For example, if the selling price of property was $500,000 and the gross rental income was $100,000, the GRM would be 5 times.

ground floor: The floor of a building closest to the building grade. Normally, the ground floor of a building is the first floor; however, a ground floor can sometimes be located between the first floor and the basement or cellar of a building. In all cases, the ground floor is part of the useable area of a building.

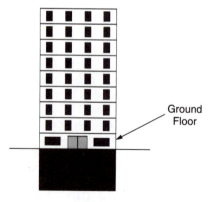

Ground Floor

ground lease: A long-term lease (such as 20 years) of only land.

ground rent: The portion of property income due to the ground value itself. It is used in a few states whereby an individual can own a structure and rent the ground to occupy a plot of land.

grout: Cement or mortar with a high moisture content developing it into a slurry solution allowing the ability to be poured or pumped into crevices, fissures, and masonry cracks and joints. Grout is widely used for filling in and providing a smooth surface material for any type of masonry or ceramic material including wall and floor tiles.

growing equity mortgage (GEM): A mortgage on which the interest rate is constant, but the payments are structured to increase, so the loan is paid off much earlier.

guarantee: A financially binding guaranty assuring an obligation or contractual agreement will be fulfilled by the guarantor.

guaranteed payment loan: An assurance a loan's financial obligation will be secured by a third party. For example, Smith has secured mortgage insurance to indemnify the mortgage on his home in the event of his demise.

guaranty: A promise to uphold a guarantor's contractual or financial responsibility in the even of default. For example, a person seeking to secure a loan is required to provide a third party's signature to guaranty the loan in the event of default.

guardian: Person serving as a property administrator (e.g., managing the property) for someone who is incompetent due to a mental or physical deficiency.

guardian's deed: Used to convey property of a minor or legally incompetent person.

guideline lives: Expected period of benefit used to depreciate business property, plant, and equipment. The guidelines may be developed by the industry or Internal Revenue Service (IRS). For example, under the modified accelerated cost recovery system (MACRS), the IRS requires specified lives to be used for depreciation for tax purposes depending upon the class of property (e.g., an office building has a longer life than an automobile).

gunite: Trademark name for shotcrete.

gutter: Metal or wood channel attached immediately below or along the eaves of a building for the purpose of channeling rainwater away from the structure. The gutter prevents rain runoff from running down the sides of a building and possibly either eroding or penetrating the structure's foundation.

habendum clause: The clause in a deed beginning with the words "to have and to hold" limiting or defining the ownership nature of the estate in the property granted by the deed. Declares the type of ownership conveyed whether it is fee simple or a life estate or some other interest.

habitable room: Room that is fit for living in. The building in which the room is located conforms with the building code and has a certificate of occupancy. Usable for all purposes, but does not include facility rooms such as a bathroom, closets, or storage rooms.

half bath: Room containing a toilet and wash basin, but does not include a shower or bath tub.

handyman's special: House that can be bought at a low price because it is in poor condition. A buyer who is handy may find it attractive because he can personally make the needed repairs without hiring others.

hangout: That portion of a loan collateralized by a leased property extending beyond the expiration date of the lease. For example, a lending institution collaterizes a 20-year loan on a commercial property being leased by a major department store for 15 years. It is estimated the $50,000 portion of the loan remaining after the lease expires will be more than covered by the value of the property.

hard money:
(1) Convertible currency which has wide acceptance. For example, the United States dollar and the Japanese Yen are considered hard money.
(2) Gold or silver coins, as compared to paper currency.

hatchway: An opening with a hinged cover allowing access from one level to another in a structure. Often installed in a roof or the floor of a building to allow the entrance of people and materials to different levels. For example, a ceiling hatchway permits access to an attic for the purpose of storing goods or providing access to perform basic maintenance.

hazard: Condition that affects the probability of losses or perils occurring. An example is possible earthquake or flood damage to a house.

hazard insurance: Insurance that lenders require borrowers to have so as to protect the lender's financial interest in a house. It guards against risks like storms or fires.

header:
(1) In masonry, the stones or bricks that are laid cross ways on a wall provid-

ing support to the horizontal stretcher bricks. The ends of the header bricks are visible in the wall.

(2) A beam providing lateral support to wall joists around an opening such as a window or finishing roof rafters.

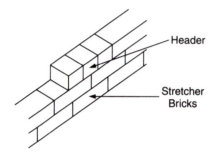

Header

Stretcher Bricks

hearing:
(1) A public procedure performed by an administrative or legislative body to investigate certain matters and encourage an exchange or views as well as to present formal evidence of fact. A hearing is not a judicial proceeding per se, but it can reach an administrative conclusion to be used as a basis for forming an administrative decision. For example, a zoning variance appeal board can have public hearings to encourage an exchange of views and present evidence of fact regarding the effects of re-zoning a certain parcel of property. Based upon the results of the hearings, a decision will be made by the zoning board of appeals as to whether or not a zoning appeal will be upheld, modified, or denied. The results of a hearing can be appealed to a judicial body.

(2) An adversary hearing allows both parties to an issue to present their views.

(3) An ex parte hearing has only one party presenting his or her views relating to some matter.

heating system: System of interconnected pipes, radiators, and/or ducts designed to heat a building utilizing a main heating unit. The system is controlled through a thermostat that regulates the average temperature of the building according to a desired setting. The two most popular energy sources are home heating oil and natural gas although some coal fired units exist. See also *baseboard heating; forced hot air; steam heat.*

hectare: Unit of metric area measurement where one hectare is equivalent to 2.471 acres or 107,637 square feet. For example, a 3.5 hectare parcel of property is equivalent to 8.6485 acres or 265,971 square feet.

heirs: Individuals who are legally entitled to inherit money and property when someone dies.

heirs and assigns: Language commonly used in a fee simple title conveyance. The significance is whether the title is clear and can be passed on to the purchaser's estate including all heirs and those who may have any interest in the estate, the assigns.

heriditaments: Any property that is part of an estate and is real or personal, material or intangible, having actual worth or is worthless and can be directly willed to an heir.

heterogeneous: Mixed assortment of either housing styles in a residential development or mixed zoning uses in an urban development plan. For example, heterogeneous nondevelopment residential area has many different housing architectures resulting from independent contractors building different style houses at different times. Heterogeneous building styles have a lower market value than a homogeneous development concept.

hidden clauses: Ambiguous contractual language that may result in an unsuspecting buyer of real property incurring obligations or risks not clearly evident.

high rise: Building more than six stories high serviced by elevators.

highest and best use: Use of a parcel of land that will produce the greatest current value.

highway easement: The construction of a highway right of way over a privately held parcel of land. Property owners are entitled to compensation for the value of the property usurped by a highway easement. See also *eminent domain.*

hip roof: Roof sloping upward from all four sides of a building with the two longer sides of the roof forming a ridge in the middle.

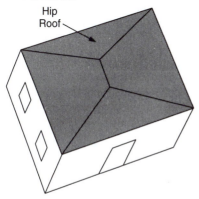

Hip
Roof

historical district: Geographic area that has been designated by local government to have historical importance. The municipality provides various incentives including tax breaks to rehabilitate and preserve the area. The district has historical structures (buildings) that will likely attract visitors. Examples are the historical district in Williamsburg, Virginia; Galveston, Texas; or Charleston, South Carolina.

historical structure: Building recognized because of its history, such as the Booth theater in Washington, DC. The demolition of historical buildings is not permitted. Historical building modifications are regulated if the building has been designated or given medallion status.

hold back: Portion of a construction loan withheld by a lender from a contractor until all construction work is satis-

factorily completed or sufficient space is rented in a floor loan. The holdback payment is usually large enough to prevent the contractor from making a profit, but still allowing enough funds to compensate subcontractors and suppliers. For example, a contractor acquired a construction to complete a $200,000 home construction project. The bank providing the construction loan had a $25,000 holdback provision until the home received a certificate of occupancy.

hold harmless clause: A contractual clause where one party assumes a liability risk for another. Thus, a hold harmless clause effectively indemnifies the named party from any liability by transferring the risk to another. For example, Smith agrees to lease a retail store from Jones under the condition that Smith will be held harmless from any structural liabilities.

holder-in-due-course: Legal ruling providing protection to home buyers of defective homes bought from a seller who then sold the contract to a third party.

holding company: Company formed for the purpose of owning securities of one or more real estate corporations and assuming control over their practices and management. The other corporations are generally referred to as subsidiaries. Holding companies control many subsidiaries in different real estate areas.

holding cost of a house: The initial cost of a home plus any expenses for final settlement that are not tax deductible plus capital improvements.

holding funds: Funds that are retained in an account until a certain event occurs. For example, a downpayment on a contract held until full payment is received whereupon the holding funds are credited to the full cost of the purchase and the merchandise is delivered to the purchaser.

holding period: The time period a real estate investment is held. The return is tied to the time period of the investment. The period is used for income tax purposes to determine whether a profit earned or loss incurred is treated as short- or long-term capital gains or losses.

holding period return (HPR): (1) The total return from holding a real estate investment for the holding period of time. The computation follows:

$$HPR = \frac{\text{Rental income} + \text{Capital gain (or loss)}}{\text{Purchase price}}$$

(2) For a mutual fund investing in real estate, the return is in the form of: dividends, capital gains distribution, and price appreciation. The annual rate of return, or the holding period return (HPR) in a mutual fund is computed as follows:

$$HPR = (\text{Dividends} + \text{capital gain distributions} + (\text{ending NAV} - \text{beginning NAV}))/\text{Beginning NAV}$$

where NAV = net asset value and (ending NAV − beginning NAV) reflecting price appreciation. For example, assume that a mutual fund paid dividends of $1.00 and capital gain distributions of $.70 per share over the year, and had a price (NAV) at the beginning of the year of $12 that rose to $14 per share by the end of the year. The holding period return (HPR) is:

$$HPR = \frac{(\$1.00 + \$.70 + (\$14 - \$12))}{\$12}$$

$$= \frac{\$3.70}{\$12} = 30.83\%$$

See also *return*.

holdover tenant: Tenant that stays in the leased property after the expiration date of the lease. He can be evicted or given a new rental agreement.

hollow wall: Wall having an air space between the two sides. A hollow wall is often covered with wallboard that is nailed to the wall studs providing an air space between the two sides.

holographic will: Will not meeting all the requirements of a valid will.

home affordability index: Measure of the typical U.S. family's ability to buy a home, published by the National Association of Realtors. When the Index measures 100, a family earning the median income has exactly the amount needed to purchase a median-priced, previously owned home, using conventional financing and a 20% down payment. For example, an index of 140.9 means that half the families in the nation have at least 140.9% of the income needed to qualify for the purchase of a home with a median price of, say, $107,400.

Some experts maintain that every one-point increase in the home mortgage interest rate results in 300,000 fewer home sales.

home equity credit line loan: See *homeowner's equity account*.

home-equity loans: Loans based on the equity of the home. Interest payments on home-equity loans are tax deductible. They come in two varieties: the traditional second trust deed (mortgage) and the home-equity line of credit.

The advantages of home equity loans include:

(1) Low interest rates because (a) the loan is secured by a house, and (b) it usually bears variable rates.

(2) No loan processing fees. There is no need to go through a loan application and incur fees each time money is borrowed.

(3) Convenience. A check may be written only when money is needed. Interest is charged only on the amount borrowed.

Pitfalls of home equity loans include:

(1) *High points.* Points imposed on a home equity loan are based on the amount of the credit line, not on the amount actually borrowed. Many home equity loans have no caps on interest rates.

(2) *Long payback period.* It is convenient to have to pay a small minimum amount each month, but stretching out the loan payback period usually means higher interest rates.

(3) *High balloon payments.* Some loans require a large balloon payment of the principal at the end of the loan period.

(4) *Risk of home loss.* Unlike other loans, there is risk of losing a home. It may be difficult to sell the home fast enough and at a fair market value to be able to meet the balloon.

(5) *Frivolous spending habit.* One may get into the habit of spending on unnecessary things.

home inspector: A certified professional who inspects homes to insure they meet satisfactory construction standards and building codes. A home inspector will examine all pertinent elements of a home including the electrical wiring, plumbing, heating systems, roof, and other structural elements. For example, before purchasing a resale home, the potential homeowner retained the services of a home inspector to provide a report on the general condition of the home.

home inventory: An individual's possessions at his residence, such as furniture. A listing of items and their costs is recommended to obtain proper insurance coverage and as support for insurance reimbursement if a loss occurs.

home loan: See *mortgage; residential mortgage.*

homeowner's association: An organized group of homeowners in a home subdivision, condominium, or cooperative complex who share common concerns regarding environmental code enforcement, maintenance issues, and organizing social events. Homeownership is a requirement in order to belong to a homeowners association, but a homeowner's fee may be charged in order to officially become a member.

In certain instances, a homeowner's association may be organized by the developer or builder of the condominium, cooperative or planned unit development. Several states statutorily regulate homeowner associations and the participation of developers.

homeowner's fee: Fee charged homeowners to belong to a homeowner's association that may include the cost of maintenance, recreation, or other services. Homeowner's fees may be levied on a regular or irregular basis.

homeownership: Residing in a structure that the individual owns.

homeowner's insurance policy: A kind of property insurance policy covering the risks of homeowners. Coverages include damage to insured's property or personal property, additional living expenses, personal liability, theft, and medical coverage for others. In computing insurance needs, replacement value (cost to rebuild, excluding land). An insured's minimum protection should be 80% of replacement cost. If the replacement cost requirement is not met, reimbursed loss will be computed using the formula:

$$R = L \times \frac{I}{RV \times 80\%}$$

where R = reimbursement, L = the amount of loss less deductible, I = amount of insurance actually carried, and RV = replacement value.

EXAMPLE: Susan has a home with a replacement value of $200,000 and incurs a $100,000 fire loss. Her insurance was for $150,000.

Insurance reimbursement equals:

$$\$100,000 \times \frac{\$150,000}{\$200,000 \times 80\%}$$

$$= \$93,750$$

There are several kinds of homeowner policies including:

(1) Homeowners-1 (HO-1): referred to as basic coverage, HO-1 provides protection against major property-damage risks such as fire, windstorm, hail, vandalism, explosion, lightening, riot, and smoke. Losses from these perils may be restricted in the amount of coverage. The policy gives protection from certain liability exposures—comprehensive personal liability, damage to property to others, and medical payments.

(2) Homeowners-2 (HO-2): known as the broad form, HO-2 provides broader coverage than HO-1. HO-2 covers major perils that cause property damages such as falling objects, collapse of structures, and freezing of plumbing. It also provides protection from the liability exposures as in HO-1.

(3) Homeowners-3 (HO-3): referred to as special form, it has "all-risk" coverage on the dwelling itself.

(4) Homeowners-4 (HO-4) Renters: it is for those who are renting an apartment or a home. It protects renters' personal property on the same basis as HO-2.

(5) Homeowners-5 (HO-5) Comprehensive: it is the most comprehensive coverage, but it is costly.

(6) Homeowners-6 (HO-6) Condominium: it is similar to HO-4 except it is designed for condominium renters rather than owners.

(7) Homeowners-8 (HO-8): it is for owners of older, remodeled buildings. It has high replacement costs. Coverage is based on actual cash value instead of replacement cost.

home owners warranty (HOW) program: Builder's ten-year guarantee that their workmanship, materials, and construction are up to established standards. The HOW provides reimbursement for the cost of remedying specified defects.

homestead: Legal status conferred by certain states on a homeowner's principal residence. In certain states, homestead status may provide protection against creditor claims or forced land sales providing the homeowner continues to maintain his or her residence there. Homestead status may also qualify the homeowner for a homestead exemption.

home warranties: Warranties issued by contractors, sellers, and real estate agencies that protect home buyers from specified defects in a house as per the contract.

homogenous: Descriptive of the architectural development of property in a certain area. For example, a housing subdivision may use very similar building architecture throughout the development. A local municipal building code may specify a homogenous building design code for the entire town. Thus, all the homes are colonials of a certain style. Homogenous development increases the value of the homes in the area as compared to heterogenous.

horizontal property laws: Body of law relating directly to condominiums and cooperative developments. Most property law provides vertical ownership of property in the sense that property owners own mineral rights as well as air rights to property. Horizontal property laws state that property owners own only the confines of the apartment unit within a condominium or cooperative building complex. Thus, horizontal property laws do not allow property owners to own the land on which their apartment unit is located.

hoskold factor: Used when determining the worth of an annuity that reinvests the amount of recaptured investment (capital) at a risk-free interest rate.

household: Group of people residing in one home, usually consisting of a family.

house poor: Buying more house than a buyer can afford based on his or her income.

house rules: Rules regarding day-to-day use of the premises.

housing code: Established federal, state, or local structural building requirements that have to be adhered to so as to receive certification by the government authority. Housing code enforcement is usually performed at the local level; however, many states have standard housing codes to be followed by all local (e.g., city, county) governments. Further, FHA-financed housing meet specified certain building code dictates. The housing code includes coverage for electrical wiring, insulation, plumbing, and roofing.

housing expenses: All expenses related to maintaining and operating a household. These expenses include the cost of rent or mortgage payments, taxes, utilities, maintenance and structural improvements. During the 1980s, one family homes made up approximately 64% of all housing. As of 1990, owner occupied housing was 64.2% of all housing; however, in the same year average rent payments increased to $374.

The cost of housing has risen in excess of increases in income. In 1982, the median price of a new home was $69,300. In early 1987, this figure had risen to $100,700. If some housing experts are correct, the problem of affordability may prevent half of those under age 30 in 1987 from ever owing a home.

Further, the proportion of income spent on housing is increasing. Current housing expenses consume, on the average, 25% of the family budget, but renters may pay more than 50% of their disposable income on housing.

housing ownership records: Records maintained as evidence of ownership of the home and any of its contents.

housing starts: A measure of actual starts of houses, condominiums, and apartment construction. When an economy is going to take a downturn, the housing sector is the first to decline. The strength in housing starts means not only that the housing industry is healthy, but suggests strength in the overall economy. At the same time, it is closely related to interest rates and other basic economic factors.

Housing starts figures are issued monthly by the Department of Commerce. Housing is a key interest-sensitive sector that usually leads the rest of the economy out of the recession. Also, housing is vital to a broader economic revival, not only because of its benefits for other industries, but also because it signals consumer's confidence about making long-term financial commitments. For the housing sector to be sustained, housing start figures need to be backed by building permits. Permits are considered a leading indicator of housing starts.

Housing and Urban Development Department (HUD): Created by Congress in 1965, the U.S. Department of Housing and Urban Development (HUD) is the agency principally responsible for federal programs relating to housing and urban improvement. HUD's programs include mortgage insurance for home-buyers, low-income rental assistance, and programs for urban revitalization that are developed in conjunction with state and municipal authorities. See also *Urban Development Action Grant.*

Originally, much of the department's efforts were devoted to subsidizing the construction and operation of low and moderate income housing. However, starting in 1982, under the Reagan administration, HUD began emphasizing the rehabilitation of substandard housing and assisting low-income tenants in paying for existing housing, either through direct rent subsidies or through a system of housing vouchers. Other programs included the designation by HUD of certain inner-city areas as "enterprise zones"; businesses that located within these zones would receive some tax and regulatory relief.

hundred percent location: See *one-hundred-percent location.*

hypothecation: Pledging of real estate as security for a loan without giving up its possession.

I.D.E.A.L: An acronym stating that real estate is the I.D.E.A.L. investment. Each of the five letters in IDEAL stands for an advantage to real estate as an investment.

"I" stands for interest deduction. ("I" could mean inflation hedge or income tax benefits). The mortgage interest paid on the first and second residential homes are tax deductible. On the average, real estate is a good hedge against inflation because property values and the income from properties rise to keep pace with inflation.

"D" stands for depreciation. The building on your land depreciates in book value each year and you can deduct this depreciation from your gross income. This is only true for investment property and not residential.

"E" is for equity buildup. This buildup of a capital asset is like money in the bank. As you amortize a mortgage, the value of your equity investment will steadily rise. In the case of income-producing property, this amortization could mean that your tenants help you build your estate.

"A" is for appreciation. Your property value goes up every year, hopefully. Be careful because this is not guaranteed.

"L" is for leverage. When you buy a house you make a down payment, say, 10% and you borrow the balance, say, 90%. You get the benefit of 100% even though you put up only 10% of your own money. You can maximize return with other people's money (OPM). The use of a mortgage and OPM means that you can use small amounts of cash to gain control of large investments and earn large returns on the cash invested.

illiquid: Unable to sell an investment to obtain cash in the short-term without incurring a significant loss. Real Estate is typically not liquid because of the inability to sell property to raise cash quickly. See also *liquid*.

immobility:

(1) Unable to move a structure (e.g., house, office building) so it must stay where it is. Except for mobile homes, property is fixed at a particular site.

(2) Inability of a person to move because he or she is attached in some way to the general locality. For example, a homeowner in New York City may be tied to his or her job and therefore cannot move to another state because of the lack of job opportunities.

impaired credit: Decline in the credit status of a prospective homebuyer.

implicit costs: Also called opportunity cost. The return foregone from an alternative employment of time or facilities. For example, if a building is rented out to a charity for a bingo night for $1,000 but it could have been rented out to a company for $10,000, the return foregone is $9,000.

implied: Something that is inferred, but not explicitly stated. The inference may be deducted from the relevant information.

implied condition: A provision not explicitly stated in an agreement, but considered as an important item. For example, the buyer of a home anticipates it to meet the seller's claims as to condition and use.

implied contract: An agreement occurring from actions of those impacted, but not communicated in writing or orally. For example, it is presumed that a real estate agent will perform his or her obligations according to the responsibilities assumed.

implied easement:
(1) Easement resulting from law such as the reasonable expectation that a purchaser of one or two homes owned by the seller will be able to use a common driveway after one of the houses is bought. If the seller wishes this not to be the case, it must be explicitly stated.
(2) Property used consistently for many years by someone without challenge from the owner.

implied warranty: Under law, a warranty in effect even if not expressly stated. It provides that real property sold is warranted to be appropriate for sale and is in proper condition even if not stated, there is an express warranty.

important land features: Factors affecting the useability and value of property. Important land features would include whether the land was flat or hilly, cleared or uncleared, high or low elevation, dry or swampy, fertile or rocky. See also *improved land.*

impound account: See *escrow account.*

improved land: Any permanent development that has been made to a parcel of land. Improved land features include whether the land has fruit bearing trees or crops produced by labor, landscaping, or permanent improvements, such as water and sewer, or roads and building structures. Any improvements made to raw land increase its useability thereby increasing its market value. See also *important land features.*

improved property: See *improved land.*

improvement: A capitalized expenditure usually extending the useful life of a building or improving it in some manner over and above the original condition. In contrast, a maintenance or repair expense is not capitalized to the building.

in escrow: The phrase used for the period in which the escrow agent communicates to both the buyer and the seller as to what documents or moneys have to be deposited with the escrow agent to satisfy the terms of the purchase and sale. The items collected include moneys to cover mortgage insurance premiums, taxes, hazard insurance, and title insurance. Title Insurance assures that no other person or entity has an ownership right to the property, confirmation that the seller has obtained an adequate loan to pay the purchase price, the property has been inspected for termites, and the seller's original deed has been obtained.

in lieu of taxes: Payments made instead of taxes. For example, a tax-exempt institution, such as a state government complex of buildings, may make an offsetting in lieu of tax contributory payment to the local government to prevent raising the property tax rate on the local citizenry.

in propria persona: Appearing in person. In propria personal is a formal judicial request to appear personally before the court to plead a particular matter. While it does not prevent an individual from obtaining counsel, it does require that the named individual appear personally rather than having the attorney represent the client before the court. Since an attorney is considered an officer of the court, allowing the attorney to represent the client in abstentia admits the court's jurisdiction which may be prejudicial.

in re: In regards to, in the matter of. Formal judicial method of entitling a matter before it.

in rem: "Against the thing." A legal term describing proceedings against property in contrast to a proceeding against individual parties. For example, because Smith has lost his job, he defaulted on his home mortgage payments. Therefore, the bank providing the mortgage began a court action seeking a foreclosure in rem against the Smith home.

inchoate: An incomplete, unfinished, interrupted right. For example, a wife has an inchoate dower's right to her husband's property that cannot be completed unless she outlives her husband.

income:

(1) Money earned or accrued during an accounting period that results in the increase in total assets.

(2) Items such as rental income.

(3) Revenues arising from the sales of real estate.

(4) The excess of revenues over expenses and losses for an accounting period (i.e., net income) of a real estate business. See also *gross income; income realization; net income; profit; revenue.*

income approach: Also called capitalization approach. A method to value income-producing property based on anticipated future income. Market value equals expected annual income divided by the capitalization rate. For example, a rental property is anticipated to generate future annual income of $50,000. The capitalization rate is 8%. Market value equals $50,000/.08 = $625,000. Approaches to real estate appraisal are the market comparison approach and cost approach.

income producing property: Also called investment property. Real property held by a business for investment potential or in order to earn income by leasing or letting it, rather than for its own use.

income property: Real estate bought and leased to tenants to obtain rental income. See also *income producing property.*

income statement: Also called profit and loss statement. A financial statement depicting a business entity's operating performance and reports the components of net income, including sales of real estate, rental income, operating rental expenses, income from rental operations, and income before tax. The income statement shows the cash flow for an entire accounting period, usually a quarter. The income statement is included in the annual report of the real estate corporation.

income stream: Cash earnings generated from a real estate investment or property. Cash earnings equals cash revenue less cash expenses. The cash earnings may or may not be discounted to its present value by using a present value of $1 table depending on the user's needs and perspective. An example is a prospective buyer of an apartment house or office building who estimates the cash earnings to be generated by considering cash rentals to be received and cash expenses associated with the rental property. In so doing, the prospective owner can estimate what price to pay for the property.

income yield: See *capitalization rate.*

incompetent: Incapable of performing duties because of a lack of knowledge and training. The individual may not possess the qualifications and credentials. For example, a prospective buyer of real estate cannot rely on an incompetent salesperson.

incorporeal property: Legal property rights that do not include possession. Examples of incorporeal property rights are air and mineral rights, riparian rights, easement and access rights.

incumbrance: A right or interest in property held by a third party, which often limits the use and diminishes the value of the property, but usually does not prevent the transferring of title. The more common forms of incumbrance are:

(1) Taxes, water rents and assessments for local improvements that have become liens upon the property to which a contract or conveyance relates.

(2) Mortgages.

(3) Property lease.

(4) Recorded judgments.

(5) Mechanics' liens for work or labor done or material furnished for use on the subject property.

(6) Lis pendens giving notice that an action or proceeding is pending in the courts affecting the title to the property.

(7) Building or other structural encroachments on the property.

(8) Easements.

(9) Restrictive covenants.

incurable depreciation: Occurs when the cost of repairing a component of a building structure exceeds the value of the structure and is therefore uneconomical to perform. For example, because of extensive settling, the foundation of an old home crumbled and had to be replaced. However, the cost of replacing the foundation with the structure on it exceeded the value of the structure. Therefore, it was considered incurable depreciation and the building was condemned and razed.

indemnify:

(1) An agreement to compensate for a loss or damage incurred by an individual or business.

(2) A legal principle in computing the amount of the economic loss reimbursed for destroyed or damaged property.

independent contractor: Self-employed contractor who may perform work on a structure such as residential or commercial property.

indestructibility:

(1) Characteristic of a material or of a design causing it to be extremely durable even under the most extreme circumstances. For example, a bomb shelter is designed to have a high level of indestructibility in order to protect its occupants under the most extreme wartime conditions.

(2) Characteristic of a trust that prevents the invasion of its principal by the trustees while providing a lifetime income to its principal beneficiary with the rest going to the son's children or to the daughter's children in the event the son fails to have children.

index:

(1) A statistical measure stated as percentages of a base period. For example, the Department of Commerce's Consumer Price Index (CPI) is based on 1982–1984 as 100. An index unlike an average, weighs prices changes by the size of the components.

(2) In real estate, the basis to set an adjustable rate mortgage, such as a 6-month certificate of deposit (CD) rate, cost of funds index, or prime rate. See also *price indices*.

index lease: A rental contact in which the tenant's rental is tied to a change in the price level, such as the Gross National Price Deflator.

Index of Leading Economic Indicators (LEI): Indicators reflecting future changes in economic conditions; referred to as the Composite Index of 11 Leading Indicators. This index indicates the direction of the economy in the next six to nine months. It helps to forecast business trends; hence, the reference "leading indicators." The Index consists of 11 indicators, and are subject to revision. This series is calculated and published monthly by the U.S. Department of Commerce. It includes as one element Residential building permits for private housing. Note that gains in building permits signal business upturns.

Index of Residential Construction Cost: Index of the costs to construct residential properties.

indexed loan: A noncurrent loan in which the principal, interest, or maturity is related to a particular index. Therefore, periodic adjustments are necessary to conform to the change in the applicable index. A case in point is an adjustable rate mortgage.

indirect lighting: Form of lighting designed to have 90% to 100% of the emitted light directed upward so that the principal illumination is reflected rather than direct. Indirect lighting is designed to have less glare than direct lighting.

industrial park: Usually a fairly large site zoned and planned for the purpose of industrial development and located outside the main residential area of a city. Industrial parks normally are provided with adequate transportation access including roads and railroads often having the explicit encouragement of local government industrial development agencies.

industrial property: Property that is zoned for industrial use, including manufacturing, research and development purposes, factory office and warehouse space, and industrial parks.

industrial subdivision: See *industrial park.*

industrial tract: Land zoned for industrial use including manufacturing, factory office and warehouse space, research and development. See also *industrial property; industrial park.*

industrial zoning: Category of property zoning that designates property to be used for industrial purposes. Industrial zoning allows manufacturing, research and development purposes, factory office and warehouse space, and industrial parks.

infiltration:
(1) Penetration of water into the earth or through a structure. For example, water infiltrates the basement of a house causing it to be damp.
(2) Air penetrating crevices in a structure.

inflation: Increasing price levels. In inflation, a dollar today is worth more than a dollar tomorrow. Inflation is caused by many factors including excess demand termed demand-pull inflation. Higher material and labor costs called cost-push inflation may be at fault. Excessive government spending and/or borrowing can also be inflationary. All of these factors may interrelate as the cause for inflation. See also *price indices.*

inflation equity: Increase in the value of property caused by inflation. For example, Smith buys a home for $150,000. Because of inflation, the home is worth $200,000 five years later. The inflation equity in the home is $50,000 ($200,000 − $150,000). Inflation equity may be used to acquire a second mortgage or a home equity loan; however, the lender risks losing its equity collateral if the housing market experiences a slowdown and the home's value recedes back to its uninflated equity value.

information reporting: Income reporting to the Internal Revenue Service using form 1099 stating income earned. For example, an employing real estate broker uses form 1099 to report commissions earned by a real estate salesperson to the IRS and to the individual.

ingress: Entrance or path to a land parcel. See also *egress.*

inharmonious: Inappropriate and possibly harmful use of land. For example, a factory located on the shore of a river discharges toxic pollutants into the waterway.

inherit: Obtaining money and/or property from a deceased person whether by will or not.

inheritance: Personal property or real property that are passed on to heirs upon one's death.

inheritance tax: State tax based on the value of property received through inheritance. The tax is paid by the recipient not the estate. See also *estate tax.*

initial payment: The down payment on the price of a piece of real estate. For example, it is customary to make a down payment of 10% of the value of a real estate parcel upon signing the purchase agreement.

injunction: A court order issued to a defendant in an action either prohibiting or commanding the performance of a defined act. A violation of an injunction could lead to a contempt of court citation: There are many different types of court ordered injunctions; however, the most frequently used are the permanent, preliminary, and temporary injunctions.

inner city: The central core of an urban area. The inner city contains the major commercial center, termed the central business district (CBD). Close to the inner city are also some of the poorest demographic groupings of the urban area's population characterized by poor housing and high crime rates.

inside lot: A building lot surrounding on both sides by other building lots.

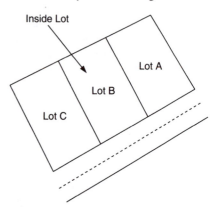

inside trim: See *interior trim.*

inspection: An on-site examination of a structure to ensure all building codes are met, and that it is in satisfactory condition. Often a real estate purchase contract will be subject to a satisfactory on site inspection. A home can be inspected by a professional home inspector.

installment land sales contract: An installment sale of land whereby the seller accepts a mortgage from the purchaser to complete the conveyance. After the mortgage has been satisfied, the deed is conveyed to the purchaser. In an installment land sales contract, the property deed is acquired after all installment payments have been completed. See also *contract for deed.*

installment note: Obligation requiring payments of interest and principal at periodic dates, usually monthly. Interest equals the balance of the loan at the beginning of the period multiplied by the interest rate. The principal reduction equals the cash payment less the interest charge.

installment sales:

(1) A sale of real estate involving periodic cash receipts. This is different from an immediate cash sale.

(2) A way to sell and finance property by which the seller keeps title but the buyer takes possession while installment payments are being made. The gain is taxed while the mortgage principal is collected.

(3) Transaction with a predetermined contract price in which payments are made on an installment basis over a period of time.

institutional lender:

(1) Large financial firm that uses depositors' money to lend to borrowers. Examples are commercial banks and savings and loan associations. Mortgages are a common form of financing. There are stringent government regulations over the activities of institutional lenders.

(2) Financial intermediaries who invest in deeds of trust and mortgages, and hold them in their own portfolio.

instrument: A legal document, such as a contract, deed, will, lease, or mortgage agreement that stipulates the rights, duties, and commitments of those involved. It is a formal notice of an agreement and is evidential in nature.

insulating board or fibre board: A board made of wood-related materials and covered with a binder primarily designed to provide high quality thermal insulation. There is a wide variety of manufactured products termed fibre board. These include acoustic board, insulating board, particle board, peg board, softboard, and others.

insulation:

(1) Material (e.g., fiber glass) used to block or restrain something from entering a house, apartment, or other structure. For example, material may be placed in a house's attic to hinder cold or hot air from entering the rooms. Insulation may also be used for noise.

(2) Person protecting himself from risk or negative consequences, such as by taking out homeowner's insurance.

insurable interest: A relationship with a person, thing, or item that is the foundation of an insurance policy. One having an insurable interest has a financial stake in preserving the insured person or property. An example is a wife having an insurable interest in her husband's real property.

insurable title: A property title evidencing ownership such as provided in an abstract of title. There are no contingent liabilities or prior unresolved ownership claims.

insurance agreement: Contract containing provisions of the insurance policy specifying who the parties are, what is and what is not covered, premium amounts and due dates, deductibles, time period, ceilings, kind of property, location of property, assignments allowed (if any), and so on.

insurance coverage: Categories and limits for perils insured against.

insurance programs: Insurance furnishes an important tool in satisfying the financial objectives of people or a business entity. The type and amount of insurance varies with age, property, rental income, and requirements of a person. Insurance is designed as a "replacement." For example, homeowners coverage indemnifies the costs of theft, accident, or fire.

insured loan: A loan indemnified against default by the borrower. Such loans may be a mortgage loan insured by a standard mortgage insurance policy or by

FHA mortgage insurance. In the event of the death or default of the borrower, the mortgage insurance policy will either pay the mortgage principal entirely, or continues making payments.

insured mortgage: See *insured loan.*

insurer: An insurance company or underwriter. An insurance policy is a legal instrument assuming the risk of loss for stated perils to real property in exchange for insurance premiums paid.

intensity of development: Square footage of space a parcel of land has.

intensive margin: Property highly leveraged. An example is when a landlord buys an apartment house paying a minimum cash payment down (e.g., 10%), and the balance on mortgage.

inter alia: Among other things. Inter alia is an ancient method of referring to statutes without reciting all of their provisions.

interest deduction: Interest deductible for taxes paid by the taxpayer. It is an itemized deduction on Form 1040 (individuals) or Form 1120 (corporations). An example is interest paid on a home mortgage for a first or second home.

interest rate: The rate, usually expressed annually, charged on money borrowed or lent. The interest rate may be variable or fixed. The higher the risk, the higher the interest rate. Mortgage interest rates are important to prospective home buyers. See also *discount rate.*

interest (rate) risk: Effect on the market price of houses as interest rates change. For example, when mortgage interest rates rise, the prices of houses tend to fall. See also *risk.*

interim loan: A loan that is to be replaced by a permanent loan. See also *bridge loan; construction loan.*

interim use: Temporary use of property until a formal zoning ruling is reached overturning it. Interim use is a form of nonconforming use of property.

interior trim: Interior building trim surrounding windows, doors, and baseboards. Interior trim is both decorative and functional. It comes in several different styles and serves to finish the adjoining surfaces between window casements and doorway edges as well as other surfaces, such as baseboards and stairwells.

interlocutory decree: An interim or provisional court decree, which is not final and can be reversed or amended, normally issued to direct additional proceedings prior to issuing a final decree. For example, an interlocutory decree is issued by a court to postpone a contested property matter until a competency hearing is held for an elderly person seeking to sell real estate in a sale being challenged by the estate's heirs and assigns.

intermediation: A court order on an issue directly related to the immediate action.

Internal Rate of Return (IRR): Real annual return on a real estate investment. It equates the initial investment with the present value of future net cash inflows from the investment. The IRR can be determined by using a financial calculator or software.

Internal Revenue Code: U.S. tax law that consists of regulations and rules to be followed by taxpayers. The Internal Revenue Code of 1954 is continually revised and amended over time.

Internal Revenue Service (IRS): Branch of the federal government responsible for collecting taxes including personal and corporate. The IRS administers tax rules and regulations, and investigates tax irregularities. Criminal prosecution may be made by the IRS for tax fraud through the U.S. Tax Court.

inter vivos: Transactions taking place between individuals who are alive rather than when one of the parties is either dead (e.g., estate) or is contemplating death. For example, a deed may transfer ownership in land while the people are living. Another example is an inter vivos trust set up by the mother for the daughter's benefit.

international architecture: A style of architecture originating in Europe in the 1920s. The international architecture design was very functional and emphasized buildings constructed of steel, reinforced concrete, and glass. The houses had smooth white surfaces with very large integral wall windows and no decoration. Also called the Bauhaus style, their functionality emphasized that "less is more." In many ways, international architecture was a reaction to the highly decorated houses of the Victorian period.

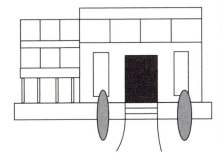

International Association of Assessing Officers (IAAO): Founded in 1934 and located in Chicago, IL with a 1993 membership of 8,300, the IAAO seeks to ameliorate assessment standards as well as to perform ongoing property assessment research. The association maintains a 10,000 volume library housing materials on tax administration, appraisal, land economics, land use, and local government standards. The IAAO conducts educational programs and offers seminars. It also awards professional designations and task forces on various professional subjects. It pub-

lishes the bimonthly *Assessment Digest* and the monthly *Assessment and Valuation Legal Reporter.*

International Right of Way Association (IRWA): Founded in 1934 and located in Gardena, CA with 1993 membership of 9,000, the IRWA is a professional association of appraisers, attorneys, engineers, negotiators, property managers, title examiners, and others having interests in the purchase of public rights of way for the construction of highways, utility rights of way and other public construction purposes. In addition to presenting awards and offering scholarships, the IRWA offers educational programs, seminars, and institutes on right of way negotiation strategies, real estate appraisal, property management, public relations, right of way valuation, transportation, and utilities. The IRWA publishes the bimonthly *Right of Way.*

Interstate Land Sales Full Disclosure Act: A federal act requiring potential purchasers and lessees of undeveloped land be provided with all necessary information required to make an informed decision regarding the desirability of the land being considered prior to making any purchase or lease decisions. The purpose of the Interstate and Land Sales Full Disclosure Act is to provide full consumer information.

interval ownership: See *time sharing.*

intestate: A person who dies without a will and having unknown intentions regarding his estate. In such a case, a court administrator is typically appointed to act as an executor in distributing any real estate. See also *executor/executrix.*

inure: To benefit an individual with property rights. For example, as a result of years of notorious and continuous adverse possession, the title to the property inured to the occupant.

inventory:
(1) A detailed list of property.

(2) The goods of a business, such as houses by a builder.

inventory checklist: List of records kept of what is owned by an individual such as the deed to a house and the title to land.

inverse condemnation: A legal action against government when property rights have been compromised or usurped by a government activity without a formal condemnation or eminent domain procedure. For example, the state constructs an interstate highway on the edge of an individual's property and blocks the view of the ocean because of the erection of fences and signs. The property owner institutes an inverse condemnation action to recover the loss in property value sustained by the construction of the expressway.

investment:

(1) A capital asset.

(2) An expenditure to buy property and other capital assets that generate revenue.

(3) Securities of real estate companies.

investment analysis: Analysis of the risks and rewards to an individual in making a particular property investment. Investment analysis considers the cost of the original investment, the investment return over a period of time, the suitability of the investment and the probability of success. Investment analysis requires many financial methods including:

(1) Break-even formulas

(2) Capitalization rate

(3) Cash flow ratios

(4) Cost of capital

(5) Cost of credit

(6) Future (compound) value

(7) Housing-affordability measures

(8) Payback period

(9) Present value

(10) Repairs and maintenance ratios

investment life cycle: Time interval between buying a real estate investment and selling it. A sound way to determine the return from a real estate investment is over its life. For example, if land was bought on February 15, 19X2, and later sold on February 15, 19X5, its life cycle is three years.

investment property: Property acquired for the purpose of value appreciation, including the possibility of earning additional income such as rental income.

involuntary alienation: Loss of property through attachment, condemnation, foreclosure, sale for taxes or other involuntary transfer of title. For example, as a result of losing his job, Smith's home was foreclosed by the bank and he was involuntarily alienated.

involuntary lien: A lien on property such as for the nonpayment of real estate taxes or mechanic's lien for repairs to the home without the consent of the owner, created by operation of law.

Inwood annuity factor: Method used by appraisers and investors to evaluate a level of payment income stream for a fixed period of years predicated on a specific interest rate. The formula used for the Inwood annuity factor is $1 - (1 + i)^n/i$ where i = the interest rate and n = number of periods the income is being received. For example, a lease pays \$400 per month for 5 years after which it expires. At an interest rate of 9%, the present value (PV) of the lease is:

$$PV = \$400 \times \text{Inwood annuity factor}$$

$$\text{Inwood annuity factor} = 1 - 1/(1 + i)^n/i$$

Where n = 5 years and i = 9%.

$$\text{Inwood annuity factor} =$$

$$1 - 1/(1 + .09)^5 \backslash .009 = 38.896$$

$$PV = \$400 \times 38.896$$

$$= \$15,558.40$$

I persona: I am the person. The person himself/herself. The actual person.

ipso facto: The result of an act or a fact.

irrevocable: Something that cannot be taken, returned, or revoked. An example is an irrevocable trust formed by a person giving her real estate to a trust administrator.

irrigation system: An agricultural technique of supplying water to land to sustain the growth of crops. Developing irrigation systems is an ancient practice being used as early as 5000 BC along the banks of such regularly flooding rivers as the Nile, by digging channels to extend the area covered by the flood. Diversion dams and water-lifting machines permitting the irrigation of lands lying above those normally reached by floodwaters were developed very early. Modern irrigation systems are still based on these two key engineering innovations.

Water distribution systems are of two broad types: surface and closed-conduit distribution systems. In surface irrigation systems, the entire land surface may be covered with water (flood irrigation), or the water may be restricted to small ditches called furrows or rills (furrow irrigation). Both flood and furrow irrigation are used although the effectiveness of water absorption by the soil is improved if the fields are graded to a uniform slope.

Closed-conduit irrigation systems use pipes to distribute water over wide areas or to the ground area around each plant. These systems can apply water uniformly, and they permit frequent light irrigations that maintain the desired level of moisture in the soil. Sprinkler systems distribute water by pumping it through a network of pipes that are either laid on the ground or lifted above the field.

The major problems of irrigation systems are increases in salinity as the water table begins to rise in areas not having good drainage. Naturally occurring salt can concentrate in irrigated fields eventually presenting a threat to the plants being cultivated.

island zoning: See *spot zoning*.

Italian architecture: Style of architecture introduced into America prior to the Civil War and modeled after Renaissance country homes in northern Italy. They were usually relatively large brick houses. Italian architecture was characterized by having an off-center square tower and a flat roof with heavy overhanging eaves supported by braces.

jalousie: Window having several overlapping glass louvers that are installed in a common window frame and pivot synchronously as a window lever or crank operating device, installed at the bottom of the frame, is turned. The lower edge of each glass louver swings outward as the window is opened.

jamb: The vertical elements of a door or window frame which provide vertical support to the overall frame.

Door
Jamb
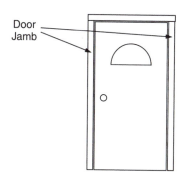

jeopardy: Danger, hazard, risk, or peril. For example, jeopardizing a piece of property by pledging it as collateral for a loan.

jetty: Projecting structure or part of a building. For example, a home was built with balconies jutting out from the sides of the building or a large rock formation constructed out into the ocean from the shoreline to preserve the beach.

J factor: Factor employed by real estate agents or appraisers to determine the change needed in operating income to obtain a desired rate of return. It is used to evaluate income-producing property. The factor is determined after considering the location of the property, rental, similar properties, and cost of maintaining.

joinder: Any of several types of legal joinders whereby one or more parties unites with or joins other parties in a legal action or proceeding even though the party may not be a direct part of the action or proceeding. A third party has a supervisory interest in an action, but does not have a direct interest to the action. For example, a guardian is appointed by the courts to oversee the property interests of a minor. The minor agrees to sell a parcel property to another party and the guardian enters into a joinder agreement approving the sale of the property. Examples of legal joinders include collusive joinder, compulsory joinder, joinder in demurrer, joinder in issue, joinder in pleading, joinder of claims, joinder of defendants, joinder of parties, joinder of remedies, and permissive joinder.

joint: Combined action of two or more people either for or against something. In real estate, used to indicate a common property ownership interest. Joint is also used to indicate a shared liability in terms of a contractual relationship.

joint note: Note having more than one maker. If one or more of the makers default on the note, all the makers are sued jointly, rather than just one or all, to make restitution.

joint ownership: Ownership of real estate in which at least two or more individuals have equal ownership. If a member of the group dies, the property is transferred to the survivor(s). For example, a husband and wife may jointly own a home. See also *joint tenancy.*

joint and several liability: Two or more people have a legal duty that can be enforced against them by joint action, against all members, and against themselves as individuals. For example, a bank can require repayment from any and all of those who have borrowed to buy real estate property. Each borrower is responsible for the entire debt, not only the percentage share. For example, Roberta and Joel are general partners. The partnership borrows $500,000 from a bank agreeing to joint and several liability. If there is a default, the bank can collect the balance of the $500,000 from either party.

joint and several liable lease: A lease having two or more joint lessees who share a common liability with a lessor. Under a joint and several liable lease the lessor may demand the full terms of the lease from one or all of the lessees and not a prorated share of the lease. For example, Smith and Jones sign a joint and several liable lease to lease a building at the rate of $1,000 per month. Smith defaults on the lease, and Jones is responsible to make the $1,000 monthly payments on the lease.

joint tenancy: A type of property co-ownership of two or more individuals to whom real property is deeded and who together have an undivided interest in it as a whole. There is only one title to the whole property. Upon the death of a joint tenant, that person's interest does not descend to his or her heirs or pass by will. Rather, the entire ownership remains in the surviving joint tenant(s). In other words, there is simply one less owner. A joint tenant can be in exclusive possession of the property or he or she can lease his or her interest to a third party without affecting the nature of the joint tenancy. Such lease will terminate upon the death of the lessor joint tenant, with the surviving joint tenants taking the interest thereon. Generally, if a joint tenant dies, the survivors(s) obtain the property, also called joint tenancy with right of survivorship.

For example, Jae and Chung are the joint tenants of a building. Each own one half of the whole building. Upon Jae's death, Chung will own the whole property, and vice versa.

joint tenancy with right of survivorship: Joint tenancy in which the death of a joint tenant (one owner) means the surviving tenant becomes the sole owner of the real property.

joint venture: Joining together of two or more business entities or persons in order to undertake a specific business venture in real estate. A joint venture is not a continuing relationship such as a partnership, but may be treated as a partnership for income tax purposes.

joist: One of a series of parallel beams directly supporting a floor or roof. Joists can be made out of wood, steel or steel reinforced concrete. Joists are in turn supported by other beams or bearing walls.

judgment:
(1) A final ruling on some aspect formed after all the facts have been taken into account.
(2) A judicial ruling in which the rights and claims of the parties have been considered.
(3) In Real Estate, a court order placing a financial indebtedness on another to pay for a claim. For example, Steve does not meet his rental obligations to Joyce. The court issues a judgment against Steve brought by Joyce.

judgment creditor: An individual for whom a court has awarded a financial judgment against a debtor. For example, a court award makes Smith a judgment creditor against Jones for $2,000.

judgment debtor: An individual against whom a court has placed a financial judgment with a creditor. For example, a court determines that Jones owes Smith $2,000 and makes Jones a judgment debtor.

judgment lien: Court order in which the (judgment) creditor is granted a lien against the property of the (judgment) debtor for the nonpayment of the amount due. Furthermore, this action extends the claim's life as far as the statute of limitations is concerned. For example, Mr. B owes Mr. A $200,000 for the purchase of an office building. Mr. A is granted a judicial order to have a lien on Mr. B's property because of nonpayment.

judicial foreclosure: Property of a defaulted borrower is sold under court order, and the judge must approve the amount received. For example, Fidelity Bank has a first mortgage balance of $100,000 on Mr. X's home. The property is foreclosed because of nonpayment. The property is sold for only $70,000. A deficiency judgment is then entered for the $30,000 balance.

jumbo loans: Loans that differ from conforming loans in that they are above the maximum conforming amount and take into account each lender's own guidelines. Jumbo loans are purchased on the secondary market by Freddie Mac.

junior lien: A lien which is secondary to a senior lien and cannot be paid until the senior lien is satisfied.

junior mortgage: Mortgage placed on a property after a previous mortgage. It can be a second, third, etc. mortgage. A junior mortgage is subordinate to the terms of a previous mortgage. Junior mortgages usually require a premium interest rate. For example Smith, buys a home for $175,000 and obtains a $100,000 first mortgage. In order to enable him to complete the financing for the property, he obtains a $40,000 junior mortgage requiring a $35,000 cash down payment. See also *second mortgage.*

jurat: Certificate of an officer stating that a sworn statement is genuine stating when, where and before whom the statement was sworn. A jurat commonly appears at the bottom of an affidavit.

jurisdiction: Geographical area for which a given governmental agency has authority and responsibility. For example, the jurisdiction of a county court is the county in which it is located.

just compensation: Compensation representing the fair market value of a property taken in an eminent domain action. For example, Jones received $150,000 for his home which was condemned in an eminent domain procedure to make way for a new highway.

Keene's cement: A hard white finishing cement with a fast setting time and a high polish capability. Consisting of anhydrous gypsum plaster and an accelerant, alum, Keene's cement is normally applied over Portland cement often using several coats.

key indication series: See *index of leading economic indicators; economic indicators.*

kicker: An income feature added to a mortgage whereby the mortgagee earns income in addition to the mortgage interest and principal payments. Also called an equity kicker, a kicker allows the mortgagee to participate in income from the mortgagor. For example, an individual buys an office condominium from a corporation selling the office unit. The corporation agrees to provide the purchaser with a mortgage if a kicker is included whereby the corporation would receive 10% of all of the business profits the purchaser would earn.

kick plate:

(1) A metal plate attached to the lower end of a door to prevent marring from people "kicking" the door in order to open it.

(2) A metal plate mounted on the open edge of a stair platform.

laches: The "Doctrine of laches" is the failure to timely assert one's rights or a claim in a given matter. The failure to take action on a timely basis misleads an adverse party that no breach has occurred. For example, an adjacent property owner constructs a roadway across the neighbor's property to gain access to a waterway. Since the neighbor never asserted his property rights in a timely manner, the doctrine of laches prevented the roadway from being withdrawn or receiving compensation at a later period.

lagging indicators: The economic indicators that trail behind aggregate economic activity. Six lagging indicators issued by the government consisting of unemployment rate, corporate expenditures, labor cost per unit, loans outstanding, bank interest rates, and book value of trade inventories. See also *index of leading economic indicators.*

land: Real estate held for productive use or investment. Land is recorded at the acquisition price plus incidental costs including real estate commissions, attorney's fees, escrow fees, title, and recording fees, delinquent taxes paid by the buyer, surveying costs, draining, and grading of the property. The cost of knocking down an old building to clear the land to construct a new building is charged to the land account. Amounts received from selling materials salvaged from the old building reduces the cost of the land. Land is usually presented under the Property, Plant and Equipment section of the balance sheet. However, land bought for investment purposes or as a future plant site is classified under Investments. If land is held by a real estate business for resale, it is shown as inventory. Land is not subject to depreciation because it is not a wasting asset.

land banking: The practice of acquiring land for a future use. For example, a franchising company is projecting rapid nationwide expansion over the next five years. In order to prepare for the expansion, they are currently in the process of land banking property by acquiring sites at the most favorable terms at this time.

land-to-building ratio: Total building area as percentage of total land area. See also *floor-area ratio.*

land contracts: Also called an installment sales contract or contract for deed. A type of creative financing in real estate allowing the seller to finance a buyer by allowing him or her to make a down payment followed by a series of periodic monthly payments of principal and interest. However, title is retained by the seller until the mortgage is paid. This means of financing can also be used to purchase improved land. Rules relating to land contracts differ among states. For instance, some states require that title be passed when a certain percentage of the loan has been paid by the borrower.

land cost: The total cost of purchasing a land parcel. Land cost includes the purchase price, closing costs, commissions, and finance charges.

land development: See *development*.

land lease: A ground lease that includes only the cost of leasing the land for a period of years. Normally, a land lease is valid for an extended period of time anticipating that improvements will be constructed on the property.

land loan: A loan used for acquiring land. Loans used to purchase unimproved land have more risk than a mortgage to purchase improved property. Thus, land loans traditionally have a somewhat higher rate of interest and may require a larger down payment than a standard home mortgage.

landlocked: Parcel of land that is totally surrounded by other land parcels not providing access to a highway. See also *easement; right of way*.

landlocked parcel: See *landlocked*.

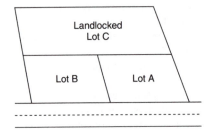

landlord: Person or business who owns property being rented out to tenants.

landlord's lien: Landlord's right to receive the value of the tenant's property to pay for unpaid rents or for damages to the leased premises.

landmark:
(1) A fixed marker or monument, either erected or naturally occurring, which serves as a boundary line for a parcel of land. For example, a stream on the eastern edge of the property serves as the landmark for that side of the property.
(2) A building, site, or historical monument, for example, the Washington Monument.

landowner's royalty: In the mining and petroleum industries, it is a portion of the profit secured from the extracted minerals or oil reserves from the property paid to the property owner. For example, a property owner in Texas and an independent oil company struck oil on the property after signing a contract agreeing to pay a 10% landowner's royalty on all profits secured from the oil recovered.

land reclamation: The process of upgrading unusable land through making physical improvements. For example, swamp land can be drained and filled in order to make it usable. Barren land can be reforested by planting and nurturing seedling trees.

land residual technique: Technique used to estimate how the value of a parcel of land will affect its ability to support a given commercial improvement leaving sufficient residual net income to maintain adequate profitability. The commercial value of the land must exceed its purchase price in order for there to be sufficient residual income. Capital land valuation is determined by capitalizing the residual net income.

Property tax appraisals and condemnation awards normally require the land residual technique. Unimproved land values are determined through this technique and the value of the improvements are added to establish a total improved land value.

In computing land residual value, an appraiser values structural improvements at their cost. Costs associated with the building are deducted from net income. The remaining value is residual to the land.

For example, a new six-unit apartment house generates a net income of $47,000 ($72,000 less $25,000 operating expenses and taxes). The apartment house cost $350,000 to construct and claims a 10% rate of return (8% interest plus 2% depreciation) which is $35,000. Using the land residual technique, the remaining $12,000 ($47,000 − $35,000) is capitalized at an 8% rate of return resulting in a $150,000 land value.

land sale–leaseback: The selling of a parcel of land whereby the original owner agrees to immediately leaseback the property. The advantage of the land sale–leaseback is that the original property owner can realize the capital value of the property while still retaining its use. For example, Smith wants to acquire another commercial piece of property. He agrees to a land sale–leaseback of the land upon which his office building is constructed. He sells the property to Jones agreeing to make rental payments to the new owner while still occupying the office building. Realizing the capital value of the land, he is now able to acquire the second piece of commercial property.

land sales contract: See *contract for deed.*

landscape: Making land more beautiful to look at by adding improvements such as lawns, trees, and bushes. Increases the value of the property.

landscape architect: Individual trained and qualified to develop landscaping designs using the most appropriate plants

on a parcel of land to achieve a particular design effect. A landscape architect may also supervise the implementation of the plant arrangements including their selection.

lands, tenements and hereditaments: An early term used to describe all types of real estate property, improvements to the land, and all rights accruing to the land.

land use intensity: Population per square mile otherwise termed density. The utilization of land in urban areas. Zoning ordinances establish levels of permissible land use intensity in an urbanized environment.

land use map: An official map indicating intensity of land use in a zoned urban area.

land use planning: Activity usually performed by a governmental planning department that makes recommendations for zoning purposes of land utilization based upon demographic and commercial patterns. Land use planning is very important for making population projections, preparing a land use map, preserving environmentally sensitive areas and developing highway rights of way.

land use regulation: Various governmental restrictions and controls placed upon land use in a given jurisdictional area. Land use regulations include zoning and building ordinances, housing codes, and subdivision regulations. The objective of land use regulation is to determine density levels as well as commercial and residential development patterns. Land use regulations consider environmental needs to be a pivotal issue in determining development patterns. These regulations add to the cost of land development.

land use succession: Changes occurring over time in the use of a neighborhood. Several factors contribute to land use succession. In a residential neighborhood, the aging of the residents and the growth and maturity of their children will eventually cause a turnover in the ownership of the housing. Residential neighborhoods bordering business districts may eventually be overwhelmed by the expansion of the business district. Other contributing factors include the physical aging of the building structures leading to obsolescence and eventual abandonment.

land value map: Map delineating property values over a designated area. Land value maps are usually developed by a governmental planning agency.

lap siding: Horizontal wood siding commonly used on the exterior of buildings which overlap each other. See also *clapboard.*

late charge: Fee payable because of late payment. For example, a mortgagor is assessed a $30 late charge by the bank for not paying the mortgage payment when due.

latent: Something that is hidden or overlooked and may be realized at a later time. For example, an individual's name is improperly spelled on a title deed, and the oversight is not noticed until the property is sold many years later. See also *latent defect.*

latent defect: A hidden or overlooked defect that may manifest itself at a later point in time. For example, a defect in a water pipe is not immediately discovered, and it later results in a massive water pipe failure resulting in severe flooding and water damage.

late payment: Payment received after the due date. A penalty and/or interest may be charged on such payment. For example, a bank may charge a penalty of $25 if a mortgage payment is received after the tenth of the month.

lateral: See *lateral support.*

lateral and subjacent support: The right of a landowner to have lateral land support from adjacent properties. The right

of lateral and subjacent support means that an adjacent land owner may not, for example, lower or undermine the soil of his or her property so as to cause a lack of support and subsequent shifting and damage to the subject property.

lath: Originally strips of wood approximately 1 to 1½ inch wide, ¼ to ⅜ inch thick by approximately 4 ft. long which were nailed across the wall studs for the purpose of supporting plaster. Subsequently newer materials, including metal wire mesh, have been introduced for the purpose of providing a foundation for plaster and they are also termed lath or lathing materials.

lawful object: An object or action which is authorized, approved, and not prohibited by law. The concept of a lawful object also implies an ethical quality in that the object under consideration is not only legal, it is also ethical and acceptable by society at large.

layering: Combination of insurance policies on property with each providing an additional increment of coverage exceeding the limits of the preceding policy. For example, policy A adds $70,000, then policy B adds $80,000, and then policy C adds $100,000, and then policy D adds $130,000, for a total coverage of $380,000. In some instances, a person may have to take out several policies from different insurance companies to obtain the total required coverage.

lay of the land: An idiomatic expression indicating the desire of an individual to understand new surroundings and all of its nuances including its quality and character. The derivation of the expression undoubtedly was from an attempt to determine the general location and incline angle of newly discovered property.

lease: Written agreement in which the lessee pays rent to the lessor for the use of real property for a stated time period. An example is the tenant's rental of an apartment or office space.

lease agreement: A contract between a lessor and a lessee to use property for a specified time period at an agreed to rental charge.

(1) *Gross lease:* A total amount of rental dollars from which the landlord must pay all taxes, utilities, insurance, and other costs.

(2) *Month-to-month lease:* There is no formal lease agreement between the landlord and the tenant. Typically, the landlord must provide a one-month notice before canceling the lease.

(3) *Net lease:* A lease in which the tenant must pay all the related property costs including insurance, taxes, utilities, and others.

leased fee: An interest a landlord has in a lease property. See also *percentage lease.*

leased fee estate: A lease contract to possess a parcel of property for a certain period of time. A leased fee estate is a conditional estate conveyance in real property for a specified period of time. The lease permits the lessee to possess, use and enjoy the property for the specified lease period. For example, Smith agrees to lease a home at the rate of $1,200 per month for two years as a leased fee estate.

leasehold: Agreement between the lessee and lessor specifying the lessee's rights to use the leased property for a given time at a specified rental payment. As rental payments are made, rent expense is charged. When the rental is paid in advance, a Prepaid Rent account (Prepaid Expense) is recorded that has to be allocated into expense over the rental period. If the prepayment is for a long-term lease, however, it is recorded as a Deferred Charge and then amortized. The amortization entry for a long-term lease is to charge rent expense and

credit leasehold. See also *leasehold improvement.*

leasehold estate: Possession and use of a property estate by virtue of a lease. There are four types of leasehold estates: estate for years, periodic tenancy, tenancy at will, and tenant at sufferance.

leasehold improvement: Upgrading made by a lessee to leased property. Examples are paneling and wallpapering. These improvements revert to the lessor at the expiration of the lease term. As improvement costs are incurred under an operating lease, the leasehold improvement account is charged. The leasehold improvement is amortized to expense over the shorter of the life of the improvement or the remaining lease term. If there is a lease renewal option and the prospect of renewal cannot be predicted with certainty, the amortization period should be the original lease term rather than the longer possible term. However, the amortization expense on a leasehold improvement is not tax deductible. Leasehold improvement is usually considered an intangible asset, because the lessee does not own the leased property.

leasehold insurance: Insurance coverage provided for an individual having a lease at a favorable rate, one which is less than the market value of the property. The insurance indemnifies the tenant for business losses in the event the landlord cancels the lease because of the occurrence of an insured peril, such as an explosion. The theory is that the loss of the favorable lease is a serious business loss that should be indemnified.

leasehold mortgage: A mortgage collateralized by a tenant's interest, usually structural improvements, in a leased parcel of property. A leasehold mortgage is subordinate to the landlord's land lease since it is a second lien by order of priority on the property. For example, Smith leases a parcel of commercial property. In order to construct a commercial office building, he obtains a leasehold mortgage to provide the necessary financing. The leasehold mortgage is subordinate to the land lease.

leasehold-sandwich: A lessee (tenant) subleases the apartment to a third party. The tenant is now sandwiched between the lessor and the sublessee. In other words, the tenant is acting as a lessee to the landlord, but the lessor to the sublessee.

lease option: An agreement specified in the lease providing the tenant the option to renew the lease for a given time period upon the expiration of the initial lease. Most lease options include the landlord's right to increase the rent upon renewing the lease.

lease with option to purchase: Provision in a lease agreement in which the lessee is given the right to buy the property at the end of the lease term. In many cases, the option price is attractive to encourage acquisition. For example, a tenant may enter into a five-year lease or an apartment with the option to buy it when the lease expires for a predetermined price.

legacy: A gift by will of real property.
(1) *Absolute legacy:* An unconditional and immediate gift.
(2) *Conditional legacy:* The bequest of a gift depends on the occurrence of something happening. For example, the beneficiary will receive the gift upon becoming married.
(3) *Contingent legacy:* A legacy dependent upon the passage of time period such as a person reaching the age of 21. A contingent legacy is tied to an event transpiring.
(4) *Specific legacy:* A specific bequest for a beneficiary. For example, a beneficiary is designated to receive a certain piece of land.

legal age: The age at which one is legally capable of entering into binding contracts, signing a deed and negotiating business agreements. In most states this is the age of majority. Normally this is the age of 18. However, for certain activities, such as drinking alcoholic beverages, the age could be higher or lower in the case of qualifying to obtain a driver's license. A contract, deed, or business agreement is not valid when signed by a minor.

legal description: A description of real property including metes and bounds, government rectangular survey, or lot numbers of a recorded plat. All property deeds have a legal description.

legal name: One's given name at birth including a first name, a possible middle name, and a surname. The legal name must be used to legally sign documents, deeds, or contracts.

legal notice: Method of official notification to an individual or the public that specific event is about to occur. Legal notice is whatever method is legally specified for official notification. Legal notice can include a registered letter, advertisement in a designated newspaper, telegram, or other methods. For example, a homeowner seeks a variance to add a bedroom and a kitchen for the purpose of providing an apartment for a family member. The municipal code specifies the homeowner must provide legal notice to adjacent property owners by registered letter the date the variance hearing will occur.

legatee: Person receiving a legacy from a will. Normally a legatee will receive personal property possibly including real property.

lender: Person who lends money to a borrower at a particular interest rate to be repaid at a later date. See also *lending agreement*.

lending agreement: Contract in which the borrower agrees to the terms of a loan including payment dates, interest rate, total cost of the loan, and late payment fees. See also *Truth-in-Lending Act.*

lessee: Individual paying a rental fee to the lessor for the right to use real property. The two methods used to account for leases by the lessee are the capital lease and the operating lease.

lessor: Owner of real property who gives another the right to use it in return for rental payments. The three types of leases for the lessor are the direct financing lease, the sales-type lease, and the operating lease. See also *lessee.*

let:

(1) *Contracts:* Awarding a contract to the bidder for the property with the best offer.

(2) *Lease:* To lease property to a lessee.

letter of intent: Document between two or more parties indicating a need to take or not take some action, sometimes subject to a previous action taking place. For example, a bank may commit to make a loan dependent on a satisfactory credit rating for the borrower.

level payment income stream: See *annuity.*

level payment mortgage: Each payment made by the borrower is equal each period, usually monthly. Each payment is comprised of principal and interest. Interest is based on the beginning balance. The cash paid less interest represents the reduction in principal.

leverage: Use of borrowed funds to enhance expected returns. It is anticipated that the investment will earn a return exceeding the after-tax cost of borrowing. See also *financial leverage.*

leverage in real estate investing: Use of other people's money (OPM) in an attempt to maximize the return but at high risk. The use of leverage in real estate investing is a way to maximize yield on a small down payment. When building real estate wealth, leverage helps one grow fast without extreme risk. High-

leveraged investing in real estate is particularly beneficial in a highly inflationary environment. The best scenario is when property values increase faster than the interest charges on their borrowed funds.

EXAMPLE: Susan pays a seller $200,000 cash for property. After one year, the property appreciates 15%. The $30,000 is a 15% yield on her investment. However, if Susan put down only 10% ($20,000) in the property and mortgaged the remainder, her return becomes an amazing 150% ($30,000/$20,000). (In this example we've omitted mortgage interest as well as the return on the $20,000 she would have invested elsewhere plus any rental income she would have earned from the property.)

Property values can also decrease such as that which occurred in California in the early 1990s. A risk is negative cash flow in which income from highly leveraged property may be inadequate to pay operating expenses, interest, and principal. See also *leverage.*

levy: The imposition or collection, usually by legal or governmental authority, of an assessment of a specified amount. An example is a tax assessment on real estate.

liability: Amount payable in dollars (e.g., notes payable) or future services to be rendered (e.g., contractor services payable). The party having the liability is referred to as the debtor. There are various types of liabilities in connection with real estate. An actual liability actually exists and has a stated amount (e.g., accounts payable). An estimated liability also actually exists, but the amount has to be predicted (e.g., estimated tax liability). These liabilities are presented in the balance sheet. A contingent liability is one that may or may not become due (e.g., a pending lawsuit). It is only footnoted in the real estate company's financial statements.

liable: Legal responsibility for something. For example, an owner of commercial property (e.g., restaurant) is legally obligated for damages on that property (e.g., restaurant patron falls and breaks his leg because of a wet floor).

libel: Written statements about a person or business that are malicious, unfounded, and damaging. It is the basis for legal action. See also *slander*.

license: Document issued by a public or private institution to perform some activity according to legal requirements. There is usually a license fee. An example is a real estate license.

licensee: Individual who lawfully retains a real estate salesperson or brokers license. A licensee has satisfactorily passed a real estate salesperson's or broker's license examination and meets the real estate salesperson's or broker's license state legal requirements. In many states, a real estate salesperson's license is retained by the employing real estate broker.

license examination: Formal written examination given in every state to those people being the age of majority and qualifying to be a real estate salesperson or broker. The examination can consist of multiple choice, fill-in, or essay questions on general matters concerning the real estate law, practices, and profession as well as mathematics and general logic. Upon successfully passing the examination, the individual will receive a real estate salesperson or brokers license depending on the type of examination taken and the applicant's qualifications. See also *license laws*.

license laws: Laws enacted by every state governing the activities and requirements of real estate salespeople and brokers. Upon satisfying the necessary age and residency requirements and satisfactorily passing a license examination, a real estate salesperson or

broker license is issued to the individual. The license will state the name of the individual, the date when the license was issued and what type of license it is, and often in the case of a real estate salesperson, the business address of the real estate broker with whom the individual is associated.

lien: Claim of a party, usually a creditor, to hold or control the property of another party to meet a debt or liability. It allows the creditor to sell the collateralized property if a default occurs. A mortgage is a lien upon property in the event of default.

lien, junior: Subordinate lien to a previous lien. Generally attached after a previous, and therefore senior, lien has been attached to property. In the event of a foreclosure action where there are insufficient proceeds to cover all the claims against the property, a junior lien can be satisfied only after all senior liens are satisfied.

lien period: Time period in which one may carry out a lien on property.

lien release: A written document terminating the terms of a lien through payment of all financial obligations. A lien release is given by the lienor, the one holding the lien, to the lienee, individual whose property is subject to the lien, as evidence of the lien's satisfaction.

lien theory state: A mortgage provides the right to the bank to have a lien on the financed property with the borrower having title to the property.

life estate: A freehold equity in an estate, restricted to the duration of the life of the grantee or other stipulated individual. See also *life tenant*.

life of loan cap: An upper limit on the interest rate that can be charged in a variable rate mortgage over its life. For example, a variable rate loan is initially offered at 7% loan rate, and its interest rates can be adjusted every three months up to a loan cap of 11%, or 400 basis points.

life tenant: The grantee who is the tenant of a life estate. When the tenant dies, the estate goes back to the grantor. For example, President Eisenhower and his wife, Mamie, were life tenants of the Gettysburg farm life estate granted by the U.S. government. Upon their deaths, the property reverted to the U.S. government as a historical site. See also *life estate.*

like-kind property: Property that is similar in characteristic and when exchanged is a nontaxable transaction. However, any property that is not like-kind, such as cash (boot), is taxed. As a result, a gain is not recognized for tax purposes until the property received is later sold.

limited liability: A liability that does not go beyond the owner's investment in a real estate business. A corporation and limited partners have this benefit. The stockholders of a corporation usually have limited liability; they risk only their investment in the business. Sole proprietors and general partners have unlimited liability. See also *partnership; unlimited liability.*

limited partner: Member of a partnership whose liability for partnership debts is limited to the amount invested in the partnership. A limited partner is prohibited from taking active part in the management of the partnership. Limited partnerships may in some cases provide tax benefits. See also *general partner.*

limited partnership: A business in which one or more persons, with unlimited liability, called general partners, manage the partnership. There are also limited partners who contribute capital, but do not manage the operations nor do they have liability for partnership debts exceeding their capital balances. Limited partnerships are popular in real estate

because of advantageous tax aspects in which double taxation of income is avoided. There also exist pass-through of losses from the partnership tax return (Form 1065) to the individual's tax return (Form 1040).

lineal: Direct line of descent as from father to son. An example of a lineal hereditament would be passing of the title of real property by virtue of a will to the first-born son.

line of credit: The maximum pre-approved amount that an individual or business can borrow without preparing a new credit request. It is a safety buffer in the event funds are needed for unexpected occurrences or emergencies.

Under the line of credit provision, a check may be written whenever funds are needed. Interest is charged only on the amount borrowed. Interest incurred on the first and second homes are deductible for tax purposes. See also *home equity loans.*

linkage: Propinquity of land to its intended use. Linkage is the time and distance between a designed use of property and the intended users. For example, if a shopping center were built several miles away from the nearest highway, its linkage would be very poor and its commercial success would rightfully be questioned.

liquidated damages: An amount of money provided for in a contract as compensation if the contract is not fulfilled. An example is an offer to buy real property that includes a provision that once the seller accepts the offer, if the buyer does not complete the purchase, the seller may keep the buyer's deposit as damages.

liquidation:
(1) Conversion of real property into money.
(2) The breaking up and selling of a real estate company for cash distribution to its creditors and then owners.

Chapter 7 of the Federal Bankruptcy Code applies to a forced liquidation.

See also *bankruptcy (business); bankruptcy (personal).*

liquidation price: Cash value or other consideration that can be received in a forced sale of real estate, such as that occurring in a foreclosure or when a company is going out of business. The liquidation value is typically less than what could be received from selling assets in the ordinary course of business.

liquidity: Immediate convertibility of assets into cash without loss. Many types of real property are illiquid.

liquidity risk:

(1) Risk that a person may not have sufficient funds to make payments on debt, rent, and so on.

(2) Risk that an individual may have to sell assets (e.g., property) at distressed prices to raise funds. An example is a homeowner who must sell his house at a low price because he cannot afford to make mortgage payments after losing his job.

(3) Risk that a business will have inadequate cash flow and/or working capital (current asset less current liabilities) to satisfy ongoing expenses, pay creditors and lenders, maintain capital facilities in proper working order, and so on. An example is an owner of commercial property that is unable to properly maintain it (e.g., new roofing, new boiler) because of a lack of funds. As a result, tenants may relocate.

lis pendens: Notice of a pending suit; a public notice given to prospective purchasers and any one else considering an interest in property that the title is being legally challenged, and the outcome is subject to a judicial ruling. For example, a municipality is about to begin an eminent domain proceeding against a parcel of property, an a lis pendens is filed giving public notice of the pending legal action.

list: To secure a listing by a real estate agent for a certain parcel of property. For example, a real estate broker wishes to list as many properties as possible to build an inventory of future real estate sales.

listing: Legal contract with a property owner empowering a real estate agent in selling, leasing, or mortgaging the principal's property. A listing has a legal description of the property, is valid for a specified period of time and gives the details of the sale. Types of listing contracts include: bilateral listing, exclusive agency listing, exclusive right to sell listing, multiple listing, net listing, open listing, and unilateral listing. See also *listing agreement.*

listing agreement: Contract allowing a real estate agent to list a property exclusively and/or with a multiple listing service and stipulating the commission rate and length of time.

listing broker: Licensed real estate broker who has a listing of property for sale.

listing form: The prepared form used to specify the terms of the listing contract. Usually a listing form consists of blanks the real estate agent fills in to provide the necessary information needed to complete the listing. This information would include the name of the property owner, the address, a detailed description of the property, type of listing, date, duration of the listing, and sales details.

litigation: Legal suit in which the plaintiff sues the defendant for some reason. A counterclaim may also be brought. The purpose of litigation is to exercise one's legal rights. There are many causes for litigation including damages made to rented facilities by a tenant, failure to pay rental payments, and divorce action to equitably distribute assets including real estate.

littoral: Land abutting a large body of water, such as an ocean or lake.

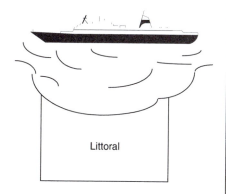

Littoral

littoral rights: Rights concerning properties adjoining a large body of water such as an ocean or lake. These rights concern the ability of the littoral property owner to use the shore and the adjoining water. See also *riparian rights.*

load (sales charge): Sales commission charged to buy shares in a real estate mutual fund sold by a broker or salesperson. Typically, the fee ranges from about 1 percent to 8 percent of the initial investment. The fee is added to the net asset value (NAV) per share when investing. However, many mutual funds do not have a load.

loan: An agreement by which the owner of property (the lender) and a borrower agree to let the borrower use the property for a particular time period and in return the borrower will pay the lender a payment (usually interest), and return the property (usually cash) at the end of the time period. A loan is usually evidenced by a promissory note. An example is a mortgage loan.

loan application: A form completed out by a borrower specifying personal and financial data to be considered by the lender in evaluating borrower risk. The information typically includes the following: (1) borrower's name and address, (2) amount and type of loan, (3) description of security, and (4) job and financial history. An application must be completed before a mortgage loan is approved.

loan closing: See *closing.*

loan commitment: Agreement by a lender to lend money to a borrower. A loan commitment typically includes the amount of money to be lent, the interest rate, and the period of the loan.

loan correspondent: See *mortgage correspondent.*

loan to facilitate: A mortgage loan where the bank provides the mortgagor the required funds to purchase property the bank has obtained through foreclosure on outstanding mortgages. For example, Smith obtains a $140,000 loan to enable him to purchase a home the bank has acquired through foreclosure on an outstanding mortgage.

loan origination fee: The lender's charge to the borrower for administrative work when preparing the mortgage including credit checks, appraisal, and title expenses. For example, Sun Bank approved a $200,000 mortgage loan with a 2% loan origination fee resulting in a charge of $4,000.

loan rates: The interest rate charged for a loan. For example, Smith obtained a $10,000 loan from the bank charging 10% interest.

loan shark: Lender who charges an exorbitant interest rate, which is typically illegal because it exceeds the interest rate allowed in the state. A borrower may go to a loan shark if he cannot obtain the loan at financial institutions such as banks and finance companies. The borrower is usually rejected because of his high risk. An example is a real estate developer going to a loan shark to complete construction because funds are not available elsewhere. Beware that loan sharking is illegal and criminal elements may be involved, and as such physical damage may be brought on the borrower for nonpayment.

loan-to-value (LTV) ratio: Percentage of the mortgage loan principal (amount borrowed) to the property's appraised value or sales price. For example, on a $300,000 house, with a mortgage loan principal of $210,000 the ratio is 70%. Home mortgages exceeding 70% (LTV ratio) usually need private mortgage insurance (PMI).

lobby: Large room at the entrance to a building designed for people to converse or move about freely.

location: Place where real estate is situated. The geographic location of property affects its value. For example, real estate in a good neighborhood is worth more.

locational analysis: The appraisal of a general geographic area for a particular use. For example, an industry may choose a location within a general geographic area which may be several hundred square miles in size because of its proximity to the general market area it serves.

Locational analysis must consider several factors:

(1) *Business climate:* The area of a growing market. What are its outstanding commercial and industrial features?

(2) *Demographic data:* Size of the population, its growth rate, composition in terms of age, family size, and educational attainment.

(3) *Employment:* Total employment data, rate of unemployment and sources of employment.

(4) *Geographic features:* What topographical features does the location have? What is its climate like?

(5) *Governmental considerations:* What is the overall governmental policy? How hospitable are they for business? What is the tax structure like?

(6) *Income:* Personal and family income is an important consideration in determining a good fit with other requirements.

(7) *Markets:* What commercial markets does the area have? What are their features and size? What are the consumer markets like?

(8) *Transportation:* Access to major highways, availability of airports and air service, and railways.

(9) *Urban growth:* What is the rate of direction of urban growth?

(10) *Zoning:* How is the land being used? What percentage is it commercial, industrial, agricultural, and residential?

Locational analysis usually begins with an economic analysis of the general area. Areas of high market activity normally have the highest economic value. Secondly, the purpose of the project has to be considered in terms of a location's characteristics. For example, a retail operation requiring high traffic volume would not be appropriate in an extremely rural area. Finally, all the characteristics of a location must be place in perspective. A judgment must be formed on the basis of the total quality of the location in terms of its suitability for a particular application.

lock: The number of days that the lender guarantees the loan's rate and terms. Without a written lock-in agreement, the lender is free to change the rate and terms at the time of loan closing. A slight increase in rate is commonly charged by lenders for lock-ins.

lock-in-clause: A clause inserted in a loan agreement by a lender guarantee a quoted interest rate on a loan for a specified period of time. The lock-in-clause is an incentive for the borrower to close the loan before the expiration date. In relatively stable economic periods characterized by a low rate of inflation, lock-in-clauses can be made for longer periods of time than during inflationary periods where there may be rapid changes in interest rates. For example, during the late 1970s and early 1980s when there was a high rate of inflation, many lenders abandoned the lock-in-clause entirely. However, during the late 1980s and early 1990s the lock-in-clause was used widely by lenders to attract borrowers.

locked-in-period: Period of time interest rates are guaranteed by lock-in-clause. The guarantee period of time is longer during stable economic periods with low rates of inflation.

loft:
(1) Space just below the roof of a house, barn, or other structure.
(2) Upper story of a factory or warehouse.

loft building: Building with large unpartitioned floor areas often used for storage. For example, a warehouse having no internal partitions is a loft building used primarily for commercial or industrial storage purposes.

log cabin: Early American frontier-style house constructed of logs. Since finished lumber was not readily available during the early frontier period of American history, homes were often fashioned out of logs. These homes were extremely durable and were either one- or two-story structures.

long-term capital goals or objectives: Capital appreciation financial goals set by a company or an individual over an extended period of time. Long-term capital goals establish a method for achieving the capital goal outcome with target ranges being established. For example, a real estate investor may set a long-term capital goal of having a net worth of one million dollars within five years through a systematic program of real estate investment.

long-term lease: A lease contract extending ten years or more. See also *ground lease.*

loss of access: The loss of an access right to a parcel of property through another property owner's property. This could materially affect the value of the property denied access.

lot: Plot of ground which may or may not be developed. An empty lot has no structure on it. Real estate taxes must still be paid on unoccupied land.

lot and block description: Method of referring to property which has been platted in a plat book in the public records. The lot and block is referenced by the number of the plat map and the lot and block within it. The plat map will give the boundaries of the properties contained within it as well as any existing easements.

lot book: See *plat book.*

lot line: A boundary line for a lot described in a plat book.

lot split: Dividing a lot into two or more parcels. Normally a variance would have to be obtained to permit a lot split. The lot cannot be split unless they meet minimum area zoning requirements unless a special variance is obtained.

louver:
(1) Series of sloping horizontal slats most frequently mounted in doors and windows permitting the passage of air while restricting vision and preventing rain from entering the building.
(2) Fins installed in air conditioning ducts and outlets primarily intended to direct air in specific directions.

low-income housing: Housing specifically intended for those people living below a specified income level. Low-income housing qualifies for tax credits up to a percentage of cost. Specific guidelines must be followed in qualifying as well as obtaining housing financing.

Urban homelessness has become a major problem in the 1980s and 1990s. Providing shelter for the poor, particularly in urban areas, is a major national concern. While the Federal Department of Housing and Urban Development has provided assistance including rent supplements and loans to developers, it is declining. As the government withdraws from active participation in housing financing and production, the amount of housing built for or filtered down to low-income households is increasingly inadequate. Assistance from Public housing accommodates only 1% of the nation's population. With roughly half a million families on waiting lists for subsidized apartments, public housing construction, in the late 1980s, nearly came to a standstill.

MAI: See *Member of the American Institute of Real Estate Appraisers.*

main:

(1) The major distribution or collection duct in an air-conditioning system.

(2) In an electrical system, the connection box where all the circuit systems are installed with a series of electrical breakers.

(3) The major pipe in a plumbing distribution system to which all other pipes are connected.

maintenance: Periodic expenditures undertaken to preserve or retain a property's operational status for its originally intended use. These expenditures do not improve or extend the life of the property. It is an expense, which is distinguished from capital improvements which are capitalized. Examples are the cost of fixing a sprinkler system or painting a wall.

majority: The minimum age required for legal competency (in most states 18 years).

maker: Any person, company, or legal entity who signs a check or note to borrow money. By signing a payment instrument, the maker assumes full financial responsibility. For example, Smith is the maker for a $1,000 check and assumes full financial responsibility for it.

mall: A public area, or plaza with a series of walkways permitting pedestrians easy access to shops, stores and restaurants. Modern malls are often enclosed enabling all weather access. Malls are often very decorative and festive encouraging a relaxed atmosphere.

management agreement: Contractual agreement between a commercial or industrial rental property owner and an individual or firm who agrees to maintain the property. Management agreements specify the nature of services to be provided and the extent of authority a property manager has. Normally, the fees charged by a property manager are a widely varying percentage of the gross rentals depending on the services required and the size of the property. For example, a management agreement provides full maintenance services for a 40-unit apartment house, and the property manager charges 5% of all gross rental receipts for the maintenance services.

management fee:

(1) A charge based on the asset value of a real estate security portfolio to manage it. For an open-end mutual fund, the management charge is included in the selling cost of the security. For an investment adviser or bank trust

department, the management charge is typically a percentage of the net asset value.

(2) In real estate, a fee to maintain property, collect rent, and keep the records.

management survey: Survey of the maintenance requirements for a commercial or industrial rental property for the purpose of preparing a management agreement.

mansard roof: A roof having two slopes on each side. The second slope is longer than the first part of the roof and extremely steep.

Mansard Roof

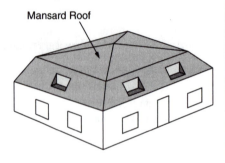

manufactured housing: Partially factory-assembled units designed to be transported in parts to the site. The structure is completed on the actual site. See also *mobile home.*

map act: Local governmental requirements regarding the subdivision of construction.

margin: Difference between the index a lender uses to compute adjustable rate mortgage (ARM) rates and the interest rate the lender actually charges the borrower. The ARM interest rate is the sum of the total of the index and the margin.

margin of security: Buffer amount between the value of the collateral and the principal balance of the obligation. For example, if the mortgage has a principal balance of $200,000 and the appraised value of the property is $250,000, the bank has a margin of security of $50,000 in the event of default. The greater the collateral value, the more protection the bank has. In troubled real estate markets because of adverse economic conditions, the market value of the property may fall substantially below the balance of the mortgage. Many homeowners in such a case have defaulted on the loan because of the decline in market values. For example, if the appraised value of a home has fallen to $60,000 while the mortgage balance is $100,000, it might be more financially prudent for the debtor to default on the mortgage.

marginal land: Land that has poor income potential, usually used in an agricultural sense meaning that the land is untillable, has poor access, is extremely steep, has suffered serious erosion, is extremely small or irregular, or is located at too high of an altitude to grow crops. Marginal land has a lower market valuation than high quality farm land. For example, property located in New England often is marginal land since it is extremely rocky and experiences harsh winters. Crops raised on this property are often marginally profitable.

marginal property: See *marginal land.*

marginal satisfaction: Increased satisfaction a buyer obtains from purchasing an additional unit of a good, service, or property. See also *marginal utility.*

marginal utility: Additional utility an individual receives when purchasing an additional unit of a commodity or service. Represents a trade off between units of cost and units of utility. For example, an individual builds a luxury home with a swimming pool. To build a tennis court would cost $50,000 and require yearly maintenance. To add two tennis courts would cost an additional $25,000. Since the probability of using two tennis courts is extremely low, the marginal utility of building the additional tennis court at $25,000 is not enough to offset the additional cost involved. However, if it cost only $5,000 to build the additional tennis court, then there may be sufficient marginal utility to justify its construction.

Marginal utility is not objectively measurable; it is more a measure of consumer desires. In order to convince consumers to buy an additional unit of a product or service, the price has to be lowered significantly enough to make the consumer desire its marginal utility.

marital deduction: Tax deduction permitted upon the transfer of property from one spouse to another. The deduction is allowed under the federal gift tax for lifetime transfers or under the federal estate tax for transfers of a decedent.

market absorption rate: The rate at which a market can absorb additional units of supply without causing market saturation and severe price distortions. For example, during a recessionary period, many homeowners may list their house for sale. Since the supply of homes entering the home resale market increased without a corresponding increase in demand, the market absorption rate has been exceeded, and the market price of the resale homes declines.

market analysis: Research on the real estate market and specific properties to ascertain future trends. This research includes all aspects of the real estate market, including psychological factors, prices, costs, timing, demography, and competitiveness. The purpose is to predict and, if possible, control trends to capitalize on opportunities. See also *market approach.*

market approach: Method of valuing a property through examination and comparison of recent sales of comparable properties. See also *direct sales comparison approach.*

market area: Regional area from which a particular product or service can expect its greatest demand. For example, a retail department store expects to attract shoppers from a market area having a 20-mile radius in the surrounding region.

market comparison approach: Method of appraising real estate based on a market comparison of neighboring properties having similar characteristics. Seeks to answer the question: What would it cost to substitute a similar property for the current one? The market comparison approach assumes that a buyer would not be willing to pay more for a property than recently paid for a comparable property. However, there still are substantial differences between two properties. This requires an individual to make a judgmental appraisal.

market data approach: Analysis of real estate sales data to appraise real estate values. Sources of real estate sales data used in the market data approach include the official records of deeds and leases available in county clerks' offices and local assessors' offices. Other sources include the real estate agents involved in specific real estate transactions, principals to a real estate sale, published transaction records and newspapers. The real estate market date must be analyzed to determine comparability in order to reach a valid appraisal value. See also *market comparison approach.*

market delineation: Method of determining the geographic extent of a market for a given commercial property. This will determine the suitability of locating a specific commercial property in a certain area. For example, a market delineation study determined that placing a retail department store will allow it to draw from a surrounding area with a range of up to 35 miles.

market price: Price at which the seller and the buyer agree to trade real estate on the open market.

market rent: Rent that a comparable property would mandate in a given real estate rental market. Market rent is a competitive rate based on rents other comparable properties receive. For example, in a given real estate rental market a one bedroom garden apartment with a kitchen and living room rents for $850 per month.

market risk: Uncertainty in the price of real estate due to market, economic, political or other conditions.

market segmentation: Process of defining submarkets within an overall market. Market segmentation is the process of defining the suitability of a submarket for a specific property. For example, a new home development with one-acre plots would appeal to families earning over $100,000 per year.

market study: Study of real estate activities including demand, price, locational influence, and current trends. See also *market analysis*.

market value: Independently appraised value of real estate in a free competitive market. Many variables must be considered in determining market value, but supply and demand are the essential ingredients. Market value determination should be based on all available information. See also *market price*.

marketable title: Title leaving no question as to who the owner is. It is the title which a reasonable buyer, knowledgeable of the facts and their legal implications and acting in a reasonable manner, would be willing to accept. A title insurance company should be retained to insure that the title is marketable.

marquee: Permanent structure protruding from the side of a building. In addition to providing shelter, a marquee is often used as an advertising format. For example, a movie theater marquee lists the current attractions.

masonry: Construction materials from stone, brick, and concrete block. Masonry materials play an important role in providing structural support as well as being used as decorative finish surfaces. There are two general classifications of masonry:

(1) Masonry made from cast-in-place concrete.

(2) Masonry made from built-up or unit masonry joined together by mortar. This type of masonry includes brick, stone, and concrete blocks.

mass appraising: Process of simultaneously appraising several pieces of property. Normally, occurs when a local government conducts a reassessment.

master deed: Filed by a condominium developer or converter for the purpose of recording all of the individual condominium units owned within a condominium development. For example, a condominium developer secured a piece of property for the purpose of developing a condominium complex. The developer then recorded a master deed showing the individual condominium units within the complex. Restrictions and covenants may be included with the master deed.

master lease:

(1) Major lease in a structure (e.g., apartment building, office building) that controls subleases. An example is a landlord and attorney entering into a main lease for the third floor offices of a building. This lease takes precedence over a sublease between the attorney and an accountant for one of the offices.

(2) A controlling property lease. Subleases are controlled by the master lease in the sense they cannot extend beyond the terms of the master lease. For example, if Smith grants Jones a

10-year master lease on a commercial office building, Jones can sublease the offices for terms not to exceed the 10-year master lease.

Master Limited Partnership (MLP): Unincorporated combination (roll-up) of limited partnerships in real estate together as a group. It is usually more comprehensive, financially sound, and marketable than individual partnerships. Shares in the MLP are typically traded on the major stock exchanges. By being unincorporated, double taxation is avoided.

master plan: Plan describing both through narrative and maps the overall land use of a designated urban area. It includes both present property uses as well as future land development plans. Private developers can develop a master plan to guide their overall development plans. Governments create master plans to help guide the development of property zoning use designations.

material fact: Significant information that if disclosed would affect an individual's decision. For example, a buyer would probably not enter into a contract with a seller of real property if it was known that the seller was a criminal.

materialman's lien: Legal lien on property on behalf of an individual who has not been paid for material (e.g., lumber) furnished in constructing property. The material enhanced the value of the property, and as such the provider of the goods must be compensated.

material participation: Significant action and duties performed by an individual in a real estate activity. An example is a partner in a real estate venture that makes key decisions and performs a lot of work.

maturity: The period when a financial debt, such as a mortgage, must be paid.

mean: Measure of central tendency, that is a measure of the center of the data; also called an average. Mean and standard deviation are the two most widely used statistical measures that summarize the characteristics of the data. Suppose a real estate agency sells 630 houses during a 30-day period. Then the mean (average) daily sales is obtained by dividing the total number of homes sold by the number of days as follows:

$$\text{Mean daily sales per day} = \frac{630}{30} = 21 \text{ per day}$$

Symbolically,

$$\bar{x} = \frac{\Sigma \, x_i}{n}$$

where $\bar{x}$ = the mean, x_i = the values in the data, Σ (read as sigma) is the summation sign, and n = the number of observations in the data.

meander: Descriptive of a property boundary that follows the course of a river or estuary. For example, a land description may say its boundary follows "the meander of the river" meaning the property boundary follows the winding of the river.

mechanic's lien: Claim on property by an unpaid workman or contractor. The property may be sold to recover the money owed. The legal justification of the mechanic's lien is that the labor and materials supplied increase the value of the property and therefore the property should be security for payment. Further, the workman should be compensated for his services. An example is an electrician or plumber who has not been paid for his work by the homeowner.

median: The midpoint in a range of numbers. For example, the median (middle value) of a house in Nassau County on Long Island in New York is $150,000.

By using median values, a prospective buyer or seller of a home may have a better idea as to whether the price being asked in the neighborhood is reasonable.

median new second-home price: Medium price for a new second home. Medium is the middle value between the lowest and highest figures.

meeting of the minds: An agreement among those involved in a contract. There is an offer and acceptance, and the property has an evaluation. A financial consideration must also exist.

meets and bounds: Method of land description that identifies a parcel by specifying its shape and boundaries.

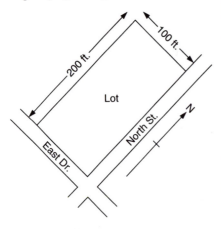

menace: Threat of violence to obtain a contract.

merchantable title: See *marketable title.*

merger: Combination of two or more real estate brokerages into one, with only one company retaining its identity. Typically, the larger of the two companies is the company whose identity is maintained. It often involves an exchange of stock.

merger of title: Forming two or more parcels of property under one title. Normally, the smaller parcel(s) are joined to the title of the larger parcel. The merger of title often occurs in an estate settlement where adjoining parcels of property are merged under one title. For example, George Smith is the heir to the adjacent property estate of his father, William. Upon William's death, a merger of title occurs whereby George's property, being the smaller of the two parcels, is joined with his father's property to form one common property.

meridians: North-south lines that encircle the earth and used as references in mapping land.

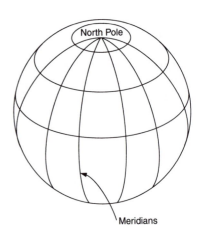

mesne: In between, intermediate, intervening; passing an interest from a principal to a second party and then to a third party.

metropolitan area: Urbanized area in and around a major city. The metropolitan area may overlap county and state boundaries and may encompass a city, its suburbs, and the towns and rural areas within the orbit of its social and economic influence. For example, the New York metropolitan area is the largest overlapping portions of the states of New Jersey and Connecticut as well as numerous counties and has more than 18 million people. The New York metropolitan area is followed in size by Los Angeles, Chicago, San Francisco, and Philadelphia. In 1983, the U.S. Office of Management and Budget termed metropolitan areas Metropolitan Statistical Areas (MSAs) and the largest metropolitan complexes, Consolidated Metropolitan Statistical Areas (CMSAs).

mezzanine: Balcony or low ceiling overhang just above the main floor and between the next story. In a theater, a mezzanine is the first balcony above the stage.

mill: One tenth of a cent. Mills are a common term in expressing tax rates per dollar of assessed valuation. For example, a property is taxed at the rate of 80 mills. If a property were assessed at $20,000 and the tax rate was 80 mills, the tax would be $20,000 × .08 cents = $1,600.

millage rate: Property tax rate whereby each mill is $1 of tax assessment per $1,000 of assessed property value. For example, a house in Los Alamitos is assessed at $200,000 and the millage rate is 10 mills. The assessment for the home would be $2,000 ($200,000 × .01).

mineral rights: Ownership rights to the minerals or other precious resources, such as petroleum, in one's property. A property owner having the mineral rights to the property can do one of three things with them:
(1) Personally recover the precious resources and sell them.
(2) Sell the rights to the resources to another party for a fee.
(3) Lease the mineral rights and receive a royalty.

minimum lot area: The smallest lot area required for building under the municipal zoning code. For example, a municipal zoning code requires all building lots to have a minimum lot area of ¼ of an acre in order to be granted a building permit.

minimum rated risk: In insurance, charging the lowest rate accorded an insurance policy covering a minimum risk classification situation. For example, a homeowner's insurance for a home located within 500 feet of a fire hydrant, having smoke detectors, a burglar alarm, and constructed from fireproof materials may qualify for the minimum rated risk.

minor: Person under the age of legal competence (most states specify 18 years).

misrepresentation: Intentionally misstated or undisclosed facts, statements or representations. Misrepresentation is a form of fraud which could lead to cancellation of a contract or other liability. For example, an individual selling a home misrepresents the fact that the home is infested with termites. Upon discovering the true situation, the new homeowner wins a court settlement for the costs of repairing the damages.

mission house: Style of the 19th century resembling an old church. It has a tile roof, arch-shape windows, stucco walls, and pyramid roof.

mistake: Unintentional error. An example is a house that the seller wants $1,000,000 for but it is mistyped as $100,000. An error may be unilateral (one party errs) or mutual (both parties err). Some types of errors are the basis to rescind a contract.

mixed use commercial project: Commercial building having several different uses blending together. For example, retail shops are on the first floor, professional offices are on floors two through ten, and a restaurant is on the top floor.

mobile home: Pre-manufactured structure, often constructed of metal, that is placed either on a minimal or no foundation. Mobile homes are typically situated in mobile home parks. An advantage is the ease of moving locations.

Mobil Home Construction and Safety Standards Act: Federal act passed in 1974 regulating mobile homes. The act defines a mobile home as a "structure, transportable in one or more sections, which is eight body feet or more in width and is forty body feet or more in length, and which is built on a permanent chassis, and designed to be used as a dwelling with or without permanent foundation, when connected to the required utilities, and includes the plumbing, heating, air-conditioning, and electrical systems contained therein." Mobile homes are well-equipped portable forms of housing including all necessities often including many luxurious appointments. Mobile homes are distinguished from vans, campers and other recreational vehicles in that they are designed for permanent residence rather than recreational occupancy.

Municipal zoning law often regulates the placement of mobile homes relegating them to mobile home park sites.

mobile home park: Site where mobile homes are located. Mobile home parks are often mandated by municipal zoning laws. They provide necessary utilities to the mobile homes often including recreational facilities. Mobile home owners rent or lease the park site from the mobile home park owner.

model furnishings: Interior furnishings included in a model unit. Model furnishings are chosen to highlight the features of the model unit often having an interior decorator assist in the design and choice of the furnishings.

model unit: Representative house, apartment, or cooperative used as a sales tool to show how the actual unit bought will probably appear in design and construction. An example is a model apartment.

modern colonial (New England) architecture: See *Cape Cod Colonial.*

modern Georgian architecture: Modeled after the English Georgian style, this architecture is a perfectly scaled grand symmetrical structure which is extremely formal and conventional in style.

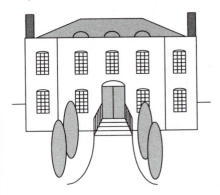

modernize: To upgrade a facility by installing up-to-date technology as well as introducing stylistic changes reflecting current patterns. Modernizing a facility can add substantially to its value and marketability. For example, a modern kitchen and baths make a house show better and sell more easily.

Modified Accelerated Cost Recovery System (MACRS): Term given to two depreciation systems defined by the Internal Revenue Service:

(1) The main system is called the General Depreciation System (GDS). Under GDS, most property is assigned to eight property classes based on their class lives. These property classes provide the recovery period to be used by establishing the number of years over which the basis of an item in a class is recovered.

(2) The Alternative Depreciation System (ADS) generally provides for a

longer recovery period and uses only the straight line method of depreciation to figure your tax deduction.

Both systems establish conventions determining how many months property can be depreciated in the first year it is placed in service and in the year of disposition.

- 20-year property. This class includes property such as farm buildings.
- Residential rental property. This class is comprised of rental buildings or structures (including mobile homes) for which 80% or more of the gross rental income is from dwelling units. Examples are living in a house or apartment. It excludes hotels and motels. Residential rental property is depreciated over 27.5 years.
- Nonresidential real property. This class includes real property that is not residential rental property. This property is depreciated over 31.5 years.

modular housing: A prefabricated house constructed in a factory with final assembly and erection on site. Because of economies of scale and modern factory production techniques, modular housing is considerably cheaper than housing constructed totally on site.

moisture barrier: Layer of material put on the outside wall or foundation to prevent the intrusion of water or humidity into the structure. A moisture barrier is constructed out of plastic, aluminum foil, or other water-resistant material. In some cases, a moisture barrier is wrapped around fiberglass insulating material and it is installed as one unit.

molding: Method of finishing edges of walls, window jams, doors, or projections with decorative strips of wood to give a better appearance as well as providing protection from jagged edges and helping in preventing drafts.

Molding may be fabricated from any material; however, almost all are made from wood. In classical times, molding was made from stone. Molding is now mass produced and can be purchased ready made although it still must be cut to size.

monterey architecture: A two-story house characterized by a balcony spanning the width of the second story. Monterey architecture was adopted from the early California Spanish period.

month-to-month tenancy: A tenancy in which no written lease is involved, rent being paid monthly. It can be renewed for each succeeding month or terminated at the option of either party with sufficient notice.

monument: An iron pipe, stone, tree, or other fixed point used in making a survey.

moratorium:

(1) Delay permitted to repay an obligation. An example is when a financial institution allows a real estate company another month to repay the balance due on a loan.

(2) Delay permitted to carryout a legal responsibility. An example is when a homeowner gives the contractor another two weeks to complete work beyond the contract completion date.

(3) Period of time that specified performance is not permitted. For example, a homeowner does not allow work to be done on his home during the Jewish holidays.

mortgage: A lien that makes property security for the repayment of debt. Mortgages can finance the acquisition of real estate such as a home. A mortgage has certain benefits compared to other debt instruments such as possibly lower interest rates, less financing restrictions, and long maturity period. See also *adjustable rate mortgage (ARM); conventional mortgage; mortgage bond.*

mortgage amortization: Amortization is paying a loan on an installment basis. The term is usually associated with a mortgage payment schedule. As a loan is amortized, the equity in the associated property is increased. However, in the early years of a mortgage, the majority of the payments are for interest rather than principal. For example, the payments on a 30 year conventional $95,000 mortgage at 9.5% would be $798.81.

mortgage-backed security: Certificates that pass-through principal and interest payments to investors.

mortgage banker: Person or business that originates mortgages and receives payments. The mortgage banker typically sells these mortgages to investors and obtains service fees for the loans. The mortgage banker is a major initiator of FHA- and VA-insured mortgages and also serves a key function in the conventional mortgage markets. Financial help is often sought from a lender, typically a commercial bank. The bank becomes a warehouse for mortgage money, and the mortgage banker draws on these funds until payment is received from the investors. Usually the mortgage banker continues to service the loan (collect debt service, pay property taxes, handle delinquent accounts, etc.) even after the loan has been packaged and sold. For this management service, a small

Amortization Schedule

Amount of *Loan:*	$95,000.00		Term of *Loan:*	30 Years	
Monthly Payments:	$798.81		Yearly Interest:	9.5000%	
Total Interest Paid:	$192,574.82		Total Payout:	$287,574.82	

Payment	Amount	Interest	Principal	Interest to Date	Remaining Balance
1	$798.81	$752.08	$46.73	$ 752.08	$94,953.27
2	798.81	751.71	47.10	1,503.79	94,906.17
3	798.81	751.34	47.47	2,255.13	94,858.70
4	798.81	750.96	47.85	3,006.09	94,810.85
5	798.81	750.59	48.22	3,756.68	94,762.63
6	798.81	750.20	48.61	4,506.88	94,714.02
7	798.81	749.82	48.99	5,256.70	94,665.03
8	798.81	749.43	49.38	6,006.13	94,615.65
9	798.81	749.04	49.77	6,755.17	94,565.88
10	798.81	748.65	50.16	7,503.82	94,515.72
11	798.81	748.25	50.56	8,252.07	94,465.16
12	798.81	747.85	50.96	8,999.92	94,414.20

percentage of the amount collected is retained before forwarding the balance to the investor. The success of the mortgage banker depends upon the ability to generate new loans. In some geographic areas, mortgage bankers are the primary source for financing real estate. All mortgage bankers try to stay in constant touch with investors and are aware of changing market conditions and lender requirements. Quite often the loan origination fee or finder's fee charged the borrower is more than offset by a lower interest rate from a lender not directly accessible to the borrower. Mortgage bankers are involved in both commercial and residential financing and also carry out related activities such as writing hazard insurance policies, appraising, and investment counseling. As with mortgage brokers, mortgage bankers are regulated by state law. See also *mortgage broker; mortgage servicing.*

Mortgage Banking Association (MBA): National trade association of people engaged in the mortgage banking business, dedicated to the betterment of the mortgage banking industry through education, legislation, and high ethical standards for its members. It is located in 1125 Fifteen Street, NW, Washington, DC 20005.

mortgage banking software: Computer software packages designed to serve mortgage banking functions, such as mortgage loan accounting/servicing, loan origination, loan processing, lease/financial/investment analysis, yield/price calculations, and portfolio management. The Mortgage Banking Association (MBA) of America has a publication entitled *Mortgage Banking Software.*

mortgage bonds: Bonds collateralized by real assets. Two kinds of mortgage bonds are senior mortgages, (having a first claim on assets and earnings), and junior mortgages, (having a subordinate lien). A mortgage bond may have a closed-end provision that prevents the firm from issuing additional bonds of the same priority against the same property or may be an open-end mortgage that allows the issuance of additional bonds having equal status with the original issue.

mortgage broker: Person or business that obtains mortgages for others by finding suitable lenders. The mortgage broker sometimes deals with collections and disbursements. Typically the mortgage broker receives a percentage of the amount financed. A finder's fee equal to 1% or so of the amount borrowed is normally paid by the borrower. The financial success of the mortgage brokerage firm depends upon the ability to locate available funds and to match these funds with creditworthy borrowers. Certain sources of funds, particularly insurance companies and the secondary sources, do not always deal directly with the person looking for capital; rather, they work through a mortgage broker. Normally, the mortgage broker is not involved in servicing the loan once it is made and the transaction is closed. See also *mortgage banker.*

mortgage commitment: The willingness of a lender to give a mortgage to a mortgagor. A mortgage commitment will give a time period the mortgage will be given and an indication of the interest rate to be charged on the mortgage. The mortgage will actually be granted at a closing. For example, Smith obtains a mortgage commitment from a bank to give him a $100,000 mortgage to buy a home for $150,000. The closing will be in six weeks and the bank gives a lock-in clause of 8% on the mortgage.

mortgage constant: Ratio of annual mortgage payments divided by the initial principal of the mortgage. This only applies to loans involving constant payment. For example, a $500,000 loan with an annual payment of $50,000, has a mortgage constant of 10%.

mortgage correspondent: Individual having permission to act on behalf of a bank or other financial institution in a specified locality to attract interested borrowers.

mortgage discount: One-time charge assessed by a bank or other financial institution at the closing of buying real property. The fee increases the effective cost to the borrower. One discount point translates to 1% of the initial mortgage amount. While the buyer typically pays these points, in some cases the seller does because of governmental law (e.g., mortgages to veterans).

mortgage guaranty insurance: See *Mortgage Guarantee Insurance Company*.

Mortgage Guarantee Insurance Company (MGIC): Private company established in 1957 and headquartered in Milwaukee, WI, providing private mortgage insurance (PMI) to mortgage lenders granting mortgages to mortgagors not having at least a 20% down payment upon application. MGIC indemnifies the mortgage lending company should the mortgagor go into foreclosure because of a default. The cost of PMI is included in the closing costs by the mortgagee.

mortgage instrument: A written mortgage document. A mortgage instrument states the terms of the mortgage including the interest rate, length of payments, payment dates, and remedies the bank is entitled to in the event of the mortgagor's failure to pay as required including late charges.

mortgage insurance: A form of life or disability insurance where a mortgagor insures a mortgage in the event of death or disability. The principal covered by mortgage insurance declines as the mortgage is amortized. Thus, mortgage insurance is a form of decreasing term insurance. For example, Smith purchased a home for $150,000 and obtained a $100,000 30-year mortgage to finance the purchase. He then obtained a $100,000 mortgage insurance policy with decreasing terms of coverage corresponding to the amortization rate.

mortgage interest deduction: Tax deduction for interest paid or accrued within the taxable year with respect to mortgage indebtedness. Interest is deductible on mortgages secured by principal and second homes. A taxpayer may not write off interest on any part of the mortgage that exceeds the original purchase price plus improvements of property, unless the taxpayer uses the money for medical or educational purposes.

mortgage lien: A lien on the property of a mortgagor. In most states a mortgage gives the mortgagee a lien—as opposed to the common-law practice of granting conditional title—on the house or property as security for the loan. A mortgage lien secures the loan. In the event of a default, a mortgage lien holder can foreclose on the property in order to satisfy the claim of the mortgagor. The priority of a mortgage lien depends on the number of previous liens on the property. If there are no other previous mortgage liens or other financial obligations against the property, then the mortgage lien is considered a first mortgage and takes priority over succeeding loan agreements. In case of foreclosure, the holder of a second mortgage lien can recover only after the first mortgage lien holder has been paid.

mortgage life insurance: Insurance coverage to pay the balance of the mortgage if the wage earner dies.

mortgage loan: See *mortgage.*

mortgage market: The interest rate and terms competing mortgage lenders are offering to potential mortgagees. The mortgage market is competitive on the basis of mortgage interest rates, points, credit history requirements, and closing costs. For example, in order for Smith to obtain a mortgage to finance a home purchase, he compared the interest rates, points charged, need for a credit check and closing costs. He finally settled on a lender whose rate was ¼% lower than the competition, charged fewer points, did not require a credit check and was extremely competitive on closing costs. The bank also guaranteed an interest rate lock-in clause until the day of the closing.

mortgage out: Obtaining all the money needed for a real estate project's development. The acquirer/developer does not need to give any of his own funds for upfront costs. The developer also does not have an equity interest.

mortgage payment table: Tables used to compute the monthly mortgage payment that consists of principal repayment and interest. A loan amortization type of formula is used. The tables have monthly payments for any combination of loan size, interest rate, and term. Table 6 (Monthly Mortgage Payments) of the Appendix gives selected combinations for $1,000 fixed-rate loans.

EXAMPLE: Monica wants to know the monthly mortgage payment on a $95,000, 10%, 30-year mortgage. Using Table 6, she needs to follow three steps:

Step 1: Divide the amount of the loan by $1,000 (that is, $95,000/$1,000 = 95)

Step 2: Find the payment factor for a specific interest rate and loan maturity. The Table 6 payment factor for 10% and 30 years is 8.78

Step 3: Multiply the factor obtained in Step 2 by the amount from Step 1. $8.78 × 95 = $834.10

The monthly mortgage payment is $834.10.

mortgage pool: A collection of packaged residential mortgage loans for sale in the secondary mortgage market to investors. Companies with mortgage pools expect to earn a short-term profit and use the proceeds to make additional mortgage loans available to homeowners.

mortgage REIT: A type of real estate investment trust (REIT) that does not own property but gives short-term financing for construction loans or for permanent mortgage loans for major projects. See also *real estate investment trust (REIT).*

mortgage release price: Amount required to payoff the full balance of the mortgage today. The amount equals the principal balance plus any prepayment penalty.

mortgage relief:

(1) One's mortgage obligation is assumed by another. An example is when the buyer of a home assumes the remainder of the seller's mortgage.

(2) Bank modifies the borrower's mortgage obligation, such as when the bank approves the homeowner's request for an extension of time to pay because of illness or loss of a job.

mortgage requirement: The amount of a periodic payment, whether monthly, quarterly, or annually, including interest and principal, required for a mortgage payment. See also *amortization; debt service.*

mortgage risk rating: The amount of inherent risk for a mortgagee in granting a mortgage. An operating principle in mortgage risk rating is that the mortgage cannot exceed 2.5 times the mortgagor's annual income, only a maximum of 28% of the mortgagee's salary can be devoted to the mortgage payment, and total debt payments including the mortgage payment cannot exceed the mortgagee's salary by 33%.

mortgage servicing: Monitoring and administrating a mortgage loan after it has been made. This may include monthly payments, record keeping, handing tax and insurance records, and foreclosure of property. A mortgage banker services the loans.

mortgage share (participation) agreement: A written agreement between institutional investors to buy or sell ownership shares in mortgages. An institution such as a bank can agree to buy a certain number of shares in a single or package of mortgages. See also *participation mortgage; shared equity mortgage (SEM).*

mortgage spreading agreement: See *spreading agreement.*

mortgagee: Lender (such as a bank) that has the property of the borrower as collateral (security, lien). If the mortgage is not paid, the property may be sold to make payment on the outstanding obligation. See also *mortgage; mortgagor.*

mortgagor: Borrower who gives property as collateral for a loan. See also *mortgage; mortgagee.*

multifamily housing: Residential structure designed to house more than one family. Smaller multifamily housing units include duplexes, triplexes, and quadriplexes. Larger multifamily housing is normally termed an apartment house. Multifamily housing can be tenant owned individually or as a condominium or cooperative or it can be rented. Multifamily housing structures of 2 to 4 units grew the most slowly during the 1980's, increasing only 1% of

Units in larger buildings of 5 or more units, increased 16%.

multiple of gross earnings rule: A rule that the price of a house should not exceed about 2 to 2.5 times your family's gross annual earnings.

EXAMPLE: If annual gross income is $70,000, the highest price one could afford would be $140,000 (2 × $70,000) to $175,000 (2.5 × $70,000).

multiple listing: System containing the real estate listings of many local agents.

Multiple Listing Service (MLS): An information and referral network among real estate agents that pools all properties offered into a common offering list. If a sale results, the listing broker and the selling broker split the commission. The members of a MLS receive the benefit of better sales exposure, which, in turn, means a better price and a faster sale. See also *multiple listing.*

muniments of title: Documentation of ownership. An example is a deed to land.

mutual consent: Two or more parties agree to something. An example is when the two parties to a contract mutually agree to make certain revisions to it.

mutual funds: Investment companies investing in investment instruments including real estate. Mutual funds are popular to investors and represent equity in a professionally managed portfolio of securities. Major benefits of investing in real estate mutual funds are:

(1) *Diversification.* Each fund share provides an investor an interest in many real estate companies.

(2) *Small minimum investment.* An investor with limited funds can accomplish diversification by owning many securities in the portfolio.

(3) *Automatic reinvestment.* Most funds permit reinvestment of dividends and

capital gains. Funds usually do not assess a sales fee on automatic reinvestments.

(4) *Automatic withdrawals.* Many funds permit shareholders to withdraw funds on a periodic basis.

(5) *Liquidity.* An investor may redeem the shares owned.

(6) *Switching.* An investor may change in his investments as his objectives change.

To aid switching among funds, usually without a fee, such companies as T. Rowe Price have "families" of funds. The value of a mutual fund share is reflected in the net asset value (NAV) equal to:

$$\frac{\text{Fund's total assets—Liabilities}}{\text{Number of shares outstanding in the fund}}$$

EXAMPLE: Assume that a fund owns 100 shares each of Rockefeller Center Properties (RCP), Union Realty (UR), and Polimeni Properties (PP). Assume that on a particular day, the market values below existed. The NAV of the fund is computed below (assume the fund has no liabilities):

(a) RCP—$80 per share
$\qquad \times$ 100 shares = $ 8,000
(b) UR—$70 per share
$\qquad \times$ 100 shares = $ 7,000
(c) PP—$150 per share
$\qquad \times$ 100 shares = $15,000
(d) Value of the fund's
$\qquad$ portfolio = $30,000
(e) Number of shares
$\qquad$ outstanding in the fund = 1,000
(f) Net asset value (NAV)
$\qquad$ per share $= \dfrac{\text{(d)}}{\text{(e)}}$
$\qquad\qquad = \$30$

If an investor owns 15% of the fund's outstanding shares, or 150 shares (15% × 1,000 shares), then the value of the investment is $4,500 ($30 × 150). There are three ways to make money in real estate mutual funds. NAV is one

way. NAV reflects the current market value of the underlying portfolio. An investor also receives capital gains and dividends.

Mutual funds are of different types, according to structure, the fees charged, means of trading funds, and investment objectives. In open-end funds, investors buy from and sell their shares back to the fund itself. An example is Fidelity Real Estate. On the other hand, closed-end funds have a fixed number of shares outstanding, which trade among individuals in secondary markets like common stocks. All open and closed-end funds have management fees. A major point of closed-end funds is the size of discount or premium, which is the difference between their market prices and their net asset values (NAVs). Some funds sell at discounts, which may make them more attractive. Funds charging sales fees are referred to as load funds. Load funds usually do not do better than no-load funds. Some analysts feel investors should buy only no-load or low-load funds. The prospectus of a real estate fund includes information as the fund's investment objectives, way of selecting securities, management and sales fees, and other costs.

mutual savings banks: A savings bank owned by its depositors. They are mostly located in the northwestern United States and are an important supplier of real estate financing. All mutual savings banks are state chartered and typically are less regulated than their closest financing relative, the savings and loan association. The percentage of their assets invested in real estate mortgages is less than the average S&L, although a higher percentage of their total mortgage portfolio is FHA and VA loans. Most mutual banks have a relatively large percentage of mortgages. Mutual banks also make personal loans which can result in capital being moved from surplus areas to deficit areas. Over two-third of the mutual banks maintain membership in the FDIC. The remaining ones are insured by state savings insurance agencies. These state agencies exercise authority over both the type of investments and the amount of their assets mutual banks can invest in particular types of real estate.

mutual water company: Business entity providing water services in a particular locality.

mutual water company: Business entity providing water services in a particular locality.

National Apartment Association (NAA):
Founded in 1939 and located in Washington, DC, the NAA has 36,000 members with 11 regional groups. It consists of 60 state and local associations of managers, investors, developers, owners, and builders of apartment houses and other residential rental property. It has certification programs dealing with apartment management, maintenance, and property supervision.

Its publications consist of the *Annual Income and Expense Survey* and *NAA Organizational Manual,* and the bimonthly *UNITS* magazine.

National Association of Corporate Real Estate Executives (NACORE):
Founded in 1969 and located in West Palm Beach, FL, NACORE has 3,273 members. Its members consist of anyone managing, administering and/or operating regional real estate departments for national and international corporations. It provides a forum for exchange of concepts and the sharing of common interests among members. It seeks to develop professionalism in corporate real estate development and management offering educational programs through its Corporate Real Estate division and defends the stakes of corporate realty interests.

Its publications include the *Corporate Real Estate Executive,* the annual *Corporate Real Estate Services Directory* and *NACORE Program,* the monthly *Employment Bank* and the quarterly *Newsletter.*

National Association of Home Builders of the U.S. (NAHB): Founded in 1942 and located in Washington, DC, the NAHB has 155,000 members with 824 local groups. Its membership consists of single, multifamily and commercial home builders. The NAHB serves as a public interest group to support legislation for the home building industry. The NAHB offers educational programs on a variety of topics of interest to the home building industry including construction and remodeling, mortgages, and management issues. It has two subsidiaries: the Home Builders Institute and the National Council of the Housing Industry. It also directs several councils including the National Commercial Builders Council, National Council of the Multifamily Housing Industry, National Remodelers Council and National Sales and Marketing Council.

Its publications include the monthly *Builder Magazine, Forecast of Housing Activity, Housing Economics,* and *Housing Market Statistics,* and the semimonthly *Nation's Building News.*

National Association of Real Estate Brokers (NAREB): Founded in 1947 and located in Washington, DC, the NAREB has 7,500 members with 15 regional groups and 6 state groups. It offers certification programs for members of the real estate brokerage industry including Real Estate Management Brokers Institute, National Society of Real Estate Appraisers, Real Estate Brokerage Institute, and the United Developers Council. The NAREB seeks to promote high ethical real estate practices in the real estate brokerage industry. It conducts research on the real estate brokerage industry, including developing reports on sales data, marketing practices and recent industry trends.

Its publications include the bi-monthly *Realtist Flyer*, the annual *Realtist Membership Directory, Souvenir Journal, Exhibitors Prospectus,* and *Catalog of NAREB's Real Estate.*

National Association of Real Estate License Law Officials (NARELLO): Founded in 1930 and located in Centerville, UT, NARELLO has 700 members consisting of state administrators managing real estate licensing laws. It seeks to improve real estate licensing examination administration, improve the effectiveness of license law management and implementation, and improve real estate licensing procedures. It conducts training workshops.

Publications include the annual *Digest of Real Estate License Laws* and the *National Association of Real Estate License Law Officials-Directory,* and the quarterly *NARELLO News.*

National Association of Realtors (NAR): Founded in 1908 and located in Chicago, IL, the NAR is a federation of 50 state associations and 1848 local real estate boards, termed either Realtors or Realtor-Associates. With over 800,000 members the National Association of Realtors promotes education, professional standards, and updates brokerage appraisal techniques, property management, and land development practices, industrial real estate and farm brokerage, and counseling methods.

Its publications include *The Executive Officer,* the monthly *Existing Home Sales,* the annual *National Association of Realtors-National Roster of Realtors,* the periodic *The Real Estate Index,* and *Real Estate Today.*

national flood insurance: Insurance based on the *National Flood Insurance Program,* enacted by Congress in 1968. The intent of this legislation is to provide insurance coverage for those people suffering real property losses as a result of floods. To encourage the buying of national flood insurance, any real property located in a flood plain area cannot be financed through a federally regulated lender unless flood insurance is purchased.

National Society of Real Estate Appraisers (NSREA): A professional society which is an affiliate of the National Association of Real Estate Brokers. The purpose of the NSREA is to formulate rules of ethics and professional conduct and enforce these rules to the benefit of its members. It awards the professional designations of "Master Real Estate Appraiser," "Certified Real Estate Appraiser," and "Residential Appraiser" to those who successfully complete a prescribed course of study and final examination.

Membership in NSREA consists of five categories. These include Candidate, Member, Junior Member, Senior Member, and Master Member. All persons who have successfully passed all qualifying procedures are entitled to use the designation Certified Real Estate Appraiser (CRA).

naturalization: Act of receiving the rights and privileges of a citizen including property rights.

negative amortization: Increase in the outstanding loan balance arising when the mortgage payment does not fully meet the interest charge on the loan. This occurs under indexed loans or when the indexed rate change does not impact the periodic debt service payments. Lower monthly payments are available with negative amortization loans, and most often, borrowers who take this risk are buying in markets with extremely high prices. Many gamble that their home will appreciate enough to cover the difference between their payments and the new loan amount.

negative cash flow:

(1) A situation where a real estate company spends more money than it receives within a stated period of time. This is an unfavorable situation that may result in financial difficulties.

(2) A situation in which real estate operating expenses and mortgage payments exceed rental income. For example, Margo buys an apartment house having a negative cash flow of $19,000 in the first month as calculated below:

Gross rental income	$50,000
Less: Vacancy loss	(4,000)
Effective gross income	46,000
Less: Operating expenses	(10,000)
Net operating income (NOI)	36,000
Less: Debt service	
Interest	(15,000)
Principal payment	(2,000)
	(17,000)
Negative cash flow	$19,000

negative leverage: A situation that occurs when borrowed funds cost more than they produce.

negotiable:

(1) A flexible price that may be adjusted.

(2) A resolved situation between two or people or parties through discussions in which common interests are modified. For example, real estate broker fees may be negotiated.

neighborhood: Local geographic area with similar characteristics. It may be referred to by name (e.g., Brooklyn Heights, Palisades) and have designated boundaries. There are major streets such as for a shopping or restaurant district. Real estate property values partly depend on how good or bad the neighborhood is.

neighborhood life cycle: Changes occurring in neighborhoods over time. The neighborhood life cycle includes the phases of birth, early growth, maturity, and decline. Not all neighborhoods pass through all of these cycles and some pass through them more quickly then others.

Neighborhoods decline for several reasons. The physical aging and deterioration of the building structures as well as the aging of the population contribute to the overall decline. Architectural obsolescence also makes these neighborhoods less attractive. Other changes include the intrusion of a business or industrial area into the neighborhood detracting from its overall quality.

net income: Also called net profit. Rental revenue less total expenses. The bottom line is the key indicator to a real estate company's operating performance for the period. See also *net loss*.

net income multiplier: Method used to calculate the price of income-producing property as follows:

$$\frac{\text{Purchase price}}{\text{Net operating income (NOI)}}$$

For example, if NOI is $20,000 and the asking price is $250,000, the net income multiplier is:

$$\frac{\$250,000}{\$20,000} = 12.5$$

See also *gross income multiplier; gross rent multiplier; capitalization rate; income approach.*

net leasable area: The floor space in a building that is actually under lease. Net leasable area is all the leasable area of a building exclusive of none leasable space such as hallways, building foyers, areas devoted to heating, air conditioning, elevators, plumbing, and other utility areas. The net leasable area produces the lease income economically supporting the building. For example, a building having 5,000 sq. ft. of area may have a net leasable area of 4,250 sq. ft.

net lease: Also called triple net lease. The lessee pays not only a fixed rental charge but also expenses on the rented property, including maintenance.

net listing: A listing wherein the commission is the difference between the selling price and a minimum price set by the seller.

net long-term gain: In taxation, the excess of total long-term gains minus total long-term losses on the sale of real estate. Long-term classification is for real estate held one year or more. This is reported on Schedule D of Form 1040 (for sole proprietors) or Form 1120 (for corporations).

net loss: The excess of total expenses over rental revenue for a real estate business. See also *net income.*

Net Operating Income (NOI): Gross income of a rental property minus allowance for vacancies and operating expenses, excluding depreciation and debt repayments. See also *cash flow.*

Net Present Value (NPV): The difference between the present value of cash inflows generated by real estate and the amount of the initial investment. The present value of future cash flows is computed using the cost of capital (minimum desired rate of return, or hurdle rate) as the discount rate. See also *net present value method.*

net present value method: A method widely used for evaluating real estate projects. Under the net present value method, the present value (PV) of all cash inflows from the project is compared against the initial investment (I). The net present value (NPV), which is the difference between the present value and the initial investment (i.e., NPV = PV − I), determines whether or not the project is an acceptable investment. To compute the present value of cash inflows, a rate, called the cost of capital is used for discounting. Under the method, if the net present value is positive (NPV > 0 or PV > I), the project should be accepted. For example, assume that

Initial investment (I)	$129,500
Estimated life	10 years
Annual cash inflows	$ 30,000
Cost of capital	12%

The present value of cash inflows (PV):

$30,000 × PV of annuity of $1 for 10 years and 12% = $30,000 (5.65) =	$169,500
Initial investment (I)	129,500
Net present value (NPV) = PV − I	$ 40,000

Since the investment's NPV is positive, the investment should be accepted.

net proceeds: Amounts received from the sale or disposal of real property less all relevant deductions (direct costs associated with the sale or disposal).

net realizable value:
(1) Expected selling price of property less costs to sell. It is the net amount received upon the sale of property.

(2) Gross receivables less allowance for doubtful accounts, representing the expected collectibility of those receivables.

net worth:

(1) *Individual:* Total assets less total liabilities less estimated taxes. It is the individual's personal equity which might be the basis for a bank loan to buy real estate.

(2) *Corporation:* Total assets less total liabilities equal to stockholders' equity.

net yield: Net return on a real estate investment. It equals the income less the expenses associated with the property.

New England colonial: Usually a $2\frac{1}{2}$ story home having a gable roof with a chimney at either end of the house. Having a traditional salt box architecture with clapboard siding, the New England Colonial was enlarged for additional family members by adding extensions, often at the rear of the home.

New England farm house: A simple box-shaped house with clapboard siding and a gable roof.

new town: Planned development having different types of homes, retail stores, recreational property (e.g., swimming pool), and employment. The planned community is typically near a metropolitan location so it can enjoy the associated amenities.

no deal, no commission clause: A clause that may be inserted in a listing agreement stating no commission will be paid to the broker until the property title has actually been transferred. Normally, a commission is payable once a ready, willing and able buyer has been found who agrees to the terms of the sale. This protects the seller from being liable for a commission in the event a sale does not actually occur.

nogging: Paneled brickwork between timber quarters, a framed wall, or partition.

nominal loan rate: The loan rate stated on the face of the loan note. The nominal loan rate is not the same as the effective interest rate. For example, if points are charged to secure a loan, the effective interest rate will be higher than the nominal loan rate.

nominee: A person or company in whose name real property is transferred. For example, real estate securities may be kept in a street name registered to the brokerage firm (nominee) irrespective of the investor being the real owner.

no money down: A method of purchasing real estate whereby a maximum amount of leverage is used. Normally the seller will finance the down payment necessary to acquire a mortgage. Thus, the purchaser is able to acquire ownership to the property with none or a marginal cash downpayment. For example, Bill wishes to purchase a home for $150,000. In order to acquire an 80% mortgage, he would need to provide a $30,000 cash down payment:

$$\$150,000 \times 80\% = \$120,000.$$

$$\$150,000 - \$120,000 = \$30,000.$$

However, the seller agrees to provide a $30,000 note in order to have the down payment. Thus, the purchaser acquires the home with the $30,000 note from the seller and the $120,000 mortgage from a mortgage lender for a total of $150,000.

nonalienation clause: A clause in a document forbidding an individual from selling or transferring the subject property to another. Frequently, nonalienation clauses are used in a trust where the grantor of the trust believes the designated beneficiary is a spendthrift. In this situation, a nonalienation clause may be inserted to prevent the beneficiary from selling the assets of the trust. This type of trust is called a spendthrift trust. See also *alienation clause.*

nonassumption clause: A clause inserted in a mortgage agreement requiring a future buyer of the subject property to obtain the consent of the lending institution prior to assuming the mortgage. In this situation, the lending institution normally renegotiates the mortgage charging the current interest rate as well as any related fees. See also *due-on-sale clause.*

nonbearing partition or wall: A partition or wall that provides no support to the structure in which it is located. For example, a nonbearing partition or wall does not support any floors above it. A partition which does provide structural support is termed a bearing partition or wall. See also *wall-bearing; wall-bearing construction.*

nonconforming use: Property use which is in violation of the current zoning ordinance, but had been in use prior to the zoning ordinance's enactment. A nonconforming use is normally allowed to continue; however, there are certain limitations that are placed on its continuance. A nonconforming use is normally not allowed to expand beyond its current boundaries and if it is a nonconforming building, the building may not be rebuilt, in the event of its destruction, without conforming to the current zoning ordinance. For example, Smith owns an automobile salvage business located in a light commercial use zoning area. Smith's use of the property is a nonconforming use which he is allowed to continue. However, he is not permitted to sell this property as an automobile salvage business to anyone else. See also *zoning variance.*

nondisturbance clause:

(1) Clause inserted into a commercial lease by a mortgagee stating the lessee's current lease will not be terminated if there is a foreclosure action against the landlord for the failure to pay a mortgage. Without this clause, a tenant could be evicted in the event of a foreclosure action by the mortgagee. For example, a tenant is concerned the landlord might be defaulting on the mortgage to the property the tenant is currently leasing. Before renewing the lease, the tenant requests a nondisturbance clause be inserted in the mortgage agreement prior to any lease renewal decision.

(2) Clause inserted in a property sale agreement, where the property owner does not have mineral rights, stating any surface improvements made by the property owner will not be disturbed by any subsequent mineral exploration and recovery activities.

nonexclusive listing: See *open listing.*

nonjudicial foreclosure sale: Foreclosure sale enabled in those states permitting the use of a power of sale clause to be inserted into a mortgage or deed of trust empowering the mortgagee to advertise and sell a property at a foreclosure sale upon the mortgagor's payment default. A nonjudicial foreclosure sale enables a foreclosure action without a formal judicial action.

nonperformance: Failure or refusal to perform a specified action. The failure to fulfill contractually agreed upon terms or actions. Nonperformance creates a liability which can enable a judicial damage action. For example, a homeowner contracts with a contractor to build an extension on his home. Because of nonperformance the contractor does not fulfill the terms of the contract. The homeowner initiates a court action awarding a judgment against the contractor in favor of the homeowner for nonperformance.

nonrecourse: Absence of personal liability such as when a creditor may seize an office building used as security for the obligation but cannot attach any other assets of the debtor. See also *recourse*.

non sequitur: Latin for it does not follow. The conclusion of a statement or phrase is illogical.

normal wear and tear: Deterioration in property resulting from its ordinary use and from the aging process. An example is an apartment building that physically deteriorates over the years.

nosing: A step's edge.

notarize: A notary public's guaranteeing the authenticity of a signature.

notary public: A public officer given the right to authenticate a document, accept a person's oath, administer depositions, and to conduct other activities in commercial business. An official seal is used by the notary. An example is when a notary public certifies the document for a real estate transaction.

note: A legally transferable debt instrument by which the issuer agrees to pay the payee within a certain time period. Notes usually pay a specified rate of interest tied to the market rate of interest. A person may sign his or her note payable promising to pay money to another party, such as a bank or creditor at a later date. The payment includes principal and interest. For example, a $50,000, one-year, 8% note

will have a maturity value of $54,000 ($50,000 principal + $4,000 interest). The $4,000 equals $50,000 × 8%. Notes may or may not be supported by collateral. Some types of notes in connection with real estate follow:

Collateral (secured) note: Note in which real estate is pledged for it.

Demand note: Note due on demand by the payee, not on the maturity date.

Joint note: Note having two or more people being obligated for it.

Mortgage note: See *mortgage loan.*

Time note: Note payable at a definite time.

Unsecured note: Note without security.

notice of cancellation clause:
(1) A notice, usually in writing, in which notice of termination is given by one individual or business to another. It is pursuant to a cancellation provision in a contract to forestall future liability.
(2) In insurance, a notice given between an insurer and a reinsurer or an insurer and an insured of the termination of a contract or policy at the time of renewal, or, in the latter case, for nonpayment of premium payments. A notice of cancellation can also be issued for a current policy when a renegotiation of its terms is desired. The cancellation of insurance on a home, apartment house, or office building is a serious matter.

notice of cessation: Actual notice to one or more individuals to cease and desist from performing a particular action. For example, a homeowner begins constructing several new rooms onto an existing house without obtaining a building permit. The municipal building department subsequently issues a notice of cessation to the homeowner ordering him to stop all further work on the renovation until a building permit has been legally obtained.

notice of default: Letter sent to an individual informing him or her they are in default on an agreement. Normally, a notice of default will give the defaulting party the terms necessary to remedy a default and the time period during which the remedy must occur. It will also state what actions will occur if the default is not remedied within the time period specified. For example, a mortgagee sends a notice of default to a mortgagor stating the total arrears which must be paid including any penalties in order to remedy the default. It also states that if the arrears are not paid within a certain period of time, the mortgagee will commence a foreclosure action.

notice of nonresponsibility: A clearly stated notice that an owner or operator will not assume responsibility for an inherent risk. For example, at a parking garage, a large notice of nonresponsibility clearly states the management is not responsible for any valuables left in a car or damage which may occur while the car is parked on the premises.

notice to pay rent or quit: Also called a three-day notice to quit. Notice by a landlord to a tenant to either pay rent due or vacate the premises. If the tenant has a long-term lease, the notice may list penalties.

notice of pendency: See *lis pendens.*

notorious possession: The clear, open, and active occupancy of real estate. For example, notorious possession is one of the tests for adverse possession.

novation: Jointly agreeing to provide an equivalent legal obligation or debt for a previous one. Persons to the contract can also be substituted. A novation requires a valid previous contract, mutual agreement of all the parties to the contract, and the termination of the original contract or discharge of the original

parties before the substitution of a new contract and/or parties to it, respectively. The new contract can have the original parties. Substituted parties can have the original or a new contract provided the major requirements for a novation are satisfied. A novation may arise when one party is experiencing financial or operating difficulty in a real estate transaction.

nuisance: An activity by a property owner that annoys or seriously disturbs other property owners making it discomforting to use their own property. A wide range of activities can be classified as nuisances. However, to be considered a nuisance, the activity must directly affect the comfort and usability of another's property. These activities can include air or water pollution activities, activities generating a large amount of sound or noise, activities which can generally affect the health and sanitation of other properties, commercial uses of a property generating high traffic volume, social activities negatively affecting an area such as the selling of drugs or prostitution. For example, a homeowner raised dogs commercially in the backyard. The noise and smell of the animals create a nuisance for the surrounding neighbors.

null and void: In law, something that is not permitted or binding and as such, is not legally enforceable. An example is an unlawful clause in a contract such as prohibiting the rental of property based on sex, race, or religion.

nunc pro tunc: Latin: now for then. Descriptive of actions which are performed after a deadline has elapsed, but retroactively have the same effect as if they were carried out in a timely manner. For example, a property title is transferred to a new owner; however, the wife of the original owner, who owned the property jointly, never signed the deed. The subsequent owner seeks to sell the property to a third buyer when the wife's missing signature is discovered by a title company prior to issuing title insurance. There is now a cloud on the title and the legality of the sale to the second owner could be challenged. However, the wife of the first owner agrees to sign the title nunc pro tunc.

nuncupative will: An oral will made by a testator/testatrix just prior to death before an insufficient number of witnesses. Nuncupative wills depend on the oral testimony of those witnesses present as proof. They are illegal in several states and are enforceable in others only if they meet specific guidelines.

obiter dictum: Opinion of a judge having no direct legal or binding effect on the outcome of a pending judicial decision. An obiter dictum is considered to be an incidental judicial remark about some point that may or may not be directly relevant to the matter before the bench. For example, while ruling in favor of a mortgagor in a foreclosure action brought by the mortgagee, a judge states an obiter dictum to the mortgagor saying "in the future, pay your bills on time."

obligatory: The legal requirement of a debtor, obligor, to pay a debt and the legal right of a creditor, obligee, to demand satisfaction of a debt or enforce payment in the event of default.

obligee: The person to whom a debt or obligation is owed.

obligor: The person responsible for paying a debt or obligation.

obsolescence: A major factor in depreciation resulting from wear and tear from use and natural deterioration through interaction of weather elements may cause depreciation to a structure. See also *economic obsolescence.*

occupancy: Residing in or using real estate. An example is a tenant in an office building.

occupancy agreement, limited: An agreement allowing occupancy of a premises for a stated period of time provided certain terms are met. A limited occupancy agreement is most frequently used when a prospective buyer is waiting for a closing to occur on a piece of property he/she wishes to occupy. For example, Smith is waiting to close on a home presently vacated by the prospective seller. Smith had to vacate his apartment prior to the closing. He negotiates a limited occupancy agreement with the seller where he agrees to pay $50 per day to occupy the premises until the closing which is scheduled in one week.

occupancy level: The number of units currently occupied in a facility, neighborhood, or city, stated as a percentage of total capacity. For example, a hotel has 80 rooms available for guests. Its average occupancy during the off season is 50. Therefore, its average occupancy level during the off season is 50/80 = 62.5%. The opposite term is vacancy rate. In this example the vacancy rate would be 30/80 = 37.5%. See also *occupancy ratio.*

occupancy ratio: The ratio of rented or leased space to the total amount of space available. For example, an 80 unit commercial office building currently has 60 units occupied. Therefore, the occupancy ratio is 60:80 or 75%. See also *occupancy level.*

offer:

(1) Proposing or presenting for acceptance a price for a property parcel.

(2) Evidence of willingness to enter into a sales agreement.

(3) The bid price in a real estate or security transaction.

offer and acceptance: Two requirements of a contract forming mutual consent.. These factors combined with valuable consideration are the major elements of a contract. For example, Smith puts his home up for sale asking $175,000. Jones makes an offer of $160,000 and Smith accepts the offer. They both sign a sales contract and Jones gives $16,000, 10% of the value of the contract, as valuable consideration. See also *agreement of sale.*

offer to purchase: A proposal to buy property at a specified price. The seller of the property has the options of accepting the offer, rejecting it, or making a counteroffer. For example, Smith signs a listing agreement to sell his home for $175,000. Jones makes an offer to purchase the property at $155,000. Smith makes a counteroffer of $165,000 as a price for the purchase of the home.

offeree, offerer: The former is the individual to whom the offer is presented, while the latter is the person proposing the offer. The same individual may play both roles. For example, an individual, acting as offerer, offers a listing of his home at $175,000. An offeror makes an offer to purchase the home at $155,000. The home owner, now acting as offeree, makes a counter offer of $165,000 to the offeror.

offering statement: See *prospectus.*

office condominium: The units are used as commercial offices. The purchaser of an office condominium owns the title to the individual office unit and not to the property. Maintenance fees are assessed to each owner.

office park: Similar to an industrial park, an office park is a planned and zoned development site for office buildings.

off-site costs: Expenditures incurred to improve a specific real estate development; however, these improvements are not directly on the property. Examples are curbs, driveways, and streets. See also *off-site improvements.*

off-site improvements: Enhancement of a property's value even though the improvement is not on it. Lighting in the street would be an example. See also *off-site costs.*

office of interstate land sales registration: Part of the Department of Housing and Urban Development (HUD), which sees that complete disclosures are made for land sales.

offset statement: An occupant's expressed interest in property that is being rented. An example is a tenant who rents a house and expresses a desire to buy it after the lease expires.

oil and gas lease: A lease granted for the right to explore for and recover oil and gas on a specific parcel of property. The terms of an oil and gas lease specify the length of time of the contract, the landowner's royalties that will be paid to the property owner, and any bonus payments including warranties to repair surface damages. For example, an oil company agrees to pay a 10% landowner's royalty on the value of all recovered oil and gas on the property.

omnibus clause:

(1) Provision in a will that stipulates that any assets not enumerated still pass to the heirs.

(2) Clause in liability insurance policies that extends coverage to unnamed others beyond the insured.

one-hundred-percent-location: Precisely the optimum location for a retail business establishment in an urban central business district (CBD). A one-hundred-percent-location normally is a square block or intersection in the CBD which could be expected to achieve the highest sales volume in terms of its exposure to the maximum traffic.

on-site improvements: Directly enhancing the physical nature of the property such as renovating the building, installing a new driveway and parking lot, and gardening.

on-site management: Managing property directly at its location. The management functions may include showing prospective tenants the facilities, collecting rents, and doing upkeep on the property.

open-end lease: A lease contract providing for a final additional payment on the return of the property to the lessor, adjusted for any value change.

open-end loan: Where the borrower may add to the principal without renegotiating the terms of the loan. Additional sums borrowed under the terms of an open-end loan will have the same rate of interest and life of loan terms as the original loan. Quite frequently a home equity loan is an open-end loan, and the borrower may add to its principal without changing its terms. For example, Smith obtains a $10,000 open-end home equity loan to make some alterations to the house. However, after beginning the alterations, he realizes additional repairs will also be necessary. Thus, he increases the principal of the home equity loan by an additional $5,000 to make the necessary repairs without changing the terms of the loan.

open-end mortgage (Deed of Trust): A mortgage or trust deed that can be increased by the mortgagee (borrower). The mortgagee may secure additional money from the mortgagor (lender) through an agreement which typically stipulates a maximum amount that can be borrowed. See also *closed-end mortgage.*

open house: Way to present a home for sale in which the house is left open for prospective buyers to see. An advertisement may be placed in the newspaper and/or outside the house. The weekends are the best time to show the house because people are typically off from work.

open housing: Housing where affirmative action is actively pursued encouraging people of all races, nationalities, and religions to purchase or rent the facilities. See also *open occupancy.*

open listing: An agreement permitting a real estate agent to sell the property while also allowing the homeowner or other agents to attempt to make the sale. See also *exclusive agency listing.*

open listing agreement: A listing agreement given to many brokers in the hope that one will produce a purchaser within a reasonable period of time. An open listing agreement is open to other brokers and/or agencies. The property owner pays a commission only to the broker who actually produces a buyer for the property.

open mortgage:

(1) A mortgage not having a prepayment clause permitting the mortgagor to repay the mortgage at any time without paying a penalty.

(2) A mortgage where the payments are overdue and open to a foreclosure action at any time.

open occupancy: Housing where affirmative action is proactively pursued protecting the housing rights of people of all races, nationalities, and religions. See also *open housing.*

open space: Unimproved property that is set aside in a developed area for environmental or recreational purposes. For example, a subdivision having 50 homes dedicates five acres for a recreational area to be maintained by the local municipality.

open space ratio: The ratio, in a development, of open space to developed land. For example, a housing subdivision containing 100 acres has devoted 10 acres to open space. Therefore, the open space ratio is 1:10 or 10 percent (10/100).

opening escrow: The deposit given by a buyer of property is delivered to the escrow agent, who retains it for the seller.

operating expense ratio: Total operating expenses divided by effective gross income.

operating expenses:
(1) Those expenses incurred in association with managing an investment property, including repairs and maintenance, legal, and management fees.
(2) Those costs associated with the selling and administrative activities of a real estate company. They are subdivided into selling expenses and general and administrative expenses.

operating lease: Regular rental of property between the lessee and lessor for a fee. An operating lease does not satisfy the criteria for a capital lease. An example is renting an apartment. A lessee recognizes rent expense. A corporate lessee should disclose the future minimum lease payments in total and for each of the five succeeding years, contingent rentals, sublease rentals, and classes (types) of property leased. The lessor recognizes rental revenue.

opinion of title: A certification of a property title issued by an attorney after examining the abstract of title. The attorney's opinion of title is essential to obtaining title insurance, a mortgage or the ability to transfer title.

optimum use: See *highest and best use*.

option:
(1) The ability or right to choose a certain alternative. An example is a lease of a property with the option to buy.
(2) The right to buy or sell an item at a specified price within a given period of time. If the right is not exercised after a specified time, the option expires.

option listing agreement: A bilateral contract where an optionor gives an option to the optionee for the right, but not the obligation, to purchase property within a certain period of time at a specified price. An option listing agreement is purchased for a consideration and entitle the optionee to exercise the right of purchase within the time specified. If the option is not exercised within the specified time period, than it will expire worthless.

optional:
(1) Not required.
(2) Right to select something or perform some act. An example is a renter of property that is given the option to buy the home at the end of the rental period or to renew the lease.

optionee: One who purchases an option. For example, Smith pays Jones $10,000 for an option to purchase property at $100,000 within six months.

optionor: Person or business that provides an option to someone else.

oral: Statement made by a person that is not in writing. An example is an oral representation made by a real estate broker to a prospective buyer of property.

oral contract: A contract not in writing. Oral contracts are legally enforceable except for those applicable to the sale of real estate.

ordinance: Law enacted by a local authority (e.g., city) applicable to the action of people or things. An example is a fine of $5,000 for littering vacant real estate.

ordinary and necessary business expenses: Tax term describing current and necessary business expenses. Ordinary and necessary business expenses do not include long-term capital losses. For example, the XYZ stationary store deducts their utility costs on their tax return as an ordinary and necessary business expense.

ordinary annuity: See *annuity*.

ordinary interest: Interest based on a 360-day year instead of a 365-day year. The former is referred to as simple interest and the latter is termed exact interest. The difference between the two types of interest can be significant when a substantial investment is involved.

ordinary loss: In taxation losses that can offset ordinary income. Assume Smith owns and operates an apartment house. Minor tenant damage to the property is used to offset rental income.

oriel window: A projecting window located above the first floor that is supported by brackets.

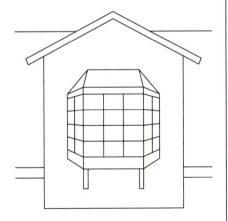

orientation:

(1) Locating a structure after considering such factors as the homeowner's desired privacy, noise, wind, and sunlight.

(2) Position of a structure on a specific location relative to prevailing winds and sunlight.

(3) Familiarizing a newly hired employee in a real estate firm with the required knowledge. An example is "breaking-in" a new real estate broker with the general neighborhood.

(4) Employee's professional background such as computer knowledge.

origination fee: See *loan origination fee*.

ostensible:

(1) Alleged to be real or genuine.

(2) What appears to be such as a real estate agent's seeming authority to act on behalf of a principal. However, the agent may not in fact have real authority. In law, one dealing with the agent may reasonably rely on the apparent representations. Assume the principal instructs his real estate agent not to sell a house for less than $200,000. If it is sold for $175,000 to a buyer who has reason to rely on the agent's actions, the property has been legally transferred. However, the principal may sue the real estate broker for breach of contract.

Other People's Money (OPM): The use of borrowed funds by people or businesses to increase the return on an investment. Examples are a mortgage to purchase real estate and buying real estate stock on margin. See also *financial leverage; leverage*.

outdoor living: Style of life emphasizing outdoor activities, amenities, and recreation. Examples are campers and barbecues. It is usually on a short-term basis.

outlawed: Something that is illegal. An example is an unenforceable debt because it has exceeded the statute of limitations.

outstanding balance: Amount still unpaid at a particular date on a loan or other financing agreement (e.g., lease).

over age 55 home sale exemption: The Internal Revenue Code (IRC Sections 1034 and 121) providing that a person over age 55 can sell a principal residence at a gain and exclude once in a life time up to $125,000 of the gain for taxes. It is allowed irrespective of the purchase of another home. The person must have used the property as a principal residence for 3 of the last 5 years. For example, Roberta, over age 55, sells her principal residence, which she has resided in for the last 3 years, at a $160,000 gain. She may exclude $125,000 of the gain from taxation. The remainder ($35,000) is a taxable capital gain. See also *1034 Exchange (rollover)*.

overage:
(1) Rental increment tied to sales or profit that is in addition to the flat rental fee. Assume a retail store in a mall is charged a base rental of $5,000 per month plus 2% of sales. If sales are $100,000, the overage would be $2,000 and total rental would be $7,000.
(2) Selling price received for property in excess of the expected amount.
(3) An excessive amount; surplus.

overage income: Rental based on a percent of sales or profit that is in addition to the constant rental amount.

overall rate of return:
(1) Net operating income (NOI) of property relative to its market value. If rental income property worth $1,000,000 results in NOI of $100,000, the overall return is 10%.
(2) NOI compared to the initial cost of the property as distinguished from its market price.

overhang: A wall or roof which extends beyond a lower wall. See also *cantilever*.

Overhang   Overhang

over-improvement: Land improvement that is more extensive than the surrounding neighborhood justifies or that can be economically warranted. For example, an individual builds a home with a higher construction cost than the neighborhood's average assessed valuation. Another example is building a second level on a house where all other houses in the neighborhood are one level. The homeowner's cost of the improvement exceeds the incremental assessed value of the house. A further example is the construction of a commercial building that is larger than its business operations can justify. The resulting empty space can be a net liability.

override: Percentage of a commission paid by a salesperson to a supervisor in an organization. For example, a real estate salesperson must pay a 25% override to the real estate broker for all successful real estate sales. If the broker earns a commission of $10,000, the override to the sales agent is $2,500. The broker's net commission is $7,500.

overriding royalty: Percentage of royalties derived from an oil and gas lease payable to someone other than the property lessor. It is a net royalty interest in the oil and gas recovered at the surface free of all operating expenses. For example, an oil company pays a 20% overriding royalty on all recovered oil and gas to a group of investors who financed the exploration costs.

owner occupant: A property owner who lives in the property he also leases or rents to others. For example, Smith owns a two-family house. He lives in one side of the house and rents out the other side to the Jones family.

ownership: Person or entity that has title or a right to something which is typically being held. Examples are real property (e.g., land, house), corporation (through stock ownership), and personal property (e.g., automobile). Ownership of property may be held by one or more people or entities.

ownership form: Methods of owning real estate. Ownership form has important consequences for income tax, estate tax, corporate income tax, and survivorship. Real estate may be owned by one or more persons. Methods of ownership include tenancy in common, joint tenancy, a tenancy by the entirety, tenancy in severalty, partnership, limited partnership, and corporation.

ownership rights to realty: The right to possess, exclusively occupy, enjoy, control, and dispose of real estate. Ownership rights to realty are granted by the ownership of a title to real property.

package mortgage: Mortgage on both the purchased real estate and personal property of a durable type. The entire amount financed is considered one mortgage. In residential real estate, a builder might include a stove, refrigerator, dishwasher, or air conditioning in the sales price. For commercial real estate, certain equipment or furniture is often included in the sales price. The advantage to the purchaser is that these items can be financed over a much longer period and at a much lower interest rate than if a separate financial instrument was used. For the builder or seller, these items serve as inducements used in financing the sale.

packaging:

(1) Transfer of both real and personal property. An example is the sale of a home with personal belongings (e.g., furniture).

(2) Putting together a group of property to be sold together, perhaps at a discount price because several items are bought in combination.

panel board: Depressed or raised framed in portion of a wall, ceiling, or door. A panel board pattern is decorative and gives the effect of a series of highlighted squares or rectangular pieces.

panel heating: Heating system hidden behind special panels, the walls, or the ceiling. Can use electric heating elements, hot air, or hot water pipes.

paper: Amount received by a seller of real property in the form of credit (e.g., mortgage, note) rather than cash. Interest is typically received on the note. If a house is sold for $300,000 of which $100,000 is cash and the balance in a mortgage, $200,000 of paper has been received. It may be risky for the seller to take paper if the buyer has significant financial problems which prevented him from getting a mortgage at the bank.

paper profit: Unrealized (holding) gain in value of real property from holding it. The increased value is not recognized in the accounts. When the property is sold there will be a realized gain or loss.

paper title: Passing of title to property that is in fact not valid.

parallel:

(1) Properties that are side by side but do not meet. They are in the same direction with a constant distance.

(2) Similar property.

(3) Comparing like property.

parapet: Protective wall along a roof or below a terrace.

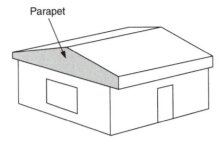

Parapet

parcel: Specific portion of a larger land tract. A parcel can also be a lot in a property subdivision.

parking area: Space reserved for specified vehicles (e.g., cars, trucks, and buses). For example, an office building may have space available for automobiles of tenants, clients of tenants, and other visitors (e.g., patrons of a restaurant). Parking facilities may be indoors or outdoors. There may or may not be a charge for parking.

parol: Statement made verbally. It is better legally to have a written statement because verbal ones without witnesses may be denied.

parol evidence rule: Permits oral evidence to augment a written contract in certain cases.

parquet floor: An inlaid stone or wood flooring arranged in tightly fitting geometrical patterns. It is decorative and often more than one color.

partial release: Release of a portion of a property from a mortgage.

partial taking: Purchase of part of property or property rights when condemnation takes place. The owner must be justly reimbursed.

participation mortgages:
(1) Involves more than one mortgagee lent on a real estate project, such as with a large commercial project.
(2) Involves more than one borrower being responsible for a mortgage, such as with a cooperative apartment.
(3) Agreement between a mortgagee and a mortgagor that provides for the lender having a certain percentage ownership in the project once the lender makes the loan.

partition:
(1) The division of real estate between owners giving each an undivided interest. For example, Smith and Jones own a parcel of property as a partnership. They dissolve their partnership and partition the parcel of property equally giving each an undivided ownership.
(2) An interior wall dividing an area into two or more rooms or separate areas.

partition action: Court action to order a compulsory sale of real estate owned jointly between two or more owners. A partition action divides the proceeds of a real estate sale among the joint owners rather than physically dividing the real estate into separate undivided interests. For example, a partition action occurs in an estate dispute between the heirs of the Smith estate where all were granted a tenancy in common for a large land parcel. The court ordered the property sold at market value with dividing the proceeds equally among the heirs.

partnership: Form of real estate organization created by an agreement between two or more individuals who contribute capital and/or their services. Advantages are: (1) it is easily established with minimal organizational effort and costs; and (2) it is free from some of the government regulations. Disadvantages are: (1) it involves unlimited liability for the individual partners; (2) it ceases to exist upon the withdrawal or death of any of the partners; and (3) its ability to raise large amounts of capital is limited. A partnership consists of general partners and limited partners.

party wall: Used to support two properties; it is attached to both.

passive income (loss): Income (loss) resulting from the rental of real property in which the individual does not significantly participate. In most cases, passive losses may not be used to reduce active income.

passive investor: Invests in rental property but does not manage that property.

passive solar heating: Solar heating using architectural design characteristics and building materials rather than an active solar heating design. For example, heavy insulation with several large windows facing south and very small windows in the northern exposure.

pass-through securities: Securities supported by a pool of mortgages. The principal and interest are due monthly on the mortgages and are passed through to the investors who bought the pool. Examples are the mortgage-backed securities guaranteed by the GNMA and Freddie Mac securities. However, Freddie Mac securities are not federally guaranteed.

patent: Exclusive right granted by the government to a company or person to use, manufacture, and sell a product or process for a 17-year period without interference or infringement by other parties. As a practical matter, the useful life is usually less than 17 years because of changes in the market place and new technology. If a patent is assigned to others, royalties may be obtained.

payback period: Time required to recoup the initial investment is computed as follows:

$$\frac{\text{Initial investment}}{\text{Annual cash inflow}}$$

Assume a real estate investment of $5,000,000 that will pay $2,000,000 a year for 6 years. The payback period is

$$\frac{\$5,000,000}{\$2,000,000} = 2.5 \text{ years}$$

The shorter the payback period, the better since by recovering the money faster it can be invested for a return. A shorter payback period involves less risk of not obtaining the investment money back.

payment cap: Limit on how much a borrower's payments can increase.

penalty: Amount to be paid by a person or business for violating a statute or legal court order. It may also be assessed for violating the provisions of a contract. Examples of penalties are a charge made by the Internal Revenue Service for underpaying corporate income taxes, penalty assessed by a municipality for failing to pay property taxes, penalty due to prepaying a mortgage, amount arising from breaking a real estate contract, and fee due from prematurely terminating a lease.

penalty clause: Contractual provision specifying a dollar amount or rate an individual to the contract must pay for not conforming to its terms. An example is the fee charged for a late mortgage payment.

pendente lite: Latin for pending the suit. A suit which is actually in progress and the outcome is pending.

penthouse: Edifice constructed on the top floor of a building usually occupying less than $\frac{1}{2}$ the roof area. A penthouse is used for two purposes:
(1) One or more luxury apartments directly accessed by a separate elevator or staircase.
(2) Structure housing elevator, air conditioning and/or other mechanical or electrical systems.

per autre vie: Time period of an estate based on how long a third party lives.

percentage-of completion method: Recognizes profit on a long-term construction contract as it is earned gradually during the construction period. This approach is preferred over the completed contract method because it does a better job of matching revenue and expense in the period of benefit. It should be used when reliable estimates of the degree of completion are possible. It is more realistic and levels out the earnings.

percentage lease: Rental due on the leased property is formulated as a percentage of sales volume. There is typically a minimum rental specified. An example is a retail store that pays rental based on its dollar sales.

percent of monthly gross income rule: Rule stating that the monthly mortgage payment, property taxes, and insurance should not exceed 25% of a family's monthly gross income, or about 35% for a Federal Housing Administration (FHA) or Veterans Administration (VA) mortgage.

EXAMPLE: A family has gross income of $120,000 ($10,000 a month). Under this guideline, the family's monthly mortgage payment, property taxes, and insurance should not exceed $2,500 (25% of $10,000).

perch: Land surveying measurement that is 16.5 feet in length, or $5\frac{1}{2}$ yards. A perch is also called a rod or a pole. Today the term perch is seldom used; however, it is found in old deeds, surveys, and contracts.

percolation test: Determines the ability of soil to absorb and draw down water. A percolation test is essential to determine the location of a drainage field for waste disposal.

performance bond: A bond, also known as a completion bond, given by a contractor and issued by an insurance company to guarantee the completion of contracted work. Public authorities often require a performance bond prior to granting a contract for work to be completed.

perimeter:
(1) Property boundaries.
(2) Outside dimensions of a building.

perimeter heating: Warm air heating system where ducts are located in the concrete slab of a building constructed without a basement. As the name implies, a perimeter heating system is located around the perimeter of the rooms of a building where the heated air from the furnace is carried through the ducts to registers located in the floor. The air is recycled through ceiling ducts back to the furnace.

periodic tenancy: Tenancy having no written lease or contract. A periodic tenancy can be on a month-to-month or week-to-week basis. See also *tenancy at will.*

perjury: Individual who gives false statements under oath, which is a criminal act punishable by imprisonment and fine. An example is signing a tax return that fraudently understates rental income, giving false testimony in a court action, and signing one's name to a legal document with willful attempt to deceive.

permanent mortgage:
(1) Mortgage for an extended time period (e.g., 25 years).
(2) Type of real estate investment trust (REIT) that gives long-term mortgages to real estate developers and contractors on new or current property.

permit: Document issued by a governmental agency permitting the recipient to do something. An example is a building permit to construct a structure.

per se: Latin for by itself. A per se matter is one that is alone and not connected to another matter. For example, age, per se, is not a determinant of health.

person: Individual with legal privileges and obligations. The legal term is sometimes used for a corporation.

personal assets: Personal property and other assets a person has in his estate.

personal financial statement: Document showing the financial health of an individual that may be requested for a loan application to buy real estate. A Statement of Financial Condition presents assets at estimated current values listed by order of liquidity and maturity. Business interests that represent a significant part of total assets should be presented separately from other investments. An example would be real estate investments. Only the person's interest (amount that person is entitled to) as beneficial owner should be included when assets are jointly owned. Liabilities are shown by order of maturity. A Statement of Changes in Net Worth is optional showing the major sources and uses of net worth. Comparative financial statements are also optional. Footnote disclosures should be made of the following: (1) individuals covered by the financial statements; (2) major methods used in determining current values; (3) nature of joint ownership of assets including real estate; (4) face amount of life insurance owned; (5) methods and assumptions used to compute estimated income taxes; (6) maturities and interest rates relating to debt; and (7) noncancellable commitments such as operating leases.

personality: Person's behavior partly genetic and partly learned through experience over time. Some people have good personal traits while others have poor ones. An individual's personality should be matched to her job. For example, a successful real estate salesperson should have an outward, persevering, and friendly behavior who feels comfortable talking to people.

personal property: Assets owned by an individual as part of his or her estate except for land and everything attached to the land. Personal property may be either tangible, having physical substance such as an auto and furniture, or intangible, lacking physical substance such as stocks, bonds, and bank deposits.

per stirpes: Type of property distribution occurring when a person dies intestate. The estate is divided by the children of the deceased and by their children. For example, if a husband dies intestate, having survived his wife, and there were four children resulting from the union, one of whom predeceased his father after having two children of his own, the estate would be divided so the three surviving children would each receive 25% of the estate, while the two children of the deceased fourth child would each receive 12.5% of the estate.

per-unit allocation: Allocating common or central costs to each unit of property. An example is assigning to each owner of an apartment based on the number of rooms occupied the cost incurred by the landlord to paint and carpet the hallways. Another example is in a condominium to allocate central maintenance costs to each condominium owner based on the size of the dwelling unit.

photovoltaic: Active photoelectric cell made of silicon and activated by electromagnetic energy in the form of light waves. They are now used in a wide range of electronic systems including modulated-light systems such as fiber optics arrays, measuring devices, and in control devices. Photovoltaic cells activated by the sun are called solar cells. Photovoltaic cells employ a solid-state diode structure with a large area on a silicon wafer. The surface layer is very thin and transparent so that light can penetrate the silicon. A typical photovoltaic cell generates approximately 0.6–1.0 volts. Typical efficiencies for solar cells currently run from 10 to 15%.

physical damage insurance: Insurance coverage for any risk that can cause physical damage to the insured item. An example is a comprehensive homeowner's insurance policy.

physical depreciation or deterioration: Decline in value of property from use.

The property's condition is aging. An example is plumbing deteriorating over time.

pier:

(1) A column designed to support a concentrated load. A pier column is made out of steel, steel reinforced concrete or wood.

(2) A structure extending out into the water supported by numerous columns providing access to water or vessels.

piggyback loan: Loan in which two or more lenders participate in the total financing of a single mortgage. The lenders in a piggyback loan do not necessarily have equal shares. For example, Smith obtains a $600,000 loan on his property. Bank A provides $400,000 and Bank B provides $200,000, all secured by the same mortgage.

pitch:

(1) The angle of a roof in relation to its horizontal axis expressed as a ratio of inches (cmm) per foot of horizontal distance.

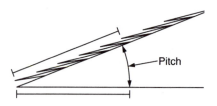

(2) The sloping of ground, such as sloping ground away from the rear of a house to prevent the flooding of a basement.

(3) A viscous tar resin used in caulking and paving.

PITI: Abbreviation for "principal, interest, taxes, and insurance," the primary elements of many monthly mortgage payments.

plaintiff: An individual's bringing a legal action against a defendant. The plaintiff wants relief from the judge against a defendant. An example is investors in a real estate investment trust (REIT) who are suing the trust for false and misleading financial statements.

plank: Long, wide piece of lumber having a minimum width of 8 inches with a minimum thickness of 1 inch for hardwood and 2 to 4 inches for softwood.

Planned Unit Development (PUD): Individually owned lots and houses with community ownership of common areas.

planning commission: Governmental body having the responsibility for planning the future development of a jurisdictional area. A planning commission is responsible for developing and managing a zoning ordinance as well as interfacing with a professional planning department.

plaster: Material used for covering the surfaces of walls or ceilings. Plaster used to be made from plaster of paris, but is now primarily made from cement mixed with sand and water. After plaster hardens and dries, it is usually covered with a coat of paint.

plaster of paris: Dehydrated gypsum that is mixed with water to form a rapidly setting material. Plaster of paris sets too rapidly to be practical for most building applications, but it is useful for ornamental creations. It is widely used for developing casts.

plat: Map that shows the location and boundaries of individual properties.

plat book: Listing of all of the plats of subdivided plots in a jurisdiction showing the location, boundaries, and plat owners. A plat book normally shows other improvements including roads, blocks, and lots.

plate:

(1) Horizontally placed timber that is connected to other timber.

(2) Smooth, flat, thin piece of metal.

(3) Electrical covering.

plat map: See *plat.*

platted land: Property that has been segregated into parts.

pleadings: Formal allegations by all of the parties to an action including complaints, answers, and replies to counterclaims.

pledged account mortgage (PAM): Method of using the buyer's down payment on a home as an interest bearing collateralized account to help offset the mortgage amortization process. The home down payment is used to supplement the early payments of a mortgage helping to qualify the mortgagor for a loan. The supplemental payments are incrementally decreased usually over the first five years of a loan to the point where the entire loan payment is assumed by the mortgagor without any supplementation. The concept of the loan is based on the theory the pledgor's increase in personal income will offset the reduction in supplemental payments by the pledged account mortgage. For example, Smith buys a home for $150,000 depositing ½ of the $30,000 down payment into an interest bearing pledged account mortgage. He secures a 30-year $120,000 mortgage at 8% annual interest for a monthly payment of $880.52. However, the mortgage payments are reduced in the first five years by the pledgee drawing upon the $15,000 deposited in the pledged account.

pledgee: Individual to whom a mortgage, or property, is pledged. See also *pledged account mortgage (PAM)*.

pledgor: Individual making the payments in a mortgage or pledging a mortgage or property. See also *pledged account mortgage (PAM)*.

plot:
(1) A parcel of land or small lot.
(2) A plat.
(3) A diagram or schematic drawing of a building or land.

plot plan: Scale drawing or diagram illustrating the proposed use of a land plat of property.

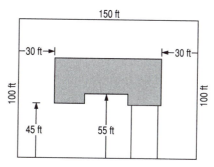

plottage: The increase in value occurring through the process of combining several contiguous land lots into one large lot held under one ownership. For example, Jones combined five contiguous lots valued at $15,000 each into one large lot worth $125,000. The plottage value is $125,000 − (5 × $15,000) = $50,000.

plottage increment: See *plottage value*.

plottage value: The result of combining two or more parcels of land so that the one large parcel has more value than the sum of the individual parcels.

plywood: Wood sheeting made from gluing together at least three layers of veneer. The grain is placed at right angles with each adjoining layer's providing additional strength.

pocket license card: Pocket-sized real estate license issued for brokers and salespersons by most states. Identifies the person as a real estate licensee.

point: Loan service charge; each point equals 1% of the amount of the total mortgage loan, which must be paid up front when a home is purchased. It is a one-time, immediate charge that increases the effective cost of borrowing. Example: $200,000 × .02 = $4,000. Costs can be added to the mortgage and paid over the lifetime of the contract.

point of diminishing returns: Point at which additional units of a specific resource no longer cause the level of satisfaction that was previously attained.

police power: Right of any government agency to enact and enforce certain regulations to provide for the health and safety and general welfare of the public.

policy:
(1) In insurance, a contract that provides coverage against given risks. Coverage limits for real estate are also specified.
(2) A real estate owner's policy and rules regarding the use of the property by the tenant.

population density: Population per square mile of a given area. For example, the population density of the United States is approximately 69 persons per square mile overall. High population density levels create crowding. The tendency of large numbers of people to live in urban areas creates congestion. For example, if the United States had a population of about 300 million people, it would not suffer from crowding; in fact much of its territory would still remain empty. On the east coast of the United States, the area from Boston to Washington, DC has been termed megalopolis because of its high population density. High population density contributes to increased energy utilization for transportation and pollution.

porosity: See *soil porosity.*

portfolio: Reducing real estate investment risk by acquiring diversified holdings.

portfolio diversification: Choosing alternative real estate investment instruments having different risk-return features. Diversification can be done by regions and types of real estate. Diversification provides a lower but acceptable overall return.

portfolio income: Income derived from a collection of asset investments. Real property investments produce rental and lease payment income. Investments in mortgages and other long term debt instruments produce interest income, while equity investments generate dividends.

positive leverage: When the return on borrowed funds exceed the after-tax interest cost. It is profitably using other people's money. See also *leverage; leverage in real estate investing.*

possession: Holding and controlling property. It includes not only custody but also having some legal right. An example is occupying real property and enjoying its benefits.

possession by adverse possession: Way to acquire title to real estate when an occupant has been in actual, open, exclusive, and continuous occupancy of property for an extended period of time. For example, Harry acquired title to the property where he resided, although he did not have a deed, he had lived there for 20 years and the actual owner was unknown.

possessory action: Litigation undertaken to obtain or maintain possession of real property.

post mortem: Investigation into the causes of death. A post mortem is normally performed by a public coroner. It might be performed to determine the cause of death of an apartment house tenant.

potential gross income: Expected revenue to be earned from a sale or the rendering of services. An example is a potential buyer of an apartment house who must estimate the gross rentals to be received in order to determine a realistic offering price for the property.

power of attorney: Legally executed and witnessed document giving another the power to act as one's attorney or agent in handling real estate dealings. The power may be general or specific. The power of attorney is revoked upon death.

power of sale: Provision in a mortgage agreement granting the lender the right to sell the foreclosed property of the borrower if the payments are defaulted upon. The borrower will only recoup the amount exceeding the selling price less legal expenses less the debt balance.

prairie house: Architectural style featuring a long low roof line with a continuous row of windows and a plain exterior. It is a very open design with long horizontal lines rather than having small secluded rooms.

preamble: Clause at the beginning of a legislative statute explaining its purpose. A preamble neither confers or increases powers contained within a statute and is therefore not an essential element of it.

preclosing: Mock closing; all information is available prior to an actual closing in order to insure all documents are properly executed by the appropriate parties. A preclosing is normally used only when it is anticipated that the actual closing could be complicated by many extraneous factors.

preemptive right: Right of a current stockholder to maintain the percentage ownership in a real estate company by purchasing new shares on a proportionate basis before they are issued to the public. It allows existing stockholders to keep the value and control they presently

enjoy. The new shares may be issued to the current stockholders at a lower price than the going market price. Further, brokerage commissions do not have to be paid. For example, if an individual owns 3% of the shares of XYZ Realtors Corporation that has a new offering of 100,000 shares, the individual is entitled to buy 3,000 shares at a favorable price to maintain the proportionate interest.

preexisting use: See *nonconforming use.*

prefabricated house: House made using standardized components that are preassembled on an assembly line in a factory rather than being built from "scratch" on a site. Normally, the prefabricated house is trucked onto the home site as a complete unit where it is installed on a completed foundation. Often times the prefabricated house is installed in preassembled components which are simply attached to each other on site. The advantages of a prefabricated house include lower cost, as a function of mass production and high quality.

premise: Land and any existing tenements that are part of a conveyance. For example, upon closing a real estate sale, the seller deeds the premises to the purchaser.

premium:

(1) Periodic fee paid for insurance protection.

(2) Amount paid for real estate above the expected prevailing price.

prepaid expenses: Expenditures paid for in advance such as property insurance, rent, and interest. Prepaid expenses are not used or consumed until later. They are typically of a recurring nature.

prepaid interest: Interest a person pays before it is actually incurred. An example is a one year's interest that a borrower agrees to pay in advance to a bank on a mortgage. This rarely occurs.

prepayment: Payment of a debt before its due such as a mortgage payment or insurance premiums. See also *due date*.

prepayment fee: Charge assessed on the remaining principal, often contained in mortgages, when an obligation is paid before its due. For example, Steve obtains a $300,000 mortgage at 12% to buy a house having a 3% prepayment fee. If he pays the mortgage immediately, he will have to pay $9,000 ($300,000 × 3%) as a prepayment fee.

prepayment of loan clause: Provision permitting a lender to charge the borrower a penalty for repaying a loan before its due date (prepaying).

prepayment penalty: Fee a borrower is assessed for the right to make a loan payment before the due date. An example is the prepayment charge for paying-off a mortgage early.

prepayment privilege: Clause in a mortgage that allows the borrower to pay more than the monthly amount and to retire the loan early without a penalty. See also *prepayment of loan clause*.

prepayment terms: Provisions of credit that apply when a loan is paid.

prerelease: Securing lease commitments to a building prior to its being available for occupancy. For example, a developer offers a discounted lease to potential tenants providing they agree to sign a lease prior to the completion of the building. A prelease agreement is often required from a mortgagee in order for a developer to obtain a permanent mortgage commitment.

presale: Selling a commercial or residential unit prior to its completion. For example, a residential home developer discounts the price of a home by $10,000 if prospective buyers will agree to a purchase prior to its completion. This enables a developer to obtain a construction loan to complete additional units.

prescription: Method of obtaining title to property through open, notorious, adverse, and continuous use of the property for a statutorily prescribed period of time. For example, John openly and continuously occupies an abandoned home. Eventually it is ruled that he has acquired title to the property through prescription.

prescriptive rights: See *adverse possession.*

present value: Current value of a future sum or stream—annuity or mixed—of dollars discounted at a given rate. Present value determination is the inverse of future value calculation. See also *time value of money.*

present value analysis: Way of valuing real estate that computes the discounted present value of an expected stream of income, including rental income and future capital gains or losses. See also *discounted cash flow; time value of money.*

present value method: See *present value analysis.*

present value tables: Precalculated tables providing the present values of $1 or an annuity of $1 for different time periods and at different discount rates. They are found in Table 3 and Table 4 in the Appendix, respectively. See also *time value of money.*

preterit: Past action(s) of a property owner or tenant.

preventive maintenance: Maintenance procedures conducted to prevent later repairs and furthering a longer useful life. For example, many boilers and burners are cleaned and serviced each year before the winter season.

price: Amount of money paid for some form of property. In real estate, the price paid for property is usually the market price; however, in the case of a forced sale, as in a foreclosure sale, the price received could be substantially lower.

price appreciation: Increase in the value of real or personal property. The price may increase because of a number of factors, such as shortage in supply, improved economy, favorable political environment, tax incentives, increased profitability. An example is the increase in the price of real estate.

price level adjusted mortgage: Interest rate on a mortgage is changed periodically based on the change in a general price index to take into account inflation, such as a yearly adjustment. An example is the consumer price index. For example, if the inflation rate increases so does the interest rate the borrower has to pay.

prima facie: Latin for at first sight. Facts assumed to be true unless subsequent evidence disproves it.

primary beneficiary:
(1) The person identified as the major beneficiary(ies) of an insurance policy. Secondary beneficiaries may also be nominated if the primary beneficiary dies before the policyholder.
(2) The person(s) to receive the benefits of a trust when distribution occurs. Secondary beneficiaries may be nominated if the primary beneficiary(ies) predecease the trust distribution.
    See also *per stirpes.*

primary financing: Loan that comes before all other loans in the event of default.

primary lease: Rental agreement directly between the landlord and tenant. If the tenant then rents it out to another, it is referred to as a sublease. The relationship takes the following form:

Owner—(*Primary Lease*)—Tenant— (*Sublease*)—Subtenant

primary location: Real property located in an excellent area for its designated objective. An example is a restaurant situated near office buildings, on the main boulevard, so it is easy to see, and has ample parking.

primary mortgage market: Mortgage market in which original loans are made by lenders. The market is made up with lenders who supply funds directly to borrowers and hold the mortgage until the debt is paid. Examples are savings and loans (S&Ls), commercial banks, mutual savings banks, and mortgage companies. The primary market is contrasted to the secondary mortgage market, which involves buying and selling of first mortgages by banks, insurance companies, and other mortgagees to free money for new loans.

prime contractor: See *general contractor.*

prime rate: Loan rate charged by commercial banks to their best customers. This is a bellwether rate in that it is construed as a sign of rising or falling loan demand and economic activity. It will affect many interest rates including mortgage rates. See also *discount rate.*

prime tenant: Major tenant in an office building or shopping center. A prime tenant occupies more space than any other tenant in a commercial development. For example, in a 20-story office building, the national headquarters of a nationwide bank occupies 11 floors.

principal:
(1) Amount being risked in a real estate investment.
(2) Person designating an agent to act for him.
(3) Primary individual having full financial liability.
(4) Owner of a real estate business.

principal broker: Licensed broker having the principal responsibility for all licensed brokers and agents in the concern. A principal broker normally receives an override on the sales of all the other licensees. For example, at XYZ real estate brokerage, John Smith, the principal broker, receives a 15% override on the sales of all other agents' and brokers' sales. See also *override*.

Principal and Interest Payment (P&I): Used to indicate what is included in a monthly payment on rental property. If the payment includes only principal and interest, property taxes, and hazard insurance would make the total payment higher.

Principal, Interest, Taxes and Interest Payment (PITI): Used to indicate what is included in a monthly payment on rental property. Principal, interest, taxes and interest payment (PITI) are the four major portions of a usual monthly payment.

principal meridian: Principal line running north and south in the government rectangular survey method. Other meridians, each 24 miles apart, are surveyed from the principal meridian.

principal residence: Primary residence of an individual. The principal residence can be a single family home, condominium, cooperative, or trailer. A principal residence may qualify for a homestead exemption in those states providing for this designation.

principle of conformity: How one's real property fits into the neighborhood. For example, if someone's house is very small and in terrible condition relative to all the other surrounding homes, it does not conform.

principle of substitution: Highest amount a property is worth equal to the amount that would have to be paid to buy equivalent property in the market place.

principle of supply and demand: Economic principle determining the market prices of goods, services, and property. The principle states there is a pricing relationship between supply and demand for real property. Economic forces interact affecting the overall pricing relationship. If demand for a given property increases and the

supply remains constant, then the price will increase. However, an increase in price will then spur increased supply which will tend to depress prices.

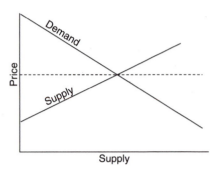

prior: Something coming before. Examples are the year before, first lien on property, and previous owner of property.

priority:
(1) Preference;
(2) Precedence;
(3) Something given prior attention; and
(4) Something having a higher level of importance or ranking. Examples of when priority apply are a prospective tenant for an apartment is the first to be called, a secured creditor coming before an unsecured creditor in bankruptcy, and a first lien on property.

Private Mortgage Insurance (PMI): Insurance for lenders against a loss if a borrower defaults on a mortgage with a low down payment. It is a policy that a home buyer can obtain from a private lender to qualify for a down payment of less than 20%. In this case, the borrower pays the premiums.

private offering: An offering of securities, stock and/or debt, directly to investors (usually large institutional investors) rather than through the public exchange markets. An advantage of a private placement to a real estate business is that the securities do not have to be registered with the Securities and Exchange Commission.

privity: Relationship between individuals or entities out of which exists a mutual interest. An example is a privity of contract among the contracting parties concerning the actions each are to take.

probate court: Court having the responsibility of performing probate of wills and administering estates. In certain states, a probate court can appoint guardians for minor children of an estate.

proceeds from resale: See *resale proceeds.*

procuring cause: Claim by a real estate broker that his/her actions were the principal cause of the completion of a property sale between two parties. A successful procuring cause claim would entitle a broker to a commission for a property sale.

professional appraiser: Expert in real estate who has an education in real estate appraisal as well as having significant professional experience. A recognized license may be obtained from the Member Appraisal Institute. However, no national requirement exists as to who may do an appraisal. If property is appraised involving a federally insured agency, the appraiser must be licensed by the state. See also *appraiser.*

profit a' prendre: Right to profit by utilizing the assets of another's land. A profit a' prendre would include the right to use and mine another's property recovering and removing any assets.

profit and loss statement: See *income statement.*

pro forma statement: Financial statement with amounts or other information that are completely or partially assumed. The assumptions supporting the amounts are usually provided. The statement may be prepared in determining the possible financial effects of buying or renting property.

progress payments: In a construction loan, payments made to a contractor as the various construction stages are completed. The contractor uses progress payments to pay the various subcontractors and suppliers as construction proceeds. For example, a bank gives a contractor a $125,000 construction loan. It pays $30,000 to the contractor upon the purchase of a building lot, and then pays additional progress payments of $25,000 upon the completion of the foundation, and $20,000 upon the completion of the framing in process, another $20,000 upon the completion of the plumbing and wiring, $10,000 upon the completion of the roof and the final payment of $20,000 upon the completion of the structure. See also *draw.*

promissory note: Formal, written, unconditional promise to pay on demand or at a future date a definite sum of money. The person signing the note and promising to pay is called the maker of the note. The person to receive payment is called the payee.

property: Ownership rights to real or other types of tangible or intangible property. Property rights include exclusive occupancy, possession, use, and the right of disposition. Individuals, groups, organizations, and governments may own property.

property brief: Summarization of the attributes and characteristics of the property such as that indicated in the legal records (e.g., title search).

property damage liability insurance: An insurance policy that promises to pay all the legal obligations of the insured due to negligence in which damage to the property has been caused.

property damage liability losses: Losses arising from damage to or destruction of property.

property depreciation insurance: Insurance protection for the replacement cost of damaged property. Thus, the accumulated depreciation is not subtracted in determining the amount of reimbursement.

property insurance: Insurance affording protection against losses due to damage to or destruction of property (such as an apartment building) or contents therein. Insurance protects assets and any future income thereon from loss, such as a fire or earthquake.

property inventory: A listing of all assets a person or business owns, their cost, and appraised value. A complete inventory record should be maintained including real estate. Documentation is needed in the event of loss and for tax purposes.

property management: Operating property for business use, such as managing an office complex.

property owner: A business or person having title to specific real property, such as a house.

property owner association agreement: A written contract of a group of property owners, typically condominium owners, describing their joint ownership obligations and rights. The association agreement usually allows members to approve new owners before a sale, and gives the right to charge each resident for agreed upon building operating expenses. For example, if the tennis court in a condominium needs $50,000 in repairs and there are 100 owners, each will be assessed $500 ($50,000/100).

property report: A report required by the Interstate Land Sale Act for the sale of subdivisions having 50 or more lots. It is filed with the Federal Department of Housing and Urban Development's Office of Interstate Land Sales Registration.

property residual technique: Approach to appraise rental property based on anticipated future earnings to be derived from it plus the estimated selling price at the end oft he period held.

EXAMPLE: A rental property is expected to generate net income of $150,000 per year for 20 years. The expected selling price after 20 years is $1,000,000. Assuming a rate of return of 15%, the property is valued at $999,850 based on the computation:

Present value of future earnings:

$150,000 $\times$ present value of ordinary annuity for n = 20, i = 15%:

$150,000 $\times$ 6.259 = $938,850

$1,000,000 $\times$ present value of $1 for n = 20, i = 15%

$1,000,000 $\times$ .061	61,000
Valuation	$999,850

property risks: Uncertainties associated with real property including lack of insurance coverage in the event of fire or injury, high crime area, and environmental problems. This risk may be reduced through adequate insurance and proper upkeep.

property tax: Tax levied on real property. It is based on the land use categorization (e.g., rural, urban) nature of improvements, fair market value, and the millage rate. Property taxes may be assessed by states, cities, special districts, and independent school districts. The property tax is usually included in the property owner's monthly mortgage payment and is added to the monthly carrying charges.

property and casualty policy: Insurance contract providing coverage for risks primarily associated with negligence and acts of omission associated with third-party injuries or property losses. Property and casualty policies normally exclude losses associated with war, riots, and unreasonable negligence.

property description: See *legal description.*

property line: Legal boundary of property.

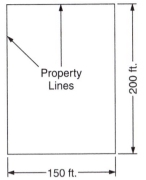

Property Lines

200 ft.

|← 150 ft. →|

property under contract: Real property being offered for sale that has received a contract for sale but has not gone to a closing. Under these circumstances, it may be possible to accept a refundable binder for sale to a different purchaser should the original contract for sale not be completed.

proportionality:
(1) Comparing properties in terms of some measure(s) such as dimensions and dollar value.
(2) Percentage relationship of a specific part of property to the whole property. An example is the square footage of one office to the square footage of all offices in an office building.

proprietary lease: Lease in a cooperative apartment building between the owner-cooperative and the stockholder tenant. A proprietary lease is granted to a tenant to occupy a specific apartment provided he/she has purchased a required number of cooperative shares.

pro rata liability clause: Clause often provided in property insurance policies that distributes the liability to pay an indemnification among several insurers in proportion to the liability exposure each has on a covered property. For example, Smith has a $3 million fire insurance policy on a commercial office building, and there is a pro rata liability clause distributed among three different insurers. Insurer A has provided a $1,500,000 fire policy while insurer B provides $1,000,000 and insurer C provides $500,000. In the event of a total loss due to fire, each insurer would be liable up to the maximum coverage provided under the terms of the policy.

pro rate: The proportionate division of expenses including taxes, interest, insurance, rents, and other property-related expenses at a closing between the buyer and the seller.

pro ration of taxes: The proportionate division of taxes at the closing between the buyer and the seller. For example, on January 1st Smith paid his property's $5,000 annual taxes. On April 15th Smith sells the property to Jones. Since 74 days have passed at the time of the closing, Jones proration of taxes is 291 (365 − 74) days @ $13.69 per day = $ 3983.79.

prospect: Potential customer or client in which there is a realistic chance of making the sale for the product or service. An example is a prospective purchaser of real estate that the real estate broker is interested in.

prospect cards: File of prospective real estate customers showing their address, telephone number, time and date of last contact, types of properties in which they are interested, and their financial capabilities. Prospect cards are a marketing tool. A real estate salesperson can use prospect cards to alert prospective customers to properties in which they have previously displayed interest.

prospectus: Document that must accompany a new issue of securities for a real estate company or partnership. It includes the same information in the registration statement, such as a list of directors and officers, financial statements certified by a CPA, underwriters, the purpose and use for funds, and other relevant information that prospective buyers of a security want to know. A preliminary prospectus, red-herring (so named because it is printed in red ink indicating the tentative nature of the document during the period in which it is being reviewed for fraudulent or misleading statements by the Securities and Exchange Commission), is issued before the final, statutory prospectus, which also contains offering instructions.

pro tanto: Partial fulfillment. Pro tanto is normally used in relation to the partial satisfaction of a claim. For example, a pro tanto settlement in an eminent domain action will not prejudice any future claims by a property owner claiming a financial settlement was inadequate.

protective covenants:
(1) Statement in a deed that specified actions, or improvements, can or cannot take place on a given property. The covenants may stipulate the use of the property, (e.g., residential, business), restrict the number of occupants, and prohibit certain actions (e.g., early morning parties, animals).
(2) An agreement restricting specified financial transactions. For example, a covenant may be agreed to in a loan agreement that a person may not borrow additional monies from another lending institution against a certain collateralized property.

proximity damage: Decline in value of real estate property because it is near something which is damaging to its worth. For example, a house located next to a pollution treatment center, drug center, or prison will be worth less.

proxy:
(1) Proxy statement, a written document that the SEC requires to be given to real estate company stockholders before they vote on corporate matters.
(2) Power of attorney by which the holder of stockholders in a real estate company transfers voting rights to another stockholder. A proxy fight may arise in which groups compete in the gathering of proxies to give them voting control.

prudent investment: Investment made rationally and intelligently as would be expected by a professional person. A reasonable degree of safety and return are expected. An example is an office building with a 99% occupancy rate of quality tenants.

public domain:
(1) Land owned by the federal, state, or county government that the public may use. This is distinguished from property owned privately by individuals and businesses.
(2) Right to an item belongs to the public at large so anyone can use it. An example is a real estate software program that is publicly available by an electronic bulletin board service.

public housing: Residence units owned by the government and available to low income families at a nominal cost.

public lands: Government owned lands, for conservation purposes or for specific uses such as dams and hydropower. Public lands are owned by federal, state, and local governments. Many public lands are rich in natural resources and, in some cases, the government has granted forestry and drilling leases to private interests.

public offerings: Offering of new securities of a real estate company to the investing public, after registration requirements have been filed with the SEC. The securities are usually made available to the public at large by a managing investment banker and its underwriting syndicate. In the public offering, unlike private placement, the corporation does not deal directly with the ultimate buyers of the securities. The public market is an impersonal one. See also *private placement*.

public record: Governmentally held records of public transactions giving constructive notice that documentation exists confirming the transaction. In real estate, deeds, subdivision plats, and assessment record cards are stored by county and municipal clerks in a publicly available filing system.

public report: A report published by a governmental unit which is publicly available. For example, the decennial census report published by the U.S. Department of Commerce is a public report.

public sale: A public foreclosure sale where public notice is given and anyone is allowed to participate. Normally, a public sale occurs because of the property owner's failure to pay taxes.

public syndicate: Group of at least two people or businesses combining to engage in a real estate project that would exceed their individual financial abilities. A syndication allows earning to be proportionately shared.

pueblo or adobe: House modeled after the dwellings constructed by the Pueblo Indians in the American southwest. A pueblo or adobe style house is made from adobe brick or materials simulating adobe brick. Typically, the pueblo or adobe styled house has roof beams, termed viga, projecting from the walls of the structure.

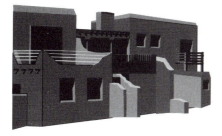

puffing: Buildup of the value of property. It is an inflated opinion of value by a seller, not a representation of fact.

punch list: Matters that need to be rectified in a home or building prior to its sale or acceptance by a new owner. For example, a leaking water pipe should be repaired prior to showing the property to prospective purchasers.

punitive damages: Also called exemplary damages. Damages achieved by a judicial award for a plaintiff in a lawsuit in addition to the actual (compensatory) damages. Punitive damages are used to penalize the defendant for bad faith, malice, fraud, violence, or evil intent. It is designed as a punishment, and to prevent future actions of the defendant.

pur autre vie: Latin for through the life of another. A life estate in property is granted to an individual so long as a third person is alive. For example, Smith grants Jones a pur autre vie in his home and property as long as Smith's son continues to live. Thus, Smith is granted a life estate pur autre vie the life of his son.

purchase agreement: See *contract of sale.*

Purchase Money Mortgages (PMM): Type of seller financing. It is a mortgage loan from a seller instead of cash for the purchase of real estate. The term has a dual meaning in real estate financing. All mortgage loans for real estate purchases are designated purchase money mortgages by lenders, and thus all the different types of mortgages explained could be classified as purchase money mortgages. The second meaning of the term explains what happens when the buyer does not have the necessary cash and the seller agrees to take back a part of the selling price in the form of a purchase money mortgage. Such a mortgage is ordinarily subordinated to take a second-lien position since the primary lender will require a first lien position before making the loan. For the purchaser, this means less cash and possibly an interest rate on the PMM less than if those same dollars were borrowed from a primary lender. The seller can possibly induce a sale not otherwise possible by agreeing to take back a purchase money mortgage. The seller is protected in that a PMM places a lien on the property the same as any other second mortgage. See also *creative financing.*

purchasing power risk: Risk resulting from possible increases or decreases in price levels that can substantially impact real estate values.

purpose of the appraisal: The reason a property appraisal is being made. The purpose of the appraisal is the first step in the appraisal process. The purpose of the appraisal should answer several questions:

(1) What specific problem will the appraisal resolve? If the purpose of the appraisal is to determine property value for the purpose of acquiring a bank loan or mortgage, then the appraisal will focus on long term property value trends in the region.

(2) If the appraisal is being used for the value insurance of the property, then replacement cost is a primary consideration.

(3) Will the appraisal assist in determining the price to be paid for a certain piece of property? If this is the case, then the appraisal should focus on comparable sales as carefully appraising specific features and improvements made to the property in question.

(4) If the major purpose of the appraisal is for the purpose of tax assessment, then comparable values of similar

properties is the main interest of the appraisal.

(5) Is the appraisal to be used in a public condemnation process or a sale resulting from a divorce? If this is the purpose, then the appraisal should focus on recent sales of similar properties not involved in a forced sale.

pyramid roof: Roof having four triangular sides forming a point at the top of a pyramid. A pyramid roof is primarily used for steeples on top of churches or certain public buildings.

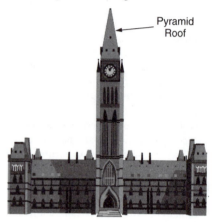

Pyramid Roof

pyramid zoning: Form of zoning regulation permitting all the uses permitted in more restrictive zoning to also apply to less restrictive zoning. The net effect of pyramid zoning is to pyramid only a few uses to more restrictive zoning regulations while allowing the broader base of uses to be applicable in less restrictive applications.

quadrangle (quad): A rectangular area bordered on all sides by buildings. Often, a quadrangle is grassy with decorative landscaping. A quadrangle can be found in a central business district or on the site of an academic institution.

quadriplex: A free-standing building having four dwelling units under one roof. Normally a quadriplex is a two-story complex with one dwelling unit located on top of and adjacent to another. However, other configurations are possible including a one story structure with all four units simply being adjacent to each other.

quadrominium: A four-unit building with four tenants in a condominium type of ownership and management.

qualifying:
(1) Process determining an individual's financial ability to meet the terms of a loan. When selling real estate, the sales broker must qualify the buyer to make certain he/she has the financial ability to purchase the property and be eligible to obtain a mortgage.
(2) In insurance, a period of time during which an individual is ineligible to receive benefits until it is determined whether or not fraud or other misrepresentation has occurred. A qualification

period is found most frequently in health insurance and pension plans.

quality of use: The type and value of real estate improvements made as well as the use to which land is put. This is controlled by zoning as well as suitability. For example, in a prime commercial downtown area large commercial department stores and high rise office buildings are constructed. See also *highest and best use.*

quantity survey:
(1) Complete estimated itemization of all costs in constructing a structure including site acquisition and preparation, material, and labor costs. A quantity survey is necessary for a contractor to prepare a project's bid price.
(2) An appraisal estimate of the replacement cost of a structure including the current cost of materials and required labor.

quarry tile: Unglazed and natural clay or shale machine extruded into ceramic tile. Quarry tile is often used for factory flooring.

quarter round: Molding used in corners simulating a quarter of a circle.

quasi: Term indicating a resemblance or analogous to a legal classification. For example, a quasi corporation, quasi contract, quasi possession, quasi offense.

quasi-contract: Legal obligation to pay for a benefit received as if a contract has actually occurred. This may arise in a few cases so that an equitable situation occurs. An example is when a homeowner allows repairs to be performed knowing that a reasonable fee will be charged. It would be unfair for the homeowner to have unjust enrichment at the suffering of the one performing the work.

Queen Anne house: Multistory, nineteenth-century house featuring turrets, high chimneys, and decorative trim.

quid pro quo:

(1) Latin term meaning something in exchange for something else. For example, a person rushes through an order for another in return for having first choice in selecting a parcel of property. (2) A business agreement ("soft dollars") whereby a real estate firm will provide business, typically referrals, to another company in exchange for receiving a service such as research of the real estate market.

quiet enjoyment: The right of possession and use of property without undue disturbance by others or adverse claims of others to title or interest.

quiet title (action): Judicial action to establish property ownership. In a quiet title action, adverse claimants are required to state their claims or be forever stopped from any future title claim. The basic purpose of a quiet title action is to clear a title from any claims arising from dower's rights, squatter's rights, or easements.

quitclaim deed: Deed conveying a right, title, or interest of the grantor. It is usually used to clear a cloud on the title such as unenforceable deed restrictions or an unused easement. Further, such a deed may be used by a wife to transfer her share of community or joint tenancy property to the husband. See also *warranty deed.*

quotation: Highest bid to buy and the lowest offer to sell a parcel of real estate in a particular market at a specified time.

QV (quod vide): Latin abbreviation for the literal translation meaning "which see."

Quit Claim Deed

This quitclaim deed is made on _____, 19____, between _____ _____,
Grantor, residing at _____, City of _____, State of _____,
and _____, Grantee, residing at _____, City of_____, State
of _____. In consideration of _____ paid by _____ the Grantor
hereby quitclaims and transfers the following described real estate to the Grantee to have and
hold forever, the described real estate located at _____, City of _____, State
of _____:

Dated _____, 19____.

_____
(Signature of Grantor)

_____
(Printed name of Grantor)

State of   _____

County of   _____

On _____, 19____, _____ personally came before me and,
being duly sworn, did state that he/she is the person described in the above document and that
he/she signed the above document in my presence.

_____
(Notary Signature)

Notary Public, for the County of _____

State of _____

My Commission expires: _____

racial steering: Directing a particular race to a certain neighborhood and away from others. An example is a real estate broker steering a black family away from a white neighborhood. This action is illegal.

radiant heating: Heating system generating heat through radiation as opposed to a convection heating system. For example, baseboard heating is a radiant heating system where the heat from circulating hot water is radiated outward through conduction by thin metal fins at the base of a wall. The surrounding air circulates around the heating unit using convection thereby warming the room.

radiator: Exposed heating unit located within a room that transfers heat generated by hot water or steam through conduction. The surrounding air circulates around the radiator using convection thereby warming the room.

rafter: One of a series of inclined structural supports supporting a roof.

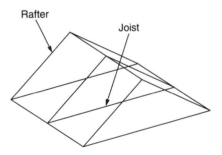

ranch style house: One-story house with a low pitched roof often having an open floor plan.

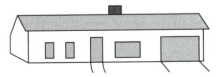

random shingles: Shingles having uniform length, but random width. Random shingles give a creative appearance to a roof.

range: Six-mile-wide column of land running north-south in the rectangular survey system.

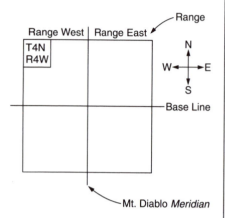

Range capacity: Number of range grassland acres needed to support one animal unit for a specified period of time or grazing season. See also *range capacity formula.*

range capacity formula: Formula for determining range capacity:

Range capacity =

$$\frac{\text{Density} \times \text{Use factor} \times \text{Surface acres}}{\text{Forage acre requirement}}$$

where Density = density of vegetation by type on the land surface; Use factor = the extent to which the herbage of range area has been consumed by livestock; Surface acres = number of acres available; and Forage acre requirement = number of acres required to graze one animal unit per species composition unit.

range lines: North-south lines used in the government's rectangular survey method. Range lines are located 6 miles apart east and west of the principal meridian and form township corners as they intersect with township lines and form a township 36 square miles in size.

range survey: Range reconnaissance, or surveying, for the purpose of preparing grazing capacity estimates. There are two parts to a range survey:
(1) Mapping of grazing cover varieties and associated topographic features affecting total grazing value.
(2) Determining livestock grazing capacity as a function of vegetation density and species composition.

ratable: In insurance, an estimable risk for the purpose of calculating an adequate and reasonable premium providing sufficient resources should the company need to pay a claim while maintaining affordability.

rate cap: In an adjustable rate mortgage (ARM), the maximum rate that can be charged during the mortgage period. For example, Smith obtained an $80,000 6% ARM having a lifetime rate cap of 10.5%. See also *annual cap.*

rate of return: See *yield.*

rate of return on investment (ROI): Income divided by the amount invested in real estate. See also *yield.*

ratification: Approval by an individual or business of a prior act (e.g., contract). Without such confirmation, the act would not be binding.

rational motives: Determination made concerning the motivation of a testator in making devises of the will. A will can be contested if it can be proved the testator did not have rational motives when making the devises of the will.

raw land: Unimproved property. It has no utilities, sewers, streets, or structures and usually must be cleared.

ready, willing, and able buyer: Real estate term describing a buyer who is prepared to comply with the terms and conditions of a purchase contract and has the financial ability to complete the transaction. In a property having a listing contract, if the real estate broker secures a client who is a ready, willing, and able buyer, then he/she is entitled to a commission.

real assets: Investments you can hold on to all your life (e.g., house) or sell for a profit when they have appreciated in value (e.g., land). Real assets are those investments you can put your hands on. Real property includes real estate.

real estate: Also called real property. Anything permanently affixed to the land, such as buildings, walls, fences, and shrubs, as well as the rights to own or use them. It is distinguished from moveable personal property.

real estate agent: Sales person or broker who sells real estate for his/her principal receiving a commission. See also *real estate broker.*

real estate board: Local real estate organization consisting of registered real estate brokers and salespeople. A real estate board is a member of the National Association of Realtors (NAR). See also *Board of Realtors.*

real estate broker: A commission broker who locates a buyer or seller of property for a principal. The broker may also arrange for financing the purchase. See also *broker (real estate).*

real estate calculators: Calculator having various financial functions including present value, purchase price, property appreciation, lease costs, loan and mortgage amortization.

real estate commission:

(1) Amount received by a real estate salesperson when a property is sold. For example, if the commission rate is 5% and the home is sold for $500,000, the commission would be $25,000.

(2) Amount a manager of real estate receives for his efforts. For example, a manager is to receive 2% of rentals collected as compensation from the landlord to manage the property. If the rentals received in a given month are $1,000,000, the manager's commission (management fee) is $20,000.

(3) Governmental agency (state or county) that enforces legal statues in connection with real estate transactions.

real estate computer software:

(1) Database program that has real estate listings including property photographs. Real estate computer software allows real estate agents and brokers to search for a particular listing by characteristics. For example, an agent may wish to locate all listings of a ranch in a particular municipality having a two-car garage, basement, four bedrooms, and two baths with an asking price within a certain range. Assuming ranch houses exist in the database having those characteristics, the real estate computer software will locate them and allow the agent to view and print them.

(2) General real estate calculation program including loan and mortgage amortization payments and schedules, present value, affordability calculations, mortgage qualifying analysis, adjustable rate mortgage amortization and payments, estimated closing costs, discount points vs. interest rates, interest paid in tax year, fixed rate loan calculations and mortgage payments, balance after Kth payment, accelerated payment schedule.

real estate counselor: Person providing advice for compensation about real estate.

real estate investment company: See also *real estate investment trust (REIT).*

real estate investment trusts (REITs): Type of investment company that invests money (obtained through the sale of its shares to investors) in mortgages and various types of investment in real estate, in order to earn profits for shareholders. Shareholders receive income from the rents received from the properties and receive capital gains as properties are sold at a profit. REITs have been formed by a number of large financial institutions such as banks and insurance companies. The stocks of many of them are traded on security exchanges, thereby providing investors with a marketable interest in a real estate investment portfolio. By law, REITs have to distribute 95 percent of their net income to shareholders, and in turn they are exempt from corporate taxes on income or gains. Because REIT earnings are not taxed before they are distributed, you get a larger percentage of the profits than with stocks. However, in exchange for this special tax treatment, REITs are subject to numerous qualifications and limitations including:

(1) Shareholder qualifications. Generally, REITs are not permitted to be closely held and must have a minimum of 100 shareholders.

(2) Qualified asset and income tests. REITs are required to have at least 75% of their value represented by qualified real estate assets and to earn at least 75% of their income from real estate investments. REIT's shares trade on the stock exchanges.

There are three types of REITs. An equity trust invests their assets in acquiring ownership in real estate. Their income is mainly derived from rental on the property. A mortgage trust invests in acquiring short-term or long-term mortgages. Their income is derived from interest from their investment portfolio. A combination trust combines the features of both the equity trust and the mortgage trust. Their income comes from rentals, interest, and loan placement fees.

Advantages include (1) dividend is received; (2) the potential for capital appreciation; and (3) liquidity from selling shares, and portfolio diversification.

Disadvantages of REITs are potential losses from market decline and high risk.

Before purchasing a REIT, read the annual report, the *Value Line Investment Survey, Audit Investment's Newsletter,* or *Realty Stock Review.* Examine the (1) track record (how long in business and dividend record); (2) debt level; (3) cash flow; (4) diversification (beware of REITs investing in only one type of property); (5) property location (watch geographically depressed areas); (6) type of property (nursing homes, apartment buildings, shopping centers); (7) aggressive management (avoid REITs that do not upgrade properties); and (8) earnings (watch earnings regularly; be prepared to sell when the market or property location deteriorates).

real estate market: The general business conditions existing between the supply of real properties and those people wishing to purchase them. Many factors influence the real estate market. Not only is the general relationship between supply and demand extremely important, but overall economic conditions including interest rates, inflation and taxation levels are critical factors. The real estate market is segmented between residential, commercial, office, and industrial properties.

real estate mortgage investment conduit (REMIC): Holding pool of mortgages. It is marketed as a tax exempt mortgage backed security for investors.

real estate office administration: Managing the day-to-day activities in a real estate brokerage office including recruiting and training new real estate agents, holding real estate closings, updating and managing real estate listings, and developing new clients.

real estate owned (REO): Real property repossessed by a lender through foreclosure and maintained in inventory.

real estate property tax: Prevalent type of property taxes assessed on real estate. It is usually collected by the local government and distributed among agencies to finance services (e.g., schools).

Real Estate Settlement Procedures Act (RESPA): U.S. law covering the procedures in some types of real estate closings. Its objective is to have uniformity in real estate settlement practices when "federally related" first mortgage loans are made on one- to four-family residences, condominiums, and cooperatives.

real estate syndicate: Group of investors pooling their money to purchase real estate. See also *syndicate; syndicate (real estate).*

real estate valuation: See *appraisal.*

real income: Inflation adjusted income relative to a base period. For example, real rental income is adjusted for changing price levels. See also *purchasing power; real return on investment.*

real interest rate: Inflation adjusted interest rate.

real property: Rights, interests, and benefits inherent in the ownership of real estate, as distinguished from personal property; frequently thought of as a bundle of rights. Real Estate may be loosely defined as land (including air rights) and other properties that are permanently attached to land such as houses, fences, and landscaping. The terms real property and real estate are often used interchangeably.

real return on investment: The yield after deducting inflation and its effects. It is the return on investment stated in real purchasing power.

realized profit or loss: Taxable profit or loss arising from a sale. It is reported in the income statement.

realtist: Member of the National Association of Real Estate Brokers, Inc.

realtor: A real estate broker or agent who, as an active member of a local real estate board of Realtors and the National Association of Realtors, adheres to standards of professionalism and a code of ethics.

realtor-associate: Membership designation for salespersons working for Realtors.

Realtor-National Marketing Institute (RNMI): An affiliate of the National Association of Real Estate Boards, engaged in educational programs and publications for its members. Its publications include *Real Estate Perspectives* and *Real Estate Today.*

realty: See *real estate.*

reappraisal lease: Lease computed as a percentage of the underlying appraised property value. Under the terms of a reappraisal lease, the rent is periodically adjusted using an independent appraisal of the property. For example, a commercial reappraisal lease provides that the rental terms can be adjusted every three years based on an independent property appraisal.

reassessment: Reappraising a decision or strategy that has been made. An example is revising the value of real estate based on new information. The valuation may be needed in contract negotiations or tax matters. The reasons for the revaluation may be many such as recent comparable sales of property, economic conditions, and new tax laws.

rebate:
(1) Amount paid back or credit given because of an overcollection or the return of property sold. Also called refund.
(2) Payment to a buyer after a purchase is made as an inducement to buy.
(3) Unearned interest refunded to a borrower if the loan is paid off before maturity.

rebuttable presumption: "Disputable" presumption that is subject to rebuttal based on evidence. However, the presumption prevails until it is rebutted.

recapture:
(1) The return by owners of a property investment usually through a depreciation allowance.

(2) A clause in a contract permitting the prior owner of real estate to recover under certain circumstances. For example, if a person sells real estate to someone on an installment land sales contract and the purchaser does not make the payments, the prior owner could recapture the real estate by taking possession of it.

recapture clause:
(1) Clause in a lease permitting the lessor a percentage of the lessee's profits above a fixed amount of rent.
(2) Clause in a percentage lease permitting the landlord to cancel a lease and recover the property if the tenant's sales fall below a specified level.

recapture rate: Annual return rate of capital invested in a wasting asset. The capital is returned from the depreciating asset's earned income.

recasting: Revising the terms of a loan such as when the borrower is experiencing severe financial difficulties. For example, a homeowner lost his job and seeks relief by requesting the lender holding his mortgage to extend the payments for five additional years and modify the interest rate on the loan downward from 10% to 9%. The lender is a family member and agrees to do so.

receipt:
(1) Written statement that something has been received such as cash, real property, or documents. The purchaser should always get a receipt. An example is the buyer of real estate getting a receipt for giving money to the seller as a down payment.
(2) Receiving something such as a cash payment.

receiver: Judicial appointed person who takes possession, but not the title, to real estate during a bankruptcy process referred to as a receivership or a foreclosure proceeding. The receiver is responsible for managing the affairs of the business prudently including collecting funds, paying bills, and carrying out normal business operations. The receiver operates under court direction and may return the real estate back to a solvent status; however, a receiver may recommend liquidation if the continuity of the business is no longer practical.

recession: A lower phase of a business cycle in which the economy is deteriorating, coupled with a declining rate of business investment and consumer spending. Real Estate prices are typically depressed in recession, although the degree varies among regions. See also *business cycle; depression; Index of Leading Indicators; unemployment.*

reciprocity: Relationship between individuals or entities whereby rights given to one are returned in kind to the other. An example is where one person has the right to use facilities of another with the understanding that the reverse privileges are granted.

recission of contract: Cancellation of a contract such as when a real estate agreement is deemed illegal.

recognized gain: The part of the amount received from selling or exchanging real property that is taxable income.

reconciliation:
(1) Adjusting the difference between two items (i.e., amounts, balances, accounts, or statements) so that the figures agree. A real estate company often has to analyze the deviation between two items, such as in preparing a bank reconciliation. For example, a reconciliation occurs when comparing the home office books account related to branch transactions with the corresponding account on the branch office books related to home office transactions. These two accounts are adjusted for the reconciling items causing the difference.
(2) In appraisal, the process of reconciling three major approaches—that is, the market comparison, cost, and

income approaches—to arrive at an estimate of the value of the subject property being appraised.

reconstructed operating statement:
(1) Income statement revised based on new information such as previous errors.

(2) Income statement destroyed by a casualty such as a fire. This requires the reconstruction of the income statement based on source records, information, and documents.

reconveyance: The transfer of a property deed to the original owner upon the satisfaction of a mortgage. A reconveyance is accomplished through a reconveyance deed. For example, upon making the final payment on his mortgage, the bank holding the mortgage reconveys the property title to Smith through a reconveyance deed.

reconveyance deed: Deed used to convey property back to the original property owner. Normally a reconveyance deed is issued upon the satisfaction of a property's mortgage.

recordation: The act of recording of deeds and other property instruments in a public registry. Recordation gives public notice of ownership claims on property as well as any other legal or financial claims. Public recording of property claims protects those who do so from unrecorded claims.

recorded map: See *plat*.

recorded plat: A subdivision map filed in the county recorder's office that shows the location and boundaries of parcels of land.

recording: The process of entering a conveyance or mortgage instruments affecting the title to real property in a public registry. Recording instruments provide public notice to the whole world of their nature.

recording fee: Fee charged by a public registry for the administrative costs of recording an instrument. For example,

a municipal registry charges $30 to record a property mortgage.

recourse loan: A loan whereby the lender, in the event of a default, has recourse beyond the collateral pledged to initially secure it. For example, Jones gave Smith a $50,000 recourse loan using Smith's house as collateral. When Smith defaulted on the loan, he only had $25,000 of equity remaining after the property was foreclosed upon by the mortgagee of a first mortgage coupled with depressed real estate market conditions. Under the terms of the recourse loan, Jones has recourse to Smith's other assets to recover the principal.

recovery fund: A fund constituted in certain states to compensate aggrieved individuals who incurred losses in a real estate transaction associated with a licensed real estate broker or agent. Normally, in states having a recovery fund, licensed real estate brokers and agents are assessed a charge as a part of their registration fee which is contributed to the recovery fund. Following an investigation and hearing, if the state's real estate commission awards a settlement to a complainant, the recovery fund's assets are debited should the implicated real estate broker or agent fail to provide a recovery.

recovery period: Period of time during which a complainant in a real estate transaction can seek a financial recovery from a licensed real estate broker or agent. The time period is determined by state statute.

rectangular survey: See *government rectangular survey*.

redemption period: Time period, as established by state statute, during which a property owner can redeem a defaulted mortgage or land contract or reclaim a foreclosed property. A property owner acting during the redemption period must pay all defaulted payments and associated charges. For example,

Smith acted within the stipulated three-month redemption period and paid all defaulted mortgage payments and late charges on his home thereby preventing a foreclosure proceeding.

redevelop: Demolition and removal of all existing structures on a building site and the subsequent construction of a totally new building structure. For example, in a downtown redevelopment project, all the older private homes were demolished and a high-rise public housing facility was constructed.

red herring: Slang reference for a preliminary prospectus that outlines the important aspects of a new issue of securities for a real estate company, partnership, or investment trust. This prospectus contains no selling price information or offering date. It is so named because of the red-ink statement on the first page instructing the reader that the document is not an official offer to sell the securities. Once the registration statement is approved by the SEC, the offering circular, the final, statutory prospectus, is printed and the security can be offered for sale.

red lining: The practice where a bank or insurance company restricts or denies mortgages or insurance, respectively, in certain defined geographic areas. See also *Federal Fair Housing Law.*

redress: Restitution or compensation for harm or wrong done. See also *recovery fund.*

reduction certificate: Lender's written statement and accounting for the remaining balance, date of maturity, and interest rate on a mortgage. The lender is certifying this information to the borrower or any other interested parties. The certificate may be issued when the property is sold and the obligation is being assumed by the purchaser. For example, Jones purchases a home from Travis and wants to take over the low-interest mortgage. A certificate should be issued from the bank indicating that the balance on the mortgage is $50,600.

referral: Recommending the use of another person or business. An example is an attorney referring a client to a CPA to handle tax planning for real estate transactions.

refinance: Modified schedule of debt payments including a mortgage. Creditors may want to refinance one's obligations if he or she cannot satisfy the original payments or if interest rates have fallen since a borrower took out the loan. For example, whether refinancing is beneficial depends on the refinancing costs including closing costs) and the time needed to recover those costs through low mortgage payments. An approximation of the closing costs is using the costs of refinancing (3% to 6% of the outstanding principal) and multiply it by the amount of the loan.

EXAMPLE: Assume that refinancing is $75,000. A 14% mortgage involves closing fees of $3,750, and the new interest rate is 10%. At 10%, the monthly payment on a 30-year fixed loan is $658. That is a savings of $231 from the monthly payment of $889 required on a 14% loan. Dividing the total refinancing cost of $3,750 by $231 gives a recovery period of about 16 months. The table below illustrates the monthly and yearly savings from refinancing to a 10% 30-year fixed-rate mortgage for $75,000. See also *15-year mortgage.*

Savings from Refinancing

Present Mortgage Rate	Current Monthly Payment	Monthly Payment at 10%	Monthly Savings at 10%	Annual Savings at 10%
12.0%	$771	$658	$113	$1,356
12.5	800	658	142	1,704
13.0	830	658	172	2,064
13.5	859	658	201	2,412
14.0	889	658	231	2,772
15.0	948	658	290	3,480

reformation: Correcting a mutual error in the original contract that did not properly portray the intent of both parties. However, if only one party is at fault, reformation does not apply unless the person's error was due to the other party's fraud.

regency house: English-style home. It is usually 2-stories high. The roof is of a hip type. The chimney is on the side of the home.

regional economics: Branch of economics that is concerned with the study of factors that explain, and policies that promote, regional economic growth and development. Regional economic factors affect property values.

regional shopping center: A large enclosed shopping mall having several national and regional retail stores acting as anchor tenants. The enclosed floor area of regional shopping centers ranges between 250,000 and 1,000,000 sq. ft. and are located in urbanized areas having a population of at least 250,000 people. They have a very large parking area.

registration statement: Document that has to be submitted to the SEC disclosing all relevant information of the new securities issue of a real estate company or limited partnership that will allow an investor to make an intelligent decision. It is a lengthy document containing (1) historical, (2) financial, and (3) administrative details about the issue.

regression: A statistical procedure using a body of measurable independent variables to compute an equation that successfully measures and forecasts the variance in another variable, the dependent variable. Regression analysis multiplies each of the independent variables by a beta coefficient and adds the results together. The beta coefficients of the independent variables are one of the most important parts of the set of results produced by regression analysis. More important, explanatory variables have higher beta values. The larger the sample size, the greater the statistical significance of the results. The total amount of variation in the dependent variable is measured by the coefficient of determination, or R^2, which ranges from 0% to 100%.

For example, the measured dependent variable is the sales prices of homes in a particular region over a 20-year period. The independent variables are property taxes, personal income, measures of municipal spending, age, and number of rooms. What impact do changes in the independent variables have on the sales price of homes? It may be determined that over the period higher property taxes and age have a strong negative beta coefficient associated with lower home sale prices while higher personal income, municipal spending, and numbers of rooms have strong positive beta coefficients associated with higher housing prices.

Regulation D: Regulation of the Securities and Exchange Commission (SEC) establishing the criteria to avoid a private offering. For example, Smith wants to sell shares in an apartment house to several investors. Smith applies to the SEC under Regulation D for an exemption from the need to have a private offering. If he is successful, the business transaction can be completed more quickly and avoid the cost of performing a private offering.

Regulation T: The Federal Reserve Bank's regulation applying to the amount of credit that may be advanced by brokers and dealers to customers to buy securities.

Regulation Z: The Federal Reserve Bank's regulation of consumer and mortgage credit transactions. A lender must provide the annual percentage rate (APR) of the loan and other essential data in mortgage credit contracts.

rehabilitate: Restoring real property (e.g., office building, residential home) to an improved state. The restoration is usually needed because the property's condition has worsened.

rehabilitation tax credit: Special tax incentive for the continued use and rehabilitation of historical buildings and old structures in an effort to arrest urban decay. Developers receive a credit based on a percentage of the cost they incur rehabilitating these structures.

reinforced concrete: Concrete with steel rods inserted into it to provide additional working load support. The premise is that both materials will act together in resisting load stress.

reinforced concrete construction: Construction method where reinforced concrete is used with concrete block and mortar to form an extremely strong building. Reinforced concrete construction is often used in conjunction with tie beams that gives the structure both vertical and lateral support.

reinstatement: The restitution of a property insurance policy that has lapsed due to nonpayment of premiums.

reinstatement clause: Provision in the insurance policy specifying that if the policy lapses due to premium nonpayment, all unpaid premiums must be paid, and any additional requirements must be satisfied before reinstatement can take place.

release:
(1) Voluntarily quitting, abandoning, or giving up any further legal right against another. For example, exercising a prepayment of loan provision would release the borrower from any further obligations.
(2) To free real estate when the mortgage is paid. When a mortgage is paid in full, a release of record is typically issued confirming the retirement of the debt.
(3) The creditor's forgiveness of the debtor's obligation.

release clause: In a mortgage, a provision that allows part of the security to be released from any further lien obligations upon the borrower's making a given payment. For example, a person may get a blanket mortgage for real estate having several structures. The mortgage may have a release provision in it allowing individual structures to be released from any later mortgage obligations when the mortgagor receives a payment from the mortgagee, either through sale of the structure or because of the payment.

reliction: An increase in land occurring from the withdrawal of a body of water. Normally, when reliction occurs, the increase in land area belongs to the individual having water rights in the area. See also *accretion*.

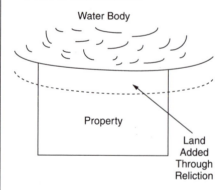

Water Body

Property

Land Added Through Reliction

relocation:
(1) The geographic moving of an individual from one region to another usually because of a change in employment. Relocation normally involves the complete moving of the individual's possessions from one area to another.
(2) An office rental tenant who moves from one area in a building to another either at the option of the landlord or the tenant. See also *relocation clause*.

relocation network: Nationwide group of independent real estate brokers who cooperate together and share information regarding clients who are seeking to relocate from one area of the country to another. The broker involved in the relocation network will contact a cooperating broker in the area to which the client is seeking to relocate to assist in locating a new home. If the client purchases real estate through the cooperating broker in the relocation network, the referring broker earns a percentage of the commission on the purchase. For example, Smith is seeking to sell his home in order to move to another region of the country. He approaches ABC real estate broker since he is also a members of a relocation network. ABC real estate brokerage lists the home for sale and contacts a relocation network broker in the national region where Smith wishes to relocate. The relocation network broker successfully arranges a purchase of a home to which the client relocates. ABC real estate broker earns a portion of the commission the relocation network broker earned completing the purchase of the new home.

relocation service: Organization that manages the relocation of the employees of client companies from one area of the country to another. A relocation service will manage home sales and purchases in another region as well as assisting in moving furniture and other personal effects. The primary purpose of a relocation service is to assist regional transitions of employees.

rem: See *in rem.*

remainder: The interest left in an estate after all costs have been deducted. For example, if a business is willed to X for life with the balance to Y upon X's death, Y has a remainder interest.

remainderman: The individual who receives an interest in a life estate after the original life tenant's interest expires. This normally occurs after the death of the life tenant. For example, Mrs. Smith received a life estate in her husband's home. Her son was chosen as the remainderman after her death to the life estate.

remodel: The process of changing, updating, and altering the appearance and structural characteristics of a building. For example, Smith remodels the kitchen in his home by replacing the cabinets, flooring, and appliances. He uses a new cabinet design as well as completely redesigning its appearance.

renegotiate: Revising the provisions, conditions, or terms of an oral or written agreement or contract. An example is when a contractor wants to increase the price of a job on a home when he realizes the original amount was considerably understated considering unexpected problems.

renegotiated rate mortgage (RRM): Also called a rollover mortgage. Provides a borrower with a fixed-rate mortgage that expires at a preestablished time, such as in four years. This permits the lender and borrower to renegotiate the mortgage rate periodically. The balance of the mortgage comes due in a balloon payment, but can be refinanced at "going" interest rates. This type of mortgage helps the lender avoid being locked into an interest rate that is below the cost of money. Here, at intervals such as 3 to 5 years, the loan is renewed at the prevailing rate; the borrower is guaranteed at least a 30-year term and can pay off the loan without penalty at any time. If rates go up, so would payments if the loan was renewed, but the borrower could shop around to get the best deal.

renewal option: The right of a person or business to renew a contract. For example, the tenant may have the right to renew a lease for a specified amount and term.

renovate: Make changes to existing property. Examples are putting in a new bathroom, kitchen, or basement; reroofing; or adding a porch.

renovation cost: Total expenditure to modernize a building to meet the owner's or tenant's needs.

rent: Payment made by the tenant to the landlord for the right to use property, such as an apartment or office.

rentable area:
(1) Square footage in an office building or apartment house that may be rented by a tenant.
(2) Geographic area that is attractive to prospective tenants.

rental agency: Business which, for a fee, aids a landlord to find a tenant or a tenant to find rental premises.

rental concession: Reduction in the normal rental charge to attract prospective tenants or keep existing tenants at lease renewal. Discounts may be given to obtain a higher occupancy rate, make it easier for the owner to derive bank financing, induce a large retailer to relocate, or stimulate a longer term lease with the tenant. A concession may also be in the form of one extra month of rental free for every two years. The property's value is worth less because the rental income base is lower.

rental contract: A lease. It is an agreement to rent property for a given amount and term specifying the terms and conditions for use. The term is mainly used when concerning residential property.

rental rate: Amount charged for each unit of rental property. An example of a unit might be square footage of space (e.g., office space) or an apartment (e.g., live-in tenants). For example, an owner of an office building might charge companies an annual rent of $10 per square foot. A landlord may charge a tenant $600 a month for a three-bedroom apartment.

rental value: How much the rental property is worth. The valuation considers the net income derived from the property and a capitalization rate.

rent bid model: Depicts the best way to allocate land to maximize usefulness and profitability.

rent controls: Governmental policy establishing the maximum amount of rent landlords can charge tenants. The objective is to prevent rent gouging. A tenant who feels overcharged, may contact the appropriate rental control office. While rent control does contain housing rental rates, it also discourages private investment in additional rental housing because of rental restrictions.

rent escalator: Provision in a lease agreement allowing the landlord to raise the rental to take into account inflation, higher upkeep costs (e.g., energy prices, maintenance), and higher interest rates. An index may be used such as the Consumer Price Index. The occupancy ratio may be another factor in setting rentals.

rent-free period: Span of time a rental agreement is free to the occupant. A landlord may offer this as an incentive to stimulate rentals. For example, an owner of an office building may provide a free rental for the first month if the tenant signs a one-year lease.

rent roll: Listing of the names of tenants, apartments, or office numbers, and monthly rentals.

rent with option to buy: Renter agrees to lease property for a designated term with the right to purchase it at a set price by a certain date.

rent-up period: How many days, months, or years are required before a new building has the desired occupancy ratio (e.g., 100%, 90%). The occupancy rate influences the amount financial institutions (e.g., banks) are willing to lend. The higher the occupancy rate and the shorter the rent-up period, the more money that may be financed.

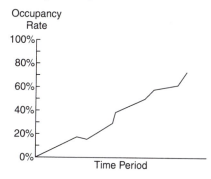

REO: See *real estate owned*.

repairs: Expenses to maintain property in satisfactory condition.

replacement cost: Current cost to replace property with similar property. An example is the cost to replace a house fully destroyed by a fire with another house. The replacement cost will typically be higher than the book value of the property because of higher prices due to inflation and appreciation in property values in that locality.

replacement cost approach: Valuation approach to real property based on what it would cost at current prices to build an equivalent new structure to replace the old one.

replacement reserve: Money set aside to buy new assets when the older ones are no longer appropriate for the intended use. An example is when the landlord must replace a deteriorating and malfunctioning air conditioner or refrigerator in the tenant's apartment.

repossession: Taking back property when the borrower defaults on the loan.

reproduction cost: Current cost to replace property with an identical property after allowing for the depreciated value of the property.

repudiation: Refusal of one party to a contract to carrying out his or her responsibilities under the agreement. An example is when a builder refuses to perform previously agreed services for the buyer of a new house, such as waterproofing and insulation.

request for notice of default: Person, such as the beneficiary of a deed, asking that he be informed if the property is foreclosed by someone else (e.g., bank, IRS).

resale proceeds: Net amount received when property (e.g., house) is sold. It equals the selling price less outstanding mortgage balance less all costs incurred in connection with the sale. These expenditures include brokerage commission, bank fees, and advertisements.

rescind: Canceling, nullifying, terminating, or dishonoring a contractual obligation. The Truth-in-Lending Act provides the right of rescission whereby a person can annul a contract without penalties, or refunding deposits. Contracts may also be terminated for fraud or improper execution. For example, a minor may rescind a real estate contract with no penalties.

rescission: Canceling a legal contract either with the permission of both parties or by one party exercising the right of rescission, based on legal grounds (e.g., minor fraud). See also *rescind*.

reservation:

(1) Stipulation in a deed giving the grantor some retained privilege or right in the property.

(2) Appointment such as meeting a real estate broker at a specific location and time to see houses for sale.

(3) Not sure about something such as suspecting the truthfulness of statements made by a real estate agent.

reserve fund: Monies set aside in the event unexpected repairs are needed to a building or apartment. It may be in the form of an escrow account in which the seller of the property puts funds away if problems with the property emerge within three months after the buyer moves in.

residence: Location where someone stays (resides) on a permanent basis. An example is a home to a family.

resident manager: Supervisor of the operation of apartments while residing in one of the apartments. Some responsibilities include showing vacant apartments to prospective tenants and assuring that the apartments are properly maintained.

residential broker: A real estate broker who lists and sells houses or condominiums, as distinguished from a commercial broker who handles business property.

residential building rate: Degree of construction of residential property (e.g., homes) measured in number of units or dollar value.

residential listing: List of dwelling units, such as homes.

residential lot: Subdivided acreage with utilities (including water, electricity, and sewerage) usually situated within or adjacent to established communities.

residential market: Availability of houses in an area.

residential member (RM): Title granted to those having expertise in valuing homes by the American Institute of Real Estate Appraisers (predecessor to the Appraisal Institute).

residential mortgage: Mortgage for residential property.

residential private investment: Investment in residential properties by private businesses and people.

residential property: Owner-occupied housing.

residential rental property: Property deriving at least 75% of the income from personal residences (e.g., living quarters).

residential service contract: An insurance contract or home warranty, usually for one year, covering electrical, plumbing, heating etc.

residential square: Neighborhood square somewhat resembling a park. It is often owned by town or row house owners situated near the square.

residential unit: Property suitable for residential living, such as a house, duplex, apartment, mobile home, or condominium.

residual: That which remains. As applied to real estate, it is the profit derived from rentals after subtracting all operating costs from the gross rental revenue. See also *residual technique.*

residual technique: Valuation method for land or improvements to property. It takes into account gross rentals less operating expenses. See also *residual.*

residue: What remains after something is removed, such as substances left after a pollution treatment facility is removed.

RESPA: See *Real Estate Settlement Procedures Act.*

respondeat superior: Term used in law stating "allow the principal to respond." An owner of property is legally liable for the improper actions of an agent representing him if it is within the scope of the duties reasonably expected to be performed. For example, a landlord may be held accountable for injury to prospective homeowners when the agent gets into an automobile accident showing them around to different apartment buildings.

restore: Refurbishing or rebuilding a property, such as a house, back to its original or earlier condition.

restraint on alienation: Restriction on conveying property that limits its transferability. The restrictions may be illegal.

restraint on transfer: Limitation on the right to convey real estate. An example is when someone must approve the sale of a home before it is sold.

restriction: Limitation or prohibition such as on what a tenant in an apartment may not do (e.g., have a dog, panel the walls). Local laws may also restrict certain actions such as failing to use the property for gambling purposes.

restrictive covenant: Legal agreement restricting the use of real property for designated purposes. It may also apply to the way in which construction of a building may be performed. The promise is typically stated as a reservation as to use. It may also be expressed as an exception in a deed.

resulting trust: See *trust.*

retail gravitation: Ability of a large group of retail stores or shopping center to take business away from other smaller or more distant shopping stores.

retail land developer: Business that transforms an underdeveloped tract of land into plots ready for construction.

retail lot sales: Selling lots of land for such reasons as building structures on them including homes, office buildings, and shopping centers.

retail property: Property to be used by a retail business in the sale of merchandise or rendering of services. An example of retail property is a store (e.g., grocery store, furniture outlet).

retainage: Funds earned by the contractor for construction activity but held back by the owner of the property until the job is finished to a greater degree. This provides the contractor with an incentive to complete the work in a timely and qualitative manner in order to receive the amount retained by the owner. An example is a contractor who has thus far completed 75% of a new kitchen, but has only received a 25% deposit with the balance payable upon the satisfactory completion of the job.

retaining wall: Keeps something under control, such as water and sand. It blocks natural flow and settling of earth. It performs the same function as a dam would for water.

retaliatory eviction: The tenant is forced to leave the premises if he complains about the poor condition of the apartment or office space he has leased. This type of eviction is illegal in many states.

retention: Storing or keeping something such as an expansion tank holding hot water.

retire:

(1) Pay in full the balance on a debt either at or before the maturity date. Penalties may be assessed on prepaying a mortgage.

(2) Person leaving from work to spend time in leisure activities.

return: Reward for investing. The real estate investor must compare the anticipated return for an investment with the associated risk. The return includes:

(1) Periodic cash payments, called rental or current income.

(2) Appreciation (or depreciation) in market value, called capital gains (or losses).

See also *holding period of return (HPR); yield.*

reuse appraisal: Appraisal performed in accordance with the National Housing Act to determine the resale value of vacant or improved property in an urban area to be or under development. The renewal project may have certain restrictions and specifications placed upon it such as square footage, use of land, and density.

revaluation: Reconsideration of the value of real property. An example is getting property appraised each year to determine its current value for tax or purposes of determining whether to sell it.

revaluation clause: Provision in a lease agreement requiring that the rental property be appraised at specified time intervals so the rental charge may be adjusted. For example, if rental is set at 2% of current value, the rent based on a new appraisal of $1,000,000 would be $20,000. It is suggested that the lessee and lessor mutually agree on the appraiser so no one is being taken advantage of. See also *reappraisal lease*.

Reverse Annuity Mortgage (RAM): Mortgage where the lender pays a borrower a fixed monthly payment based on the value of the property. It allows the borrower to receive monthly receipts against the equity in his or her home. It is designed for senior citizens who own their homes and require additional funds to pay current living expenses, but do not wish to sell their homes. At the end of the payment term, usually 10 or 15 years, the mortgage on the borrower's home equals a predetermined sum so that the value of the equity is reduced by the amount. The loan is not repaid until sale of the property or the death of the borrower when it is settled through normal probate procedures.

reverse leverage: Also called negative leverage. The interest rate on the obligation exceeds the return rate on the real estate investment. As a result, losses are magnified. See also *positive leverage*.

reversion: Also called estate in reversion. A vested interest or estate in which a person has a fixed interest in the future. For example, if a grantor is required by the IRS to pay a substantial sum in back taxes, the part remaining reverts to the estate for later distribution to the beneficiaries.

reversionary factor: Factor used in present value computations to determine the current value of future cash flows. It is used to get the current value of what the selling price would be when the property is sold at a future date. For example, the present value of selling a home for $300,000 ten years from now at a 10% interest rate equals:

$$\$300,000 \times \text{present value of \$1}$$
$$\text{for } n = 10,\ i = 10\%$$

$$\$300,000 \times .386 = \$115,800.$$

reversionary interest: Property interest a person has that is presently possessed by another. Upon the termination of the possession, the property reverts to the grantor. For example, the income from an estate is given to the wife for her lifetime. Upon her death, the income reverts to the estate whereupon the children will then share in the income.

reversionary lease: Future rental agreement to start after the current rental arrangement expires.

reversionary value: Estimated value of property after a specified time period.

revocation:
(1) Person or business making an offer decides to nullify it before it is accepted.
(2) Canceling the authority given to another such as when a real estate owner takes away the right of an agent to represent him.
(3) Terminating a financial instrument before issuance.

rezoning: Modification made by a municipality to the zoning of a locality. A change in zoning typically has to be requested and approved by a zoning commission and then the legislative body. It can be requested by individuals or businesses. The rezoning will only take place if no negative effects result to the affected citizens and properties within the area.

rider: Written modification to an insurance policy that alters its provisions. The rider may update the policy, and change the coverage of real property.

ridge:
(1) Significant elevation of land.
(2) Connection of edges between different sloping surfaces (e.g., roofs).
(3) Narrow upward strip.

ridge board: Material installed at the roof's edge for support.

right: Claim of a person or business to real property such as by exercising an option.

right of access: See *access right*.

right of courtesy: The spouse's legal right, upon the death of his wife (or her husband), to a life estate in all lands she (or he) owned.

right of dower: A life estate right of a widow on the demise of her husband, if he dies intestate, to all his lands and possessions for her and her children's support. If she dissents from his will, the widow is entitled to one-third of all the assets of husband's estate. The right of dower has been abolished in almost all states and significantly changed in others.

right of entry: Right to enter and start construction or furnishing property that is in the process of being purchased.

right of first refusal: Right of an individual to be offered something before it is offered to others. For example, a tenant whose apartment is going to be converted to a cooperative has the first right of refusal before the unit may be sold to others. The existing tenant is usually given a lower insider price.

right of redemption:
(1) The right to recover property taken away by foreclosure by paying the lender the total amount owed plus foreclosure costs.
(2) The right of a debtor in bankruptcy to recover personal property under lien by making restitution to the creditor.

right to rescind: A person has the option of canceling a contract previously agreed to.

right of rescission: Borrower's right to cancel, within three business days, a credit contract in which his or her residence is used as collateral. This right does not apply to first mortgage loans. See also *cooling-off period.*

right of subrogation: The substitution of one person or business for another when the substituted person or business has the same rights and obligations as the original party. An insurance company can subrogate for the insured when the insured is being sued.

right of survivorship: Survival right of a person to the property of another when an interest was involved. This right is implicit in a joint tenancy or a tenancy by the entirety.

right of way: An individual is typically allowed by law to walk over another individual's land to get some place. It may arise from repeated use or written agreement. Examples are passing a store's property to get to a highway, and going through a neighbor's property as a short cut to a community pool. See also *access; easement.*

rigid conduit: Stiff pipe used to cover electrical wiring for safety purposes.

riparian owner: Owner has rights to water on his land. He also has a reasonable privilege to water adjacent to his property that flows through it or abutting it.

riparian right: The common law right of a landowner whose land borders a river or stream to use and enjoy that water.

riser: Board behind steps or stair going upward. See also *high rise.*

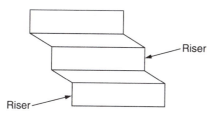

risk:
(1) Fluctuation in sales, profits, rate of return, etc.
(2) Likelihood of declining value.
(3) A peril insured against.
Types of real estate risk include *risk of*

principal—the possible decline in the amount invested; *liquidity risk*—represents the possibility that the property may not be sold on short notice for its market value. If the property must be sold at a substantial discount, then there is substantial liquidity risk; *business risk*—involving variations in rental income, vacancies, or operating expense; *market rental risk*—caused by a long-term lease that may lock the property owner into below-market rents; and *interest rate risk*—variability in property values as the mortgage rates and money market conditions change.

rod: Survey measurement that is 16.5 feet long.

rollover: See *1034 Exchange Rollover.*

rollover loan:

(1) A delay in making a principal payment on a mortgage that a bank allows a debtor for current financial difficulties.

(2) The extension of a loan at maturity at the "going" market interest rate.

(3) A mortgage loan in which the amortization of principal is long-term based but the interest rate is short-term.

rollover mortgage: Mortgage in which the rate of interest is constant but the entire loan is negotiated, or rolled over, after a stated time period. See also *renegotiated mortgage.*

roof: External top of a structure such as for an office building or house.

roofer: Contractor who constructs new roofs or repairs old ones.

rough hardware: Metal hardware within the construction that is typically not visible, such as bolts, nails, and screws.

round timber: Timber in an original form, such as a pole.

row house: Single-family dwelling attached to other units by common walls.

row stores: Retail businesses next to each other with common walls on each side and the same roof.

royalty: Monies paid to use property, such as the use of natural resource extractions. The royalty payment is typically based upon some percentage of the income or fee for substances generated from the use of such property.

rubble: Rough, fractured parts of brick and stone that may be left over after an old structure is destroyed to make room to build a new structure.

rubblework: Masonry of rough stones constructed irregularly.

rule of 72 and rule of 69: Rule of thumb approach used to determine how long it takes to double an investment in real estate. Under this approach, dividing the number 72 by the fixed rate of return equals the number of years it requires for annual earnings from the real estate investment to double. That is,

$$\frac{72}{r \text{ (in percent)}}$$

EXAMPLE: Bill bought a piece of property yielding an annual return of 20%. The investment will double in less than three years.

$$\frac{72}{20} = 3.6 \text{ years.}$$

The rule of 69, which is similar to the rule of 72, states that an amount of money invested at r percent per period will double in

$$\frac{69}{r \text{ (in percent)}} + .35 \text{ periods.}$$

EXAMPLE: Using the same information from the prior example,

$$\frac{69}{20} + .35 = 3.45 + .35 = 3.80 \text{ years.}$$

rule of 78: Also called the Rule of the Sum of the Digits. An approach that banks use to formulate a loan amortization schedule. It results in a borrower paying more interest in the beginning of a loan when he/she has the use of more of the money, and less interest as the obligation is reduced. Interest can be saved by prepaying the loan.

EXAMPLE: Ruth borrows $3,180 ($3,000 principal and $180 interest) for 12 months, so her equal monthly payment is $265 ($3,180/12). She wants to know how much interest will be saved by prepaying the loan after six payments. Ruth might incorrectly guess $90 ($180 × 6/12), believing that interest is charged uniformly each month. It is not! Rule of 78 works as follows:

(a) First, add up all the digits for the number of payments. In this case, 78 = (1 + 2 + 3 . . . + 12) one can easily compute the sum of the digits (SD) using the following formula:

$$SD = \frac{n(n + 1)}{2} = \frac{12(12 + 1)}{2}$$

$$= \frac{(12)(13)}{2} = \frac{156}{2} = 78$$

where n = the number of months. (The sum of the digits for a four year (48 months) loan is 1,176 [(48)(48 + 1)/2 = (48)(49)/2 = 1,176)]. See *Loan Amortization Schedule.*

(b) In the first month, before making any payments, Ruth has the use of all the amount borrowed. She thus pays 12/78ths (or 15.39%) of the total interest in the first payment. In the second month, she pays 11/78ths (14.10%); in the third, 10/78ths (12.82%); and so on down to the last payment, 1/78ths (1.28%). Thus, the first month's total payment of $265 contains $27.69 (15.39% × $180) in interest and $237.31 ($265 − $27.69) in principal. The 12th and last payment of $265 contains $2.30 (1.28% × $180) in interest and $262.70 in principal.

(c) In order to find out how much interest is saved by prepaying after the sixth payment, Ruth should add up the digits for the remaining six payments. Thus, using the above formula, 6(6 + 1)/2 = 21. This means that 21/78ths of the interest, or $48.46 (21/78 × $180), will be saved.

(d) To determine the amount of principal still owed, subtract the total amount of interest already paid,

Loan Amortization Schedule
Based on a loan of $3,180 ($3,000 principal and $180 interest)

Payment Number	Fraction (Percent) Earned by *Lender*	Monthly Payment	Interest	*Principal*
1	12/78 (15.39%)	$ 265	$ 27.69*	$ 237.31**
2	11/78 (14.10%)	265	25.39	239.61
3	10/78 (12.82%)	265	23.08	241.92
4	9/78 (11.54%)	265	20.77	244.23
5	8/78 (10.26%)	265	18.46	246.54
6	7/78 (8.97%)	265	16.15	248.85
7	6/78 (7.69%)	265	13.85	251.15
8	5/78 (6.41%)	265	11.54	253.46
9	4/78 (5.13%)	265	9.23	255.77
10	3/78 (3.85%)	265	6.92	258.08
11	2/78 (2.56%)	265	4.62	260.38
12	1/78 (1.28%)	265	2.30	262.70
78	78/78 (100%)	$3,180	$180.00	$3,000.00

*$27.69 = $180.00 × 12/78 (15.39%)
**$237.31 = $265 − $27.69

$131.54($180 − $48.46), from the total amount of payments made, $1,590 (6 × $265), giving $1,458.46. Then subtract this from the original $3,000 principal, giving $1,541.54 still owed.

(e) Is Ruth better off paying the loan after the sixth payment? It depends on how much return she can obtain from an alternative investment. In this case, she needed $1,541.54 to pay off the loan to save $48.46 in interest. For loans of longer maturities, the same procedure applies, though the actual sum of the digits will vary. Thus, for a 48-month loan, you would pay in the first month 48/1176ths of the total interest, in the second month, 47/1176ths etc.

See also *amortization schedule; loan amortization.*

run with the land: Privileges, rights, obligations, or restrictions associated with owning land. They are directly associated with the land regardless of who owns it. Examples are the dimensions of the plot, and local restrictions on how the property may be used.

rural: Geographic location external to populated cities. It usually has a low population and may be a small town with farms.

rural-urban fringe: Area that is located between a rural and urban area.

rurban: Geographic location that is gradually being developed as an urban area.

R value: Heat resistance measure commonly used with insulating material, outside walls, and roofs. The higher the R value, the more heat transfer resistance a material has.

S

sale-leaseback: Situation in which an owner of property sells the property to an investor and then leases the property back, usually for a 20- or 30-year term. EXAMPLE: Jay sells a property to Laura for $500,000 and agrees to lease it at a net rental to give her a 10% return on her investment. Jay will receive $500,000 in cash and will keep the property, and pay Laura a net amount of $50,000 each year. At the end of the term, the property will revert to Laura.

sales-assessment ratio: Selling price of a property divided by its appraisal value. If real estate has a selling price of $400,000 but its assessed value is $380,000, the ratio is 1.053.

sales commission: Amount earned by a real estate broker for his or her services upon the sale of real estate. It is usually expressed as a percentage of the selling price.

sales contract: Agreement between the seller and buyer involving the terms of sale.

sales deposit receipt: Receipt given for a partial payment made on the sale of property. It shows the buyer has made a down payment.

sales expenses: Charges incurred in making a sale of real estate such as real estate commissions and attorney fees.

sales incentive: Extra compensation given to a real estate broker who has surpassed his sales quota (e.g., number of houses sold, total sales dollars of houses sold, number of apartments rented, square footage of office space rented). The incentive may be a flat fee or a percentage of the extra sales dollars above the quota. For example, if the sales goal is $3,000,000 but actual sales generated was $4,000,000 and an incentive of 1% on extra sales is given, the real estate broker would receive a bonus of $10,000 (1% × $1,000,000). While sales incentives are typically in money, it may be in other forms such as a new car, free vacation, and gift certificates.

sales kit: Literature, samples, equipment, tools, and other useful information that real estate brokers or agents can use for demonstration purposes to prospective buyers.

salesperson: Individual engaged in selling a product or service. The product may be an investment in real estate. In some instances, state law may require licensing to safeguard the public by requiring specified professional and ethical standards.

sales price (gross): The price the seller charges the buyer for real estate. The net sales price received by the seller will be less after taking into account the selling costs (e.g., brokerage commission, closing costs).

sales price list: Written enumeration of the desired selling prices associated with homes or office buildings for sale. The prospective buyer can then determine if the properties for sale are within his buying range.

sales-ratio analysis: Evaluation of the reasons for the difference between the expected selling price of a property and its appraisal value. Perhaps the discrepancy is due to a poor appraisal, emergency nature of selling or buying property (e.g., owner is ill and must sell immediately), or unexpected deteriorating local conditions (e.g., sudden crime wave in the community).

sales value: What a piece of property could be sold for on the market.

salt box architecture: Style of architecture popular during the American Colonial Period. The 2-story house is square or rectangular. The steep gable roof extends down to the first floor in the rear.

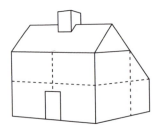

sandwich lease: The lessee becomes a lessor by subletting the property to a third party. Typically, the sandwich leaseholder does not own or use the property.

sandwich panel: Insulation covered on each side by a material, such as metal.

sanitary sewer: Sewer whose sole purpose is to carry away domestic waste water.

sash: Frame surrounding a door or window to block adverse weather. It may be made of wood, metal, or other material. The frame may be fixed or moveable.

satellite cities: Subordinate neighborhoods that are tied to an urban area economically. For example, office buildings in a city are the workplace for residents in surrounding communities.

satisfaction:

(1) An individual is pleased with something such as work performed by an electrician at his home. Sometimes payment for work is made contingent on the recipient's expressed satisfaction and signature.

(2) Discharge of an obligation through payment or the rendering of a service.

(3) Fulfilling a person's needs or desires such as obtaining a real estate license or certificate. In this case, professional requirements have been met.

satisfaction of lien: Release and discharge of a lien on property because the terms of the lien have been met.

satisfaction of mortgage: Written statement of the lender (e.g., bank) that the buyer of real estate has paid-off the entire mortgage.

satisfaction piece: Lender's written assurance that the borrower has fully paid the obligation. The borrower may then show this instrument to interested parties.

savings and loan association: Financial institution that channels the savings of its depositors mostly into mortgage and home improvement loans. It concentrates on originating, servicing, and holding mortgage loans. Traditionally, they have been the largest supplier of single-family owner-occupied residential permanent financing, although S&Ls are not limited solely to this type of financing. Savings and loan associations also make home-improvement loans and loans to investors for apartments, industrial property, and commercial real estate. Approximately 40% of the S&Ls are federally chartered, the rest are state chartered. If federal, the association must be a member of the Federal Home Loan Bank System (FHLBS), and its funds must be insured by the Federal Savings and Loan Insurance Corporation (FSLIC). All federally chartered S&Ls are mutually owned (owned by depositors) and the word "federal" must appear in their title. State chartered S&Ls can be either mutually owned or stock associations. (In a stock association, individuals buy stock that provides the equity capital.) They have optional membership in both the FHLBS and the FSLIC. In some states, these lenders are known as building and loan associations or cooperative banks.

saw-tooth roof: Pitched roof that looks like a saw.

scale: Model depicting on paper what a structure physically looks like. The dimensions are drawn on a proportionate basis to the real thing. An example is a scale of an existing or proposed office building.

scantling lumber: Yard lumber about 2 inches by 8 inches.

scarcity: Inadequate supply of real estate in a particular area will result in a favorable demand supply relationship resulting in price increases for the property. This benefits the current owners of the property. An example was the explosive growth in Orlando, Florida, causing property value to skyrocket in selected areas.

scenic easement: Easement with the objective of keeping scenic beauty or to forbid constructing something else blocking that view. The property is retained in its natural setting.

schedule E: Schedule which is part of Form 1040 showing income or loss from real estate transactions including

net rental income (rental revenue less rental expenses).

schematic plan: Outline or diagram of a structure or group of structures (e.g., community development) used for planning purposes.

scratch cost: Initial plaster used on a lathe.

seal:

(1) Attesting to something such as the validity of an instrument used in real estate.

(2) Identifying marker of a company.

seasoned loan: Loan such as a mortgage that the borrower has consistently made payments on when due over many years. The borrower has proven his credit worthiness.

secondary financing: See *junior mortgage.*

secondary location: Real property situated in a less advantageous area. Examples are a supermarket located in a crime area, or one that is difficult to see because it is off the main street, or one that has inadequate parking space.

secondary mortgage market: Market where mortgage loans can be sold to investors. The availability of funds for financing real estate is affected by economic conditions, both local and national. The result is that at certain times or in certain geographic locations little or no capital is available for mortgages; consequently, few if any loans are made. From the viewpoint of the lender, another problem is that real estate loans can be highly illiquid; thus, the supplier of funds can have a difficult time converting loans into cash. For these reasons, the need exists for some means by which a lender can sell a loan prior to its maturity date. The secondary mortgage market attempts to meet these needs. Capital can be made available during times of tight money and at capital-deficit locations. By selling mortgages in the secondary mortgage market, a lender can convert existing mortgages into cash which can in turn be used to fund new mortgages. Likewise, an investor in the secondary market can buy existing mortgages, pay the seller a small servicing fee, and avoid the time and expense of originating and servicing the loans.

second deed of trust (mortgage): Deed of trust or mortgage in real estate in which the lender subordinates her loan to another lender whose priority is first if there is nonpayment by the borrower.

second home: Another residence in addition to the main residence where a person or family resides. An example is a second home out of the city used on weekends and during vacations. Interest and real estate taxes on a second home are deductible for tax purposes.

second lien: Lien which is over and above a first lien. A second lien is subordinate to the first lien and can be satisfied only after the initial lien is satisfied.

second mortgage: Mortgage debt with a subordinated claim to the first mortgage. A second mortgage is senior to subsequent liens, and may be used to reduce the amount of a cash down payment or in refinancing to obtain cash for some purpose (e.g., home improvement, investment in a business). The interest rate on the second mortgage is higher because of the greater risk. The second mortgage usually has a repayment term much shorter than the first mortgage with a fixed amortization schedule. There may also be a balloon payment. For example, a home costs $300,000 and the first mortgage is for 85%, or $255,000. Therefore, a $45,000 down payment is required. If a second mortgage is available for $30,000, then the down payment will be $15,000.

section: Measure of land representing one square mile. A section equals 640 acres.

section 8 housing: Federal program in which the U.S. government subsidizes much of the rent paid by low-income people. It applies to rentals of privately owned apartments.

section 167: Section of the Internal Revenue Code relating to depreciation. Capital improvements made to real property are depreciable.

section 1031 tax-free exchange: Section of the Internal Revenue Code that addresses tax-free exchanges of certain property. The general provisions for a tax-free exchange of real estate are that the properties must be (1) like-kind property (real estate for real estate); (2) exchanged; and (3) held for use in a trade or business or held as an investment. Delayed exchanges are permitted within certain limits.

section 1034: Provision in the Internal Revenue Code applicable to the sale of an individual's house. The gain or loss is deferred by adjusting the cost basis of a new house bought within two years of the date of sale of the old house. The replacement cost for the new house must be equal to or greater than the net selling price of the old house. The net selling price equals the gross selling price less expenses associated with the sale such as brokerage fees. For example, Charles has a gain on the sale of his home of $30,000. He replaces it in six months with a higher priced home costing $300,000. The gain is deferred and adjusts the cost basis of the new home to $270,000.

section 1221: Section of the Internal Revenue Code explaining what a capital asset is and is not. Capital assets include real estate such as buildings and raw land. It excludes from the definition receivables, inventory, and intangibles.

section 1231: Section of the Internal Revenue Code applies to assets used in a trade or business. In general, gains on section 1231 assets are taxed at capital gains rates (excluding depreciation recapture), and losses are considered ordinary losses for tax purposes. Assets included under section 1231 are apartments, warehouses, hotels, and office buildings.

section 1245: Provision of the Internal Revenue Code applying to gains from the sale of personal property subject to depreciation. In most cases, the gains are at the capital gains tax rate limited to the amount of accumulated depreciation taken.

section 1250: Rule within the Internal Revenue Code applicable to capital gains from selling real estate that has been depreciated for tax purposes. Most buildings must be depreciated using the straight-line method.

sections I and II (homeowners' policy): Sections of a homeowner policy. Section I relates to the home, contents, and accompanying structures. Section II provides comprehensive coverage for personal liability and the medical payments and property damage incurred by those other than the insured.

secured loan: Requires collateral to secure the debt. An example of collateral might be one's home.

secured note: Written obligation of a borrower that is backed by collateral in the event of default. The lender must assure himself that the market value of the security equals or exceeds the amount of the debt.

secured party: Lender who possesses the collateral of the borrower if the loan is defaulted upon.

securities and exchange commission (SEC): Federal government agency monitoring and regulating corporate financial reporting and disclosure, use of accounting principles, auditing practices, and trading activities. Its regulations apply to publicly held real estate companies. SEC requirements promote full disclosure to protect investor interests.

securitization: Process of the borrower giving the lender security to obtain the loan.

security:
(1) A certificate of ownership in a real estate company (e.g., stock), or other ownership rights.
(2) Pledged assets for a borrowing. An example is an office building serving as collateral for the mortgage.
(3) Way of protecting property from improper access or use, such as posting a security guard in an apartment building.

security agreement: Legal contract in which the lender controls the pledged property being financed. The agreement describes the property and its location. If default occurs, the lender may sell the collateral. There may also be loan covenants such as required insurance coverage for the collateralized property.

security deposit: Prepayment to a landlord for refurbishing the unit beyond what would be anticipated from customary wear and tear. It is like a damage deposit. The security deposit may be refunded at the end of the lease provided the premises are satisfactory.

security interest: Creditor's control over property. When a loan is secured with pledged assets, the creditor has the right to go to court to obtain possession of the property if the borrower defaults. The creditor can usually sell the property, apply the amount received (less expenses) to the balance owed, and sue for any still remaining unpaid balance. State laws differ as to creditors' rights and obligations.

seed money: Funds put up by venture capitalists to finance a new business. Often, involves a loan or investment in preferred stock or convertible bonds. A major purpose of seed money is to form a basis for additional financing to aid in a real estate firm's growth.

seizin: Individual who enjoys a freehold land right.

select lumber: High quality, premium wood to be used in construction such as for home building.

self-amortizing mortgage: Mortgage being reduced through periodic principal and interest payments.

self-supporting walls: Walls that support themselves, and thus do not need external supports.

seller financing: If buyers are considering a home with an assumable mortgage at a fair interest rate or if the sellers have already paid their mortgage, remember to consider seller financing. With seller financing, the seller determines the sales price and then acts much like a lender. He or she determines the amount of down payment and the other terms of sale. Seller financing becomes more common when interest rates are high and buying a home is out of reach for many who could otherwise not afford it. But regardless of interest rates, this option helps qualify people to buy who might not be able to qualify for a loan through a lending institution or who may have the income to afford monthly payments but not the cash for a down payment. With seller financing, borrowers whom lenders might consider marginally qualified not only may qualify to buy but also may save money because closing costs are often non-existent or less expensive than with lender financing. Often, seller financing produces returns that are substantially higher than those of most other investments. Also, seller financing is treated as an installment sale for tax purposes, and the seller will be taxed only on the proportional amount of gain received each year. Finally, if the buyer defaults, the seller can take the property back under the contract or, if absolutely necessary, he can foreclose on the property. A seller can also offer a wraparound mortgage to a buyer who already owns a home. With this option, the seller makes a money advance to cover or "wrap" the balance due on the old mortgage and the amount on the new loan at an interest rate below market levels. The term of the wrap is the time left on the old mortgage. So with the seller's help, the buyer's monthly payment is substantially less than for a new first mortgage at the higher interest rate.

seller's market: Real estate market in which the seller has the upper hand because demand exceeds supply. This will increase property values. See also *buyer's market.*

selling broker (agent): Holder of a real estate license who solicits a prospective buyer of property and receives a commission for his efforts.

semiannual: Also called biannual; twice a year. An example is when lease payments are due January 1 and July 1.

senior lien: Lien prior to another lien taking precedence over it. A senior lien may not necessarily be a first lien.

sensitivity analysis: Simulation that enables investors to determine variations in the rate of return on an investment property in accordance with changes in a critical factor (e.g., how much will the rate of return change if operating expenses rise 10% or rental income drops 5%?). It is an experiment with decision alternatives using a what-if approach.

sentimental value: Emotional value of property to the particular person. An example is an owner of a house who is attached to it because his deceased parents lived there.

separable property: Property wholly owned by one spouse, which was the spouse's before marriage or was received as a gift or an inheritance. This property legally belongs to that spouse and cannot be taken away in a debt action against the other spouse or for estate valuation.

septic system: System for human waste disposal where sewers do not exist. Pipes transport waste into septic tank and a leaching field purifies the fluids that come out of the septic tank before they join the ground water. It is used when county sewers have not yet been installed.

septic tank: Tank placed beneath the ground to accumulate sewage. See also *septic system.*

sequence sheet: Listing of items in priority or sequential order. There may be a succession or series of steps to result in a desired outcome. An example is what logical order should occur in building a home. The first step might be constructing a foundation for the house.

service contract: Agreement bought by a homeowner for servicing of household items. This contract may be taken out with the contractor or a third party. Examples are service contracts on household appliances (e.g., stove, refrigerator). A service contract provides the owner with the assurance of knowing the item will be repaired at a set fee if problems arise. However, a service contract is usually more costly than paying for the repairs as incurred.

servicing:
(1) The periodic, routine maintenance of household items.

(2) The handling of an account, as a mortgage serviced by a mortgage banker. See also *loan servicing.*

servient tenement: Land subject to an easement.

servitude: Work required as a court judgment because of a crime committed.

setback ordinance: Local zoning law or private limitation on how far in feet a structure might be situated from the curb or other appropriate marker.

set-off:
(1) *General:* Showing the net amount by reducing the gross amount for the contra effect. An example is offsetting against a payable of $50,000 a receivable to that same party of $30,000.

(2) *Law:* Defendant in an action counterclaims an amount the plaintiff owes him so as to reduce the possible recovery for the plaintiff. For example, if the plaintiff is suing for $100,000 in damages the defendant may try to reduce that amount by $25,000 by arguing that the plaintiff has wronged the defendant in some other way.

(3) *Taxation:* Offsetting an amount you owe the government in taxes against what the government owes you in taxes. For example, you can reduce your tax liability by a carryforward loss.

settlement statement: Accounting statement at the settlement of a real estate transaction that shows each item charged or credited, to whom, and for how much.

severalty: Person's sole ownership of real property.

severalty ownership: Person's title to real estate giving him exclusive power and rights over it.

severance damages: Amount awarded by a government when a person's property is condemned and he must move.

sevient estate: Land subject to an easement.

sewage: Waste matter carried off through a series of conduits to a waste disposal facility.

sewage tax: Levied on those benefiting from the installation of a sewer.

sewer: Drain facility usually underground for waste and water disposal consisting of connected pipes.

sewer line easement: Easement to build, maintain, and operate a disposal line for sewage.

shakeout: Decline in real estate values occurring during economic hardships such as depression or recession. The late 1980s and early 1990s experienced a depressed real estate market. Many office buildings remained totally, or almost totally vacant. One region of the country may be doing well while another is doing poorly. Further, it is possible that even though commercial real estate values are declining, prices of residential homes may be increasing, or vice versa. During a shakeout, huge losses may be experienced by real estate owners with some declaring bankruptcy.

shakeup: Sudden, drastic change in organization, direction, objectives, strategies, or functioning. It is often associated with a new owner who wants things his way. Managers and employees may experience tension and fear of losing their jobs.

Shared Appreciation Mortgage (SAM): A type of equity participation loan where, in exchange for charging a below-market interest rate, the lender receives a predetermined percentage of any increase in value of the property over a specified period of time. To illustrate, a lender who would otherwise charge 10% interest, might agree to take 7% interest plus one-third of the appreciation of the property. For the lender, the money received from the appreciation of the property increases the effective yield on the investment.

The borrower, by agreeing to share appreciation in property value gets a lower interest rate, which in turn reduces the monthly mortgage payment. A SAM is normally written so that at the end of the shared appreciation period, the property will be appraised and the amount due to the lender through appreciation is due at that time.

shared equity mortgage (SEM): Bank receives equity participation in the house as a result of lending the homeowner money. When the house is sold, the bank will receive its proportionate share of the proceeds. In such an arrangement, the bank sometimes pays the down payment for the house because of the homeowner's poor financial condition.

sheathing: Covering studs on the outside.

shed roof: Roof with one side that is at a sloped angle.

Shed Roof

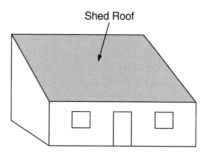

sheriff's deed: Title to property being given under a court order because the original owner failed to pay the mortgage payments and/or real estate taxes. A judgment in a lawsuit may also have forced the original owner to lose the property in order to pay damages. The deed is often associated with a foreclosure.

sheriff's sale: Foreclosed property is sold via a sheriff's deed. The amount received is used to pay the balance of any obligations against the owner or real estate.

shingles: Thin wood that is shaped in a wedge and laid together in rows. An example is a roof on a house.

shopping center: Retail businesses in the same locality having a parking lot servicing them. The center may contain a department store, small retailers, and restaurants. There may also be a movie theater. The shopping center may or may not be enclosed in a mall.

short-form: Condensed appraisal report covering the major items.

short-term *capital* **gain or loss:** The profit or loss from selling an investment that is held one year or less. Short-term gains are ordinary income, while short-term losses are deducted from current income. Short-term gains or losses do not qualify for any special tax treatment. See also *short-term gain or loss.*

shotcrete: Mortar or concrete which is pumped or "shot" through a hose at high velocity onto a surface. See also *gunite.*

siding: Material placed on the outside surface of a structure such as aluminum or vinyl siding on a house. It is cost-efficient because it eliminates the need for repeated painting. Siding provides insulation and makes the exterior of the home more attractive.

sight line: Visible area that can be readily seen by outside traffic. This is particularly important for a commercial business.

silent partner: Partner in a real estate business who remains anonymous but has legal rights and obligations.

sill: Bottom of a frame such as a window sill.

simple interest: Interest computations based only on the original principal. For example, the simple interest on a $100,000, 8% loan is $8,000. It is compared with compound interest which is applied to the original principal and accumulated interest. For example, $100 deposited in a savings account at 10% simple interest would yield the interest of $10 per year (10% of $100). The same $100 at 10% interest compounded annually would yield $10 interest in the first year. In the second year, however, the interest will be $12.10 (10% of $110, the first year's principal and interest). See also *compounding; future value; time value of money.*

simple rate of return: Also called accounting or unadjusted rate of return. The return computed by dividing the anticipated future annual net income by the required investment in real estate. Sometimes the average investment instead of the initial investment is used as the required investment, which is called average rate of return.

EXAMPLE: A real estate investment resulted in the following:

Initial investment	$650,000
Estimated life	25 years
Expected annual rental income	$ 75,000

The simple rate of return is $75,000/$650,000 = 11.5%. Using the average investment (one-half of the original investment), the average rate of return will be doubled as follows:

$$\$75,000/(\$650,000/2) = \$75,000/\$325,000$$

$$= 23.0\%$$

single family dwelling: House designed and zoned for one-family use. Other dwellings may be attached to a single family dwelling, but do not share the same plumbing, heating, or electrical system. Single family dwellings may be detached housing, condominiums, cooperatives, and townhouses.

single property syndicate: Sponsor sells interests to real estate investors in one property only (e.g., apartment house). The total amount received from the equity investors is used by the sponsor to buy the property for the partnership.

single purpose property: Property devoted to only one use such as a medical building.

sinking fund: Fund set aside for periodic payments, aimed at reducing a financial obligation taken out to buy real estate, or to accumulate enough funds to buy property or for plant expansion. The principal deposited into the sinking fund earns interest. The total amount accumulated is then used for the desired purpose.

site: Geographic location where a vacant or occupied structure exists. It usually means the land reserved is for a future building.

site analysis: Evaluating a locality to determine its value and appropriateness for designated objectives.

site assessment: Appraisal of a location before the purchase is made of it for potential environmental problems (e.g., hazardous waste).

site built home: Potential homeowners buy land at a location they like (e.g., near the water front) and then build their house on it.

site development cost: The total expenditures required to make a locality suitable for the designated purpose. An example is how much it would cost to build a shopping center on a lot.

site survey: Determining the measurements of a specific location.

situs: Geographic location of land based on its economic significance. Property values are directly impacted by economic factors in the particular locality. For example, a fashionable boutique or Lexus dealership might do well in a wealthy neighborhood but not in a poor one.

skin: Outside layer or covering for a structure. It may be a coating of material for protection against inclement weather.

skylight: A window in a roof or ceiling of a structure from which light enters the house.

slander: Oral defamation of the character or reputation of another. It is the basis for a lawsuit. See also *libel.*

slow-burning construction: Building a structure in such a way as to reduce the process of destruction in the event of fire. Fire-resistant materials are used.

slum area: Depressed, poorly kept locality that may include vacant businesses. It may be a high crime area. The people living in the area are typically poor and there may also be homeless people.

small claims court: Special court for the purpose of providing fast, inexpensive, and informal settlement of small financial claims between plaintiff and defendant. The parties represent themselves. A landlord of an apartment building might sue a tenant for nonpayment of a rent in this court.

Society of Industrial and Office Realtors (SIOR): Branch of the National Association of Realtors. Members are involved in real estate transactions for businesses applicable to office space. Membership requires many years of business experience with industrial and business firms as well as ethical standards. The organization may be reached at 777 14th Street, NW, Washington, DC 20005. Telephone: (202) 383-1150.

soft market: Real estate market where supply significantly exceeds demand enabling potential buyers to obtain lower prices and good deals.

soft money:
(1) Money paid for a real estate project or investment that can be taken off on the tax return as an expense.
(2) Expenditures made during construction of a building that do not go directly into the building. Examples are permit fees, interest on borrowed funds, attorney fees, and real estate taxes.

softwood: Conifer wood, such as pine and redwood.

soil: Upper layer of ground.

soil bank: Government compensation to farmers not to grow products to preserve the land and maintain stable agricultural products.

soil capability: Appropriateness of the soil for the designated purpose(s). An example is soil suitable for the growing of vegetables and fruit, or grazing for horses.

soil map: Map showing the kinds of soil in a designated locality.

soil pipe: Pipes from a structure to a sewer for the purpose of sewage disposal.

soil porosity: Extent to which soil has cavities or pores, thereby allowing water to pass through.

soil productivity: Ability of the soil to accomplish the desired objective such as its capacity for harvesting crops.

soil survey: Surveying the land to determine its suitability for a specific purpose, such as building a high-rise apartment house.

soil tests: Examining and testing the ground to determine the conditions for building something, such as an office building.

solar heating: Warming method using sunlight. It involves special glass panels.

Soldier's and Sailor's Civil Relief Act: Federal law protecting someone in active service from bank foreclosure of their property that was bought before entering the armed services.

sole ownership: See *sole proprietorship.*

sole plate: A two-by-four used for wall resilience and partitioning. Studs rest on it.

sole proprietorship: Real estate business owned by one person having all the rights and obligations.

southern colonial architecture: Building that is elaborately built with columns in a symmetrical way, generally with three floors and a gabled roof.

space merchandising: Marketing attractive space at the appropriate location at a good time in the correct square footage at a reasonable price or rental charge. An example is the renting out of space for retail businesses at a mall.

span: Spread between girders or heavy walls.

Spanish architecture: Designing a home with a Spanish cultural flavor.

Spanish villa: Home of 1 to 3 stories with stucco outside and a roof made of red tiles.

spec house: New homes built on speculation that a buyer will be found. They vary in price, size, and other features and can be found in various stages of construction.

special agent: Person retained to perform on behalf of another individual with restricted responsibility and power. An example is a broker hired by a home owner to solicit buyers. The agent typically is engaged to do one specific function.

special assessment: Charge levied against property owners to finance an improvement made by the local government which benefits the homeowners and commercial businesses. Examples are sidewalks and sewers.

special use permit: Authority given by a municipality to perform specified operations in a certain zoning area. Conditions are sometimes attached by the zoning group. An example is permission to have a commercial business activity for three months in a residential area, such as a street fair.

special warranty deed: Property deed in which the grantor limits the title warranty to the grantee. A grantor does not warrant a title defect to the property occurring from a happening before the time of his ownership.

Specialist in Real Estate Securities (SRS): Individual who by his expertise, education, and experience prepares syndication reports.

specific lien: Lien on a given property, such as an person's house as a collateral for a loan.

specific performance: Situation in which a person guilty of breaking a contract is required by the judge to fulfill his duties. Specific performance is required only if the item or subject of the contract is unique and money damages are not adequate. An example is a person's failure to deliver a specific property.

specifications: Details relating to the construction of a structure. The specifications, usually designated in the blueprints of construction, will indicate the building procedures to be followed by the contractor, the type of materials that must be used, the styles and designs that are to be incorporated, the dimensions requested, and so on.

speculative value: Value that a speculator believes an investment will reach at some point in the future.

speculator: Individual who attempts to maximize his or her profitability by investing with the anticipation that a particular investment will go up in value. A speculator will generally be willing to incur a significant degree of risk in the hope that a significant profit can be made in a short time. For example, a real estate speculator may purchase large amounts of land based on the assumption that high demand for the land in the near future will substantially boost its price.

spendable income: Net amount of cash that an investor requires from an income-producing property, after taxes, for a period of time, usually a year. It is computed by accumulating all rental receipts for the period and deducting from them all cash-related expenditures applicable to the property, such as the mortgage principal payments, mortgage interest, insurance, taxes. Depreciation, a noncash expenditure, is deducted initially for purposes of computing operating income upon which income taxes are based. However, since it is a noncash expenditure, it is in the end added back to get spendable income.

spot zoning: Zoning a portion of land in a given area for different purposes than its surrounding functions. For example, a locality may decide to spot zone a vacant lot in a residential area for commercial purposes. Historically, spot zoning has not received favorable support in court.

spouse: A married partner. Property may be jointly held by spouses.

spread: The difference between the price offered by a buyer and the price asked for by the seller of real property.

spreading agreement: Agreement between a lending institution and borrower where the borrower agrees to extend or spread the collateral of a loan to additional properties beyond the original mortgaged property. The effect of this agreement is to reduce the risk of collection by the lender by enlarging the security base of the loan.

springing power of attorney: To obtain the right through authorization to act as a legal representative and agent for another.

sprinkler system: In-ground watering system generally controlled by a digital timer that waters the grass and shrubbery of a property.

square footage: Standard unit of area that is used to measure a parcel of real estate. Square footage is computed by multiplying the length and width dimensions of a room, building, lot, etc. For example, if a room is 18 feet by 15 feet, its area is 270 square feet.

square foot cost: Cost of the standard unit of area that is used to measure a parcel of real estate. Commercial property rentals are generally quoted on the basis of square foot cost. For example, a property in a city might rent at a cost of $5 per square foot per month.

square foot method: Represents a means of appraising a building by simply multiplying its square foot cost by the total amount of square feet in the structure being evaluated. Two or more buildings may then be compared by analyzing their total square foot costs.

squatter's right: Right to use property in the absence of forcible eviction by another. Some state laws allow squatter's rights to convert to bona-fide title over time. For example, if it cannot be ascertained who owns a parcel of property then a squatter may acquire title to the real estate because he has been an occupant of the property continually for some minimum period required by law.

SRA: See *senior residential appraiser.*

SREA: See *senior real estate analyst.*

SRPA: See *senior real property appraiser.*

stabilization:

(1) Rentals that may be charged from landlord to tenant are stabilized by a government. For example, rent stabilization in New York City exists for certain types of apartments. The landlord is restricted on rental increases by law.

(2) Economic policies designed to reduce the fluctuation in the business cycle. An example is Federal Reserve monetary policies.

(3) An attempt by an underwriter to prevent a market price of a new security from going below the public offering price.

stagflation: Increasing prices during a slowdown in economic activity.

stair landing: The landing at the bottom and/or top of a stair case providing support for the structure.

standard depth: Depth of land used as the standard to appraise its value. An example is 100 feet used for residential land.

standard metropolitan statistical area (SMSA): Area or county used in the census or other data gathering functions that has a population of 50,000 inhabitants or more.

standard of living: The quality of life enjoyed by a person depending on factors such as spendable income, housing conditions, health, and education.

standby commitment: Commitment by a lender to a borrower (e.g., contractor or real estate developer) for a given amount of money at specified terms for the financing of a project. The borrower pays a fee for the privilege of either executing the loan or allowing the commitment to lapse. See also *standby fee.*

standby fee: Fee charged by a lender to a borrower for a standby commitment.

standby loan: Short-term loan that is made to bridge the term between the end of one loan and the beginning of another. See also *bridge loan.*

start rate: Also called a teaser. The starting interest rate of an adjustable rate loan. It generally lasts between 1 and 12 months, at which time the loan rate increases based on prearranged criteria.

state housing act: Law of the state establishing guidelines and requirements for constructing buildings. The standard may differ between the states.

statement of consideration: Enumeration of the consideration given by each party to a contract which in some cases must be in written form to be enforceable. For example, the statute of frauds requires that all contracts for the sale of real estate (transfer or ownership in real property by sale) be in writing.

status:

(1) Condition of real property.

(2) Degree of completion or accomplishment such as a home that is 70% completed.

(3) Position of an item.

(4) Legal standing such as of a case.

status quo: Existing state of affairs with respect to the real estate market and conditions.

statute: Legislative written decree (rule) stipulating prescribed action and conduct designed to be in the public's best interest. Laws may cover civil and criminal matters.

statute of frauds: Requirement based on law that certain types of contracts must be in written form in order to be enforceable. With respect to real estate, although negotiations and preliminary agreements may be oral, the final agreement must be in written form. Thus, all deeds, mortgages, and real estate contracts must be evidenced by a written form and may not be oral.

statute of limitations: Legal time restriction for prosecuting an improper act, or civil or criminal offense. Proceedings must be brought before the expiration date of the applicable federal, state, or local statute of limitations. Most states allow up to six years to file a claim for violation of a written contract and five years for civil liability claims.

statutory liens: Charges resulting in involuntary encumbrances against real property derived from legislated law rather than from debts owed to organizations (e.g., banks) or individuals (e.g., contractors). For example, if a homeowner does not pay his real estate taxes, the tax assessor may statutorily place a lien on his or her property for the back taxes owed.

statutory redemption period: Limited period of time granted by state law to an individual who has had his or her property foreclosed on and sold to regain possession of the property by repaying the debt that was defaulted on.

steep land: Land located on a precipice.

steering: Illegal practice of restricting the houses that are shown to a purchaser because of race, religious, or ethnic reasons.

stepped-up basis: An increase in the income tax basis of a property that is a result of a tax-free exchange. As a result of an inheritance, for example, the basis of the inherited property was stepped up to its current market value.

step-up lease: Lease that incorporates increases in agreed-on payments over the term of the lease contract. For example, a particular step-up lease may require that the lessee pay a 10% increase each year over the 5-year term of the lease.

stick style of carpenter gothic: Style of construction made popular in the 1800s. Its characteristics include very steep roofs, ornate trim, diagonal braces, and exposed framing members.

stipulations: Conditions and terms agreed to in a contract.

stock in trade: Inventory that is marketed and sold by an entity.

stock of housing: Number of housing units of a particular category that are available.

stoop: Stairs or porch by the front door of the house.

stop clause: Provision in a lease agreement indicating the maximum amount of operating expenditures (e.g., utilities—gas, electric) that must be incurred by the landlord in a given year. Any amount incurred in excess of this amount must be paid by the lessee.

stop notice: Directing the bank not to pay a check when presented at the bank. There is a service charge for this. If a contractor loses the check given to him, he may ask that the payor stop payment and replace the check.

store decisis: Legal practice followed in the American and English judicial systems of following the precedents of former decisions in deciding new cases. The application of this doctrine has not only enhanced the uniformity and stability of the law throughout the country, but has also enabled the courts to be more efficient by providing guidelines for current cases.

storm sewer: Sewer system built into the streets of a neighborhood that is capable of accommodating the excess water flow of a heavy storm without backing up or flooding.

story: One of the horizontal levels of a building that is constructed one above another as part of the building's overall construction.

straight bankruptcy: See *bankruptcy; Chapter 7.*

straight lease: Lease that requires periodic equal (e.g., monthly) rental payments that will not change for the term of the lease. A straight lease is also known as a flat lease.

straight-line depreciation: The depreciation method where an equal amount of depreciation expense is allocated to each full period of the asset's useful life. The amount of depreciation is computed as follows: Annual depreciation = (Original cost − Salvage value)/ Useful life. For example, assume that the building costs $800,000 and has an estimated useful life of 20 years. The estimated salvage value at the end of the 5-year period is $200,000. Then the straight-line depreciation per year is ($800,000 − $200,000)/20 years = $30,000/year.

straight-line recapture rate: Capitalization rate used to convert the expected income derived from a property into its estimated asset value (capitalized value). The estimated asset value may

be computed by dividing the annual income generated by a property by its capitalization rate. The capitalization rate that is used is generally viewed as having two components: (1) rate of return on investment and (2) straight-line recapture rate that represents the percentage of cost that the investor believes that he or she must recover each year in order to recoup the entire cost of the asset over its useful life. For example, an investor decides that the capitalization rate for a particular piece of real estate is 15% consisting of a rate of return of 12% on his investment and a 3% straight-line recapture rate.

straight mortgage or deed of trust: Device that places the ownership of real property with one or more trustees for security until the loan is paid by the debtor. It is used in place of a conventional mortgage contract in some states. The deed of trust stipulates that in the event of default by the debtor the trustee would liquidate the property for the benefit of the lender in a trustee's sale.

straight note: Loan agreement that generally requires payments of interest only over the term of the note. At the end of the term, the entire debt balance becomes payable in a single balloon payment.

straw man: Individual who purchases property for another for the purpose of not identifying to the seller and other interested parties the real identity of the true acquirer. The individual who makes the purchase is an agent of the true purchaser and will convey the property to him or her after the sale has been consummated.

street improvement: Repairing the street for safety and attractiveness. In some localities, such as on Long Island, the home owner is responsible for properly maintaining the street surrounding his home.

stretcher bricks: A method of brick construction where the bricks are laid with their sides facing outward. See also *brick masonry.*

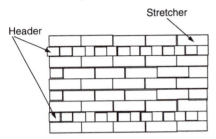

string stringer: Large heavy piece of wood or other material generally running horizontally through a building providing support for other parts of the structure. The stringer usually runs in the direction of the greatest length of supporting beams that are dependent upon it.

strip development: Construction of commercial property in a manner that enables each lessee or tenant to have access to the main strip or thoroughfare running through the property. For example, this mode of development is very common in the building of a shopping center to insure maximum exposure of each store or unit to shoppers.

strip lumber: Lumber of no more than 8 inches wide and 2 inches thick.

structural analysis: Evaluation of the dimensions (e.g., shape, size, layout) of a building to determine its ability to meet the needs of the occupants.

structural lumber: A strong piece of lumber at least two-by-four. It is used for studs and beams to hold a building or structure up. The structure is in effect, attached to, or built onto the structural lumber of a building frame.

structure:
(1) Something that has been built and physically exists at a specific location, such as a building, garage, and fence.

(2) Something consisting of related parts, such as the organization and terms of a written agreement for a real estate transaction.

studs or studding: Post-like components of wood that comprise a building frame. For example, a building code in a locality might require that studs measuring two-by-six be used for the exterior part of the frame of newly constructed housing units.

subchapter S corporation: Corporation whose stockholders are taxed as partners. That is, income is taxed as direct income to the shareholders. The key advantage of this tax treatment is that shareholders escape double taxation (taxes on corporate net income and taxes on the distribution received are included in the individual's tax return). To qualify as an S corporation, (1) there must be 35 or fewer stockholders; (2) there can be only one class of stock; and (3) no nonresident foreigners may be shareholders.

subcontractor: Party that receives part or all of a construction job to do from the general contractor.

subdivider: Individual or entity that divides up a large piece of owned land into smaller pieces generally for the purpose of developing them into homes for sale in the future.

subdivision: Piece of land that is divided into smaller pieces by its owner for the purpose of improving them (building homes, etc.) for future sale. See also *subdivider.*

subject property: In appraisal jargon, property currently being appraised.

subject to: Said of property that is bought subject to the existing loan against it.

subject to mortgage or trust deed: Situation in which a purchaser acquires mortgaged property and continues to pay the mortgagee for the debt outstanding.

Although the new buyer continues to pay the mortgagee for the debt due, the new buyer is not liable for the amount due. In the case of a default, the seller of the property (original mortgagor– signer of the promissory note given to the lender) is liable for the remaining debt. In the case of default, only the new purchaser's equity in the property is lost.

sublease: Lease agreement between the lessee (one who leases property from another) of an original lease and a new lessee. For example, Jones signs a lease for an apartment with Smith that allows Jones to sublease it to another, if desired. Jones unexpectedly is offered a position in Europe and decides to sublease the apartment for the remaining term of the original lease to Stevens. The sublease represents the agreement between Jones and Stevens. Smith, the original lessor, is not a party to the sublease.

sublessor: The initial lessee of rented property who then leases it to a subtenant.

subletting: Process by which a lessee leases the property to another lessee.

submarket: Accumulation of housing units deemed substitutable by homogeneous households, such as those having comparable attractiveness and usefulness.

subordinate: To reduce the priority of payment of a debt or lien. For example, in order to enable a tract of land to be developed, the first mortgagee agrees to subordinate his or her loan to a new development mortgage loan (taken by the owner) that will now become the first mortgage. Although both debts are now secured by the same property, in the event of default and subsequent liquidation of the property to pay-off the liabilities, the second mortgage will not

be paid until the first mortgage is fully satisfied.

subordination agreement: An agreement by which a mortgage is made subject (junior) to a junior mortgage. For example, a loan on a vacant lot is made subject to a subsequent construction loan.

subordination clause: A provision that allows a mortgage recorded at a later date to take preference over an existing mortgage.

subpoena: Writ issued by the court requiring a person to appear as a witness or to provide written information in the case. A contempt of court citation may occur for failure to observe the subpoena. An example is when a tenant subpoenas another tenant to appear in court in litigation against the landlord.

subpoena duces tecum: Legal order for a person to present at a deposition or trial documents in his possession, such as related to a real estate transaction.

subrent: Process by which a lessee rents his apartment to another. See also *sublease*.

subrogate: Substituting one party for another in an action giving that party full rights or claims. For example, an insurance company pays the insured for a fire loss caused to the home by a third party (e.g., electrician who did a faulty job). After the insurance company reimburses the insured for the loss, the insurance company "now stands in the insured's shoes" and sues the third party for the damages.

subrogation rights: Rights allowing an insurer to act against a negligent third party (including its insurance company) to receive reimbursement for payments made to an insured.

subsequent: Something which occurs at a later date. It follows a prior occurrence. An example is that after a contract is signed new circumstances arise requiring a revision to the original terms.

subsidized housing: Housing whose rental payments are reduced because of aid granted by the federal, state, or local governments, private enterprises, or individuals. For example, monthly rental payments for elderly individuals living in senior citizen subsidized housing complexes are significantly lower than the fair market value of these payments due to federal subsidies.

substitution: In valuing real estate, substitution is the principle that the market value of a property can be relatively accurately estimated by determining market value of similar properties in the general vicinity. Thus, by substitution, an appraiser can ascertain the market value of a piece of real estate by analyzing the sales prices of comparable units in the neighborhood sold in the recent past.

subsurface easement: Owner of land allowing another to use space under the ground, such as to install a sewer or gas line.

subsurface rights: The owner of real property generally has exclusive rights to the soil and minerals underneath the land. Significant limitations on subsurface rights have to be disclosed in the title deed at the time of acquisition. If no restrictions are indicated, the buyer can expect to exercise full rights to the property. It is important to note, however, that in some states, the owner of land is not automatically assumed to also be the owner of the subsurface. That is, land ownership may be separated. In many areas, subsurface rights can be extremely valuable because of the existence of oil, natural gas, and minerals, and those must be acquired separately. See also *mineral rights.*

subtenant: Person who leases rented premises from the initial lessee. The

sublease is for a time not exceeding the original lease period. See also *subletting.*

suburban: Description of an area that is located at the outskirts of a city composed primarily of residential units. The city frequently provides employment, cultural activities, and other support services for the suburban commuters.

succession: Transfer of real property by legal means such as through inheritance.

successor: Individual coming later in a sequence. An example is a keeper of a home succeeding the seller as the owner.

sui juris: Latin term meaning legal capacity to act on behalf of oneself.

suitability standards: Financial characteristics or standards that a potential investor is evaluated on to judge his or her suitability for a particular investment program. For example, to determine whether a particular large scale investment program in apartment buildings is appropriate for an investor, an individual's net worth, liquidity, knowledge of the real estate industry, outstanding debt, overall financial sophistication, and other attributes will all be considered and evaluated.

sum-of-the-years'-digits (SYD) method: Accelerated depreciation method in which the amounts recognized in the early years of the property's (e.g., building) useful life are greater than those recognized in the later years. The SYD is found by estimating the property's useful life in years, assigning consecutive numbers to each year, and adding the numbers. For n years, a short-cut formula is $n(n + 1)/2$.

The yearly depreciation is then computed by multiplying the total depreciable amount for the asset's useful life by a fraction whose numerator is the remaining useful life and whose denominator is the SYD. Annual depreciation equals:

(Original cost − Salvage value)

$$\times \frac{\text{Remaining useful life}}{\text{SYD}}$$

EXAMPLE: A building is bought costing $100,000 with an estimated salvage value of $10,000 and a life of 5 years. The SYD is: 5(5 + 1)/2 = 15. The depreciation computation follows:

Year	Fraction	Cost − Salvage value	= Depreciation
1	5/15	$90,000	$30,000
2	4/15	90,000	24,000
3	3/15	90,000	18,000
4	2/15	90,000	12,000
5	1/15	90,000	6,000
Total			$90,000

summary possession: Act of actual eviction or removal of a lessee from a property. The eviction may be either voluntarily through due process of law or involuntarily by force. This generally occurs when a lease is violated by a lessee for nonpayment of rent.

summary proceeding: Way to obtain a faster decision in a legal case than going to a trial. Procedural rules are followed so there is less time involved in gathering the facts of the dispute and in questioning. Many landlord-tenant contracts provide for the controversy to be settled through the summary proceeding instead of the court trial.

summons: Notice sent from a plaintiff to a defendant requiring the defendant to appear before a court or judge. For example, a landlord might send a summons to a tenant regarding a notice of eviction due to nonpayment of rent. The tenant must then appear in court to defend the landlord's eviction request.

sump: Pit or cavity built into the basement of a building to avoid or minimize flooding. It allows for the

drainage of excess water and moisture. See also *sump pump.*

sump pump: Pump installed in the sump of a building to pump out and drain any water or liquids that have accumulated.

sunspace: Room in a building used to collect solar heat. To provide for such collection, a room is generally constructed with a glass roof and walls.

supermarket: Large, high-volume food store where customers serve themselves by going through the aisles and selecting their groceries to be paid at the cash register on the way out.

surety: One who agrees to pay the debts of another in the event that the debtor does not pay. The creditor can demand payment from the surety as soon as the debt becomes due. Although a surety agreement does not have to be in writing to be enforceable, most of them are.

surrender: Expiration of a lease or insurance policy by mutual consent of the parties, also to give up.

survey: Accurate measurement of land for the purpose of determining the boundaries of its perimeter, its contours, and area. Surveys are generally required by banks and other lending institutions as part of making mortgage secured loans to individuals and other entities. See also *surveyor.*

surveyor: One who is trained in the measurement of land for the purpose of determining its perimeter boundaries, contours, and area.

survivorship benefit (on an annuity): Part of the premiums and interest that have not been returned to the annuitant before his death.

sweat equity: The equity in property because of work in it by the buyer or holder which directly increases its value.

swing loan: See *bridge loan.*

syndicate:

(1) A group of investment bankers underwriting and distributing a new or

outstanding issue of securities of a real estate business.

(2) A professionally managed limited partnership investing in different types of real estate.

syndication: Way of selling real estate in which a syndicator sells equity interests to investors. Examples include a real estate investment trust, limited partner-

ship, and corporation. For example, a partnership interest may be sold to investors in a shopping center.

syndicator: Sponsor of a syndicate involving people or companies buying an interest in a real estate investment or unit. The group of investors are in effect engaged in a joint venture for profit.

tacking: Adding a period of time onto another. An example is a mortgagor who successfully restructures his loan by tacking another five years onto the term.

take-out loan: Form of financing that replaces or "takes-out" a construction loan to a developer. The take-out loan is a permanent mortgage loan which replaces the construction loan when, commonly, the builder has successfully sold, at minimum, a majority of the units under construction. A developer must arrange take-out financing before he can hope to get a construction loan.

taking: Act of obtaining land through condemnation. For example, when an interstate highway must be constructed, the land for the new road is obtained through takings. Usually, the government will exercise its right to "take" only after it is determined that the owners of the acquired property is unwilling to settle for a reasonable price. See also *eminent domain.*

tandem plan: Government program of providing low interest rate mortgages to low-income qualified buyers. In the tandem program, the Federal National Mortgage Association (FNMA) purchases low interest rate mortgages at a discount from the Government National Mortgage Association (GNMA). In doing this, GNMA subsidizes the low-income home buyer and incurs a loss on the transaction.

tangible: Anything that has physical substance and form, such as land and buildings.

tangible asset: One having physical existence and a life exceeding one year. It is not kept for resale in the ordinary course of business. An example is a building.

tangible property: Items of real and personal property that usually have a long life, such as housing and other real estate.

tax and insurance escrow: When a mortgage loan is provided to a borrower, the lender (frequently a bank) establishes a fund called a tax and insurance escrow to accumulate the debtor's monthly payments for property taxes and insurance premiums for the mortgaged property. As the taxes on the property and insurance premiums change from year to year, the amounts needed to fund the tax and insurance escrow account also change (on a monthly basis).

tax assessor: Government official who values real estate property for tax purposes and ascertains the annual property tax assessments that must be collected.

tax avoidance: Payment of the minimum tax by using legal tax planning opportunities such as estate planning. The use of tax avoidance strategies is a sound approach to retaining cash flow. On the other hand, tax evasion uses illegal ways to accomplish this objective.

tax base: The value of property subject to tax. The tax equals the tax rate multiplied by the property's value.

tax basis: The cost basis of property, such as a home owned for tax purposes. For example, a home was purchased for $150,000. Capital improvements to it (e.g., roof, walls, boiler) cost $15,000. The house was later sold for $230,000. The gain on sale is $65,000 ($230,000 − $165,000).

tax book: Compilation of all tax maps of a given tax district that are bound together and kept at the local tax office. The tax book is a public record that may be accessed by an individual for review upon request.

tax credit: Reduction in taxes payable to the IRS or local government. A tax credit is more beneficial to the taxpayer than an itemized deduction because it reduces taxes on a dollar-for-dollar basis. Assume a taxpayer's calculated tax is $25,000 before considering a tax credit of $2,000. The tax due after the credit is $23,000. Examples of tax credits on real property are the low-income housing credit and the investment tax credit.

tax deed: Document evidencing the passage of title to a purchaser of property sold for taxes. The tax deed is issued upon foreclosure of the property lien. Typically, there is a grace time period permitting the owner to make good on the delinquent taxes in order to redeem the property.

tax district: Region or locality that assesses real estate taxes on the properties located within its borders. Frequently, the local county or city is the property taxing jurisdiction which is empowered, by law, to assess taxes on real property.

Tax Equity and Fiscal Responsibility Act of 1982 (TEFRA): Federal tax legislation notably establishing 10% withholding on interest and dividends.

tax-equivalent yield: See *tax-exempt bond.*

tax evasion: Not paying taxes legally due the government. Examples are the failure to report rental income received and claiming false deductions on real estate holdings. The penalty for tax fraud is 75% of the underpaid tax. There may also be criminal prosecution.

tax exempt: Tax-free status given to certain nonprofit organizations and governmental entities. Churches, charities, and government buildings do not pay property tax because of their tax-free status.

tax-exempt bond: Bond whose interest is free of federal, state, or local tax in the state of the issuer. It is typically a municipal bond of a state or county agency. For example, a New York City resident does not pay federal, state, or city tax on the interest received from a New York City obligation. It is triple tax-free, though this is not necessarily the case with other states. The return on a tax-exempt bond is equivalent to a higher return on a taxable corporate bond because of the tax savings. The dollar advantage of a tax-exempt security increases as the tax rate rises. Assume a taxpayer in the 31% tax bracket receives 5% on a tax-exempt bond. The equivalent taxable yield on a corporate bond is 7.2% (5%/.69).

tax flaw: Defect in the tax law that either may provide a loophole to minimize the tax payment or result in higher taxes than there should be.

tax foreclosure: Property taken over by the government because the owner has failed to pay taxes on it. The property may revert back to the owner when the taxes are paid. If not, the government may sell the property to collect the amount due.

tax-free exchange: Transfers of real estate from one taxpayer to another that are exempt from federal income taxes. An example is an exchange of property in which ownership of transferred real estate is still kept. In the year of exchange, there is no recognized gain or loss. However, there is an adjustment to basis of the property received in the transfer, in effect deferring the gain upon future disposition.

tax liability: Legal obligation to pay taxes associated with owning property or earning income. For example, a real estate owner must pay property taxes.

tax lien: Claim made by a federal or local government agency against a taxpayer's property for delinquent or overdue taxes. The tax lien is effected through tax assessment, demand, and failure to pay. In some cases, a lien may be applied to property held by a third party. Once the taxes are paid, the lien is released.

tax map: Map which documents the area, perimeter location, dimensions, and other data relating to land for purposes of assessing annual real estate taxes. See also *tax book.*

tax participation: Standard portion of a lease which indicates that in the event of an increase in annual assessed real estate taxes during the lease term, the lessee will be responsible for higher monthly payments to cover the increase.

tax planning: Evaluation of different tax options of investing in real estate with the purpose of reducing the tax liability in current and future years. Examples are the timing of buying and selling real estate, and real estate tax shelters. Tax software can be used in tax planning.

tax preference item: Item falling under Section 57 of the Internal Revenue Code that may result in the imposition of the alternative minimum tax (AMT). These items of otherwise exempt income or deductions or of special tax benefit were targeted to ensure that taxpayers who benefit should pay the minimum amount of tax. An example is contributions of appreciated property.

tax rate: Amount of tax to be paid based on taxable income. The tax rate usually changes as the unit of the tax base changes.

(1) *Individual:* Tax rate depends on whether the tax return is for a single filer, joint filer, or head of household. For example, the maximum tax rate for a joint filer in 1994 is 39.6% for taxable income over $250,000. The tax rate is 36% for taxable income over $140,000 but less than $250,000.

(2) *Corporation:* The maximum tax rate in 1994 for a corporation is 35%.

tax rate schedule: Used to compute the tax on a specified taxable income. The marginal tax rate usually increases as the taxable income rises. For example, for tax returns filed on a joint basis, the tax rates in 1994 are:

Tax Bracket	Taxable Income
15%	0–$38,000
28%	$ 38,000–$91,850
31%	$ 91,850–$140,000
36%	$140,000–$250,000
39.6%	Over $250,000

tax refund: Amount the taxpayer gets back when he or she files the tax return at the end of the reporting year because taxes were overpaid for that year. The tax overpayment equals the tax payments remitted less the tax actually due.

tax return: Generic name of the form used to file taxes payable to a federal, state, or local government. The tax return includes items such as gross income, deductions, tax credits, and tax due. Individual taxpayers file on a calendar year basis using Form 1040, which is due 3½ months after the tax year. Corporations prepare Form 1120 on a calendar year or fiscal year basis. It is due 2½ months after the tax year. The partnership tax return is Form 1065.

tax roll: Compilation of all real estate properties in a given tax district that are subject to real estate taxes. The tax roll indicates the taxable assessed values of all properties in the district and enables the tax assessor to establish the required tax rate that must be assessed in a given fiscal period to meet the budgeted financial requirements of the locality.

tax sale: When a property owner defaults on his or her tax payments, the taxing jurisdiction may force a liquidation of the property or tax sale for the purpose of collecting the owed real estate taxes. Many states have laws that provide for a redemption period in which the property owner may redeem the property that was sold if the purchase price, back taxes, and other related costs (interest, legal fees, etc.) are paid in a specified period of time following the tax sale.

tax shelter: Investments, usually in limited partnerships, that can protect of defer (shelter) part of the income from current taxes. Under current law, passive leases can be applied up to passive income. Typically, a large amount of capital along with a significant amount of debt is needed. Allowable deductions are typically allowed only to the amount at-risk. A tax shelter is advantageous by the taxpayers in high tax brackets so they can take losses from it to reduce their taxable income. A number of real estate tax shelters exist. There is a penalty of 1% of the total amount invested for the failure to register a tax shelter. The failure to report a tax shelter identification number has a penalty of $250. Penalties for "abusive" shelters may be staggering. Tax shelters have been significantly restricted in recent years.

tax shield: Deductions that result in a reduction of tax payments. The tax shield equals the amount of the deduction times the tax rate. An example is depreciation of rental property by the landlord. If depreciation is $50,000 and the tax rate is 40% (federal plus local), the tax shield equals $20,000 ($50,000 × 40%). The higher the depreciation, the greater will be the tax savings. This is a major reason why landlords prefer an accelerated depreciation method.

tax stop: Restriction in a lease that sets a maximum limit on the amount of property taxes that a lessor will pay. The lessee is required to pay any taxes in excess of that limit.

taxable income:

(1) *Individual:* Adjusted gross income less itemized deductions and personal exemptions. After taxable income is computed, the tax to be paid can be determined by looking at the tax rate schedules.

(2) *Corporation:* Gross income less allowable business deductions.

teaser rate: An enticingly attractive initial rate below the market offered in an adjustable rate mortgage. For example, the teaser rate may be offered at 2% below market. A borrower who cannot qualify at the market rate might be able to do so at the teaser rate. See also *adjustable rate mortgage (ARM)*.

tenancy:

(1) The period for which a tenant has the right of possession; it may be for a

fixed period of several years, or a period tenancy, such as month to month. (2) The right or interest to have real estate, whether by title or by rental. See also *joint tenancy; tenancy in common.*

tenancy in common: Ownership of property by two or more people in undivided interests (not necessarily equal), without the right of survivorship. Each co-owner's interest may be conveyed separately by its owner. Tenancy in common dissolved by conveyance of a co-tenant interest to another new tenancy in common is created between grantees and remaining co-tenants. In the event that one of them dies, his or her interest passes by a will to his or her devises or heirs by intestate succession and not to the other tenants in common. See also *joint tenancy; tenancy by the entirety.*

tenancy by the entirety: Type of ownership by husband and wife, recognized in 27 states, in which the rights of the deceased spouse pass to the survivor. It is the same as joint tenancy, except that one spouse cannot sell his or her share without approval of the other spouse.

tenancy in severalty: Ownership of property by one individual.

tenancy at will: Tenancy that may be terminated by one party—the tenant or the landlord—at any time. The agreement may be in writing or oral. For example, John has an oral agreement to use Joanne's property. Joanne may ask John to vacate the premise at any time; John may also vacate at any time.

tenant: Individual renting a residential or office unit.

tenant changes: Changes made by a lessee to property during the term of the lease. In general, if the changes are permanent, such as the addition of a building to lease land, the ownership of the building reverts to the lessor at the end of the lease. On the other hand, the lease contract may specify that all tenant fixtures, that is fixtures added to the property by the lessee may be removed when the lease terminates. The lessee, therefore, may remove a machine, for example, that was attached to a leased factory building when the lease term terminates.

tenant at sufferance: Interest in real property that exists when a tenant remains in possession of leased premises or a "hold over" after his right to possession has ended. In a tenancy at sufferance, a tenant is called a holdover tenant. For example, Jill is a tenant at sufferance. Jim, the landowner, is entitled to evict her and recover the possession of the property, provided he does so in a timely manner.

tenants' union: Group of rental occupants acting together.

tender: To present something of value for another's acceptance. An example is making a bid at a public auction for real property.

tenement:
(1) City apartment building that is overcrowded, poorly constructed or maintained, and generally part of a slum.
(2) In law, a tenement also refers to possessions of an individual that are real property, that is, attached to the ground, such as land and buildings.

tentative map: Map presented to a municipality's planning agency by a real estate developer for consideration and approval.

1031 tax-free exchange: Also called a like-kind exchange. An exchange in which tax benefits are available to real estate owners planning to sell their investment, rental, business or vacation real estate, and reinvest the net proceeds in other real estate. Real Estate held for these purposes are called like-kind/1031 properties. Property owners may sell like-kind properties and defer taxes on the sale's profits by meeting the requirements of Internal Revenue Code (IRC) 1031 exchange. The purpose of the 1031 exchange is to allow sellers of like-kind property to buy replacement property of like-kind within a specific time period and defer taxes. The deferred profit tax benefit applies despite a time lapse between the sale of the taxpayer's former property and his purchase of replacement property. This sell-now, buy-later situation is called a delayed exchange. The 1031 exchange applies only to property other than the personal residence or dealer property. Specifically included for exchange are properties used or held for rental income, business purposes, investment, or as vacation homes.

Taxwise, investment properties include vacant land held for profit (not income), ground leases and management-free triple net leases. An owner of these qualifying like-kind properties can complete a 1031 exchange, but he must follow the to time constraints. A 1031 exchange differs from the more informal 1034 tax deferred rollover, which applies to a personal residence and has more lenient deadlines. Unlike a 1034 rollover, a 1031 exchange has different deadlines and other criteria. The replacement property must be acquired before 45-day and 180-day deadlines have run. Note that often, brokers are unable to arrange a nearly simultaneous closing for both legs of an exchange.

See also *1034 rollover exchange (sale or exchange of the residence)*.

1034 rollover exchange (sale or exchange of the residence): Tax-free exchange that allows a seller two years after escrow closes on his former principal personal residence to buy like-kind property and defer taxes. Profits from the sale of a principal residence are not taxed if, essentially, the purchase price of the new residence is equal or greater than the sales price of the old residence. Also, the new residence must be acquired and personally occupied within 24 months before or after the sale of the old residence, for a 48-month period. To accurately set the amount of profit deferred, the net sales price and adjusted sales price of the old residence must be calculated. From these respective figures are derived the actual profit and minimum purchase price of the new residence to fully avoid taxes on the profit. The 24-month sale-to-replacement period offers the homeowner the opportunity to use the net sales proceeds from the old residence for short-term, high-yield money market investments. These investments are liquid and generally more lucrative than real estate acquisitions during periods of high interest rates. See also *1031 tax-free exchange.*

1034/121 rolldown: Combination of IRC 1034 and 121 dealing with the sale of a personal residence with the once-in-a-lifetime $125,000 exclusion that may be available to the "over-55" seller. Should the over-55 homeowner buy a new home of lesser value, the $125,000 exclusion can be used to avoid some or all of the taxes on the sale of the old residence. See also *over age 55 home sale exemption.*

1040: Yearly tax return filed by an individual or couple. It is due to the federal taxing authority on April 15 for the preceding calendar year. The taxpayer reports gross income, adjustments to gross income, personal exemptions, deductions, and taxable income. The tax rate is graduated, based on taxable income. Income or loss from real estate property is reported on Schedule E.

tenure in land: Classification of one's ownership rights in land. One may either buy the land and own all rights to it or lease it where one's rights are described in and limited by the lease agreement.

tenure property: The right and duties of using and holding property.

term:
(1) A stated number of years.
(2) The length of time something is effective, such as a two-year rental.
(3) A condition specified in an agreement. An example is that the tenant must not have a dog in the apartment.

term loan:
(1) Loan requiring only interest payments until the last day of its term, at which time the full payment is due.
(2) Intermediate- to long-term (usually, 2 to 10 years) collateralized loan granted to a business by a commercial bank, insurance company, or commercial finance company such as to finance the purchase of real estate. The loan is amortized over a fixed period. See also *straight loan.*

termination clause: Provision in a contract that upon a certain occurrence or event the contract is canceled. An example is a contractual term that the written agreement is terminated if one of the party's commits a criminal act in the use of the property.

termite clause: Provision in a contract for the sale of real property that gives the purchaser the right, at his or her expense, to have the property inspected for the existence of termites. If, in fact, termites are determined to be present, the clause generally requires that the seller remedy the situation, that is, treat the property for the infestation. If the seller chooses not to exterminate the termites, the buyer has the right to cancel the sales contract.

termite inspection: Inspection required in certain types of sales of property to determine if termites are present within a building.

termite shield: Aluminum or metal treated barrier that is placed between the concrete and wood of the foundation of a newly constructed building to prevent termites from infesting the wood. Many experts say that such a shield is ineffective because the termites simply go around the shield to get to the wood in the foundation.

termites: Insects that destroy the support wood in the structure of a building. Termite inspection should be periodically performed to detect their existence. If an infestation is confirmed, the termites should be eradicated through extermination.

terrace: Unroofed, paved area built adjacent to an apartment building or residence.

terrazo: Type of flooring, made up of tiles of colored stone or marble that is set in concrete.

testament: Also called a will. Describes the disposition of property.

testamentary capacity: Having the intellect to comprehend the terms and conditions of a will and their impact. A testator must understand his or her estate and its eventual disposition and effects in order to validate the will.

testamentary intention: Interpreting the objective of a testator in his or her will. The disposition of the testator's estate must be understandable or it could be legally challenged.

testamentary trust: Also called settlor. A trust created by a will starting upon the donor's death. It empowers a trust administrator to implement the terms of the trust.

testate: Person who dies leaving a will specifying the distribution of the estate.

testator/testatrix: Man or woman, respectively, who makes a will.

testimonium: Portion of a deed that states the act and date of the transfer of the property.

thin market: Market in which there are comparatively few bids to buy or offers to sell real estate. The term relates to a single investment or to a particular investment market, such as the real estate market. In a thin market, buying or selling a few homes can impact disproportionately. Price volatility is generally wider than liquid markets.

third party: Person or business indirectly having an interest in an occurrence, transaction, or situation.

35-percent rule of thumb: A lender uses this rule to determine a borrower's housing affordability. It says that a borrower can afford no more than 35% of monthly take-home pay.

EXAMPLE: Steve's gross annual income is $50,000 and take-home pay is $2,095 per month. At 35%, Steve could not afford a monthly payment of $1,050. Using this amount, the mortgage rate (variable or fixed), the mortgage term, and a mortgage payment schedule, the lender can calculate how much Steve can qualify for.

thrift institution: Depository institution, such as mutual savings banks. If organized as mutual associations, depositors are shareholders. They offer mortgages.

tie: Once of a set of timbers used in the construction of a building or for esthetic purposes, the land around a property for beautification.

tie beam: Concrete or timber beam that serves as a support in the wall structure of a building. Concrete tie beams are often reinforced with steel rods.

tier:
(1) Series of rows.
(2) Townships moving as a row from east to west. It covers a 6-mile area in width. The term is employed under the rectangular survey method.

tight market: Market in which the spreads between the asking and offer price of real estate are small. The property may be in abundant supply and actively traded.

tight money:
(1) Less funds available to prospective home buyers by lenders. Attractive mortgages are difficult to get.
(2) A decrease in spending dollars because of a decrease in the money supply.
See also *easy money*.

tile: Thin layer or slate of baked clay, linoleum, or some other material that is used for covering floors, roofs, or as an ornament in a building.

time is of the essence: Contract clause that makes it essential that the provisions be carried out at the specified time or the contract is voidable.

time-share homes: Homes with division of ownership or use of a resort unit on the basis of time periods. For example, a resort home may be divided into 25 time shares of two weeks each, with two weeks left open for maintenance.

time sharing: Segregation of ownership in real estate property over a stated time period. An example is a co-owned vacation apartment, used by co-owners for one month each.

time value of money: A dollar today is worth more than a dollar at some future date. It is the rationale behind compounding for future value or discounting for present value.

title: The legal right of an ownership interest in a property. It is evidence of ownership and lawful possession.

title abstract: See *abstract*.

title check: An investigation to ascertain who legally has the title to property. For example, when a house is sold, the attorney for the purchaser will do a title search to guarantee that the seller owns the house.

title company: An insurer who researches the title to real estate for the purpose of discovering any unknown liens or encumbrances on the property that may have come into effect before the current purchase of the property. Mortgage bankers lending money to home buyers generally require the purchaser to purchase title insurance. If, after the purchase, a recorded encumbrance surfaces that was not discovered by the title company, it is paid by the title company to the insured as a claim.

title defect: Title deficiency that prevents a seller from successfully transferring property to a buyer. A title company may discover a title defect (due to encumbrances against the property or failure of a former co-owner of the property to sign a deed transferring the title, etc.) in preparation for a closing, effectively blocking the sale of the property until the defect is resolved.

title insurance: Insurance required of home buyers by lenders, to protect against losses arising from disputes over the ownership of a property (i.e., defective titles). The policies are issued by a title insurance company.

title search: An investigation of the property to ascertain if there are any restrictions or deficiencies of title, including mortgages, encumbrances, or liens.

title theory states: Some states make the legal assumption, based on title theory, that the mortgagee is a partial owner (based on the extent of the money borrowed) of the real estate securing the mortgage and remains as is until the debt is fully paid. That is, if the borrower defaults, the lender may take immediate control of the property for purposes of satisfying the outstanding debt. In other states where lien theory is followed, the mortgage lender may not take immediate possession of the property, but rather must initiate foreclosure proceedings.

toll:
(1) Fee assessed to use someone else's property.
(2) Fee to use a bridge or tunnel.

topography: Art of mapping the physical features of a region. The topography describes the characteristics of an area, such as its contours, flatness, maintainousness.

torrens system: Named after Sir Robert Torrens, a British administrator in Australia. The torrens system is a state-sponsored system of land title registration, not applicable in states, such as California.

tort: Wrongful act that causes injury or damages. Examples are trespassing on someone's property destroying part of it, and the landlord's negligent failure to repair defective electrical wiring resulting in a fire. The perpetrator is legally liable to the aggrieved party.

tortfeasor: One who has committed a tort. A tort is a civil wrong (not a criminal act) that occurs as a result of a breach of legal duty owed to someone, e.g., negligence. A tort does not arise from a breach of contract.

tort liability: Legal obligation stemming from a civil wrong or injury for which a court remedy is justified. A tort liability arises because of a combination of a direct violation of a person's rights, the transgression of a public obligation causing damage, or a private wrongdoing.

total return: Return earned on an investment over a given time period. It includes two basic components—the current yield, such as rental income and capital gains, or losses in property values. It is typically stated as an annual percentage. See also *holding period of return; return; yield.*

townhouse: An attached dwelling in a multiple housing complex having at least two floors and usually a garage. Such dwellings are typically found in condominiums and cooperatives.

township: Six-by-six mile square area of land designated by the intersection of range lines and township lines in the rectangular survey system.

Township 4 North
Range 4 West of
Guide Meridian

township lines: Lines determined by a government rectangular survey laying out a standard six-mile square area of land.

tract: Extended area of land commonly held for subdividing and development into residential units.

tract house: Structure that has the same blue print and design as all the other homes in a given development; the opposite of custom built.

tract index: System for listing recorded documents affecting a particular tract of land.

trade fixture: Articles of personal property installed by a tenant under the terms of a lease for purposes of use in his or her trade or business. Trade fixtures are removable by the tenant before the lease expires and are not true fixtures.

trade-in: Amount received for old property when exchanged for new property.

trade name: Word, or group of words, that identifies a business or one of its products. The name is registered with the U.S. Patent Office and provides legal protection for an indefinite number of renewals for periods of 20 years each. In effect, the name has an unlimited life.

trading on equity: Also called financial leverage. The use of borrowed funds to magnify return. Trading profitably on the equity, also called favorable financial leverage, means that the borrowed funds generate a higher rate of return than the interest rate paid for the use of the money. The excess accrues to the benefit of the owner because it magnifies, or increases, his or her earnings. See also *leverage*.

trailer park: Area containing running water facilities, electrical outlets, recreational accommodations, etc., for the short-term and long-term parking of trailers.

transaction cost: Expenditure to make a specific security or real estate transaction. Real estate transaction costs include survey costs, mortgage points and origination fees, recording fees, state transfer taxes, survey costs, title insurance, and title search fees.

transfer: Changing property ownership. An example is the sale of a home to another.

transfer development rights: Rights granted to owners of property restricted to conservation use, historic preservation, or some other low density function to sell to other landowners allowing them to develop their properties in other areas at higher densities (to build additional structures on these properties) than existed previously. The owners of restricted-development properties get these rights as compensatory consideration for the building constraints on their lands. They may sell these rights to any landowner in other areas who is not restricted regarding development densities.

transfer fee: Fee charged by a mortgage lender to a buyer, seller or both for transferring a mortgage when the mortgage property is sold.

transfer tax:
(1) A state-levied tax upon the transfer or sale of property. Some states base the tax on selling price.
(2) Federal tax on gifts made and estate proceeds.

treads: Width of a stair.

trespass: To enter illegally. For example, entering property without permission.

trim: To clip or prune shrubbery, etc.

triple net leases: A lease requiring tenants to pay all utilities, insurance, taxes, and maintenance costs.

triplex: A free-standing building having three separate housing units all under one roof. See also *duplex; multifamily housing; quadriplex.*

truss: In construction, a bracket or braced framework of triangulated bars, beams, and ties used for support in the construction of a roof.

trust: An agreement in which the trustee takes title to the property (called corpus) owned by the grantor (donor) to protect or conserve it for either the grantor or the trust's beneficiary. The trust is set up by the grantor. The trustee is typically given authority to invest the property for a return. Trusts may be revocable or irrevocable.

trust deed: See *deed of trust.*

trustee: Third party to a bankruptcy proceeding. The trustee's responsibility is to value and recapitalize the real estate firm if it is to be reorganized.

trustee in bankruptcy: Person selected by a judge or creditors of a bankrupt individual to handle matters including the sale of the bankrupt's assets, management of the funds from the sale

of those assets, payment of expenses, and distribution of the balance to creditors. The trustee is usually compensated with a specified percentage of the liquidation value.

trustee's deed: Deed given by a trustee at a deed of trust foreclosure sale.

trustee's sale: When a debtor defaults on a loan for which a deed of trust is given, the trustee is required to have a sale (trustee's sale) of the real estate security for the benefit of the lender. A deed of trust is used in place of a mortgage in many states. When a loan is made by a lender which is collateralized by real estate, a deed of trust is signed by the parties giving legal title of the collateralized property to a trustee for the purpose of insuring that the property is used to satisfy the debt in the event of default.

trustor: Individual creating a trust.

Truth-in-Lending Act (TILA): Also called Consumer Credit Protection Act of 1969 or Regulation Z. A federal statute protecting buyers. The key provision is that both the dollar amount of finance charges and the annual percentage rate (APR) must be disclosed before extending credit. The finance charge includes a disclosure of the following: interest, finder and origination fees, discount points, service charges, credit report fees and other charges paid by the consumer directly or indirectly which are imposed as an incident to the extension of credit. The regulation also applies to all advertising seeking to promote credit. This advertising is required to include specific credit information. The intent of Congress was to assist consumers (residential, noninvestment customers) with their credit decisions by providing them with specific required disclosure and does not attempt to establish minimum or maximum interest rates or other charges.

tudor: English style of architecture characterized by carving and paneling and flattened arches.

turnaround property: A deteriorated property that can be restored and sold for a gain.

turnkey project: All the new tenant has to do is "turn the key" to the apartment or office in a newly constructed building because everything is completed and ready for occupancy. For example, Bob moves into a new building and the apartment is fully in condition as far as the landlord's responsibility is concerned (e.g., painting, air conditioning, and heating). Bob only has to buy personal items (e.g., furniture).

turnover:

(1) Movement or change of people such as tenants.

(2) The sale of one average real estate inventory item within a specified time.

type of use: Stipulation in a contract on how property can or cannot be used. For example, a rental agreement may stipulate that an apartment may not be used for retail trade.

ultra vires: Action that is beyond that allowed legally. Examples are charging illegally high interest rates on mortgages and real estate exceeding the amount permissible by legal statute, and a real estate company performing duties it is not authorized by the corporate charter to perform. Violations may result in lawsuits.

underfloor wiring system: Wires, such as for electricity, places beneath the floor of a structure.

underimprovement: An improvement to property that is below the standard, usual expectation. An example is when a contractor's work on a house is below the quality that the homeowner reasonably expected for the price paid.

underlying mortgage: The first mortgage on property when other mortgages exist as well, as in the case of a wraparound loan. For example, the total amount financed might be $200,000 of which the first lien is for $80,000 while the balance of the wraparound is $120,000.

underpinning:
(1) Reinforcing a building with supports.
(2) Using beams on an interim basis while a structure is being built.
(3) A property.

undersupply: Lack of supply of real property. When demand exceeds supply, price of the property goes up. For example, if there are only a few homes in a town that everyone desires to reside in, the prices of those homes will increase.

underwriting: The acceptance of risk in return for payment. In a new securities issue, the underwriter, known as the investment bank, may perform an underwriting function by purchasing the securities of a real estate company at a fixed price from the issuer, expecting to sell them at a higher offering price and making a profit on the spread. Underwriting is the function of investment bankers, who usually form an underwriting group, also called a syndicate, to pool the risk and assure successful distribution of the issue.

undisclosed principal:
(1) A major party to a transaction, such as a seller or purchaser of property, remains anonymous. An example is when someone acts on behalf of a purchaser who wishes his identity not to be disclosed.
(2) Person is not informed by an agent that there is a principal. In this case, the agent has legal ability under the contract.

undivided interest: Ownership by two or more persons that give each the right to use the entire property.

undue influence: Someone acts in an extraordinary way because of fear, excessive influence, or other reason. The person is being forced to do something against his will. The injured person can use this pressure tactic as a basis to void the contract. An example is when an employee of a real estate company is threatened with his job unless he signs a contract agreeing to unreasonable terms in a real estate transaction.

unearned increment: Unexpected increase in the price of property not due to any effort on the owner's part. An example is when the appraised value of a house increases because of a population increase in the region.

unemployment: The nonavailability of jobs for people able and willing to work at the prevailing wage rate. It is an important measure of economic health, since full employment is generally construed as a desired goal. As firms fail and as individuals struggle, mortgages and other loans go unpaid. This causes real estate values to go down and hurts lenders. Loan defaults rise. See also *recession.*

unencumbered: Real property that is without any obligations, liens, or anything else against it. It is free and clear such as a house without a mortgage.

unenforceable: Oral or written contract that is not enforceable by the judicial system. Examples are contracts with minors, fraudulent agreements, and contracts that exceed the statute of limitations.

Uniform Residential Landlord and Tenant Act: Legislation in 13 states providing protection to people who rent their residences. The act deals with landlord-tenant contractual relationships and obligations.

unilateral contract: An agreement in which one individual or business agrees to do or not do something in return for the actual performance of another person or business.

unilateral listing: Listing of property that is open, meaning there is no one real estate agent who has the sole right to sell the property.

unimproved land: Raw land in its natural condition which has in no way been improved.

unincorporated group: Association of people not treated as a corporation. Examples are a limited partnership and a group of cooperative owners.

unit: Segregated part of a structure such as an office in an office building or a residence in an apartment house.

unit in place method: Approach to valuing property based on its replacement cost. The cost of each major element of the property per square foot is added together and multiplied by the total space (total square footage) to estimate what it costs to rebuild the structure. Assume the cost per square foot for the following components of a building:

Walls	$ 4.50
Ceilings	1.50
Floors	2.50
Other	8.00
Total	$16.50

If the total square feet are 20,000, the property's estimated value is $330,000 ($16.50 × 20,000).

United States Government securities: See *treasury securities.*

unities: Peculiarities necessary to form a valid joint tenancy. They are unity of time, title, interest, and possession.

unity: Legal dictate that must exist for property to be owned as joint tenants.

unity of interest: In joint tenancy, the joint tenants must acquire their interest by the same conveyance and the interest must be equal.

unity of possession: Principle stating that the joint tenants must have equal rights to possession of the whole property.

unity of time: Principle stating that all joint tenants must acquire their title at the same time.

unity of title: Principle stating that all joint tenants must acquire their interests from the same deed or will.

unjust enrichment: Person or business that benefits from the work of another person or business. The recipient has not compensated the other party for this gain. In law, the one being enriched at the sacrifice or detriment of the other party must provide restitution. Assume an electrician did work for Mr. Jones who suddenly died before making payment. The new owner of the house is legally obligated to pay the bill.

unlawful detainer: Illegally keeping or holding on to someone else's property. An example is a tenant staying in the apartment after the lease has expired. A court order may be sought to evict the tenant.

unrealized gain: Increase in the value of property arising from holding it. The gain is realized only when the property is sold at which time it is taxable. An example is the increase in the appraised value of a house arising from better economic conditions and real estate market.

unrecorded deed: The transfer of a property deed from one person to another without publicly recording it. The recording of a deed in a public office gives constructive notice of the act of the sale and helps prevent possible fraud.

unsecured loan: Loan that is not secured by a mortgage on a specific property. It is backed only by the borrower's credit rating. Unsecured loans are typically short term. The disadvantages of this kind of loan are that, because it is made for the short term and has no collateral, it carries a higher interest rate than a secured loan and payment in a lump sum is required. See also *signature loan.*

unsecured note: Credit note in which a lender's only security is the borrower's personal financial situation and credit history.

unsolicited listings: Listing of real estate property done without any effort on the part of the real estate broker. An example is when a homeowner calls the real estate brokerage firm on his own without having first been solicited.

up-front fee: Received immediately when an investment is made or contract signed. For example, a real estate limited partnership may require that an investor pay a 3% sales fee at the time of initial investment. Thus, for a $10,000 investment only $9,700 is actually put to work as the investment into the limited partnership since $300 is taken "off the top."

upland: Land that is adjacent to water such as a stream.

upset date: Provision in a written agreement allowing the prospective purchaser the right to cancel the contract if occupancy requirements are not satisfied as of a specific date.

upset price: Judicially determined minimum selling price for auctioned property. For example, a judge rules that a foreclosed home may not be sold for less than $200,000.

upside potential: An approximation of the possible appreciation of value in real estate. One would consider several factors in evaluating the upside potential in the value of real estate, including location, amenities, and potential increase in rental income. The opposite of upside potential is downside risk, which is an approximation of the possible comparative decline in value of a property. Real estate investors always evaluate individual properties in terms of the upside potential compared to the downside risk.

urban: Metropolitan locality such as a city. It is heavily populated with many residents and businesses. An example is New York City. See also *rural.*

Urban Development Action Grant: The Urban Development Action Grant, is intended to stimulate private investment in distressed cities and urban counties by providing federal "seed money" to attract private funds for such projects as industrial parks and revitalized waterfront areas. The Community Development Block Grants program transfers HUD funds directly to cities and states for urban renewal projects.

urban economics: Branch of economics that applies the tools of economic reasoning to the analysis and solution of urban economic problems.

Urban Land Institute (ULI): Nonprofit entity disseminating advice and data on the best utilization of land. The address is 1090 Vermont Avenue, NW, Washington, DC 20005, telephone (202) 289-3307.

urban property: Real property located in a metropolitan, heavily populated area.

urban renewal: Older property is bought usually by a governmental agency to be modernized and improved. In many cases, the deteriorating property is torn down and a new structure built. An example is public housing designed to redevelop a slum neighborhood. Some private foundations may also engage in community development. Urban renewal projects are often directed at a particular depressed area in the city. Development might also include sports arenas and parks to make the area more attractive.

urban space: Availability of land in an urban area.

urban sprawl: Unexpected growth in an urban locality.

use density: Percentage of land that may be used productively to the total square footage of the land. For example, if total square footage is 40,000 but only 30,000 square feet may be built upon because of zoning requirements, the use density rate is 75% (30,000/40,000).

use tax: Levy charged to use something such as water supplied by the town.

useful life: Usual operating service life of property for the purpose it was acquired. The useful life used for depreciation accounting does not necessarily coincide with the actual physical life or any commonly recognized economic life. An example is a building that can be used for 30 years.

usufructuary right: An individual's option to fairly utilize another's property. An example is privileges under an easement. For example, a person receives permission to use a lake on the private property of another.

usury: An interest rate charged on a loan that exceeds the legal maximum interest rate within the state. It is illegal to do so. The maximum interest rate may depend on the type of lender and nature of the loan. Federal laws may also apply.

usury laws: State laws limiting the interest rate that can be charged to individuals borrowing money in that state. These laws affect all lenders in a state regardless of what federal or state agency issued their charter. If there is a national economic emergency, the federal government may temporarily suspend state usury laws.

utilities: Services provided to a parcel of land by public utility companies, such as gas, water, and electricity.

utility:
(1) An economic and highly subjective term describing satisfaction of a specified want. Utility and usefulness are not necessarily synonymous terms.
(2) The value of a certain outcome or payoff to someone; the pleasure or displeasure that person would derive from that outcome.

utility easement: An easement granted to a public utility.

utility room: Contains the appliances necessary for the maintenance of an establishment.

vacancy and credit losses: Losses incurred by a landlord because (1) apartments or offices are unoccupied and/or (2) tenants fail to pay the rent due.

vacancy factor: Percentage of rentals estimated not to be made because of actual and anticipated vacancies.

vacancy rate: Percentage of rental property that is unoccupied. For example, a vacancy rate of 25% means that 25% of the rental unites are not being used. Idle space can cause a significant cash drain to the landlord who is not receiving cash inflows to offset the cash outflows of maintaining the property. An office building, shopping center, or hotel must have a minimum occupancy rate to break even.

vacant land: Property that is unoccupied and thus not being used. It is usually raw land with no structure or improvements theron.

vacate: To leave property. An example is a tenant who moves from the apartment and takes all her possessions at the termination of the rental period. If a tenant leaves before the lease expires, the tenant is still legally responsible for the rent due as long as the apartment remains unoccupied.

vacation home: Second home. The interest and real estate taxes on the second home are tax deductible on the family's 1040 tax return.

valid: Information that is factual, such as representations made by a real estate broker to a prospective buyer. See also *valid contract*.

valid contract: One that is legally binding because it is in conformity with legal requirements and conditions. See also *contract*.

valid deed: Legally proper instrument under seal that transfers title to real property from the seller to buyer. See also *deed*.

valley: Low level of land positioned between mountains or hills.

valley flashing: Waterproofing the joint of a roof.

valley roof: Roof having a concave angle.

VA loan guarantees: Home loans backed by the Veterans Administration. The Veterans Administration issues a 60% loan guaranty for a sum not to exceed $27,500. The mortgaged home must be a principal residence. VA loans are granted with no down payment to qualified veterans.

valuable consideration: Value is exchanged by the parties to an agreement involving current or future performance making it legally enforceable. Without reasonable consideration for performance, the contract may not be valid.

valuation: Process of valuing a real estate property, such as through appraisal. It is the worth of the property. A valuation is often required by the county or city for property tax purposes.

In determining the value of a real estate business, it may be based on the fair market value of its net assets (assets less liabilities), gross revenue multiplied by an appropriate multiplier, or the weighted-average earnings over five years multiplied by a relvant multiplier. See also *gross income (rent) multiplier; net income multiplier.*

value: Highly subjective term, usually an expression of monetary worth applied to a particular piece of real estate property.

value after the taking: Worth of the property part which is left subsequent to a condemnation action.

value before the taking: Market price of all the property prior to a condemnation proceeding.

value in exchange: Giving money, a good, or service that is worth something in exchange for another good or service provided by the other party. An example is paying cash for the market price of a home.

value in use: Discounted value of net cash receipts to be obtained from a property. The present value calculation includes consideration of annual cash inflows plus the disposal value.

variable interest rate: Interest rate on a mortgage that moves up or down based on some variable such as an index of the lender's cost of funds, inflation rate, or prime rate.

Variable Rate Mortgages (VRM): Mortgage in which the interest rate charged by the lender can vary according to some reference index not controlled by the lender, such as the interest rate

on 1-year U.S. T-bills or the 11th District Cost of Funds Index.

For the lender, this means that as the cost of money increases, the interest being charged on the existing mortgage can be increased, thus maintaining the gap between the cost of money and return. Either the monthly payment, the maturity date, or both can be changed to reflect the difference in interest rates. In addition, the mortgage usually stipulates a maximum annual charge and a maximum total increase in the interest the lender may charge.

Under current regulations established by the FHLBB, the interest rate may not be raised more than 2.5% points above the initial rate. The rate can be changed each six months, with no more than $\frac{1}{2}$ of 1% change each six months.

Variable rate mortgages are more popularly known as adjustable-rate mortgages (ARM). See also *adjusted rate mortgage (ARM).*

variance: The right to deviate from the use of land prescribed by an existing zoning ordinance.

vault:

(1) Where something of value is kept in a secured place. An exmaple is important real estate documents and/or money kept in a bank vault.

(2) Ceiling or roof designed as an arch.

vendee: One who buys real property.

vendee's lien: Legal right of the buyer of real estate for the acquisition price paid if the seller does not render the deed to the property. The buyer's lien is not only for the purchase price paid but also for any direct costs associated with that property's acquisition (e.g., legal fees).

vendor: One who sells real estate or other products.

vendor's lien: Also called purchase money mortgage. A seller's claim to property held by a buyer as collateral for a debt or charge.

veneer: Outside of a structure covering a lower quality or cheaper surface to make the structure look better. Examples of veneer exteriors are bricks covering concrete, or a thin surface layer of better quality wood covering lower quality wood. See also *brick veneer.*

vent: Opening so that air or gas may enter or leave. For example, an air conditioner has a "vent open" or "vent closed" knob for outside air. The "vent closed" switch must be on for air conditioning to work.

ventilation: An opening that lets the outside air come in or out of a structure (e.g., house). A ventilation fan lets the structure have access to outside air when the switch is in the open position.

venture: Buying real property subject to risk. For the high risk undertaken, the expected return is higher. However, the investor may lose all or part of the initial invesment.

venture capital: Financing source for new real estate businesses or turnaround ventures that usually combine much risk with potential for high return. There are various stages of venture capital, such as beginning with seed money and then proceeding to the development stage. Sources of venture capital include wealthy individuals, small business investment companies, and limited partnerships.

venue: Geographic location (e.g., county, city) where a court action and trial takes place. The legal proceedings should occur in the place where jurisdiction applies. A "change of venue" may occur in a criminal action if a fair trial is precluded. In this case, another district is used for the proceeding.

versus: Compared to; relative to; against.

vest: Giving another an immediate benefit. Examples are (1) an employee in a real estate company receiving pension or health care benefits after five years of employement, and (2) passing title to property. Once vesting has occurred, a legal right exists to the recipient. However, one can have title without possession, such as when there is a life estate from Phil to Bob, but Bob only obtains possession upon Phil's demise.

Veterans Administration (VA): Federal agency that aids veterans of the armed forces. For example, it guarantees a home loan for up to a predetermined dollar amount or percentage of the loan balance, whichever is less.

Veterans Administration Loan Guaranty Program (VA): Loan guaranty program included in the Servicemen's Readjustment Act of 1944. Its provisions cover the compensation to lenders for losses they might sustain in providing financing to approved veterans.

The maximum guaranteed amount, which has periodically been increased, is set by the VA as is the maximum interest rate charged by lenders. There are no provisions on the upper limits of the loan-to-value ratio, which means that it is quite common for an approved veteran to receive 100% VA financing. It should be noted that some lenders set limits on how much they will finance using VA financing. The VA guarantees loans up to 30 years.

To qualify for VA financing, the veteran applies for a certificate of eligibility. The property as well as the borrower must qualify. If the property is approved, a certificate of reasonable value is issued. As is true with FHA, junior financing is essentially prohibited under VA. (Junior financing is rare.) Coverage also extends to the financing of mobile homes and condominiums.

A VA loan is assumable; however, unless released by the lender, the veteran who borrowed the funds initially remains liable to the lender. Lenders cannot insert prepayment penalties under either VA or FHA loans. A mortgage without a prepayment penalty is commonly referred to as an open mortgage, while one that cannot be prepaid is a closed mortgage. The VA limits the points charged to the buyer to one. Any other points must be paid by the seller.

Veterans Administration mortgage: Mortgage guaranteed up to 30 years by the Veterans Administration to veterans meeting minimum requirements. Originally established by the Servicemen's Readjustment Act of 1944, amended provisions state the maximum guaranteed mortgage amounts and interest that can be charged. There are no provisions on the loan to property value permitting qualified veterans to obtain 100% financing, although some mortgagees will independently establish loan limits. A borrower must receive a certificate of eligibility and the property to be mortgaged must also have a certificate of reasonable value. A veterans administration mortgage is assumable, mortgagees cannot have prepayment mortgage penalties and only one point can be charged.

view:

(1) What something looks like at a distance. An example is looking out the window of a home or office providing a beautiful view of a lake or mountain.

(2) How one looks at things; opinion. An example is a prospective buyer of a house who considers the askng price to be a great deal.

violation: Any abuse, disobedience, law-breaking, transgression, or wrongdoing. It may result in punishment or litigation.

visual right: Occupant's right in a structure (e.g., home, apartment, office) to see out of the window without being hindered. For example, if someone wants to construct an office building adjacent to a home that will significantly block the homeowners' view of the outside, his visual rights may be violated.

vitrified title: Clay-baked, glazed piping that is not damaged by water. It is often used in underground drainage.

viz: Namely.

void:

(1) Canceling something such as voiding a check that was written.

(2) Having no legal consequence such as the cancellation of a contract by both parties.

voidable: Descriptive of a contract that may be annulled by a party to it due to some illegality (e.g., fraud), incompetence, or a clause to rescind it.

volatile market: Real estate market characterized by sudden and unpredictable short-term price movements.

voluntary alienation: Conveying title to real estate between individuals or businesses through a deed.

voluntary bankruptcy: Bankruptcy declared by any insolvent person or business. In contrast to involuntary bankruptcy, which is applied for by the creditors. See also *Chapter 7; Chapter 11; Chapter 13.*

voluntary lien:

(1) Encumbrance on property without being objected to by the owner.

(2) An obligation of the owner of property that is recorded with his permission such as a mortgage.

wage earner plan: See *Chapter 13*.

wainscot: Wood panels on a wall.

waiver: Deliberately and voluntarily giving up or delaying a claim or right arising from a contractual agreement or surrounding circumstances. An example is when a lender waives his right to receive a $10,000 monthly payment on June 30, and agrees to delay receipt of such payment for one month. Another example is when a bank waives its right to foreclose on a house.

waiver of lien: Voluntary giving up of a right of a lien, usually on a temporary basis. The waiver may be explicitly stated or implied. An example is when a lender (e.g., bank) waives its right of lien against secured property of the borrower because of missed payments on a mortgage.

walkaway risk: Risk involved when a potential buyer or seller of property decides not to buy or sell. For example, if a seller does not sell at the offered price, he runs the risk of not being able to sell the property to another or if later sold, it will be at a much lower price.

walkup: Residential or commercial building of two or more floors that can only be accessed through stairs. It is more common in urban areas.

wall: Divider made of plasterboard (in newer structures) or plaster (in older structures) used to partition rooms. A room is created by the walls surrounding it.

wall-bearing: Supports a structure.

wall furnace: Small furnace placed between the studs of a wall. It is typically electric, but in the past more frequently was gas.

wall panel: Exterior wall not supporting a load, mostly found in office buildings.

wall tile: Tile placed on a wall as decoration, such as in a bathroom or kitchen.

wallboard: Eight-by-four sheet of material attached to a wall's studs. It can be made attractive by wallpapering or painting.

warehouse property: Building or other structure used to receive, hold, and issue products and other goods for a fee. A warehouse is a commercial property typically located in an industrial area.

warehousing:

(1) Interim loans from banks to other lenders for their underwritten stocks or bonds. The stocks and bonds are issued to investors, household and institutional, for their portfolios.

(2) A mortgage banker puts together mortgages issued to borrowers and sells these mortgages in the secondary market to raise funds and/or reduce risk. (3) Storing of assets expecting them to be sold at a later date.

warehousing requirements: Structural, storage, and shelving characteristics associated with a warehouse.

warranted price (value): Justifiable and fair amount for a real estate transaction based on the conditions and limitations involved in the exchange.

warranty: Guarantee by a seller to a buyer to satisfy, for a specified time period, problems in the quality or performance of items within the home. There is usually no additional charge during the warranty period. See also *express warranty; implied warranty.*

warranty deed: Assures that the title is free of any legal claims including encumbrances. It includes covenants of (1) seizin, (2) freedom from encumbrances, (3) express warranties of title, (4) right to quiet enjoyment, and (5) further assurance. See also *quitclaim deed.*

warranty of habitability: Implied assurance from a landlord to a prospective tenant that an apartment is safe and void of health problems.

warranty insurance: Taken out on property to replace or repair it if it malfunctions. It covers parts and/or service. An example is a warranty a homeowner takes out on a stove, refrigerator, or dishwasher. It offers protection as added insurance to the homeowner.

waste: Misuse, alteration, destruction, or neglect of land by an individual rightfully in possession that breeds a significant and permanent reduction of its value to the legal interest owned by another individual.

waste pipe: Gets rid of unwanted substances and materials from a residence or office building. Waste includes solids and liquids, hazardous and nonhazardous materials.

wasting asset: Natural resource, such as oil, coal, and timber, having a limited useful life and subject to depletion. Such assets decrease in worth primarily due to the extraction of the valued commodity held by these assets.

water-holding capacity: How much water may be retained in a unit, such as an expansion tank in a home.

water level: Surface level of water.

water mains: Pipes transporting water.

water right: Landowner's legal right to the water found on his property. For example, there might be a stream of water adjacent to the land. The water might be used for irrigation or other purposes.

water table: Distance from the location of natural ground and water to the actual ground level.

waterfront property: Residential or office structure adjacent to water such as a lake. Such property has a higher value because of the greater demand for it.

waterproofing: Putting a waterproofing substance on the exterior cement walls of the structure (typically the basement) to prevent water from entering the interior of the structure. The cracks in the walls are patched up.

weak market: Characterized by a low volume of real estate sale transactions. See also *depressed market.*

wear and tear: Physical decline in a property's value caused from use, old age, and environmental factors.

weatherstriping: Additions made to a structure to protect it from damage due to inclement weather. An example is reinforcing the wood surrounding windows.

weep holes: Number of small holes in a wall allowing water to drain from it. This makes the walls able to withstand water pressure.

wet plaster: Water/plaster mix used as a surface for walls and ceilings.

wetlands: Land located next to water that has and will continue to experience water damage. The land generally is not suitable to build a structure on. In some cases, federal or local government may take over the land to preserve it.

widow's walk: Platform erected on a roof in some New England homes having a view of the sea. It was said widows of lost seaman would walk on the platform looking out at sea for their husbands to return from sea.

will: An individual's written statement of how he or she wants property to be distributed upon death. There must be witnesses for the will to be enforceable.

windbreak: Something offering protection against the wind such as trees and fences.

winder, wheel step: Wedge-shaped step found on a spiral staircase with a wider tread on its outside portion.

window: Opening in the wall of a structure to let in air and light.

Windowsill: Bottom frame of wood supporting a window. It should be strong in order to support something put in the window such as an air conditioner.

wing: Part of a building that is connected to but leads away from the main structure.

wire glass: Glass containing wire support to make it stronger. There is less chance of glass being broken into pieces and hurting people.

without recourse: The company is not responsible to a third party if an account or financial instrument is dishonored by the debtor. The creditor's recourse is solely to the debtor's property. An example is when a company sells accounts receivable to a factor to obtain money. If the customer defaults, the factor cannot recover the amount due from the company.

witness:

(1) An individual providing evidence in a trial under penalties of perjury. The witness's testimony is under oath.

(2) Observing the occurrence of an event or the transacting of a transaction or contract. An example is witnessing a will and signing to its authenticity.

Women's Council of Realtors (WCR): Organization that is part of the National Association of Realtors and is designed to promote women activities in real estate transactions. Those interested in the council may write to 430 North Michigan Avenue, Chicago, Illinois 60611, telephone (312) 440-8083.

wood-destroying insect: An insect, such as a termite, that "eats into" the wood and destroys it. This can cause significant damage to the home. Most states have laws that require termite inspection and certification when a house is sold. Many homeowners take out policies for an annual fee with termite companies as protection.

woodland:

(1) Land that has trees on it.

(2) Farm land.

working drawing: Drawing for the entire structure or part of it that is detailed and in scale so that engineers and construction workers may readily follow it.

workout:

(1) Trying to resolve a problem between two individuals up with some compromise or common ground. It occurs more often during times of poor economic conditions. An example is a creditor offering an accommodation to a borrower to avoid a bankruptcy situation.

(2) A debt which is in default but which the creditor allows the debtor to rectify by lengthening the time period of the loan, reducing the interest rate, or some other accommodation. An example is a bank that elects not to foreclose on a mortgage because of the homeowner's nonpayment, but agrees to stretch out the payments.

wraparound mortgage (trust deed): Also called all inclusive trust deed (AITD). A mortgage (trust deed) that encompasses existing mortgages and is subordinate to them. The existing mortgages stay on the property and the new mortgage wraps around them. The existing mortgage usually carries a lower interest rate than the one on the new mortgage loan. This loan is a type of seller financing. It is often used with commercial property where there is substantial equity in the property, and the existing first mortgage has an attractive low interest rate. By obtaining a wraparound, the borrower receives dollars based on the difference between current market value of the property and the outstanding balance on the first mortgage. The borrower amortizes the wraparound mortgage which now includes the balance of the first mortgage, and the wraparound lender forwards the necessary periodic debt service to the holder of the first mortgage. Thus, the borrower reduces the equity and at the same time obtains an interest rate lower than would be possible through a normal second mortgage. The lender receives the leverage resulting from an interest rate on the wraparound greater than the interest paid to the holder of the first mortgage.

EXAMPLE: The sale price is $300,000. There is a mortgage balance of $200,000 payable at 9% interest. The buyer will pay $30,000 cash down and agrees to pay the balance at 11%. By using the wraparound mortgage, the seller can have the buyer agree to a mortgage of $270,000 at 11%; the buyer makes the applicable monthly payment to the seller. The seller, in turn, continues to make payments on the underlying first mortgage which was written at 9%. This means that the seller, in his or her role as a mortgagee, now earns 11% on $70,000 (the difference between the new mortgage of $270,000 and the existing mortgage of $200,000) and 2% on the existing $200,000 loan.

The seller grants a deed to the buyer in the regular way. Note that for this method to work, the original lender must be agreeable to the seller transferring title. See also *creative financing*.

writ: Judicial order requiring the named person or business to act or not act on something. An example is an order to a tenant to make rental payments to a landlord.

writ of ejectment: Court order granted in favor of the landlord to remove a tenant from the property because of nonpayment of rent and/or damaging the property. The writ directs an officer of the law to execute it and contains any needed directions.

writ of execution: Court order to seize and sell property because of the nonpayment of taxes, or foreclosure of property.

writ of mandamus: Court order stopping or directing a judicial directive.

write-down: Reduction of part of the balance of property by charging an expense or loss account. The reason for a write-down is that some economic event has occurred indicating that the asset's value has diminished.

wrought iron: Type of material or substance typically made for railings around the outdoor front patio and for both sides of the stairs in the front and rear of house. Other examples are chairs and tables for the kitchen and patio. It has to be painted with special paint to preserve it so it does not rust. It is usually painted black or white.

yield (rate of return): The income earned on an investment, typically stated as a percentage of the market price.

Z

zero lot line: Individual residences are on separate lots which are attached in some way. An example is a building having clusters of individual units on its sides.

zero rate loan: Loan with a significant down payment with the balance being paid in equal periodic payments over a short time period. There is no interest charge. An example is when a seller of real estate is anxious to sell the property and in so doing offers a zero percent financing rate.

zone: Geographic location by itself with designated boundaries. An example is a district.

zone representative: One who represents a zone such as an elected leader of a region. He or she may have dealings with the county's officials in matters affecting that zone.

zoning: Local governmental ordinance breaking down the country into districts that are restricted on how private property is to be constructed and used. It applies to the land and buildings. The particular community's needs are taken into account. Zoning helps in maintaining or increasing property values. Zoning may be divided into residential, commercial, industrial, and agricultural. Each of these may be subdivided

further. For example, residential may be segregated into single family homes, two-family homes, apartment buildings, and so on. Zoning may also make a district an historical one because of its importance in federal or local history. Zoning typically imposes height limitations on structures to protect other property owners. There are also restrictions on how many structures may be constructed in a particular geographic area. Zoning requirements may also exist as to parking and open space. Restrictions may also be placed on pollution and noise.

zoning board of appeals: A municipal or county local government board that resolves zoning disputes.

zoning hearings: Request of a local government's planning body to alter the zoning requirements based on a justifiable reason.

zoning laws: Local government ordinances governing real estate development including structural and design aspects. Zoning ordinances usually define (1) various usage classifications ranging from agricultural to heavy industry; (2) building restrictions including minimum-square-footage building requirements; and (3) violation penalties and procedures.

zoning map: Divides a locality into districts for differing purposes. The map is continually kept current. It reveals the status of each district.

zoning ordinance: Local regulation on how real property may be used in a particular locality. The county may establish different zoning classifications and restrictions (e.g., height of a building, absence of commercial buildings). If the ordinance is violated, penalties may be assessed. There may be circumstances in which a variation to the ordinance may be allowed.

zoning records: Documentation of zoning requirements and changes thereto.

zoning variance: Permission to do something that differs from the basic zoning requirement. An example is a homeowner receiving special authorization to build a two-family house in a single family zoned area.

APPENDIX

Table 1   The Future Value of $1.00 (Compounded Amount of $1.00)

Periods	4%	6%	8%	10%	12%	14%	20%
1	1.040	1.060	1.080	1.100	1.120	1.140	1.200
2	1.082	1.124	1.166	1.210	1.254	1.300	1.440
3	1.125	1.191	1.260	1.331	1.405	1.482	1.728
4	1.170	1.263	1.361	1.464	1.574	1.689	2.074
5	1.217	1.338	1.469	1.611	1.762	1.925	2.488
6	1.265	1.419	1.587	1.772	1.974	2.195	2.986
7	1.316	1.504	1.714	1.949	2.211	2.502	3.583
8	1.369	1.594	1.851	2.144	2.476	2.853	4.300
9	1.423	1.690	1.999	2.359	2.773	3.252	5.160
10	1.480	1.791	2.159	2.594	3.106	3.707	6.192
11	1.540	1.898	2.332	2.853	3.479	4.226	7.430
12	1.601	2.012	2.518	3.139	3.896	4.818	8.916
13	1.665	2.133	2.720	3.452	4.364	5.492	10.699
14	1.732	2.261	2.937	3.798	4.887	6.261	12.839
15	1.801	2.397	3.172	4.177	5.474	7.138	15.407
16	1.873	2.540	3.426	4.595	6.130	8.137	18.488
17	1.948	2.693	3.700	5.055	6.866	9.277	22.186
18	2.026	2.854	3.996	5.560	7.690	10.575	26.623
19	2.107	3.026	4.316	6.116	8.613	12.056	31.948
20	2.191	3.207	4.661	6.728	9.646	13.743	38.338
30	3.243	5.744	10.063	17.450	29.960	50.950	237.380
40	4.801	10.286	21.725	45.260	93.051	188.880	1469.800

Table 2 The Future Value of an Annuity of $1.00[a] (Compounded Amount of an Annuity of $1.00)

Periods	4%	6%	8%	10%	12%	14%	20%
1	1.000	1.000	1.000	1.000	1.000	1.000	1.000
2	2.040	2.060	2.080	2.100	2.120	2.140	2.200
3	3.122	3.184	3.246	3.310	3.374	3.440	3.640
4	4.247	4.375	4.506	4.641	4.779	4.921	5.368
5	5.416	5.637	5.867	6.105	6.353	6.610	7.442
6	6.633	6.975	7.336	7.716	8.115	8.536	9.930
7	7.898	8.394	8.923	9.487	10.089	10.730	12.916
8	9.214	9.898	10.637	11.436	12.300	13.233	16.499
9	10.583	11.491	12.488	13.580	14.776	16.085	20.799
10	12.006	13.181	14.487	15.938	17.549	19.337	25.959
11	13.486	14.972	16.646	18.531	20.655	23.045	32.150
12	15.026	16.870	18.977	21.385	24.133	27.271	39.580
13	16.627	18.882	21.495	24.523	28.029	32.089	48.497
14	18.292	21.015	24.215	27.976	32.393	37.581	59.196
15	20.024	23.276	27.152	31.773	37.280	43.842	72.035
16	21.825	25.673	30.324	35.950	42.753	50.980	87.442
17	23.698	28.213	33.750	40.546	48.884	59.118	105.930
18	25.645	30.906	37.450	45.600	55.750	68.394	128.120
19	27.671	33.760	41.446	51.160	63.440	78.969	154.740
20	29.778	36.778	45.762	57.276	75.052	91.025	186.690
30	56.085	79.058	113.283	164.496	241.330	356.790	1181.900
40	95.026	154.762	259.057	442.597	767.090	1342.000	7343.900

[a] Payments (or receipts) at the *end* of each period.

Table 3 Present Value of $1

Periods	4%	5%	6%	8%	10%	12%	14%	16%	18%	20%	22%	24%	26%	28%	30%	40%
1	0.962	0.952	0.943	0.926	0.909	0.893	0.877	0.862	0.847	0.833	0.820	0.806	0.794	0.781	0.769	0.714
2	0.925	0.907	0.890	0.857	0.826	0.797	0.769	0.743	0.718	0.694	0.672	0.650	0.630	0.610	0.592	0.510
3	0.889	0.864	0.840	0.794	0.751	0.712	0.675	0.641	0.609	0.579	0.551	0.524	0.500	0.477	0.455	0.364
4	0.855	0.823	0.792	0.735	0.683	0.636	0.592	0.552	0.516	0.482	0.451	0.423	0.397	0.373	0.350	0.260
5	0.822	0.784	0.747	0.681	0.621	0.567	0.519	0.476	0.437	0.402	0.370	0.341	0.315	0.291	0.269	0.186
6	0.790	0.746	0.705	0.630	0.564	0.507	0.456	0.410	0.370	0.335	0.303	0.275	0.250	0.227	0.207	0.133
7	0.760	0.711	0.665	0.583	0.513	0.452	0.400	0.354	0.314	0.279	0.249	0.222	0.198	0.178	0.159	0.095
8	0.731	0.677	0.627	0.540	0.467	0.404	0.351	0.305	0.266	0.233	0.204	0.179	0.157	0.139	0.123	0.068
9	0.703	0.645	0.592	0.500	0.424	0.361	0.308	0.263	0.255	0.194	0.167	0.144	0.125	0.108	0.094	0.048
10	0.676	0.614	0.558	0.463	0.386	0.322	0.270	0.227	0.191	0.162	0.137	0.116	0.099	0.085	0.073	0.035
11	0.650	0.585	0.527	0.429	0.350	0.287	0.237	0.195	0.162	0.135	0.112	0.094	0.079	0.066	0.056	0.025
12	0.625	0.557	0.497	0.397	0.319	0.257	0.208	0.168	0.137	0.112	0.092	0.076	0.062	0.052	0.043	0.018
13	0.601	0.530	0.469	0.368	0.290	0.229	0.182	0.145	0.116	0.093	0.075	0.061	0.050	0.040	0.033	0.013
14	0.577	0.505	0.442	0.340	0.263	0.205	0.160	0.125	0.099	0.078	0.062	0.049	0.039	0.032	0.025	0.009
15	0.555	0.481	0.417	0.315	0.239	0.183	0.140	0.108	0.084	0.065	0.051	0.040	0.031	0.025	0.020	0.006
16	0.534	0.458	0.394	0.292	0.218	0.163	0.123	0.093	0.071	0.054	0.042	0.032	0.025	0.019	0.015	0.005
17	0.513	0.436	0.371	0.270	0.198	0.146	0.108	0.080	0.060	0.045	0.034	0.026	0.020	0.015	0.012	0.003
18	0.494	0.416	0.350	0.250	0.180	0.130	0.095	0.069	0.051	0.038	0.028	0.021	0.016	0.012	0.009	0.002
19	0.475	0.396	0.331	0.232	0.164	0.116	0.083	0.060	0.043	0.031	0.023	0.017	0.012	0.009	0.007	0.002
20	0.456	0.377	0.312	0.215	0.149	0.104	0.073	0.051	0.037	0.026	0.019	0.014	0.010	0.007	0.005	0.001
21	0.439	0.359	0.294	0.199	0.135	0.093	0.064	0.044	0.031	0.022	0.015	0.011	0.008	0.006	0.004	0.001
22	0.422	0.342	0.278	0.184	0.123	0.083	0.056	0.038	0.026	0.018	0.013	0.009	0.006	0.004	0.003	0.001
23	0.406	0.326	0.262	0.170	0.112	0.074	0.049	0.033	0.022	0.015	0.010	0.007	0.005	0.003	0.002	0.001
24	0.390	0.310	0.247	0.158	0.102	0.066	0.043	0.028	0.019	0.013	0.008	0.006	0.004	0.003	0.002	
25	0.375	0.295	0.233	0.146	0.092	0.059	0.038	0.024	0.016	0.010	0.007	0.005	0.003	0.002	0.001	
26	0.361	0.281	0.220	0.135	0.084	0.053	0.033	0.021	0.014	0.009	0.006	0.004	0.002	0.002	0.001	
27	0.347	0.268	0.207	0.125	0.076	0.047	0.029	0.018	0.011	0.007	0.005	0.003	0.002	0.001	0.001	
28	0.333	0.255	0.196	0.116	0.069	0.042	0.026	0.016	0.010	0.006	0.004	0.002	0.002	0.001	0.001	
29	0.321	0.243	0.185	0.107	0.063	0.037	0.022	0.014	0.008	0.005	0.003	0.002	0.001	0.001	0.001	
30	0.308	0.231	0.174	0.099	0.057	0.033	0.020	0.012	0.007	0.004	0.003	0.002	0.001	0.001	0.001	
40	0.208	0.142	0.097	0.046	0.022	0.011	0.005	0.003	0.001	0.001						

Table 4 Present Value of Annuity of $1

Periods	4%	5%	6%	8%	10%	12%	14%	16%	18%	20%	22%	24%	26%	28%	30%	40%
1	0.962	0.952	0.943	0.926	0.909	0.893	0.877	0.862	0.847	0.833	0.820	0.806	0.794	0.781	0.769	0.714
2	1.886	1.859	1.833	1.783	1.736	1.690	1.647	1.605	1.566	1.528	1.492	1.457	1.424	1.392	1.361	1.224
3	2.775	2.723	2.673	2.577	2.487	2.402	2.322	2.246	2.174	2.106	2.042	1.981	1.923	1.868	1.816	1.589
4	3.630	3.546	3.465	3.312	3.170	3.037	2.914	2.798	2.690	2.589	2.494	2.404	2.320	2.241	2.166	1.879
5	4.452	4.330	4.212	3.993	3.791	3.605	3.433	3.274	3.127	2.991	2.864	2.745	2.635	2.532	2.436	2.035
6	5.242	5.076	4.917	4.623	4.355	4.111	3.889	3.685	3.498	3.326	3.167	3.020	2.885	2.759	2.643	2.168
7	6.002	5.786	5.582	5.206	4.868	4.564	4.288	4.039	3.812	3.605	3.416	3.242	3.083	2.937	2.802	2.263
8	6.733	6.463	6.210	5.747	5.335	4.968	4.639	4.344	4.078	3.837	3.619	3.421	3.241	3.076	2.925	2.331
9	7.435	7.108	6.802	6.247	5.759	5.328	4.946	4.607	4.303	4.031	3.786	3.566	3.366	3.184	3.019	2.379
10	8.111	7.722	7.360	6.710	6.145	5.650	5.216	4.833	4.494	4.192	3.923	3.682	3.465	3.269	3.092	2.414
11	8.760	8.306	7.887	7.139	6.495	5.988	5.453	5.029	4.656	4.327	4.035	3.776	3.544	3.335	3.147	2.438
12	9.385	8.863	8.384	7.536	6.814	6.194	5.660	5.197	4.793	4.439	4.127	3.851	3.606	3.387	3.190	2.456
13	9.986	9.394	8.853	7.904	7.103	6.424	5.842	5.342	4.910	4.533	4.203	3.912	3.656	3.427	3.223	2.468
14	10.563	9.899	9.295	8.244	7.367	6.628	6.002	5.468	5.008	4.611	4.265	3.962	3.695	3.459	3.249	2.477
15	11.118	10.380	9.712	8.559	7.606	6.811	6.142	5.575	5.092	4.675	4.315	4.001	3.726	3.483	3.268	2.484
16	11.652	10.838	10.106	8.851	7.824	6.974	6.265	5.669	5.162	4.730	4.357	4.033	3.751	3.503	3.283	2.489
17	12.166	11.274	10.477	9.122	8.022	7.120	6.373	5.749	5.222	4.775	4.391	4.059	3.771	3.518	3.295	2.492
18	12.659	11.690	10.828	9.372	8.201	7.250	6.467	5.818	5.273	4.812	4.419	4.080	3.786	3.529	3.304	2.494
19	13.134	12.085	11.158	9.604	8.365	7.366	6.550	5.877	5.316	4.844	4.442	4.097	3.799	3.539	3.311	2.496
20	13.590	12.462	11.470	9.818	8.514	7.469	6.623	5.929	5.353	4.870	4.460	4.110	3.808	3.546	3.316	2.497
21	14.029	12.821	11.764	10.017	8.649	7.562	6.687	5.973	5.384	4.891	4.476	4.121	3.816	3.551	3.320	2.498
22	14.451	13.163	12.042	10.201	8.772	7.645	6.743	6.011	5.410	4.909	4.488	4.130	3.822	3.556	3.323	2.498
23	14.857	13.489	12.303	10.371	8.883	7.718	6.792	6.044	5.432	4.925	4.499	4.137	3.827	3.559	3.325	2.499
24	15.247	13.799	12.550	10.529	8.985	7.784	6.835	6.073	5.451	4.937	4.507	4.143	3.831	3.562	3.327	2.499
25	15.622	14.094	12.783	10.675	9.077	7.843	6.873	6.097	5.467	4.948	4.514	4.147	3.834	3.564	3.329	2.499
26	15.983	14.375	13.003	10.810	9.161	7.896	6.906	6.118	5.480	4.956	4.520	4.151	3.837	3.566	3.330	2.500
27	16.330	14.643	13.211	10.935	9.237	7.943	6.935	6.136	5.492	4.964	4.525	4.154	3.839	3.567	3.331	2.500
28	16.663	14.898	13.406	11.051	9.307	7.984	6.961	6.152	5.502	4.970	4.528	4.157	3.840	3.568	3.331	2.500
29	16.984	15.141	13.591	11.158	9.370	8.022	6.983	6.166	5.510	4.975	4.531	4.159	3.841	3.569	3.332	2.500
30	17.292	15.373	13.765	11.258	9.427	8.055	7.003	6.177	5.517	4.979	4.534	4.160	3.842	3.569	3.332	2.500
40	19.793	17.159	15.046	11.925	9.779	8.244	7.105	6.234	5.548	4.997	4.544	4.166	3.846	3.571	3.333	2.500

Table 5   A Table of Monthly Installment Loan Payments (to Repay a $1,000 Simple Interest Loan)

Rate of Interest	Loan Term						
	6 Months	12 Months	18 Months	24 Months	36 Months	48 Months	60 Months
7½%	$170.33	$86.76	$58.92	$45.00	$31.11	$24.18	$20.05
8	170.58	86.99	59.15	45.23	31.34	24.42	20.28
8½	170.82	87.22	59.37	45.46	31.57	24.65	20.52
9	171.07	87.46	59.60	45.69	31.80	24.89	20.76
9½	171.32	87.69	59.83	45.92	32.04	25.13	21.01
10	171.56	87.92	60.06	46.15	32.27	25.37	21.25
10½	171.81	88.15	60.29	46.38	32.51	25.61	21.50
11	172.05	88.50	60.64	46.73	32.86	25.97	21.87
11½	172.30	88.62	60.76	46.85	32.98	26.09	22.00
12	172.55	88.85	60.99	47.08	33.22	26.34	22.25
12½	172.80	89.09	61.22	47.31	33.46	26.58	22.50
13	173.04	89.32	61.45	47.55	33.70	26.83	22.76
14	173.54	89.79	61.92	48.02	34.18	27.33	23.27
15	174.03	90.26	62.39	48.49	34.67	27.84	23.79
16	174.53	90.74	62.86	48.97	35.16	28.35	24.32
17	175.03	91.21	63.34	49.45	35.66	28.86	24.86
18	175.53	91.68	63.81	49.93	36.16	29.38	25.40

Table 6 Monthly Mortgage Payments (Amortization Table Monthly Payment per $1,000 of Loan)

Interest Rate per year	5 years	10 years	15 years	20 years	25 years	30 years	35 years	40 years
				Life of the Loan				
5%	$18.88	$10.61	$ 7.91	$ 6.60	$ 5.85	$ 5.37	$ 5.05	$ 4.83
5½	19.11	10.86	8.18	6.88	6.15	5.68	5.38	5.16
6	19.34	11.11	8.44	7.17	6.45	6.00	5.71	5.51
6½	19.57	11.36	8.72	7.46	6.76	6.32	6.05	5.86
7	19.81	11.62	8.99	7.76	7.07	6.66	6.39	6.22
7½	20.04	11.88	9.28	8.06	7.39	7.00	6.75	6.59
8	20.28	12.14	9.56	8.37	7.72	7.34	7.11	6.96
8½	20.52	12.40	9.85	8.68	8.06	7.69	7.47	7.34
9	20.76	12.67	10.15	9.00	8.40	8.05	7.84	7.72
9½	21.01	12.94	10.45	9.33	8.74	8.41	8.22	8.11
10	21.25	13.22	10.75	9.66	9.09	8.78	8.60	8.50
10½	21.50	13.50	11.06	9.99	9.45	9.15	8.99	8.89
11	21.75	13.78	11.37	10.33	9.81	9.53	9.37	9.29
11½	22.00	14.06	11.69	10.67	10.17	9.91	9.77	9.69
12	22.25	14.35	12.01	11.02	10.54	10.29	10.16	10.09
12½	22.50	14.64	12.33	11.37	10.91	10.68	10.56	10.49
13	22.76	14.94	12.66	11.72	11.28	11.07	10.96	10.90
13½	23.01	15.23	12.99	12.08	11.66	11.46	11.36	11.31
14	23.27	15.53	13.32	12.44	12.04	11.85	11.76	11.72
14½	23.53	15.83	13.66	12.80	12.43	12.25	12.17	12.13
15	23.79	16.14	14.00	13.17	12.81	12.65	12.57	12.54
15½	24.06	16.45	14.34	13.54	13.20	13.05	12.98	12.95
16	24.32	16.76	14.69	13.92	13.59	13.45	13.39	13.36
16½	24.59	17.07	15.04	14.29	13.99	13.85	13.80	13.77
17	24.86	17.38	15.39	14.67	14.38	14.26	14.21	14.19
17½	25.13	17.70	15.75	15.05	14.78	14.67	14.62	14.60
18	25.40	18.02	16.11	15.44	15.18	15.08	15.03	15.02
18½	25.67	18.35	16.47	15.82	15.58	15.48	15.45	15.43
19	25.95	18.67	16.83	16.21	15.98	15.89	15.86	15.85
19½	26.22	19.00	17.20	16.60	16.38	16.30	16.27	16.26
20	26.50	19.33	17.57	16.99	16.79	16.72	16.69	16.68
20½	26.78	19.66	17.94	17.39	17.19	17.13	17.10	17.09
21	27.06	20.00	18.31	17.78	17.60	17.54	17.52	17.51
21½	27.34	20.34	18.69	18.18	18.01	17.95	17.93	17.92
22	27.62	20.67	19.06	18.57	18.42	18.36	18.35	18.34
22½	27.91	21.02	19.44	18.97	18.83	18.78	18.76	18.75
23	28.20	21.36	19.82	19.37	19.24	19.19	19.18	19.17
23½	28.48	21.70	20.20	19.78	19.65	19.61	19.59	19.59
24	28.77	22.05	20.59	20.18	20.06	20.02	20.01	20.01
24½	29.06	22.40	20.97	20.58	20.47	20.43	20.42	20.42
25	29.36	22.75	21.36	20.99	20.88	20.85	20.84	20.84

Table 7   Corner Influence

Depth in Feet	%	Depth in Feet	%	Depth in Feet	%	Depth in Feet	%	Depth in Feet	%
1	2.6	21	30.2	41	40.5	61	45.2	81	48.1
2	4.9	42	30.9	42	40.8	62	45.4	82	48.2
3	7	43	31.6	43	41.1	63	45.6	83	48.3
4	9	44	32.3	44	41.4	64	45.8	84	48.4
5	10.9	45	33	45	41.7	65	46	85	48.5
6	12.7	46	33.6	46	42	66	46.2	86	48.6
7	14.4	47	34.2	47	42.3	67	46.4	87	48.7
8	16	48	34.8	48	42.6	68	46.6	88	48.8
9	17.5	49	35.4	49	42.8	69	46.8	89	48.9
10	19	50	36	50	43	70	47	90	49
11	20.4	51	36.5	51	43.2	71	47.1	91	49.1
12	21.7	52	37	52	43.4	72	47.2	92	49.2
13	22.9	53	37.5	53	43.6	73	47.3	93	49.3
14	24	54	37.9	54	43.8	74	47.4	94	49.4
15	25	55	38.3	55	44	75	47.5	95	49.5
16	26	56	38.7	56	44.2	76	47.6	96	49.6
17	26.9	57	39.1	57	44.4	77	47.7	97	49.7
18	27.8	58	39.5	58	44.6	78	47.8	98	49.8
19	28.6	59	39.9	59	44.8	79	47.9	99	49.9
20	29.4	60	40.2	60	45	80	48	100	50

Source: Sander A. Kahn and Frederick E. Case, *Real Estate Appraisal and Investment* (New York: John Wiley & Sons, 1976), p. 561.

The purpose of the corner influence table is to calculate the equivalent inside lot front footage and its relationship to property depth. For example, a corner lot has 60 front feet and is 75 feet deep. It sold for $125,000. The table gives a percentage of 47.5% for corner influence as follows:

Actual Cost per front foot = ($125,000/60′)	= $2083.33

Number of front feet in the lot	= 60.0′
Corner-influence factor with 75′ depth = 47.5% × 60′	= <u>28.5′</u>
Total equivalent inside lot front feet in plot	= 88.5′

Unit front-foot value = selling price/equivalent inside front feet

($125,000 / 88.5′) = $1412.43 per front foot

Net Corner Influence/Front Foot = $2,083.33 − 1,412.43   = $670.90

Many factors are important in determining the appraised value of a corner lot. The corner influence table is only one tool in appraising corner influence.